It's another Quality Book from CGP

This book is for anyone studying <u>Resistant Materials</u> at GCSE.

Let's face it, D&T is pretty hard-going — you've got a whole load of technical stuff to learn on top of doing your project.

Happily this CGP book helps to take the headache out of all that learning. We've explained all the technical stuff — and drawn plenty of pictures to make the whole thing that bit clearer. Plus we've stuck in some handy hints to help make your project a winner.

And in true CGP style it's got some daft bits in to try and make the whole experience at least vaguely entertaining for you.

What CGP is all about

Our sole aim here at CGP is to produce the highest quality books — carefully written, immaculately presented and dangerously close to being funny.

Then we work our socks off to get them out to you — at the cheapest possible prices.

Contents

Section One — The Design Process

Design Brief 1
Research 2
Design Specification 3
Generating Proposals 4
Development 5
Evaluation 6
Manufacturer's Specification 7
Planning Production 8
Revision Summary for Section One 9

Section Two — Tools and Processes

Hand Tools 10
Machine Tools 11
Machine and Power Tools 12
Deforming 13
Reforming 15
Assembly and Finishing 16
Fabricating — Screws and Bolts 17
Fabricating — Nails, Rivets and Adhesives 18
Fabricating — Joints 19
Fabricating — Joining Metals. 20
Computerised Production 21
Revision Summary for Section Two 22

Section Three — Materials & Components

Properties of Materials 23
Metals 24
Plastics 26
Wood 27
Manufactured Boards 28
Composites and Smart Materials 29
Fixtures and Fittings 30
Adhesives 31
Choosing the Best Material to Use 32
Revision Summary for Section Three 33

Section Four — Systems and Mechanisms

Systems 34
Gear Mechanisms 35
Belt Drives, Chains and Pulleys 36
Cams and Cranks 37
Levers and Links 38
Revision Summary for Section Four 39

Section Five — Market Influences

Product Analysis 40
Quality Assurance and Control 41
Social Responsibility 42
Consumers 43
The Environment 44
Health and Safety 45
Revision Summary for Section Five 47

Section Six — Industrial Awareness

Scale of Production 48
Manufacturing Systems 49
CAD/CAM and CIM in Industry 50
Advertising and Marketing 51
Good Working Practice 52
Jigs, Moulds and Templates 53
Revision Summary for Section Six 54

Section Seven — Project Advice

Tips on Getting Started 55
Tips on Development 56
Tips on Evaluation 57
Tips on Presentation 58
Summary Checklist 59

Index 60

Published by Coordination Group Publications Ltd.

Contributors:
Martin Chester
Charley Darbishire
Stephen Guinness
Brian Kerrush
Simon Little
John Nicolls
Andy Park
Julie Schofield
Karen Steel
Claire Thompson

With thanks to Stephen Guinness, Brian Kerrush, Katherine Reed, Glenn Rogers, Angela Ryder and Karen Steel for the proofreading.

ISBN: 978 1 84146 792 4

Groovy website: www.cgpbooks.co.uk
Jolly bits of clipart from CorelDRAW®
With thanks to TECHSOFT UK Ltd for permission to use a screenshot from 'DESIGN TOOLS — 2D DESIGN'

Printed by Elanders Hindson Ltd, Newcastle upon Tyne.

Text, design, layout and original illustrations © Coordination Group Publications Ltd. 2002
All rights reserved.

Section One — The Design Process

Design Brief

The process of designing and making something is called 'the design process' (gosh). The whole process can take a while — so, like many pineapples, it's usually broken down into smaller chunks.

The Design Process is Similar in Industry and School

It's no accident that the things you'll have to do for your Design and Technology project are pretty similar to what happens in industry.

- The best products are those that address a real need.
- That's why companies spend so much time and money on customer research. The more people there are who would actually use a product, the more chance it stands of being a roaring success.
- The best ideas for Design and Technology projects are also those that meet a genuine need.

The rest of this section describes a typical design process.

It shows the sort of thing that happens in industry every day.

It also shows the stages you need to go through while you're putting a Design and Technology project together.

First get your Idea for a New Product

First things first... whether you're working in the research and development department of a multinational company, or you're putting together your project, you need to explain why a new product is needed.

It could be for one of the following reasons:

1) There are problems with an existing product.
2) The performance of an existing design could be improved.
3) There's a gap in the market that you want to fill.

The Design Brief explains Why your Product is Needed

The design brief explains why there might be a need for a new product.
It should include the following:

1) an outline of the problem and who it affects
2) the need arising from the problem
3) what you intend to do about it (e.g. design and make...)
4) how your product will be used
5) the environment it will be used in

DESIGN BRIEF FOR: BACKSCRATCHER / TURNIP HOLDER
No currently commercially available backscratcher has an in-built capacity for turnip storage.
So we will manufacture a product to meet this need for those people having itchy backs and modest turnip storage requirements (up to 4 turnips).

Basically, the design brief should concentrate on the problem you're trying to solve.

Remember — your project doesn't have to involve turnips...

Your design brief should be simple and concise, and allow you room for development. A design brief should not be a detailed description of what you intend to make — you can only say this after you've designed it and tried stuff out. Got that... describe the problem first. The rest comes later.

Research

Once you've written your design brief, you can start researching your project.
This is what life is all about.

Research can help you get Ideas

It's worth doing your research carefully — it can give you loads of ideas for the rest of the design process.
The point of doing research is to:

1) check that people will actually want your product (although you might have done this already when you chose your project).

2) find out what makes an existing product good or bad — talk to people who actually use this kind of product, and see what they like or dislike.

3) find out the materials, pre-manufactured components, techniques and ingredients that you can use, and how they will affect the manufacturing and selling costs.

4) give you a good starting point for designing.

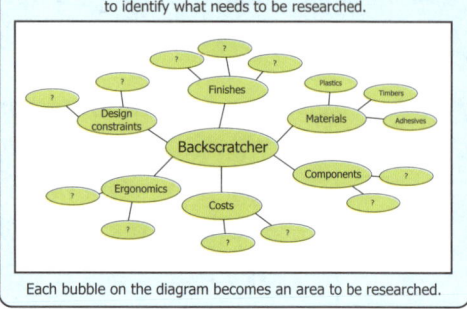

A simple spider diagram can really help to identify what needs to be researched.

Each bubble on the diagram becomes an area to be researched.

There are Different Kinds of Research

You can do different kinds of research. This might include:

① **Questionnaires** — to find out people's likes/dislikes and so on. This will help you identify your target group and find out market trends (e.g. what things are becoming more popular).

② **Disassembling a product** (i.e. taking it apart) — this will help you find out how a current product is made and how it works. It could also give you information about different materials and processes used, and how existing products meet potential users' needs.

③ **Measuring** — to find out the weights and sizes of current products. This might give you an idea of the possible size, shape and weight of your product. You could also do some kind of sensory analysis (e.g. you could see how it tastes, feels, looks and smells).

Research Analysis means Drawing Conclusions

Once you've done your research, you'll need to come to some conclusions. This means deciding how to use the information to help you with your design. This is called research analysis.

Try to do the following:
1) Pick out the useful information.
2) Explain what impact the research will have on your designs.
3) Suggest ways forward from the research gathered.

By the time you've done all this, you should have some ideas about how to tackle your project.

I disassembled my dog — he doesn't work any more...

Research is important. Trust me. More important at this stage than cutting wood or moulding plastic. And one more thing while I'm ranting... you could also spend some time doing 'book research', e.g. finding out about any British or European standards your product will have to meet.

Section One — The Design Process

Design Specification

Once you've picked out the main points of your research, you're ready to put together a design specification. So put that chisel away... you're not ready to do anything practical yet.

The Design Specification is a List of Conditions to Meet

The design specification describes the restrictions and possibilities of the product.
It's a good point to start from when you get round to doing the more creative stuff.

1) The design specification gives certain conditions that the product will have to meet. Try to put your specification together in bullet form as specific points, rather than a paragraph of explanations.

   > E.g. if your research tells you that people would never buy a backscratcher weighing 300 grams or more, then your design specification might include the statement, "Must weigh less than 300 grams."

2) Once you've come up with a design, you need to compare it to the specification and confirm that each point is satisfied.

   > E.g. If your design specification contains these two points, then all of your designs should be at least 400 mm long and have a variety of colours.

   > "The minimum length will be 400 mm."
   > "The product should be multicoloured."

3) Some points might be harder to compare to your specification simply by looking at the product.

   > E.g. "The product should feel comfortable."

   For this, you'll need to get someone to test the product once it's been made/modelled.

4) Include points to describe some or all of the following:
   - a description of how it should look
   - details about what it has to do/be
   - materials, ingredients and joining methods
   - details of size/weight
   - safety points to consider
   - financial constraints

You might need to make More than One Specification

You'll probably need to produce several specifications as your project develops:

> Initial Design Specification — this is your first design specification. It should be done after your research analysis.

1) As you develop your design, you'll probably want to make some changes to your design specification. This is fine, as long as your design brief is being met and you have taken your research analysis into account.

2) Maybe as a result of some of your modelling (see page 5) you'll find that certain materials aren't suitable. You can add this information to an updated specification.

3) You can keep doing this until you end up with a final product specification.

I'd never buy a backscratcher that didn't glow in the dark...

If I told you that design specifications were going to get your pulse racing, you'd probably suspect I was lying. And of course, I would be lying. To be honest, they're a bit dull. But making a design specification is a vital step in designing and manufacturing a new product. So learn about it.

Section One — The Design Process

Generating Proposals

Now hold on to your hats, my wild young things — this is where it all starts to get a bit more interesting. This is the creative bit. This is where you start generating ideas.

There are a few Tricks that can help you Get Started

The following are suggestions to help you get started with designing:

1) Create a mood board — this is a load of different images, words, materials, colours and so on that might trigger ideas for your design.

2) Brainstorm — think up key words, questions and initial thoughts relating to your product. (Start off by just writing whatever ideas come into your head — analyse them later.)

3) Work from an existing product — but change some of its features or production methods so that it fits in with your specification.

4) Break the task up into smaller parts — e.g. design the 'look' of the product (aesthetics), then look at the technology involved and so on.

You need to Come up with a Range of Designs

1) You need to annotate (i.e. add notes to) your designs to fully explain your ideas. These notes could be about:

   - materials
   - size
   - user
   - shape
   - cost
   - production method
   - functions
   - advantages and disadvantages

2) You need to produce a wide range of appropriate solutions that you think could actually be made.

3) Try to use a range of techniques for presenting your designs. A good thing to do is to use different drawing techniques — for example:

   - perspective
   - orthographic projection
   - cross-sections
   - freehand sketching
   - digital camera photos
   - isometric projection

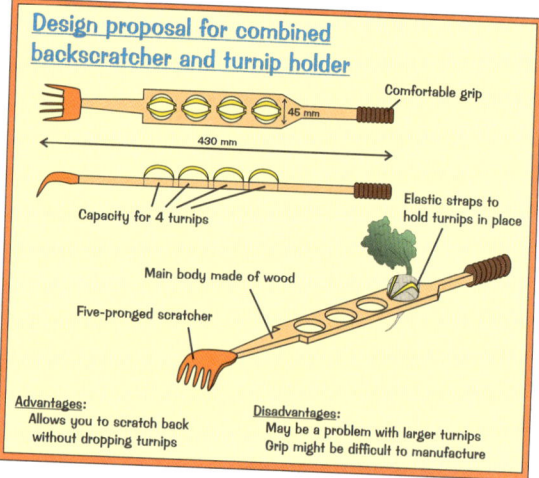

4) Once you've got a few possible designs, you need to check that each one matches your specification — any that don't will not be suitable.

5) Finally, you need to choose one of your suitable designs to develop further.

Write whatever comes to mind — no hope for me then...

Think what someone will need to know to fully appreciate your design, and include this information on your proposal. And remember — you need to do quite a few of these so that you can choose the best one to develop and improve. This is the bit where you need to get your creative head on.

Section One — The Design Process

Development

Once you've decided on a design, you can begin to develop it further.
This is when your design should start to really take shape.

You can Develop your Design in Different Ways

Depending on the type of product that's being produced, further development might involve:

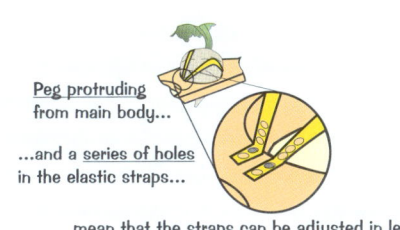

Peg protruding from main body...
...and a series of holes in the elastic straps...
...mean that the straps can be adjusted in length by putting the peg through a different hole.

1) producing further sketches — but in more detail e.g. recording the sizes of fittings and components, and dimensions for component positions. Also sketching how parts should be constructed and fitted together.

2) modelling and testing your idea. Or experimenting with different aspects of the design. E.g. you could try various materials, sizes and production methods.

3) using people's opinions about developments to help you arrive at a satisfactory solution.

Modelling means Trying Things Out

It can be useful to prototype or model your idea, especially if it's difficult to draw.

1) Try out different aspects of your design. If your design is quite complex it may help to break it down into smaller, more manageable parts and test them individually.

2) Use a camera (digital or otherwise) to record your models.

3) Evaluate the models (see next page), identifying reasons for selecting or rejecting different designs.

The peg was originally made using a nail, but when the elastic was pulled, the nail came out of the wood too easily. This was remedied by using a screw.

> This is a vital part of the design process. Ideally you should solve all the potential problems with your design at this stage.

Use the Results to Make Modifications

1) Results from your modelling and from your evaluation (see next page) will help you make important modifications (changes) to improve the product, and help it meet the design specification.

2) Suggested improvements could be:
   • ways to make the product itself better,
   • suggestions to make it more suitable for mass production (see page 48).

3) But make sure you keep a record of whatever it is you find out (see next page).

4) Once you've made a modification to your design, you'll need to try it out to see if it actually improves things.

5) You might find that you end up modifying something, then trying it out, then making another modification and trying that out, then making another modification and trying that out, and so on. That's just the way it goes sometimes.

Modification — wear a parka and ride a scooter...

Modelling and evaluation (see next page) go hand in hand. It's pointless building a model and trying it out if you're not going to bother learning anything from it. So keep your thinking trousers on at all times and make the most of your modelling time.

Section One — The Design Process

Evaluation

Evaluation's an important part of any product development process, and needs to be done at various stages along the way.

Keep Records of your Research and Testing

1) As you develop your product, keep records of any testing or market research you do. Write it all down, keep it, and refer back to it.

2) You might have tested materials for suitability, or tested components to see how well they work — but whatever you did, you need to write down all the results.

3) Compare the good and bad points of existing products with your model or prototype. Ask yourself if your product does the job better. Record your results.

4) Find out people's opinions and preferences about your models and prototypes (see previous page). This will help you to refine your ideas so you can arrive at the best solution.

5) Questionnaires help here — relevant market research questions might include:

- Does the product work well?
- Does the product work as well as similar products on the market?
- Does the product look good? Is it well styled and modern-looking?
- Are you unsure about any of the features? If so, which ones and why?
- If this product were on the market, would you consider buying it?
- If you were buying it, which price range do you think it would fall into?
- Do you prefer another similar product to this one?

This type of evaluation is called formative evaluation — it's being used to help form the final design.

Now You should Know Exactly What You're Making

By the time you've finished developing your ideas and have arrived at a final design, you should have found out / worked out:

1) The best materials, tools and other equipment to use (and their availability). This might include identifying any pre-manufactured components you're going to use.

2) The approximate manufacturing time needed to make each item.

3) How much it should cost to manufacture each item.

4) The most appropriate assembly process — this is going to be important information when it comes to planning production, and can be in the form of a flow chart (see page 8).

If you don't know what you're doing now, you never will...

At this stage of the process it should be crystal clear in your own mind how your final product should look, and how you're going to make it. But you're not finished yet. No, no, no, no, no... There's still the little business of actually making your pride and joy. Oh what fun... what fun...

Section One — The Design Process

Manufacturer's Specification

Now that you know <u>exactly</u> what you're going to make, you need to <u>communicate</u> all that info to the person who's actually going to <u>make</u> it.

You need to produce a Manufacturer's Specification

A manufacturer's specification can be a written <u>series of statements</u>, or <u>working drawings</u> and <u>sequence diagrams</u>. It has to explain <u>exactly</u> how the product will be made, and should include:

1) clear <u>construction</u> details explaining <u>exactly</u> how each bit's going to be made,
2) <u>sizes</u> — <u>precise measurements</u> of each part,
3) <u>tolerances</u> — the maximum and minimum sizes each part should be,
4) <u>finishing</u> details — any special sequences for finishing,
5) <u>quality control</u> instructions — where, when and how the manufacturing process should be checked. (See page 8 for time planning and page 41 for quality control.)
6) <u>costings</u> — how much each part costs, and details of any other costs involved.

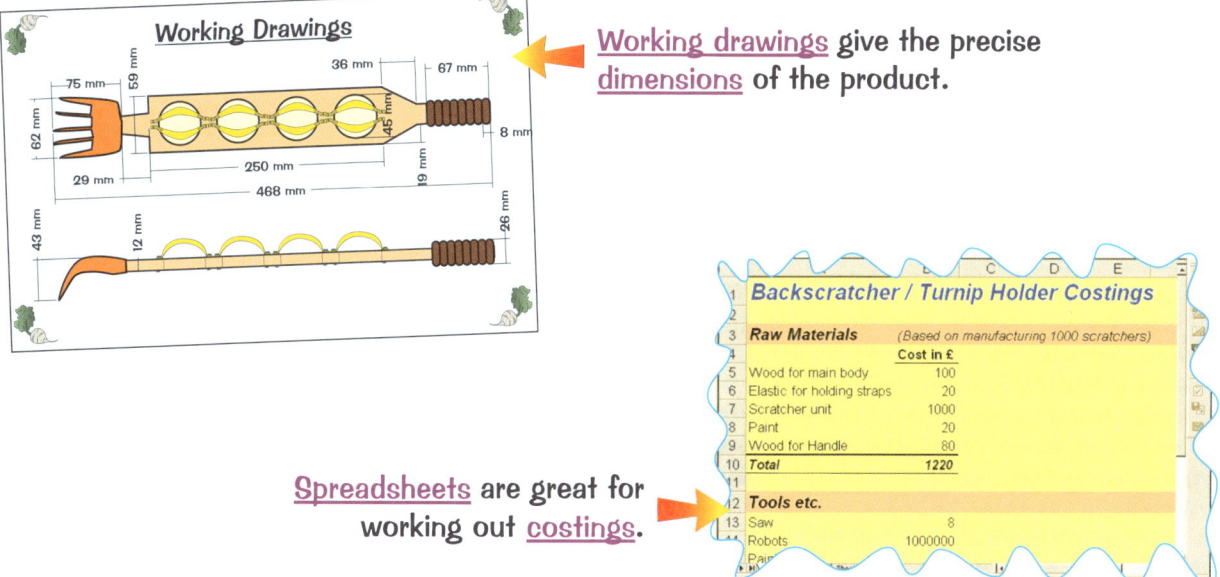

<u>Working drawings</u> give the precise <u>dimensions</u> of the product.

<u>Spreadsheets</u> are great for working out <u>costings</u>.

Plan how long the Production Process should take

When you get to this stage of product development, you also need to plan:

1) how your methods might have to <u>change</u> to produce the product <u>in volume</u>
2) <u>each stage</u> of the process in a great deal of <u>detail</u>
3) <u>how long</u> each stage will take
4) what needs to be <u>prepared</u> before you can start each stage
5) how you will <u>ensure consistency</u> and <u>quality</u>

See the <u>next page</u> as well for some different ways to help with this planning.

Clear construction details — "Insert tab A into slot B..."*

You know what they say... the devil's in the detail. Yeah, well, I don't know exactly what that means, but it's probably got something to do with being really precise. And that's what you've got to do with your manufacturer's specification, or your masterpiece could end up as a dog's dinner.

* ...which doesn't fit, so try it in every other slot before widening slot B until it does actually fit. Repeat for tabs C, D and E.

Planning Production

Making one or two examples of your product is (relatively) easy. But mass-producing it is a whole different ball game. And it takes a shed-load of careful planning.

Use Charts to help you

You need to work out how long each stage will take, and how these times will fit into the total time you've allowed for production. There are different ways of doing this:

① **Work Order** This can be produced as a table or flow chart. The purpose of a work order is to plan in sequence each task to be carried out. This will also include: tools and equipment, quality control stages, safety, and so on.

Start and **end** a flow chart with a sausage-shaped box.

Processes go in rectangular boxes.

Decisions go in diamond-shaped boxes. These let you show where quality should be checked.

Day	Process	Tools needed
1	Cut main block of wood	Panel saw
	Cut 4 turnip-holder holes	Drill, fret saw
2	Paint main block of wood	Paint, paint brush

② **Gantt Chart** This is a time plan showing the management of tasks. The tasks are listed down the left-hand side, and the timing plotted across the top. The coloured squares show how long each task takes, and the order they're done in.

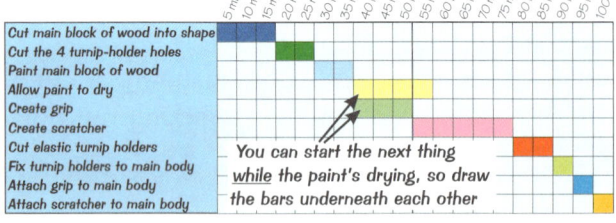

You can start the next thing while the paint's drying, so draw the bars underneath each other

Test that the Product Works and Meets the Specification

1) When you think you've got the final product, it's vital to test it. Most important of all, you have to make sure it works, and meets the original design specification.

2) More questionnaires or surveys may help here. Ask a wide range of people to give their opinions about the finished product.

3) If your product fails to match any part of the specification, you must explain why. You really have to stand back and have a good hard think about your work. If you aren't satisfied with the way any part of the process went, think of how you could put it right for next time. Write it down in the form of a report.

4) This type of final evaluation is called summative evaluation — it summarises what you've learnt.

There's nothing like a good chart...

So, that's all you have to do when it comes to your project. Just do in a few short weeks pretty much what it takes people in industry several months to complete, and you've got no worries.

Section One — The Design Process

Revision Summary for Section One

So that's the section over with, and what a roller-coaster ride full of fun and excitement it was. Yeah, well, the fun's not over yet, so don't look so disappointed. There's still some exciting revision questions for you to tackle. So try the questions, and then have a look back through the section to see if you got them all right. If you did — great. But if you got any wrong, have another careful read of the section and then <u>try the questions again</u>. And keep doing this until you can get all the questions right. That way, you know you're learning stuff.

1) What is the name given to the whole process of designing and making something?
2) Give three reasons why a new product might be needed.
3) Describe the kind of information you should put in your design brief.
4) Give three ways in which research can help you when you're designing a new product.
5) Explain how a questionnaire can be useful.
6) Give two other methods you could use to carry out research.
7) What is the name given to the process of drawing conclusions from your research?
8) Explain what is meant by a design specification.
9) Why might some points in a design specification be hard to assess just by looking at the product?
10) When would you compile an initial design specification?
11) Give three ways of getting started on your ideas.
12) What does the word 'annotate' mean?
13) What information should you include in your designs?
14) Why should you aim to produce a number of design ideas?
15) Give three techniques for presenting your designs.
16) Name two ways of developing your designs further.
17) Explain why it's useful to model your designs.
18) Describe two kinds of improvement you could make to your design.
19) When should you make an evaluation of your design? a) at the end of the project b) throughout the project c) evaluation is for wimps and sissies.
20) Describe two ways of evaluating your work.
21) What is meant by the phrase 'formative evaluation'?
22) Explain why a manufacturer's specification needs to be very precise.
23) Give four kinds of information that need to be on a manufacturer's specification.
24) When using a Gantt chart, what information goes down the left-hand side?
25) Describe two methods of planning how long the manufacturing process should take.
26) Describe the process of 'summative evaluation'.

Section One — The Design Process

SECTION TWO — TOOLS AND PROCESSES

Hand Tools

It's not all fancy high-tech stuff in this section. You need to know about hand tools too.

Saws are the Main Cutting Tools

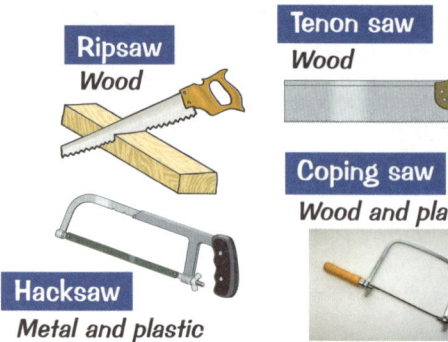

1) Different saws have teeth designed for cutting different materials. Tenon saws and ripsaws are used on wood. Hacksaws are used for cutting metals and plastics. Coping saws can be used on either wood or plastic, and are mainly for cutting curves.
2) Saws have to be kept sharp, either by sharpening (e.g. tenon saw) or replacing the blade (e.g. coping saw).

Planes and Files are Used for Shaping and Smoothing

1) This is a bench plane:
2) It has an angled blade that shaves off thin layers of material.
3) It's used on wood for removing material (shaping).

1) Files have hundreds of small teeth to cut away at a material.
2) Different cuts of file make them suitable for different processes: rough cuts are for removal of material, fine cuts are for finishing (final smoothing).
3) Most files are meant for metals and plastics, but there are special ones with very coarse teeth called cabinet rasps for use on wood.

Drills Make Holes (no kidding...)

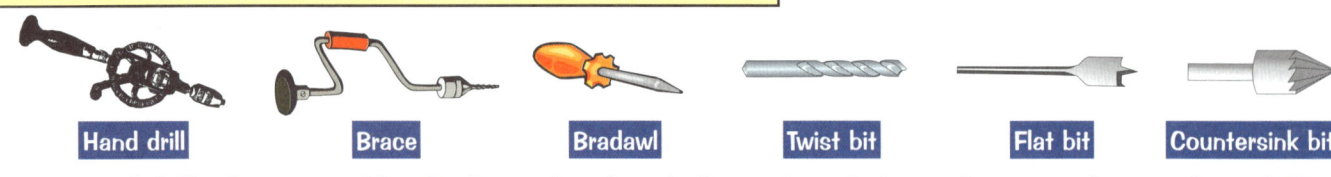

Hand drill   Brace   Bradawl   Twist bit   Flat bit   Countersink bit

1) Hand drills, braces and bradawls are hand tools for making holes. There are also machine drills and hand-held power drills. All drills rotate the drill bit clockwise and press it against the material.
2) Twist bits are used for drilling small holes into wood, metals and plastics.
3) Flat bits are used on wood and plastics to drill large flat-bottomed holes.
4) Countersink bits make holes for screw heads to sit in.
5) Different bits are suitable for different materials. Spade bits and auger bits are used on wood. High speed steel (HSS) twist bits are used on metals and plastics.

Chisels are Used for Shaping Woods and Metals

1) Chisels are used to cut away and shape materials.
2) Wood chisels (bevel-edged, firmer and mortise chisels) are used on wood and are hit with a mallet.
3) Cold chisels are used on metals and are hit with a hammer.
4) Gougers are chisels with grooves in them — they're used for sculpting.

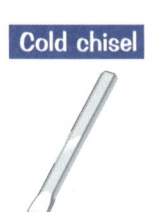
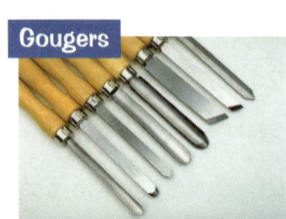

Learn about tools — you know the drill...

Before removing material always mark out what's to be removed and then double-check your marking out. It's a bit tricky to stick stuff back on if you've cut it off by mistake.

11

Machine Tools

Machines tools do the same jobs as manual tools — but a lot quicker and more accurately.

Machine Tools are Quick and Accurate

1) These are usually stationary and are often bolted to the workbench or the floor.
2) They can be used for processing large quantities of material accurately and quickly.
3) Most machines used for wood are attached to a dust extractor.
4) Safety glasses should be used and clothing tucked in to avoid catching in machines.

There are some Ace Machines for Cutting and Drilling

Whether you have these tools in your D&T workshop or not, you still need to know that they exist and what you'd use them for.

The circular saw or saw bench has a round blade and is used to cut wood and man-made wooden materials like plywood to size. It makes straight cuts only.

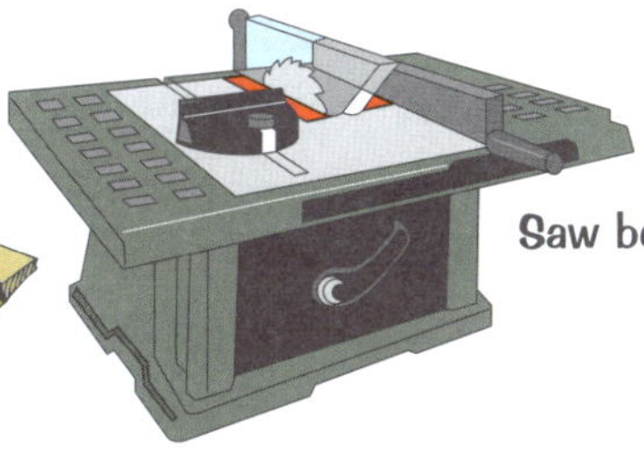

Saw bench

Circular saw

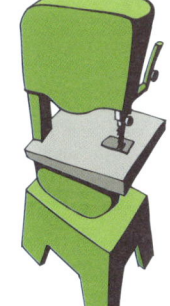

The band saw has a blade in a long flexible loop and is normally used to cut wood, but special blades can be bought for use on plastics and softer metals. The blades come in different widths and can be used for straight or curved cuts.

A planer and thicknesser (either separate or both in a single machine) are used for flattening the surface of pieces of wood and for reducing their thickness to a specified measurement.

A pillar drill or pedestal drill is used with HSS twist bits, or other types of suitable bit (see page 10), to make round holes. They can be used on all kinds of materials, depending on the bit used.

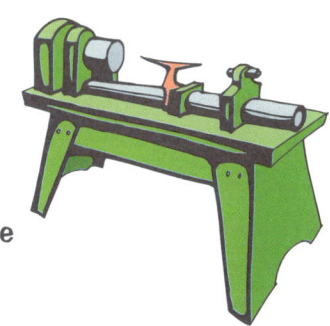

Lathes come in two types — wood lathes and engineers' lathes (for working metal). A piece of material is held and rotated by the lathe, while the turning tool or cutting bit is pressed onto the material to cut it. Lathes are used to produce round objects.

All this information is giving me a saw head...

Machines are cool, don't you reckon — especially compared with doing it by hand. Personally, I'm hopeless at sawing — never get it in a straight line and generally cut myself. Not fun. But give me a saw bench and I'm your... um... person. Lovely neat edges and no missing fingers. Smashing.

Section Two — Tools and Processes

Machine and Power Tools

Just wait till you see these Sanders and Grinders

Aah... these little beauties...

1) A sanding disc spins a disc of abrasive paper which the material's pushed against.
2) It's used for trimming accurately to a line.
3) Different types of abrasive are available for use on wood, metal, and plastics.

1) A bench grinder contains abrasive wheels of different grades (coarse to smooth).
2) It's used to remove metal for shaping or finishing purposes, as well as for sharpening edged tools such as chisels.

1) A milling machine is used to remove metal one thin layer at a time to produce the required size or shape.
2) It can also be used to make a surface absolutely flat.
3) It can produce a very accurate finish.

Power Tools are Hand-held Motorised Tools

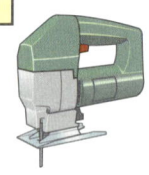

1) A jigsaw has interchangeable blades and variable speeds.
2) You can make straight or curved cuts in all materials, but it is quite slow. (See page 53 for more on jigs.)

1) You can get a hand-held version of the circular saw (see page 11).
2) In this case the wood is held stationary and the saw is moved along it, using adjustable fences for guidance.
3) It's good for making straight cuts very quickly in wood.

1) A planer is used like a bench plane to remove shavings of wood. It's used either to reduce the material to the required size, or for rough shaping.
2) The advantage of a power planer is that it takes much less effort and is much faster — but it's not as accurate as a bench plane.

Don't let this page grind you down...

It goes without saying, but don't be an idiot with power tools. Waving a circular saw around might seem amusing at the time but you'll probably regret it if you accidentally cut someone's head off.

Section Two — Tools and Processes

Deforming

Deforming means changing the shape of a material.

Laminating is Gluing Thin Strips of Wood Together

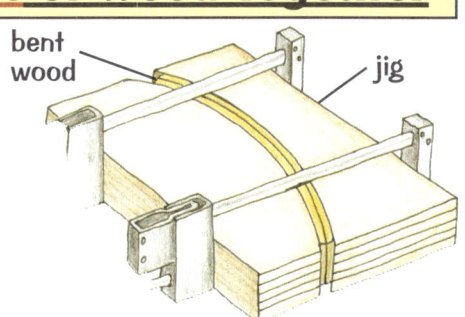
bent wood — jig

1) Thin strips of wood (usually 2-6 mm thick) are glued together, like plywood.
2) This 'sandwich' is held in a jig, which keeps it in the shape of the finished product whilst the glue dries.
3) Items produced this way include chair and table legs, roof beams and rocking chair runners.

Most Metals need to be Heated before Bending

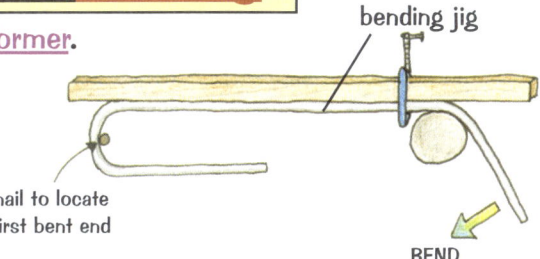
bending jig / nail to locate first bent end / BEND

1) Some thin pieces of metal can be bent cold on a jig or former.
2) Thicker or harder metals have to be heated or annealed first (see p25) and allowed to cool.
3) This makes them soft enough to bend easily, but the annealing process might have to be repeated as bending makes them go hard again ('work hardening').

Sheet Metals can be Folded...

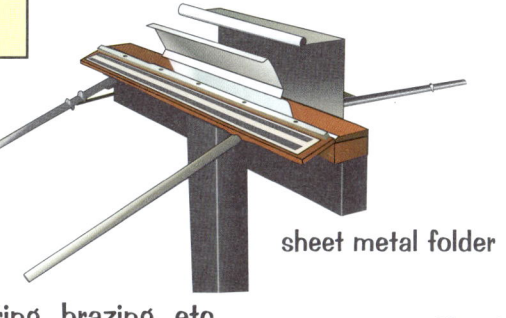
sheet metal folder

1) This is a method of shaping sheet metals such as aluminium and tin plate.
2) The outline of the product, e.g. a box, is marked out and cut from a flat sheet of metal.
3) The sides are then bent or folded up using folding bars, formers and mallets.
4) The corners are then joined using rivets, soldering, brazing, etc.

...and so can Plastics...

The element heats the plastic along the line where you want to bend it.

1) Line bending is ideal for use with acrylic sheets — e.g. for making picture frames and pencil holders, etc.
2) It can be done manually or with a line bender or strip heater.

Iron and Steel are Forged

1) Metal, especially iron and steel, can be heated in a forge. A forge is a fire with air blown into the middle of it to produce a very hot flame.
2) When the metal's hot enough to have softened sufficiently, it's taken out and hammered into shape on an anvil.

Dave said he'd deform my nose if I kept seeing his girlfriend...

If you're making something out of metal, you might find that you end up using iron or steel. Now, iron and steel can be forged. But if I were you, I'd use the real stuff. It's probably better.

Section Two — Tools and Processes

Deforming

Most of these processes involve heat — so take necessary safety precautions (see p45).

Press Moulding is Used to Shape Thermosets

1) A 'slug' of thermosetting plastic powder is put into a 'female' mould.
2) A former is pressed onto it and pushes the plastic into the mould.
3) Very high temperatures and pressures liquify the powder, and the plastic is set into a permanent shape.

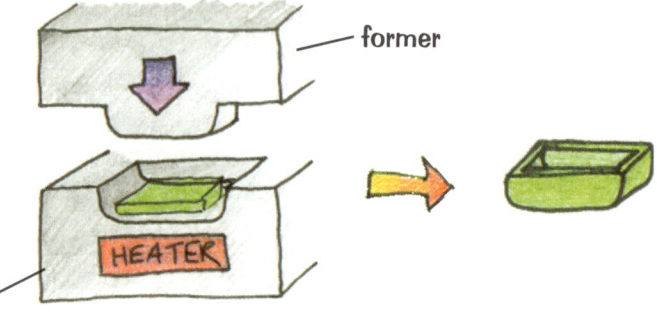

In Vacuum Forming, Air is Sucked from Round the Mould

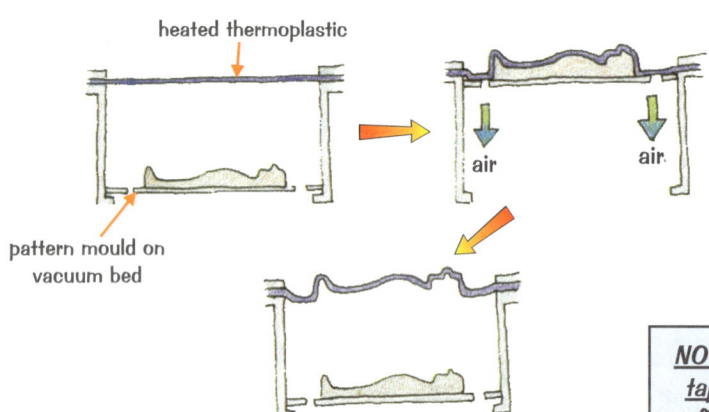

1) A sheet of thermoplastic is heated until it goes soft.
2) A pattern (or male mould) is put onto the vacuum bed. The bed is then lifted close to the heated plastic.
3) The air is sucked out from under the plastic. Atmospheric pressure forces the plastic onto the pattern mould.

NOTE: The sides of the pattern must be slightly tapered and the corners rounded to allow the finished product to release from the mould.

Blow Moulding Uses Air

1) A sheet of thermoplastic is clamped to the bed of the former and is heated until soft.
2) Air is blown under it, which forces the plastic up through a large hole in the bed.
3) This forms a bubble or dome, and is used to make dome-shaped products.

thermoplastic bowl

A more versatile method is where the softened plastic sheet is blown into a solid mould:

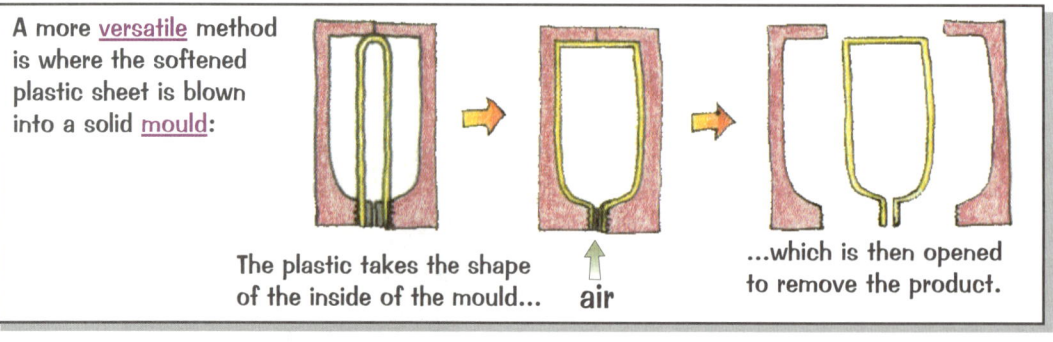

This method is often used to produce bottles and containers.

Pop Idol moulding is used to make Darius, Gareth, Will... yuk...

It's not that hard to remember this stuff — press moulding uses pressure, vacuum forming works by creating a vacuum and blow moulding works by blowing air into the plastic. Once you've got that, you need to learn the diagram for each, and an example of what you could make that way.

Section Two — Tools and Processes

Reforming

Reforming is where metals or plastics are liquified, usually by heat and pressure, and then shaped in some form of mould. How absolutely amazing. This stuff really keeps me on the edge of my seat.

Die Casting is Used to Mould Metals and Thermoplastics

1) Die casting is a process used to mould metals and thermoplastics.
2) The material is melted and poured into a mould which is in the shape of the product.
3) Some plastic resins can be cold-poured into moulds (without heating). They harden or set through a chemical reaction.

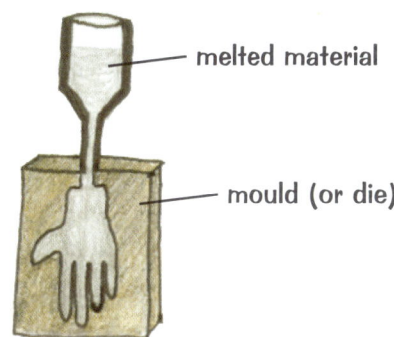

– melted material
– mould (or die)

Injection Moulding Uses Pressure to Mould Plastics

1) This is similar to casting, but the molten material is forced into a closed mould under pressure.
2) The plastic is often melted using built-in heaters.
3) This is an industrial process which is usually automatic and continuous.

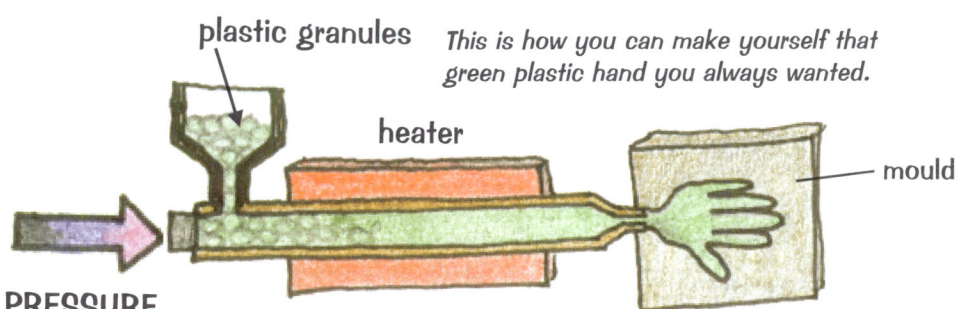

This is how you can make yourself that green plastic hand you always wanted.

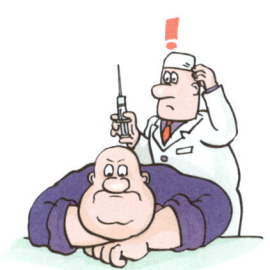

Plastics expert Brian had doubts about his new job.

Extrusion Produces Long, Continuous Strips

1) Used for some metals and thermoplastics, this process is very similar to injection moulding.
2) The material is melted and forced under pressure through a die.
3) It produces long, continuous strips of the moulding, such as plastic-covered wire, and plastic and aluminium edgings.

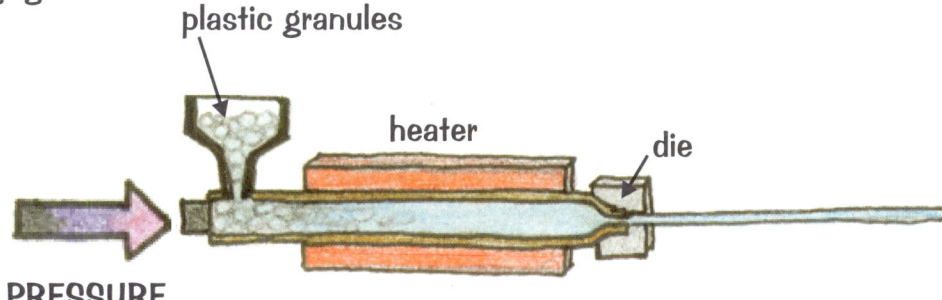

Don't eat this book — because this page is all mould-y...

Reforming processes are usually industrial processes for mass production, and are not usually economically viable for small quantities of products. Like my life-size model of Eamonn Holmes.

Section Two — Tools and Processes

Assembly and Finishing

This is the putting together of components to build the final product.

Assembly — Putting the Product Together

1) If permanent joining methods are to be used, it's vital to double-check the fit of the parts before final assembly. The project could be ruined if you can no longer get access to carry out other processes you might have forgotten.

2) Sometimes it is easier to clean up (e.g. with glasspaper) and apply a finish (e.g. paint) before final assembly, because access to inside areas for finishing is easier.

3) When gluing, soldering, brazing, or welding it's vital to get the joint areas clean and free from dirt and oil, etc.

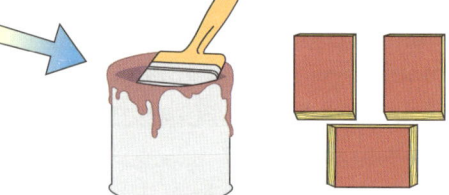

4) It's important not to touch areas to be joined after cleaning as fingerprints can leave enough grease on the surface to stop the joint from working.

5) When gluing, make sure you've tried the parts together first in a 'dry run'. This avoids getting halfway through gluing and finding that a part won't go on properly.

6) Gluing up (and often soldering, brazing and welding) needs clamps to hold the work securely whilst joining. Removing clamps too early can break the joint. Some glues require the joint to be clamped for 12 hours or more.

Finishing — Making it Look Pretty

Finishing is the final process in the making of any product. It makes the product look good and protects it from moisture and dirt.

1) Before finishes are applied it is important to remove any visible tool marks and blemishes with files, emery cloth, glasspaper, etc.

2) If paint of any type is to be applied, the surface must first be cleaned to remove grease and dust.

3) Different paints are produced for different materials and for use in different situations. It's important to select the correct type — otherwise it might not stick to the material, and it could even damage it. You've got to be especially careful when painting particular plastics.

4) Cellulose paint is generally applied to metal. It's sprayed on and looks great because it gives a very smooth finish. However, it's expensive as spraying means that much of the paint doesn't end up on the product.

Assembly — where all the teachers and kids are really bored...

Before starting assembly of your project stop and think — have you completed all the other necessary processes to the required standard first? And, can you put it off till another day?

Section Two — Tools and Processes

Fabricating — Screws and Bolts

Fabricating is the joining of pieces using the most appropriate method.
Different methods are used for different materials and in different situations.

Screws and Bolts are Used with Woods, Metals and Plastics

1) There are different types of screws for use with wood, metals, and plastics.

2) Woodscrews often require 'pilot' and 'clearance' holes to be drilled before the screw is inserted. As the screw is turned by a screwdriver, the thread (the twisty bit around the outside of the screw) pulls it into the wood. Different types of head are available for different jobs, e.g. round, countersunk, slotted and cross heads.

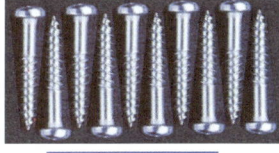
Woodscrews

3) Self-tapping screws have hardened threads and are designed to cut their own threaded holes in hard materials such as metals and hard plastics.

4) Machine screws have a straight shank and are used with washers and nuts. Heads vary (round, pan, countersunk, etc.). Some are tightened with a screwdriver (cross and slotted types), and some with an Allen key (socket head).

Self-tapping screws

5) Bolts are similar to machine screws but have a square or hexagonal head and are tightened with spanners.

6) Screws and bolts are usually made from steel, brass or stainless steel, and are 'self-finished' or plated with zinc, brass, chrome, or black japan (a black varnish).

Bolt — head, thread, shank

Threading is Often Used to Make Joints More Secure

1) Threading is a method of fastening machine screws and bolts directly into a metal or plastic component without using nuts.

2) A hole is drilled and a set of 'taps' used to cut a female thread in the hole. The screw is inserted into it and tightened until it stops.

3) A round rod can be made to fit a threaded hole by cutting a male thread onto the outside of the rod. Male threads are cut either with a 'split die' or on a lathe. This allows components to be joined directly without the use of bolts or screws.

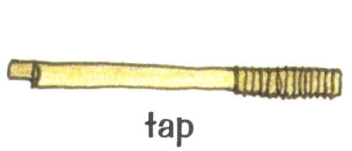
tap

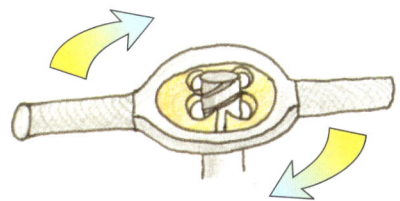
split die

If you don't learn this page you'll be scr... um... scuppered...

Remember, screws are much like people in some ways — they have different shaped heads. But in other ways they're very different — for example, I've never seen anyone with a countersunk head.

Section Two — Tools and Processes

Fabricating — Nails, Rivets and Adhesives

Nails and rivets and threads — the fun never stops with Resistant Materials. Ah, no, I tell a lie — the fun always stops with Resistant Materials. Much better — that first one didn't sound right at all.

Nails are Used for Joining Bits of Wood Together

1) These are similar in use to woodscrews but have a straight shank with no thread.
2) They're inserted with a hammer and can be punched below the surface with a nail punch to hide the head.
3) Nails are only used in wood and wooden products, e.g. plywood. They're much quicker to use than screws, but the joint they make is nowhere near as strong.
4) Nails are mostly made from steel, but special ones can be made from other metals, e.g. brass for use in boat building. Like screws, they come with a variety of head and shank shapes for different uses.

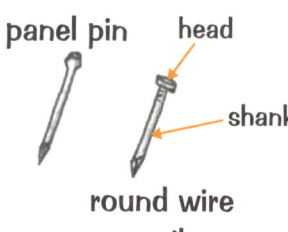

Rivets are Mainly Used for Joining Sheet Metal

1) A rivet is a metal peg with a head on one end. Rivets are used mostly for joining pieces of metal.
2) A hole is drilled through both pieces of metal and the rivet is inserted with a 'set' (hammer-like tool). The head is held against the metal whilst the other end is flattened and shaped into another head with a hammer.
3) 'Pop' (or 'blind') rivets are now very common. They can be used where there is only access to one side of the material (hence 'blind' rivet). It's a fast and easy method of joining sheet metal.

standard rivets

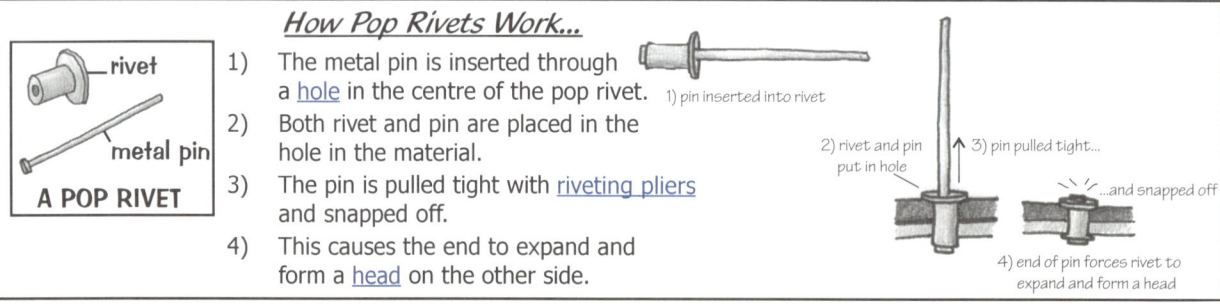

How Pop Rivets Work...
1) The metal pin is inserted through a hole in the centre of the pop rivet.
2) Both rivet and pin are placed in the hole in the material.
3) The pin is pulled tight with riveting pliers and snapped off.
4) This causes the end to expand and form a head on the other side.

You Need to Choose the Right Adhesive for the Job

1) There are many different types of adhesive for use with different materials and for different jobs, e.g. PVA and animal glue (for wood), contact adhesive and epoxy resin (for lots of materials).
2) Adhesives will only work properly if the right one is chosen for the job, and if the surfaces to be joined are thoroughly cleaned.
3) Some plastics can't be glued as they're too smooth, and have a greasy texture which stops the glue from 'keying in'.
4) Adhesives are often used to reinforce other methods of fabrication, e.g. joints in wood.

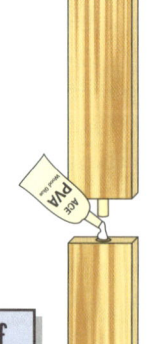

You often get a little tube of PVA wood glue with flat-pack furniture to reinforce joints.

See p31 for more about adhesives.

That page was riveting...

When deciding which method of fabrication to use on a product, think carefully about which is more important — speed of assembly or strength. It's often a trade-off between the two.

Section Two — Tools and Processes

Fabricating — Joints

Wood can be joined together in several ways — either by the traditional method of cutting joints and nailing and gluing together, or by using special fittings which can be taken apart again.

Some Joints are More Permanent than Others

1) There are dozens of different joints, e.g. <u>dovetail</u>, <u>mortise & tenon</u>, <u>housing</u>, <u>halving</u> and <u>mitred</u>, for use in different situations. It's important to use the right joint in the right place.

2) Joints are often <u>glued</u> to make them <u>secure</u> and <u>permanent</u>.

3) <u>Marking out</u> and <u>cutting</u> joints takes a lot of skill. <u>Accuracy</u> is vital if the joint is to fit and hold together (as well as look good).

BUTT JOINT

Pretty <u>feeble</u> but very <u>quick</u> and <u>simple</u>. Often used for joints in <u>cheap pine furniture</u>.

MITRED JOINT

Mitred joints are <u>similar to butt joints</u> but prettier and <u>trickier to cut</u>. Used for <u>picture frames</u>.

DOWEL JOINT

Dowel joints use a <u>wooden or plastic peg</u>, called a dowel, which fits into aligned <u>holes</u> to <u>reinforce the joint</u>. Often replace traditional joints in <u>factory-made furniture</u>.

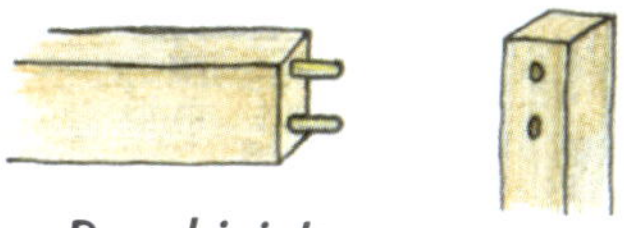

MORTISE AND TENON

Mortise and tenon joints (cut with a tenon saw and mortise chisel) are <u>dead strong</u>. Often used in <u>tables</u> and <u>chairs</u>.

LAP JOINT

Lap joints have a <u>larger surface area</u> for gluing than butt joints, so they're a <u>bit stronger</u>. Used in some <u>drawers</u> and <u>boxes</u>.

HALVING JOINT

Halving joints are <u>fairly strong</u> — again, due to the large surface area for gluing. Sometimes used in <u>frame construction</u>.

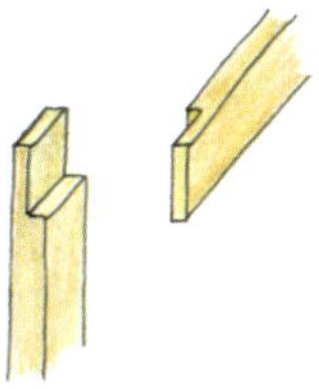

HOUSING JOINT

Housing joints are often used in shelving units as they provide a <u>good surface area</u> for gluing, and the shelf is supported all the way along its depth.

DOVETAIL JOINT

Dovetail joints are <u>very strong</u> and look <u>attractive</u>. They're often used in <u>drawer</u> construction. They're the <u>bee's knees</u>, but they're a <u>pain in the neck to make</u>. Unless you have a dovetail jig (see p53).

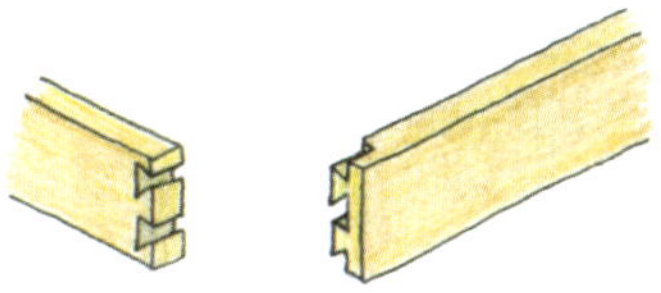

Knock-Down Fittings are Non-Permanent Joints

1) These are <u>blocks</u>, <u>brackets</u> (plastic or metal) and other fittings which enable furniture to be assembled and taken apart again easily.

2) They are used instead of traditional joints, and are very <u>fast</u> to use, but are nowhere near as <u>strong</u> as glued joints.

3) Most types are assembled with <u>screwdrivers</u> or <u>Allen keys</u>.

4) They are usually used for cheap '<u>flat-pack</u>' furniture.

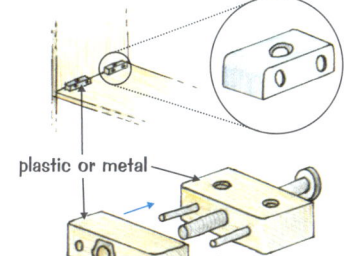

Butt joint... Nope, nothing funny about that...

So, just to wrap up... which joint you use depends on:
a) whether you're a traditionalist, b) how much time you've got, c) how good you are at woodwork,
d) whether you want to take the thing apart again, e) how strong you want the joint to be.

Section Two — Tools and Processes

Fabricating — Joining Metals

It's the page you've been waiting for — it's all about welding and stuff. Splendid.

Soldering, Brazing & Welding are for Joining Metal

These are methods of joining metal by the use of varying amounts of heat.

1) Soldering is a relatively low temperature process. Solder, made from tin and lead, is melted onto the components to be joined, sticking them together when it cools and solidifies. A soldering iron or blow torch can be used for this process.

Soldering Iron

2) Brazing is a higher temperature process which uses brass spelter as the joining material. It's much stronger than soldering. Either a gas brazing torch, a blow torch, or a brazing attachment for an electric-arc welder is used to heat the joint.

Blow torch

3) Welding uses a very high temperature from an oxyacetylene torch, an electric-arc welder or a TIG welder to actually melt the edges of the joint so that they flow together. Thinned metal or slight gaps are filled with metal from a welding rod. This is by far the strongest method of joining metal.

Welding equipment — the mask protects your face, particularly your eyes, from heat and sparks.

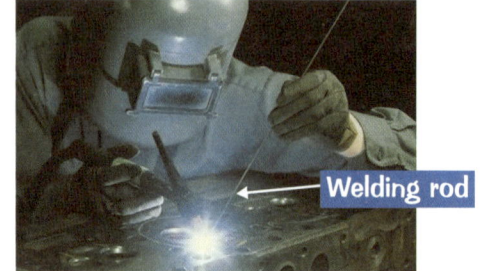
Welding rod

The Joint Needs to be Carefully Prepared

For all three of the above processes careful preparation of the joint is vital:

1) Joints have to be well-fitting with minimal gaps.
2) They must also be very clean and free from grease. Fingerprints on the surface can stop solder or brass spelter from 'taking'.
3) 'Flux' has to be used when soldering and brazing and on some metals when welding. This stops the air oxidising the surface of the metal whilst heating it, as this too would stop the joint from taking.

Doughnuts — for while you work.

Marty has to get to 88 mph to make the flux capacitor work...

Extra care needs to be taken with heat processes. And make sure you use the safety and protective clothing and equipment provided. And don't try and solder your hand to your face. It'll hurt.

Section Two — Tools and Processes

Computerised Production

Almost everything is designed on computer now — washing machines, hoovers, cars, planes, houses, cameras, computers. It's much easier and quicker than doing it all on paper.

CAD — Computer-Aided Design

See page 50 for how this is used in industry.

1) Computer Aided Design involves designing products on a computer, rather than the traditional methods on paper.
2) Software ranges from 2-D engineering drawing programs to 3-D frame and solid modelling packages.
3) CAD allows designers to model and compare designs cheaply and relatively easily. Also, many problems can be ironed out before the production of prototypes.
4) In 3-D programs, finished products can be viewed from all angles, and scales of components can be worked out in relation to each other.
5) Finished drawings can be printed off on large format inkjet printers or plotters, or can be distributed electronically and instantly to production teams at factories across the world.

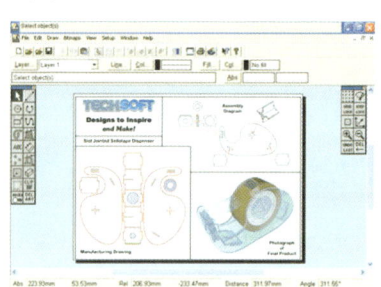
This is 'TECHSOFT DESIGN TOOLS — 2D DESIGN'. (Nice blue background...)

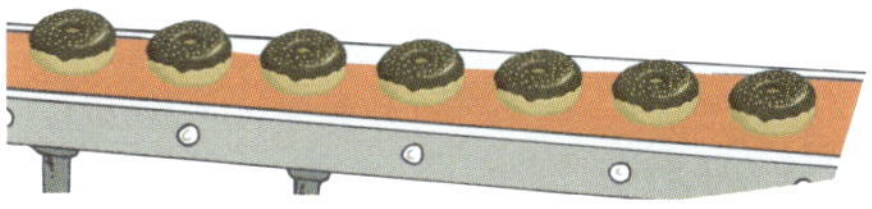

CAM — Computer-Aided Manufacture

Mmmmmmmmm

1) Computer-Aided Manufacture is usually linked with CAD.
2) Components and products are made on machines, such as milling machines, which are controlled and operated by computers rather than by people.
3) Products are designed with CAD software and control data is downloaded from the computer to the control unit of the machine.

a milling machine

Machines used in CAM are Computer Numerically Controlled — CNC

1) The machines used in the CAM process are Computer Numerically Controlled.
2) This means the CAD/CAM program works out the necessary movements of the tool head and sends the data to the machine in the form of numbers. The machine's onboard processor interprets the numbers and controls the movement of the tool head.
3) Machines which can be controlled in this way include lathes, milling machines and drilling machines.

a CNC cutter and plotter

ADVANTAGES of CNC:
1) Less cost due to less need for separate specialised machine tools for each product.
2) Less chance of human error.
3) The product can easily and quickly be changed without expensive retooling.

DISADVANTAGES of CNC:
1) High initial cost of the machines.
2) High cost of training programmers and operators.
3) Fast special purpose machines are cheaper than CNC machines for large-scale production runs.

My sister's pants were manufactured by a computer — they're CAMiknickers...

End of section. Now you should know all you have to about 'tools and processes'. But if you don't, go back over the section again and really try and ram it into your head. Then have a doughnut.

Section Two — Tools and Processes

Revision Summary for Section Two

Well here we are again... at the end of a section and at the start of a Revision Summary. What could be better. What a beautiful place to be. Sit back and relax. Look forward to answering thirty-one questions all about 'tools and processes'. Bet you can't wait. I know how much fun I had when I was writing them. There I was, about to go out with my mates, when I realised I hadn't done these questions. "What a wonderful place the world is," I thought, "and how lucky I am to be able to stay in and write questions about Resistant Materials instead of going out with my friends."

1) Define the terms 'deforming', 'reforming', 'fabricating', 'assembling' and 'finishing' in the context of resistant materials.
2) Name four different types of hand saw. What is each one used for?
3) Name three different types of drill bit. Say what each one is used for.
4) a) Describe a saw bench, and say what it is used for.
   b) What is the name of the hand-held version of a saw bench?
   c) What is the main difference between the way you use the two saws?
5) Describe how a band saw works.
6) Name two uses of a bench grinder.
7) Which power tool would you use to cut along a curved line?
8) Describe the process of laminating.
9) What is 'work hardening'.
10) What is a forge?
11) Describe the process of press moulding.
12) Draw a series of diagrams to illustrate vacuum forming.
13) How does blow moulding work, and what shape is produced in this process?
14) Explain the difference between casting and injection moulding.
15) What shapes are produced by extrusion? Describe the process.
16) Name three things you must do before permanently assembling a product (using solder).
17) Give one advantage and one disadvantage of using cellulose paint.
18) Name the three main types of screw. How do they differ, and what are they used for?
19) Explain the difference between a bolt and a machine screw.
20) Name the tool used to cut a female thread.
21) Describe two different ways of cutting a male thread.
22) Give one advantage and one disadvantage of using nails rather than woodscrews.
23) Why can some plastics not be glued?
24) How does a pop rivet work?
25) Name four types of wood joint.
26) What is the main disadvantage of using dovetail joints?
27) What are 'knock-down' fittings?
28) Describe the main differences between soldering, brazing and welding.
29) Why do you need to use flux when soldering and brazing? What does it do?
30) What do the abbreviations CAD, CAM and CNC stand for?
31) Give three advantages and three disadvantages of CNC over specialist machines.

Section Two — Tools and Processes

SECTION THREE — MATERIALS & COMPONENTS

Properties of Materials

Different materials have different physical and mechanical properties. I kid you not.

Mechanical Properties — Learn 'em All...

You need to be totally familiar with these terms — if you start getting strength and hardness mixed up, or get confused between malleability and ductility, you'll drop marks all over the place.

STRENGTH:
1) A material's strength is a measure of its ability to withstand forces without breaking.
2) Tensile strength resists pulling forces — e.g. the rope in a tug-of-war.
3) Compressive strength resists squashing forces — e.g. bridge supports.
4) Bending strength resists forces trying to bend — e.g. surfboards.
5) Shear strength resists strong sliding forces — e.g. a rivet needs to withstand shear forces.
6) Torsional strength resists twisting forces — e.g. drill bits need to withstand twisting forces.

HARDNESS:
1) The ability to withstand abrasive wear and tear, denting and bending.
2) Very important for tools that cut, like files and drills.

PLASTICITY:
1) If a product can change shape permanently, without breaking or cracking, it's said to have good plastic qualities.
2) This could mean that a material is malleable (changes shape under pressure so can be moulded, e.g. by hammering) or ductile (can be drawn into wires).

BRITTLENESS:
1) Brittle materials can't withstand much stretching.
2) Brittle materials are more likely to crack or break than change their shape.
3) Glass and acrylic react like this under force.

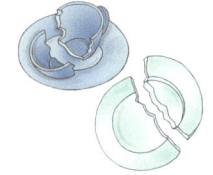 

TOUGHNESS:
1) Tough is the opposite of brittle.
2) If a material is tough, it's hard to break or snap.
3) Armour and bulletproof vests need to be tough.

DURABILITY:
1) If a product is durable it is able to withstand repeated use.
2) Durable products also withstand wear and tear, weathering and corrosive attack.

Wouldn't like to be that duck...

Not a bundle of laughs, sure, but darn important stuff. Learn it, then turn over the page and write down: 1) a definition of each of the six words 2) anything else interesting about that property.

Metals

Some metals are pure metals and others (alloys) are mixtures of different metals.
Both types of metal can be classified into two basic groups — ferrous and non-ferrous.

Ferrous Metals contain Iron

1) These are the metals that contain iron.
2) Because of this, almost all of them are magnetic.
3) Examples: mild steel
   high-carbon steel
   stainless steel

METAL	PROPERTIES	USES
MILD STEEL	Quite strong and cheap but rusts easily and can't be hardened or tempered.	car bodies, screws, nuts, bolts, nails, washing machines
HIGH-CARBON STEEL	Harder than mild steel and can be hardened and tempered. But it's not as easy to work and also rusts.	drills, files, chisels, saws
STAINLESS STEEL	Hard and won't rust, but is more expensive.	medical equipment, sinks, kettles, cutlery (e.g. knives)

Non-Ferrous Metals — guess what? — Don't contain Iron

1) If a metal doesn't contain iron, it's non-ferrous.
2) Examples: aluminium
   brass
   copper

METAL	PROPERTIES	USES
ALUMINIUM	Lightweight and corrosion-resistant but expensive and not as strong as steel	aeroplanes, cans, ladders
BRASS	Quite strong, corrosion-resistant, malleable, ductile and looks good	door handles, electrical parts
COPPER	Relatively soft, malleable and ductile and a very good electrical conductor	wiring, pipes

An Alloy is a Mixture, e.g. Brass = Copper + Zinc

1) An alloy is a mixture of two or more metals, or a metal mixed with another element.
2) An alloy is a new material with different properties and different working characteristics.
3) Alloys can be grouped as ferrous (contains iron), e.g. steel = iron + carbon, and non-ferrous (doesn't contain iron), e.g. brass = copper + zinc.

— Different types of steel also contain varying quantities of other metals, such as chromium.

You can Buy Metals in Loads of Shapes and Sizes

1) Metal is extracted from the earth in the form of metal ore. It's then refined and processed to produce usable materials.

2) Metals are commonly available in a wide range of shapes and sizes, because it can be very difficult to convert one shape to another.

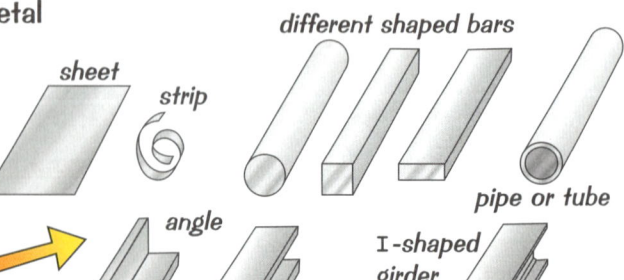

sheet, strip, different shaped bars, angle, pipe or tube, I-shaped girder, U-shaped channel

Metals — hahahaha...

Okay then, metals. Well, you've got your pure metals — like iron, copper and zinc, and you've got your alloys, which are mixtures — like brass and steel. Ferrous metals contain iron, e.g. steel and... err... well, iron. For your non-ferrous metals, remember ABC — Aluminium, Brass, Copper.

Section Three — Materials and Components

Metals

Metals are rarely used in their raw form without treating them first. Most need some kind of surface finish — either for aesthetic (appearance) reasons or to provide protection.

Heat Treatments — for Softening or Toughening

Metals can be heat-treated to change their properties and characteristics. The three main types of treatment are listed below:

1) **Annealing** — softening metal by heating and leaving to cool.

2) **Hardening** — heating and rapidly cooling a metal.
   The metal is heated to its upper critical temperature then plunged into cold water. It leaves the metal brittle, so is often followed by a process known as tempering...

   At the upper critical temperature, the atoms in the metal 'rearrange themselves' into a different structure.

3) **Tempering** — to make the metal tougher and less likely to break.
   When steel is tempered, it's first cleaned to make it bright in appearance and then gently heated. As it gets hotter, it changes gradually from a pale straw colour to blue — and the colour shows you how tough it's become.

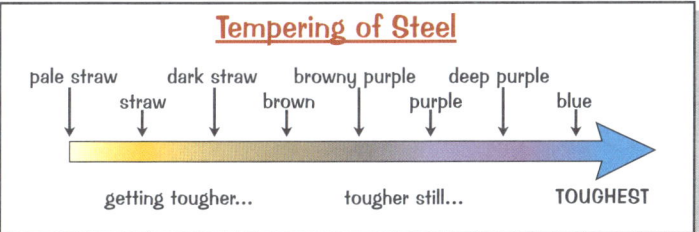

Tempering of Steel

Surface Finishes — for Protection and Looks

You need to know about a few different kinds of surface finish...

1) **Painting**

   A primer such as red oxide or zinc chromate is needed for steel (so that later coats of paint aren't absorbed by the metal). Hammerite is a durable top coat that's available in a range of colours and finishes — it offers protection and is quick drying.

2) **Plastic coating**

   A metal is heated evenly in an oven and then plunged into fluidised powder (i.e. very fine powder that's made to act like a liquid by passing gas through it) for a few seconds. The metal, with its thin coating of plastic, is then returned to the oven to completely fuse it to the surface.

3) **Polishing**

   This may be carried out by hand or by using a buffing wheel. The wheel is coated with abrasive polish and the metal is held against the spinning wheel until the required surface finish is achieved.

4) **Lacquering**

   This provides a barrier against tarnishing and oxidising, and is often used on decorative items such as jewellery. A thin layer of cellulose, gum or varnish is applied to leave a transparent coating.

Heat treatment? — sounds like the hairdresser's...

The metal must be thoroughly cleaned (e.g. with paraffin or white spirit) before adding a finish. You wouldn't want that Hammerite peeling off now would you — what a disaster that'd be.

Section Three — Materials and Components

Plastics

Most plastics are produced by industry using water, oil (or coal or gas), air and salt.
There are two families of plastics — thermoplastics and thermosetting plastics.

Thermoplastics — Recyclable and Bendy

1) Thermoplastics are recyclable.
2) They don't resist heat very well, so they can be ground down, melted and re-used — very important in today's society of increasing waste.
3) Thermoplastics are easily formed into shapes.
4) A moulded shape can be reheated and it will return to its original state — the material is known as having plastic memory.
5) Examples of thermoplastics: acrylic, ABS, polystyrene and polyethylene (polythene).

Thermosetting Plastics — Non-Recyclable and (usually) Rigid

1) These types of plastic are non-recyclable.
2) They resist heat and fire so are often used for electrical fittings and pan handles.
3) These types of plastic undergo a chemical change when heated (unlike thermoplastics) to become hard and rigid. They're not used in schools very often.
4) Examples of thermosetting plastics: melamine-formaldehyde, polyester resin, epoxy resin and urea-formaldehyde.

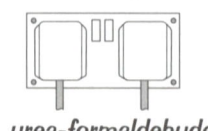
urea-formaldehyde

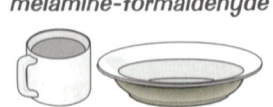
melamine-formaldehyde

...an' ye can get 'em in loads of different forms...

1) Plastics can be bought in many different forms — from powders, granules, pellets and liquids (for processing into finished products), through to films, sheets, rods, tubes and extruded mouldings (complex shapes).
2) Plastics don't need protective surface finishes, due to high resistance to corrosion and decay.
3) But for a nice appearance, wet and dry paper (silicon carbide paper) is applied to remove scratches from the plastic, and followed up with a mild abrasive polish or anti-static cream.
4) Alternatively, a buffing machine can be used. No Spike jokes, please.

New Plastics are still being Developed

The following materials are fairly recently-developed and have loads of uses:

1) Plastizote is a closed-cell polyethylene foam that has eliminated the need for the toxic chemicals presently used in the foam industry. It's suitable for a wide range of products, including shoe insoles, buoyancy aids and reusable packaging.
2) Plastics that conduct electricity can be made by putting stainless steel fibres into plastics.

Life in plastic — it's fantastic...

Thermosetting plastics can't be remoulded — i.e. once they're set, they're set permanently. Like when you pull a funny face and the wind changes. Something like that, anyway.

Section Three — Materials and Components

Wood

Woods can be divided into two main catagories — <u>softwood</u> and <u>hardwood</u>.
This is not a description of the wood — it just means what <u>type of tree</u> it comes from.

Softwood — Evergreen Trees, like Pine

1) Most softwood trees are <u>coniferous</u> (cone bearing). They typically have thin needle-like leaves and are <u>evergreen</u> — e.g. pine, cedar and yew.
2) They grow in colder climates and are <u>fast growing</u> — most reaching maturity within 30 years. This makes them easy to <u>replace</u> with new trees, so they're usually <u>cheaper</u> than hardwoods.

Pines:
1) There are several types of <u>pine</u> but they're all generally <u>pale yellow</u> with <u>brown streaks</u>.
2) <u>Scots pine</u> is fairly strong but knotty.
3) <u>Parana pine</u> is more expensive — it's hard and is best used for interior joinery.

Pine trees — before and after the 'chop'.

Hardwood — Deciduous Trees, like Oak

1) Most hardwood trees are <u>broadleaved</u> and <u>deciduous</u> (they shed their leaves annually) — e.g. oak, mahogany, beech and elm.
2) <u>Broadleaf</u> trees grow in warm climates and are usually <u>slow growing</u>. They can take around a hundred years to mature, so they're generally <u>more expensive</u> than softwoods.

Colours of the common hardwoods:

<u>mahogany</u>	reddish brown	<u>elm</u>	light reddish brown
<u>beech</u>	creamy/pinkish	<u>oak</u>	rich light brown

A deciduous tree in autumn. Ah, innit pretty...

The Bit about Woodstain...

Most woods need <u>protection</u>, particularly if they're going to be used <u>outdoors</u>.
Most hardwoods have an attractive grain and often don't have paint as a surface finish.

1) <u>Polyurethane varnish</u> can be used to seal and protect the surface of the wood, and give it a smooth surface finish. You can buy it clear or in a wide range of colours.
2) <u>Woodstain</u> can be applied to wood to enhance the appearance of the wood's <u>grain</u>. It's available in natural colours but also in bright blues, reds etc. Stains usually don't protect the wood, so varnish may need to be applied afterwards.
3) <u>Oil</u> can be used to maintain a <u>natural</u> appearance of the wood. Some oil-based finishes also offer protection to wood used outdoors.
4) <u>Paint</u> is often used to colour and <u>protect</u> wood. Emulsion paints are cheap, but they are <u>water-based</u>, so they don't protect wood from water. <u>Polyurethane paint</u> is more expensive but is <u>waterproof</u> and much <u>tougher</u>.

I wood have put two pages in on this if I could...

Ah... wood's lovely, isn't it. Except for the splinters. Or 'spelks', as my friend Tim would have it.
If he got splinters, he'd say, *"Ayaz — spelks!"* (Don't worry, that's just how they talk in my part of the world.)

Section Three — Materials and Components

Manufactured Boards

Solid woods (see p27) are cut straight from the tree. Man-made woods (boards) are made from the bits of waste that are produced when the trunks and branches are cut into planks.

Plywood — Loads of Layers

Plywood is a very popular man-made board, used for building and general construction.

1) Plywood is very strong for its weight and thickness, compared with solid wood.
2) It's made up of several layers — always an odd number of them.
3) The layers are glued with their grain at 90 degrees to each other — which is why it's so strong.
4) The outside of the board can be finished with a nice veneer (a thin layer of good quality wood) to make it look better.

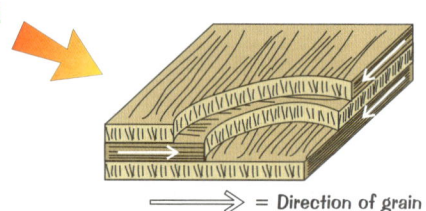

= Direction of grain

Blockboard and Laminboard — Blocks in a 'Sandwich'

Blockboard and laminboard are boards of similar construction. Although not as strong as plywood, they're a cheap substitute, especially when thicker boards are required.

1) Strips of softwood are glued together, side by side, and sandwiched between two veneers. The veneers add strength and make the board look nicer.
2) The outer veneers are glued with their grain at right angles to the grain of the inner core — this makes the board stronger.
3) The softwood used is usually pine or spruce. (Some countries use hardwood instead.)
4) The width of the softwood for laminboard is between 5 mm and 7 mm.
5) The width of the softwood for blockboard is thicker, at between 7 mm and 25 mm.

Cross-section of blockboard/laminboard.
Veneers
Strips of softwood

MDF and Chipboard — MFI eat your heart out...

Medium Density Fibreboard

1) Medium density fibreboard (MDF) is a popular board that's very cost-effective (cheap).
2) MDF has smooth faces and takes paint and other finishes well.

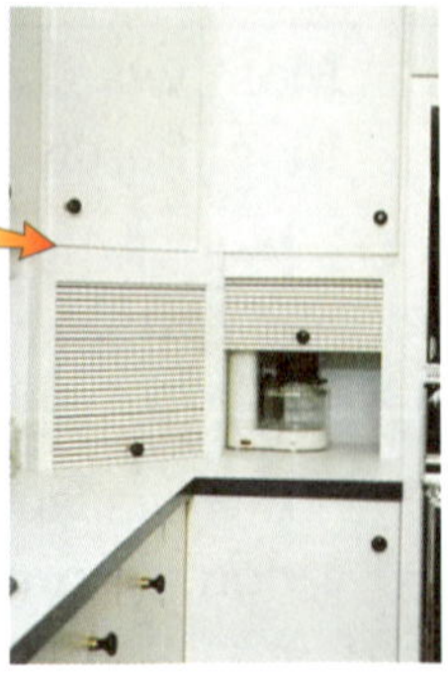

I reckon this kitchen's made with painted MDF.

Chipboard

1) This is produced by compressing wood particles together with glue.
2) It's cheap but not very strong, so is usually used with a hardwood or plastic veneered surface in cheap furniture.

A little bit of chipboard.

"Enjoying learning about wood?" — "No, I'm board"...

Man-made boards are available in large sizes — because they're not restricted by the size of the tree, like solid wood is. Knock-down (KD) joints (see p19) are the easiest way to join these boards.

Section Three — Materials and Components

31

Adhesives

Adhesives are used for joining materials together. The kind you need to use depends on what materials you're joining. So seatbelts on — here we go...

Polyvinyl Acetate (PVA) is used for Wood

1) Polyvinyl acetate (PVA) is a white woodworking glue.
2) There are two types of PVA — interior and exterior.
3) Interior will join wood as long as it doesn't get wet.
4) Exterior is more expensive, but is able to join wood in damp or wet conditions.
5) PVA is white and creamy and easy to use.

Contact Adhesive is very Strong

1) This glue is rubber based, and forms a very strong bond.
2) It's applied to both surfaces, and then the surfaces are kept apart for about 10 minutes until the glue goes tacky.
3) Then when the surfaces are brought into contact, the sticking is instant.
4) Contact adhesive has a strong, unpleasant odour — so it's best used in a well-ventilated area.

Epoxy Resin sticks almost Anything

1) The trade name for epoxy resin is Araldite.
2) Two separate substances are mixed in equal parts — they're both thick, sticky liquids, but one is yellow and one is clear.
3) Once mixed, epoxy resin will stick almost anything — ceramic to ceramic, metal to wood, wood to plastic, etc.
4) It takes about 15 minutes to harden and is expensive.

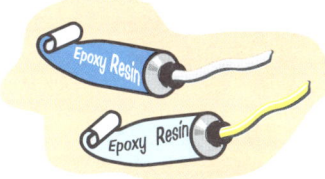

Superglue also sticks Most Things

Simon instantly regretted not removing the superglue from his fingers.

1) Superglue is even more expensive than epoxy resin but will stick to most things.
2) It certainly sticks to skin, so you have to be very careful.
3) It's a thin, clear liquid.
4) After applying the glue, slight pressure is required for a very strong bond.

Acrylic Cement is used for Plastics

1) Known as Tensol, this adhesive is used for plastics.
2) It's a watery, clear liquid.
3) It isn't particularly strong, but is ideal for plastic objects where the joints aren't going to be knocked about.

Adhesives — a gripping topic for sure...

I said it would be good, didn't I. And I wasn't lying, as I'm sure you'd agree. Well, let me tell you something else about adhesives... PVA is the most common wood glue used in schools.

Section Three — Materials and Components

Choosing the Best Material to Use

Selecting the right materials isn't <u>easy</u>. But it's something you've got to be able to do, otherwise you can end up in a right <u>pickle</u>.

Different Factors affect your Selection of Material

You should be able to make a good choice as long as you understand a material's <u>properties</u>, and know what it's being <u>used</u> for.

Functional Requirements — What does the product have to do?

Ask yourself the following questions:

1) What <u>demands</u> will be made on the material? (Will it have to withstand heavy loads or chemicals? Will it have to conduct heat or electricity?)

2) Will it be for <u>outdoor</u> or <u>indoor</u> use? (If it's for outside, you'll need to consider whether your material will <u>corrode</u>.)

3) Does it need to fit in with an <u>environment</u>? (Your material might need to be a particular <u>style</u> or have a certain <u>look</u>.)

Most of this car seems to have rusted away, leaving just the boot and half the back wheel. Probably the result of a poor choice of material.

Economics — How much money have you got?

You'll need to consider the following points:

1) The <u>size</u> of the product — materials like pewter are <u>expensive</u>, but may be a good choice for a small item of jewellery.

2) <u>Scale of production</u> — is your product a <u>one-off</u>, or will it be <u>batch</u> or <u>mass produced</u>? Stainless steel could be a possible material for a one-off product. But if you're mass-producing something that would be equally as good made from some kind of plastic, that might be cheaper.

Nowadays most cars are assembled by robots.

Availability of Supply — What can you get hold of?

Can you get hold of the material you want? And if you can, can you get it in a suitable form? Most materials are only available in <u>standard forms</u> and <u>sizes</u>, and it can be <u>very expensive</u> to get a material in any other form. This will have a direct effect on the <u>cost</u> and the <u>method of manufacture</u>.

For example, materials might be available as granules, strips, bars, tubes, rough sawn, planed...

Manufacturing Method — How will the product be made?

1) Some materials are easier to <u>join</u> than others (which will affect the production method used).

2) Also, the <u>material</u> must be suitable for the intended <u>production method</u> (and vice versa). For example, you can make something out of certain plastics using <u>injection moulding</u>, but it's no good planning to use this technique for wood.

I reckon you should just make everything out of cheese...

You need to know about different materials so you can choose the right one for the job in hand. Don't make a fireguard or teapot from chocolate, for example — they won't be much use. It sounds obvious, but it's a mistake that amateurs make all too often. Be smart — don't be one of them.

Section Three — Materials and Components

Revision Summary for Section Three

Yowzers — what a section that was. Yep, that was one for the thrill seekers among you, make no mistake. Lots of facts about wood and plastic. Boy oh boy, I can feel my pulse quickening at the very mention. Okay... perhaps I'm overstating things just a tad... maybe it wasn't that exciting. But it's definitely stuff you need to know, otherwise you might end up making something well dodgy when you come to do your project. So try these questions, and if you get any wrong, go back, check the section and then try them again. And repeat this process until you get every single question right.

1) Name six mechanical properties, and describe what they mean.
2) Explain the difference between ferrous and non-ferrous metals. Give two examples of each.
3) What is an alloy?
4) What is meant by the following terms:
   a) annealing   b) hardening   c) tempering?
5) Suggest two surface finishes for metal.
6) Name the two different kinds of plastic. How are they different? Give two examples of each.
7) What is plastizote?
8) What are the two main categories of wood? Why are they different? Give two examples of each.
9) Describe three types of protective coating you could apply to wood.
10) Name one type of paint that is waterproof.
11) What is the main advantage of using plywood compared to solid wood?
12) Why are the layers in plywood glued at right angles to each other?
13) What is a 'veneer'? Why are veneers used?
14) Describe the main difference between blockboard and laminboard.
15) What does MDF stand for?
16) How is chipboard made?
17) What is a composite material?
18) Name two composite materials and explain why they are so useful.
19) Describe the special properties of a shape memory alloy.
20) What are the four main types of hinge? Describe when each type might be used.
21) Explain the difference between a lock and a catch.
22) Name five different types of adhesive. Explain when each type might be used, and what properties make it suitable for this use.
23) Name four factors that would affect your choice of material for a product you were going to make. Explain how each factor might influence your choice.

Systems

It's often handy to think of a device as a 'system'.
A system has various parts that work together to perform a set function.
In D&T systems may include the use of mechanisms, electronics, pneumatics and structures.

Systems can be broken down into three simple elements: Input, Process and Output.

Subsystems — Small components of a Larger System

1) All complex systems can be broken down into a number of smaller systems, called subsystems.

2) A simple example of this is a bicycle. As a whole system it has an input — movement of your legs, a process — turning the pedals, which link to the wheels, and an output — forward motion. You can break it down further into smaller subsystems like this:

   Wheels and frame — a structural subsystem.
   Pedals and gears — a mechanical subsystem.
   Braking system — a mechanical or pneumatic subsystem.

Mechanical Systems — Systems that Use Mechanisms

1) In Resistant Materials you need to look in detail at mechanical systems.
2) All mechanical systems will have mechanisms which transform an input motion and force into a desired output motion and force.
3) They will be designed so that you can gain some advantage from using them — in other words they make something easier for you to do. This idea is known as 'mechanical advantage'.
4) For example, a car jack lets you lift up a car, a job you couldn't do without it (unless you're Super lift-cars-without-a-jack Man). The mechanism gives you an advantage.

Super lift-cars-without-a-jack Man

Motion — Different ways of looking at How Things Move

In this section you will be looking at a number of different mechanisms, many of which are designed to change one type of motion into another. You need to understand four different types of motion:

1) Linear Motion — moving in a straight line.
2) Rotary Motion — moving in a circle, e.g. a wheel.
3) Oscillating Motion — moving backwards and forwards in an arc, e.g. a swing.
4) Reciprocating Motion — moving backwards and forwards in a straight line.

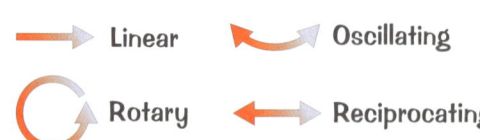

Do your ears hang low, can you oscillate them to and fro...

So the idea is — devices have an overall function, but you can break down this big system into small subsystems — each doing a specific task. It's a bit like football — you've got strikers, midfielders, defenders and the goalie, all doing different jobs, but with the overall aim of winning the game.

Gear Mechanisms

The 'process' part of a system could include one or more mechanisms. The next few pages are dedicated to making sure you know about all the main kinds of mechanism. First up — gears...

Gears are toothed wheels which interlock (or mesh) together as a way of transmitting rotary motion.

Gear Train — Linking Gears Together

Where two or more gears are linked together it is called a gear train.

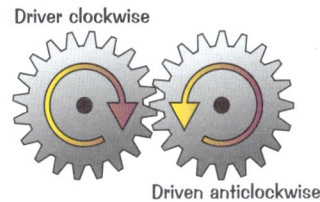

Driver clockwise
Driven anticlockwise

The DRIVER GEAR, turned by hand or motor (the input), turns the driven gear (the output). Both will automatically turn in different directions. If the driver is turning clockwise, the driven will turn anticlockwise and vice versa.

By using a third gear called an IDLER, the driver and the driven gears will both turn in the same direction. The size of the idler will not alter the speed of the other two gears.

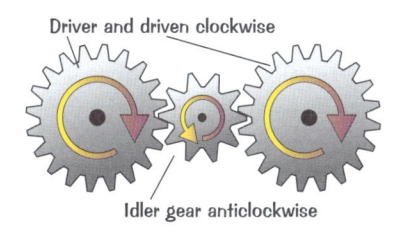

Driver and driven clockwise
Idler gear anticlockwise

Driver 20 Teeth 1 Turn
Driven 10 Teeth 2 Turns
Ratio = 1 : 2

If linked gears are different sizes, they will turn at different speeds. The GEAR RATIO is the relationship between the number of teeth on the driver gear and the driven gear. Any idler gears will have no effect on the gear ratio.

A COMPOUND gear train is where more than one gear is fixed to the same shaft. This is handy because it lets you change the gear ratio easily.

Main Shaft

Gears can change the Type and Direction of Motion

RACK AND PINION gears are used to turn rotary motion into linear motion. The pinion, a round gear, is turned to move a flat gear, the rack.

Pinion gear
Rack

A WORM DRIVE AND WORM WHEEL change the direction of rotation through 90°. The worm drive (the driver) only has one tooth and will turn much faster than the worm wheel, which with many teeth will turn very slowly.

BEVEL GEARS also change the direction of rotation through 90°.

worm drive
worm wheel

This is a bit like a threaded pole (see p17 on threading). This thread acts as one big 'tooth'.

This one's called Richard. It's a very old one, not very popular these days...

The teeth are angled at 45° so the gears fit together at right angles.

Have no fears, dry those tears, it's a wonderful page all about gears...

For a gear enthusiast like myself this is a very special page. Just look at those beautiful, grey, perfectly-crafted lumps of spinning metal — mmm... Anyway, even if they don't excite you, you still need to learn them all. There's nothing difficult here, just 7 gear types to sketch and learn.

Section Four — Systems and Mechanisms

Belt Drives, Chains and Pulleys

And the fun continues on page 36 with exciting stories about belt drives, chains and pulleys...

Belt Drive — Transfer of Power and Movement

1) A belt drive transfers power and movement from one rotating shaft to another.
2) Belt drives are used in pillar drills. The flexible belt links the motor to the drill shaft, and can be put in different positions to make the drill turn faster or slower.

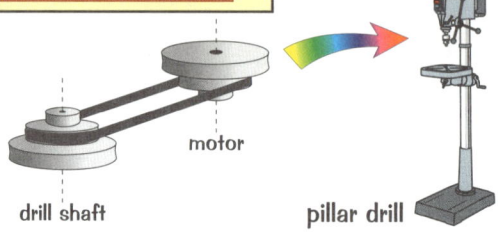

Chain and Sprocket — Transfer of Power and Movement

1) A common example of a chain and sprocket mechanism is on a bike.
2) There are two sprockets (toothed wheels) linked with a chain (made up from loads of links).
3) This has the advantage that it can't slip like a belt drive could.

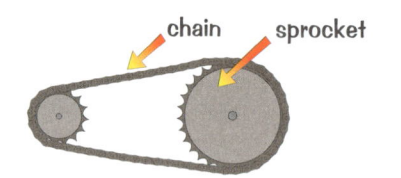

Velocity Ratio — To Work Out Speeds

1) With both of the above systems, if you alter the size of the wheels or sprockets, you change the speed that they turn.
2) The relationship between the two is summed up by the velocity ratio.
3) With both systems, simple formulas will help you calculate the velocities:

Belt Drives

$$\text{RPM of the driven pulley} = \frac{\text{RPM of driver pulley} \times \text{diameter of driver pulley}}{\text{diameter of driven pulley}}$$

Chain and Sprockets

$$\text{Velocity ratio} = \frac{\text{Number of teeth on the driven sprocket}}{\text{Number of teeth on the driver sprocket}}$$

Pulleys — Can help gain Mechanical Advantage

1) Pulleys are another way to gain mechanical advantage when lifting a load.

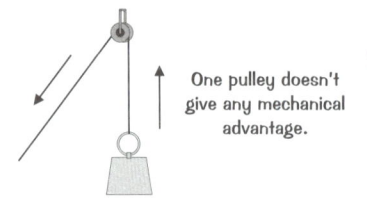

   One pulley doesn't give any mechanical advantage.

2) One pulley on its own will not make a load lighter, but it will reverse the direction of the force required. You will be able to lift the load by pulling.

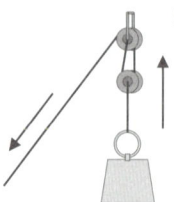

   Simple Block and Tackle
   Weight can be lifted using half the effort.

   You don't need to know why this works — but if you've got a burning desire to find out, I suggest starting with an A-Level mechanics book...

3) If set up in the correct way pulleys can make things appear a lot lighter than they actually are. For example, one fixed pulley and one moving pulley (a block and tackle) will mean you only need half the force.

Baby don't break my heart, pulleys stay and we can work it out...

Make sure you learn those formulas. Make up a few simple examples (and sketch them) and try out the formulas on them — they make a lot more sense when you try them with actual numbers. I'm going to make myself a lovely cup of tea now because I reckon I deserve one.

Section Four — Systems and Mechanisms

Cams and Cranks

Cams — Change Rotary Motion into Reciprocating Motion

1) A cam is a mechanism that converts rotary motion into reciprocating motion.
2) The cam mechanism has two main parts — the cam itself and the follower.
3) The cam is a rotating shape that comes in many different shapes and sizes.
4) The follower follows the shape of the cam. It may simply rest on the cam, or it may have a small wheel to reduce friction.

Here are a few basic cam shapes that you need to be able to recognise:

① CIRCULAR CAM — Also called offset or eccentric — produces a uniform reciprocating motion.

The circular cam rotates about an off-centre pivot...

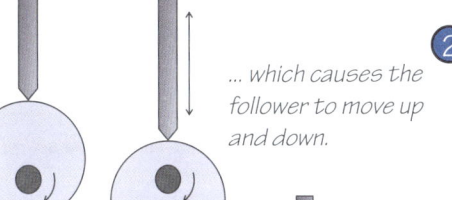

... which causes the follower to move up and down.

② SNAIL CAM — For half of the revolution the follower will not move, then it will gently rise, and then suddenly drop. It will only work in one direction.

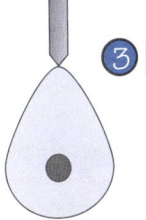

rotates in one direction only

③ PEAR CAM — Again for half a revolution the follower will not move, then it will gently rise and fall.

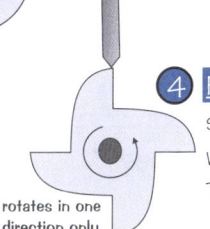

④ FOUR-LOBED CAM — Has four lobes (bits that stick out). For each turn of the cam the follower will rise and suddenly fall four times. This cam shape will also only work in one direction.

rotates in one direction only

Cranks — the Simplest Crank is a Handle on a Shaft

Cranks are used all over the place — from simple mechanical toys to car engines, valves and pumps.

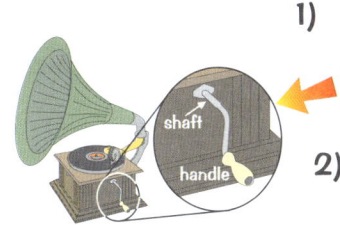

1) A crank can be as simple as a handle on a shaft. As you increase the distance between the handle and the shaft, the handle gets easier to turn (you have a greater mechanical advantage).

2) Cranks can be used with connecting rods to turn rotation into reciprocating motion (up and down), like in a toy car where the driver's head bobs up and down.

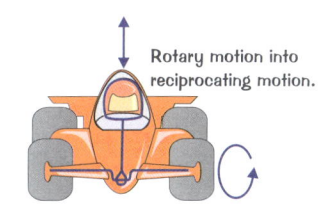

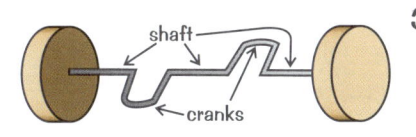

Rotary motion into reciprocating motion.

3) When a crank or several cranks are directly on the shaft it is called a crankshaft (will wonders never cease?). They're used on kids' go-carts as a simple pedalling mechanism.

Crank and Slider — as seen in Pistons

1) This mechanism can be found in steam engines. The reciprocating motion of a piston is turned into rotational motion.
2) Both parts are joined together with a connecting rod. The mechanism won't work unless the rod can move at both ends.

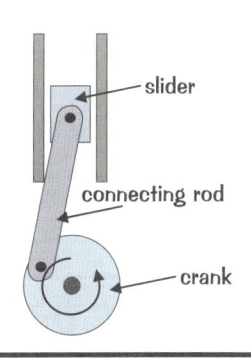

Revision can be tough, but I know you cam do it...

Blimey, that's a very bad pun. Why do they bother? They must be so bored...

Cams turn rotation into reciprocating motion. Cranks can do the same and they can also do the opposite.

Section Four — Systems and Mechanisms

Levers and Links

Levers are used to help move or lift things.
There are three different types of lever that you will need to know about.

First Class Lever — Pivot in the Middle

1) All first class levers have the pivot between the effort and the load.
2) By using this type of lever a large load can be lifted using a smaller effort — the lever can give you a mechanical advantage.
3) As you move the pivot closer to the load it becomes easier to lift.

Second Class Lever — Load in the Middle

1) Here the pivot is at one end of the lever and the effort is at the other end.
2) Again the closer you put the pivot and the load, the easier it is to lift.

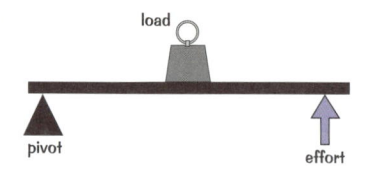

A wheelbarrow is a good example of a second class lever.

Third Class Lever — Effort in the Middle

1) In a third class lever the effort is in between the load and the pivot.
2) Third class levers can be things like fishing rods, cricket bats and garden spades.
3) Moving the effort and pivot apart makes it easier to move/lift the load.

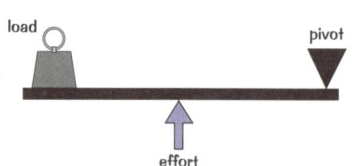

Double-Acting Levers — First Class Levers Joined Together

Sometimes levers can be joined together. A double-acting lever is when you have two first class levers hinged together at the pivot point. A common example of this is a pair of scissors.

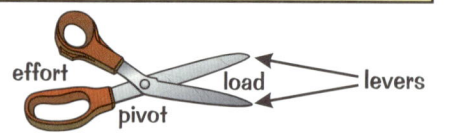

Links Connect Different Parts of a Mechanism

A link is something that connects different parts of a mechanism together. Here's a few common examples:

1) Simple links can:
   - transfer forces and
   - change the direction of motion.

   In this example the input and output motions are in opposite directions.

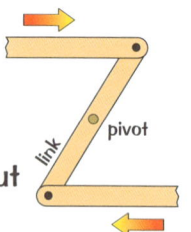

2) A bell crank changes the direction of a force through 90°.

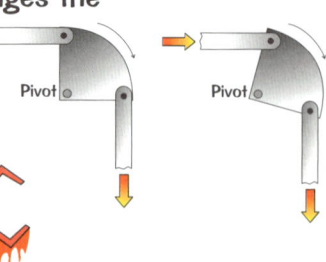

3) Lazy tongs use loads of levers linked together.

Treat me bad, do me wrong, just say you'll never lever me...

That sounds like a song doesn't it. Don't know which one though. If you think you know, send your answer to me at... err actually, don't bother — I don't really care. Anyway, it's another easy page. As usual, the best way to learn is to scribble (and sketch) what you remember until you know it all.

Section Four — Systems and Mechanisms

Revision Summary for Section Four

OK, so mechanisms probably wasn't <u>the most</u> fascinating topic you've ever read about. But it wasn't too bad... and it's pretty easy, really. It's not very hard, so there's <u>no excuse</u> for not learning all the examples in this section. There's nearly always a mechanisms question in the exam. You might have to incorporate a particular mechanism into a design and for this you need to know a <u>range of examples</u>, <u>what they do</u> and <u>how they do it</u>. Anyway, <u>enough of me rambling</u>...
GET ON WITH THESE QUESTIONS.

1) Describe the three elements that any system can be broken down into.
2) Some large systems can be split into smaller systems. What are the smaller systems called?
3) Describe three subsystems of a bicycle.
4) What is mechanical advantage?
5) List and describe, with the aid of simple diagrams, four different types of motion.
6) Give a simple explanation of what gears do.
7) What is a gear train?
8) What is the difference between a driven gear and a driver gear?
9) Describe the purpose of an idler gear.
10) What happens if you change the size of an idler gear?
11) Explain the term 'gear ratio' and give an example of how it is calculated.
12) What's the advantage of using a compound gear train?
13) Sketch a rack and pinion gear mechanism. Describe the motion involved.
14) Which turns faster — a worm drive or a worm wheel? Explain your answer.
15) What does a bevel gear do?
16) Explain what a belt drive is and give a simple example.
17) What is the advantage of a chain and sprocket mechanism?
18) What does 'velocity ratio' mean?
19) How can a pulley system give you mechanical advantage? Draw an example.
20) Briefly describe a cam mechanism.
21) Sketch and describe four different cam shapes.
22) Which cam shapes can only rotate in one direction?
23) Give an example of where you might find a crank.
24) Where might you find a crank and slider mechanism?
25) Sketch and describe a first class lever, and give an example.
26) Sketch and describe a second class lever, and give an example.
27) Sketch and describe a third class lever, and give an example.
28) What is a double-acting lever?
29) Write a simple definition of a link.
30) What two things can a link do?
31) Sketch a bell crank and describe what it does.
32) Sketch a pair of lazy tongs.

Section Four — Systems and Mechanisms

Product Analysis

You've no hope of designing good products if you don't look at other people's stuff first — all designers do it. You need to work out what makes them work and what makes the designs good.

Analysing Existing Products Makes You a Better Designer

Product analysis is <u>essential</u> (for all designers) because it helps you:
1) <u>practise thinking about design</u> — <u>practice</u> means <u>improvement</u>,
2) get familiar with <u>manufacturing methods</u> — important D&T stuff,
3) understand the <u>uses of different materials</u>,
4) get <u>ideas</u> to use in your own designs, or <u>modify</u> existing designs based on what you find out,
5) pick out <u>examples</u> of good or bad design, manufacture and material selection,
6) make <u>better judgements</u> about what products people might buy.

Consider all the Factors when Analysing a Product

① **FUNCTION:** Function is what the product is <u>intended</u> to be <u>used for</u> — and <u>how it works</u>. <u>Disassembling</u> (taking apart) a product can be very useful for finding out how it all works — it's useful to make <u>careful notes</u> as you disassemble it, and <u>record</u> what <u>parts</u> it has and how it's <u>structured</u>, using <u>sketches</u> or <u>photos</u>. *(See also page 2.)*

② **FORM:** In other words, the <u>shape</u> and <u>look</u> of the thing — e.g. colour, texture and decoration. A product could be <u>old-fashioned</u> or <u>modern-looking</u>. It could have <u>flowing curves</u> or it might be very <u>angled</u> with lots of corners. This is also known as '<u>aesthetics</u>'. *(See also p4.)*

③ **ERGONOMICS:** Ergonomics is about how easy the product is to use — whether it's <u>safe</u> and <u>comfortable</u>. A hand-held product needs to <u>fit well</u> in the hand, for example. Controls and buttons need to be <u>easily reachable</u>. Designers have to take all of these things into account. *(See also page 42.)*

④ **COST:** You need to consider <u>value for money</u>. If you were investigating a hairdryer, say, you could conduct a survey and find out if it's cheaper or more expensive than similar hairdryers.

⑤ **COMPETITION:** How it performs compared to <u>other similar products</u> on the market.

⑥ **ENVIRONMENT:** Some parts or components might be <u>recyclable</u> when the product reaches the end of its life. Some parts might be made from <u>biodegradable</u> materials. Manufacture is important, too — it might involve <u>environmentally unfriendly</u> processes. *(See also pages 42-44.)*

⑦ **MATERIALS:** Product analysis should include looking at <u>what materials</u> have been used, <u>why those materials</u> were chosen and <u>how</u> those materials were formed or <u>shaped</u>.

⑧ **MANUFACTURE:** Consider all the <u>processes</u> that have been used to manufacture the product. This includes things like which <u>technique</u> was used to <u>mould</u> any plastic in the product, and how electrical parts have been used. Don't forget to check if any parts have been assembled separately and plonked into the product later — the term for that is <u>sub-assembly</u>.

⑨ **DEVELOPMENT:** Development is stuff that the manufacturer could do to <u>improve</u> the product. Development includes things they could do to make it more popular and <u>increase sales</u>.

Become a better designer — learn when to add go-faster stripes...
Nine factors to learn. That's all.

41

Quality Assurance and Control

Quality assurance (QA) is all about standards — setting standards and meeting them.
Quality control (QC) is how you check that you're meeting those standards.

Products are Monitored for Quality

Products are monitored for quality right through design and development to manufacture, end-use performance and degree of customer satisfaction. Top companies that do QA well are awarded ISO 9000 — an international standard of quality.
Factors such as equipment, materials and staff training are constantly checked.

Quality Control is Making Sure You're Within Tolerances

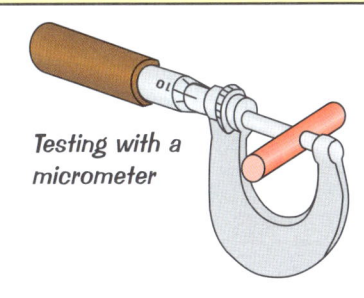

Testing with a micrometer

Quality control involves testing a sample of a component at every stage of production. It stresses the importance of working to specific tolerances — i.e. margins of error.

Tolerance in testing is expressed as an upper (+) and lower (−) deviation. For example, if a spindle is specified as being 20 mm (± 0.5), then a micrometer reading of between 19.5 mm and 20.5 mm would be OK.

Quality control makes sure a product does these things:
1) conforms to the design specification
2) does the job it was designed to do
3) meets relevant standards institutions' criteria (p43)
4) keeps the customer happy

There are Different Kinds of Testing

Failures at testing can identify faults with machining and tool settings and eliminate costly waste.

1) Measuring every component with a micrometer is a time-consuming (and therefore costly) business — this process can be speeded up using limit gauges. These are usually double-ended, one end being machined to the lower limit and the other end to the upper limit.
2) Some testing is visual and may include using X-rays to spot defects, e.g. of a welded joint. This is non-destructive testing.
3) Some testing is physical and destroys the product to see how fractures develop or to examine the nature of collapse. This is destructive testing.

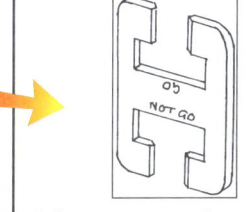

If the component fits through the upper limit but not the lower one, it's within the acceptable range.

In your own project, your work needs testing and checking. You might need to make your own gauges and measuring tools, as well as using the trusty micrometer.

Total Quality Management — a whole lotta quality control

'Total quality management' (TQM) introduces quality-control systems at every stage of manufacture and management. TQM aims for right first time, every time.

How good is this page? — dunno, it's hard to gauge...

You know, 'gauge' must be one of the world's most difficult words to spell. Anyway, the important thing here is that you know how to do quality checks, and how to make sure that your components are the right size and shape and that they match your specification.

Section Five — Market Influences

Social Responsibility

Social responsibility in design is all about making sure you <u>don't</u> make products that <u>mess up</u> people's <u>health</u>, people's <u>lives</u> or the environment. Hmm. Serious stuff.

Design Must Be <u>Socially</u> and <u>Environmentally Responsible</u>

When you're selecting <u>materials</u>, <u>components</u>, and <u>manufacturing processes</u>, you need to take these factors into consideration:

1) whether <u>using the product</u> might <u>harm</u> people or the environment
2) whether any <u>materials</u> used, including paints and varnishes, are <u>toxic</u>
3) whether the <u>manufacture</u> of the product harms the environment, e.g. consider how much <u>waste material</u> will be produced by the manufacturing process, and how it's going to be disposed of
4) whether <u>recycled materials</u> could be used to make the product or packaging — or <u>biodegradable or recyclable</u> materials if the product's designed to be <u>thrown away</u> after use
5) <u>conditions for workers</u> during manufacture of components, e.g. whether <u>child labour</u> was used
6) whether any <u>social</u>, <u>cultural</u> or <u>religious groups</u> may be <u>offended</u> by the product

Products Must be <u>Safe</u> and <u>Easy to Use</u>

See p45-46 for more on safety.

When you finalise a design, think about how people are going to use the product.
1) The product must be <u>safe</u>. It's not socially responsible to injure your customers.
2) The product must be <u>user-friendly</u>. Take responsibility for the experience of using it. If the product is <u>frustrating</u> and <u>difficult</u> to use, it <u>isn't well designed</u>.
3) Think whether the product could be <u>misused</u>. If people use a product for something that it hasn't been designed for, it might be <u>dangerous</u>.

How do you flush this thing...

<u>Ergonomics</u> means Making the Product Fit the User

1) Products need to be designed so that their <u>size</u> and <u>proportions</u> make them fit the needs of the user — e.g. a chair for a five-year-old needs to be a different size from a chair for a fifteen-year-old (obviously).
2) Designers use <u>body measurement data</u>, known as <u>anthropometrics</u>, to make sure that the product is the <u>right size</u> and <u>shape</u> for people to use.
3) For example, a <u>chair seat</u> needs to be the <u>right height</u> off the ground so that the person sitting in it has their feet on the floor, and their knees at a right angle. The back of the chair should support the person's back in the <u>right place</u>.
4) <u>Badly designed</u> products can have <u>long-term health impacts</u>. They might well be safe to use on a day-to-day basis (e.g. there's no risk of losing a limb), but end up causing things like <u>eye strain</u> or <u>backache</u> after long-term use.

There are <u>Social Issues</u> with Products Aimed at <u>Kids</u>

1) <u>Parents</u> have strong views on what sort of products they want their kids to use.
2) <u>Society</u> has an axe to grind, too — e.g. a <u>hand-held games console</u> might be criticised because it encourages kids to sit around all day, <u>hunched over a tiny screen</u> instead of running about and getting fresh air.

Anyone nodded off yet?...

Social responsibility is a bit gloomy, but it's just about making sure that products are the <u>right shape</u> and <u>size</u> for people to use without <u>pain or injury</u>, and that no one is <u>damaged</u> by making them.

Section Five — Market Influences

Consumers

What the customer wants or needs drives all design briefs. Without customers, there's no need for the product. If no one buys a manufacturer's products, the manufacturer will go bust.

Customer Satisfaction is what Manufacturers Want

If you just think about design as what you do in D&T lessons, you might see evaluation as the end of the design process. In the world of manufacturing, the end of the process is customer satisfaction...

See pages 5, 6, 8 & 57-58 for more on evaluation.

Customer satisfaction is achieved when the product works, it's great to use, and it's good value for money. For this to happen, product development, design, production, engineering, marketing and finance all need to work properly together and become a quality system. The key features of a quality system are quality control (QC), quality assurance (QA) and total quality management (TQM) — see p41 for more on these.

Designers do market research to find out what customers want. See p51.

Consumer Protection keeps us Safe from Dodgy Products

Manufacturers who produce unsafe or unreliable products may be prosecuted under one or more of:

1) **The Trade Descriptions Acts** ensure that any claims made about a product (e.g. that it is hard-wearing, long-lasting, waterproof) must be true.
2) **The Consumer Safety Act** legislates over fire regulations and specifications for clothing, toys, electrical goods, etc.
3) **The Sale Of Goods Act** ensures that products perform as you would expect and that goods last a reasonable length of time.
4) **Fire Safety Regulations** cover new and second-hand furniture, stuffed furnishings and fabrics, to ensure resistance to ignition and low toxicity fumes.

As well as the law, consumers can get help from:
1. The Office of Fair Trading
2. The British Standards Institution
3. The Environmental Health Department
4. Local Authority Trading Standards Officers
5. Local Authority Consumer Protection Departments

These places give advice on consumer matters:
1. The Citizens' Advice Bureau
2. The Consumers' Advice Council
3. The National Federation of Consumer Groups
4. The National Consumer Council

Labels Tell Consumers What's Safe

Safety labelling is important to consumers.
Official labels show that standards have been met for safety, quality or design. These are awarded by the British Standards Institution (BSI) *(their label is the Kitemark)*, the British Electrotechnical Approvals Board (BEAB) or the British Toy and Hobby Manufacturers' Association (BTMA).
If the product is to be sold within the EU, it also must be marked "CE" to show that it meets Central European Standards.

The British Standards Kitemark

1) Labels also help consumers use and maintain a product.
2) They can give useful safety instructions, such as "this way up", "ensure catch is fully locked before use" or "danger — this part gets extremely hot during use".
3) Or they can give maintenance instructions such as "clean with warm water only", "do not use abrasives", "oil frequently" or "do not immerse in water".

Learn it now or learn it later — that's your consumer choice...

When you do your design and manufacture project, you need to take all this into account. That includes putting all the right labels on and knowing the appropriate laws and safety codes.

Section Five — Market Influences

The Environment

Humans exploit and use up the Earth's non-renewable resources simply by using so much stuff. We pollute the water and air and produce large quantities of waste. Not very clever really.

Which Material You Choose Matters to the Environment...

1) The rainforests are a prime example of a threatened resource. They produce valuable and exotic hardwoods which are (mostly) not being replaced. Softwoods (which can regenerate themselves in a person's lifetime) are a greener choice, as are recycled materials that use waste wood, e.g. chipboard. There are sustainable hardwood plantations in some countries, but it costs money to organise them and to check that they're all above board.

2) Metal ores are taken from the Earth's crust. There's only a limited amount of each ore.

3) Most plastics come from oil, which will eventually run out.

4) Recycling and using recycled products is environmentally responsible.

5) Energy efficiency is not only "green", but cost-effective, too. Manufacturing processes need to be chosen for energy efficiency. If manufacturers wanted to be extremely responsible, they'd try to use renewable energy sources like wind power or hydroelectricity. This is most relevant when choosing where to site a factory.

Throwing Away Old Products Causes Pollution

1) At the end of its life, an old product needs to be disposed of to make way for a shiny new one. Most waste goes into landfill sites. Some chemicals used in products cause serious problems when they get into watercourses or into the soil. There are laws about what can be dumped into landfill sites — and what has to be recycled or specially treated to make it safe.

2) Britain's recycling rate stands at 11% — which is about a quarter of what some of its North European neighbours manage. By 2016 EU law will force Britain to cut down to 22% the 80% of its waste which is currently going into landfill.

3) Packaging contributes to the problem of waste. Designers need to assess how much packaging is actually needed for a product, and how it will be disposed of or recycled.

Audits and Assessments Check Environmental Impact

Industry measures waste, emissions and by-products as part of environmental audits. Life cycle assessments evaluate the environmental impact of a product from design brief to obsolescence. Every step along the way is examined for environmental friendliness.

Three examples of environmentally friendly design — all to do with laundry:

1) Biological washing powders use enzyme technology to enable them to wash clothes at lower temperatures, producing an energy saving of nearly a third.

2) The latest washing machines have forward-tilting drums which require less water to get the clothes wet — and therefore less energy to heat the water up.

3) Some industrial washing machines have polypropylene drums which are cheaper than using stainless steel. And they're still 'green' because, like steel, the polypropylene can be recycled instead of being scrapped at the end of the drum's life.

Balancing consumer demands against environmental concerns can be difficult. Recycling can be more expensive than using fresh materials and the cost needs to be got back by raising the price of the product. Also some recycled products aren't of such high quality as non-recycled ones.

Landfill sites are the future? — what a load of rubbish...

It's a bit of an eye-opener — only 11% of our rubbish recycled. It'll make me think twice before I throw away a bottle. But whether you lose sleep over this stuff or not, you still need to learn it.

Section Five — Market Influences

Health and Safety

Safety is essential for the person <u>making</u> the product, and the person <u>using</u> the product. The person making the product is <u>responsible</u> for finding out the hazards, and taking action to <u>minimise the risks</u>.

Wear the Right Clothing...

Always wear <u>appropriate protective clothing</u>:
1) While working, especially with machine tools, make sure your <u>sleeves are rolled back</u>, apron ties are tucked in and if you've got <u>long hair</u>, it's <u>tied back</u>.
2) Protect yourself from <u>hazardous</u> material by wearing <u>strong protective gloves</u>.
3) If material is <u>hot</u>, wear protective gloves, an apron and a face mask.
4) Wear goggles or a face mask if using <u>hazardous materials</u> or if a lot of <u>dust</u> or <u>vapours</u> are involved — and make sure there's adequate <u>ventilation</u>.
5) When <u>casting</u>, always wear <u>thick all-body suits</u>, <u>face visors</u>, <u>gauntlets</u> and <u>spats</u> (to protect legs and feet).

Maybe that's a bit excessive.

a leather gauntlet

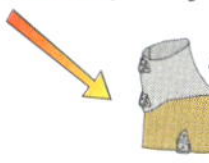

a leather spat

...be Careful with Tools and Machinery...

1) Use the <u>safety guards</u> on lathes and drilling machines.
2) Remove <u>chuck keys</u> from chucks <u>before</u> switching on.
3) Know how to <u>switch off</u> and isolate machines in an emergency.
4) <u>Never</u> adjust a machine unless you've <u>switched it off</u> and isolated it <u>first</u>.
5) <u>Never</u> leave machines <u>unattended</u> while switched on.
6) Always <u>secure</u> work safely — e.g. you should clamp work securely for drilling.
7) Don't use <u>machines</u> or <u>hand tools</u> unless you have been <u>shown how</u>.
8) Ensure that any <u>dust extraction</u> equipment is connected and working properly.
9) Carry tools safely.
10) <u>Never</u> operate machines unless <u>allowed to</u>, and under supervision where appropriate.
11) Know where the <u>EMERGENCY STOP</u> buttons are (but only use them when needed).

Chucks and Chuck Keys...
A chuck key is one of those things you use to tighten a drill bit holder (a chuck). You get chucks on various tools.

You'd want to know where the stop button was, wouldn't you...

...Handle Materials and Waste Sensibly...

1) <u>Choose</u> your materials sensibly (only use <u>hazardous materials</u> where <u>necessary</u>).
2) Moving <u>long lengths</u> of <u>metal</u> and <u>timber</u> is a possible hazard to others.
3) Make sure materials are <u>safe to handle</u>. <u>Deburr</u> metal (file down any rough edges) before you start work. (And if metal is greased, degrease it first.)
4) Beware of <u>naked flames</u> or red-hot heating elements — and keep them away from <u>flammable liquids</u>.
5) Make sure you <u>dispose of waste properly</u> (this is also an environmental issue — see p44).
6) When <u>storing</u> material, make sure it's <u>put away safely</u> so it can't fall or slide and injure anyone.
7) Never clear away metal shavings/dust with your bare hands — <u>use the brush</u> provided.

...basically, just don't be a Moron

1) <u>Don't run</u> or move quickly around the workshop.
2) <u>Never throw anything</u> across the workshop.
3) Be tidy — put tools away when not in use.
4) Report any <u>accidents</u>, <u>faults</u> or <u>breakages</u> to your supervisor (teacher in your case) — <u>immediately</u>.
5) Speak up if you see someone else behaving dangerously in the workshop.

Learn this page — it'll help you avoid horrific injury...

Blimey, that's a lot of stuff to learn. OK, safety rules are mainly common sense — but that's no excuse for not learning them. Remember two key points — "identify hazards" and "minimise risks".

Section Five — Market Influences

Health and Safety

Safety is also important for the consumer.
People don't want to risk death every time they boil the kettle.

Design Safe Products — Think About the Consumer

When designing products, think 'safety'. Products which may harm the end user are generally inappropriate. Sometimes it's impossible to avoid potential harm completely (e.g. sharp tools), but for these products effort should be made to at least minimise the risks.

1) Toys and tools should have unnecessary sharp corners and edges smoothed so that consumers can't cut themselves. (This includes any attachments — e.g. attaching the eyes of a teddy bear by 10 cm metal spikes would be a thoroughly bad and unsafe idea.)

2) Toys often end up in children's mouths, so don't finish the surface with any toxic paint or varnish. Check this out at research stage and choose a non-toxic range of surface treatments.

3) Small components must be firmly attached so that a young child can't pull them off — this would be a choking hazard.
(Toys with detachable components would be unsuitable for small children.)

4) Use standard components wherever you can, because these have already been rigorously tested by the manufacturer — this helps make sure that safety standards are met.

There are Laws on Safety

To protect consumers, there are safety standards applied to many products by the British Standards Institute (BSI). Products which meet these standards are awarded the Kitemark (see p44). Manufacturers usually incorporate this in their label. Many plastic products have it moulded on.

The Health and Safety at Work Act and COSHH (Control Of Substances Hazardous to Health) relate to safety in the workplace. They're designed to protect you from hazardous (mainly chemical) products or dangerous working practices which may pose a risk to your health.

Risk Assessment is Important for Workers and Consumers

Risk assessment is a procedure which is carried out to identify and minimise any potential risks of using chemicals, machinery or equipment. It may also be carried out on a product to highlight any potential risk to the end user and ensure precautions are taken to minimise potential danger.

Employers, workshop managers and your technology teacher must assess the risks involved in using workshop facilities and justify the level of precaution taken, e.g. placing warning or caution signs on machines, installing non-slip flooring or erecting barriers and guards.

Choose a piece of machinery you use in school and ask yourself these questions:
1) What could go wrong?
2) What effect would this have?
3) What can I do to prevent it happening?
4) What system could I implement to make sure the risk is minimised?

You'll never pass your D&T Exam if your product kills people...

Risk assessment comes down to working out what might go horribly wrong and finding the best way to prevent it going horribly wrong. Toys are a good example of safety in design — kids put things in their mouths, and you don't want them to choke or poison themselves.

Section Five — Market Influences

Revision Summary for Section Five

You can't go just yet. Oh no. You have to do these little questions first, to check you've learnt everything in this section. Think of it as Learning Quality Control. ☺

1) Why do you need to do product analysis?
2) What are form and function?
3) Name five other factors that you should look at when analysing a product.
4) What is quality assurance?
5) What are tolerances?
6) If a component had to be 35 mm ± 0.2 mm, what would be the upper and lower tolerances? Would 34.7 mm be OK?
7) Give an example of non-destructive testing.
8) Do you need to do quality control on your own work?
9) Should a manufacturer and designer care about the safety of manufacturing workers?
10) If you were being environmentally responsible, what kind of material might you choose for a disposable product?
11) What is ergonomics?
12) What's the fancy name for body measurement data?
13) What sort of impact can a badly designed product have on the user's health?
14) What are the Trade Descriptions Acts about?
15) What is the Sale of Goods Act for?
16) Whose symbol is the Kitemark? What do they do?
17) Give an example of a safety label that you might see on a ladder.
18) Give an example of a maintenance/safety label that you might see on a hand-held electric blender.
19) Name two non-renewable resources.
20) Give three examples of ways that manufacturers and designers can reduce the environmental impact of a product.
21) Why is packaging such a big deal?
22) Where should a chuck key be before you operate a drill?
23) What should you use to clean up metal shavings (swarf), e.g. after drilling?
24) If you see someone breaking safety rules in the workshop, what should you do?
25) When should you wear goggles? (In the context of D&T.)
26) Why are small removable parts inappropriate to use on toys for very small children?
27) Why must surface treatments on toys be non-toxic?
28) What is COSHH?
29) What is risk assessment? Who does it?

Section Five — Market Influences

Scale of Production

The term 'scale of production' is all about the <u>quantity</u> of products that you're going to manufacture. Commercially there are <u>four main categories</u> for you to learn...

Jobbing Production — Making a One-Off Product

1) This is where you're making a <u>single product</u>.
2) Every item made will be different, to meet the customer's <u>individual</u> and <u>specific requirements</u>.
3) This type of production is very <u>labour intensive</u>, and requires a <u>highly skilled</u> workforce.
4) Examples are wide-ranging, from made-to-measure furniture to one-off buildings like the Millennium Dome.

Batch Production — A Specified Quantity of a Product

1) This is where you're making a <u>specific quantity</u> of a particular product.
2) Batches can be <u>repeated</u> as many times as required.
3) The <u>machinery</u> and <u>labour</u> used need to be <u>flexible</u>, so they can quickly change from making one batch to making another batch of a similar product.
4) The time <u>between</u> batches, when machines and tools may have to be set up differently or changed around, is called <u>down time</u>. This is <u>unproductive</u> and needs to be kept as short as possible so the manufacturer doesn't lose money.

Mass Production — High-Volume Production

1) Making products on a really <u>large scale</u>, such as cars or electrical goods.
2) Often uses <u>expensive specialised equipment</u> including computer-aided manufacturing (CAM) and industrial robots.
3) As well as all this equipment, you need a <u>large workforce</u>. The different stages of production and manufacture are <u>broken down</u> into simple <u>repetitive tasks</u> which people are able to learn easily.
4) <u>Recruitment</u> is relatively <u>easy</u> — you don't need to employ skilled people.

Continuous Production — Non-Stop Production 24hrs/day

1) This involves <u>non-stop</u>, uninterrupted production.
2) The specialised equipment required costs so much that it would be too <u>expensive</u> to turn it off. So it has to keep running and producing continuously.
3) Examples of continuous production include <u>oil</u> and <u>chemical</u> manufacture.

Which Category Do I Use in the School Workshop?

If you're making a <u>single product</u> that you've designed, with its own specification, it will be <u>jobbing production</u>. Sometimes you may work with the rest of the class in small <u>teams</u>, all making different parts of a product which you then bring together and assemble to produce a number of <u>identical products</u>. This will be <u>batch production</u>.

It's not what you've got — it's how much you've got of it...
Yup, all that this lot boils down to is quantity.

Manufacturing Systems

Take a look at these five main manufacturing systems, and learn how they work.

Cell Production is Working in Teams to Produce Components

1) Production stages are split into individual components, which are each made by a different production cell.
2) Each cell has a team of people working to produce a single component.
3) Within each cell the team is responsible for all aspects of production, including quality control and maintenance of the machines.
4) Advantages of this method include teamwork, communication and quality.

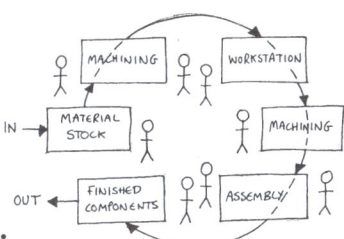

In-Line Assembly is Used for Mass Production

1) Most of the production line is automated.
2) Unskilled labour is used mainly for assembly, with a small number of semi-skilled operators making sure there's a continuous flow along the production line.
3) A disadvantage of this system is the lack of flexibility when compared with cells.

Flexible Manufacturing Systems Use Semi-Skilled Workers

1) The FMS approach is based on the belief that the key to successful manufacturing is a flexible workforce and flexible machinery.
2) Individual people are semi-skilled, being able to do a variety of jobs.
3) It works well with batch production, where change and flexibility are essential.

Concurrent Engineering Needs Good Communication

1) This is where different stages of the design process can overlap (one can start work before the other has finished) — which saves time.
2) It's essential to make sure there are good communication links between all the stages of the design process, e.g. marketing, research, design, planning, manufacture and distribution.
3) The overall aim is to design and make the product with maximum efficiency.

Just-in-Time Manufacturing Needs Detailed Forward Planning

1) For just-in-time manufacture (JIT), you only buy materials and components as and when you need them.
2) This removes the need for large stockpiles of resources, saving money and space.
3) Everything has to be kept on time, or things can easily go wrong.

Cell production — hold on, am I in the Biology book by mistake...

Darned useful stuff this — especially if you're going to go anywhere near the manufacturing industry when you leave school. Well, even if you're not, you still have to learn it for the old GCSEs.

Section Six — Industrial Awareness

CAD/CAM and CIM in Industry

All this computer-aided stuff is here to make life a little bit easier for everyone. You need to learn what all the abbreviations mean, and how they're useful in industry. *(More on this on page 21.)*

CAD/CAM — Computer-Aided Design and Manufacture

1) CAD (Computer-Aided Design) is all about using computers to help design a product.
2) CAM (Computer-Aided Manufacture) refers to any part of the manufacturing process that's controlled by a computer system.
3) CAD/CAM (Computer-Aided Design and Manufacture) is the process of joining CAD and CAM systems together. This involves the use of specialised computer software that converts data from drawings into machining instructions.

CIM — Computer-Integrated Manufacturing

1) CIM is the system by which different stages of the design process are linked together by a central computer system.
2) A lot of different people are involved in making even the simplest of products and they all need to be aware of what the others are doing.
3) CIM helps coordinate all the different stages in the process using a central computer database.
4) With this system no stage is carried out in isolation, as communication is made easy through the central computer system. 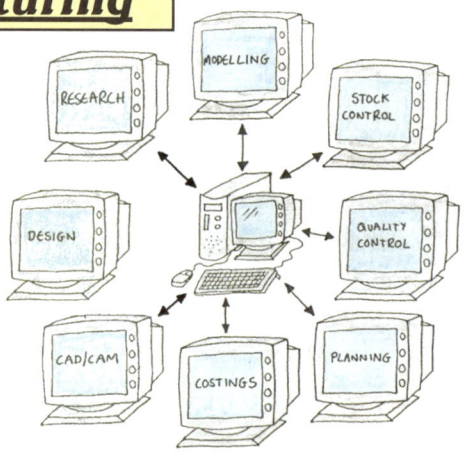 
5) The really clever bit is the software held on the central computer. It will automatically update any changes made and alert all the related stages. For example if a change is made in a CAD program, the software will automatically change the corresponding CNC program that controls the manufacturing machines. This can save a lot of time and eliminate some costly mistakes.

Confused Between your CADs & CIMs or your CANs & CATs?

1) CAD — Computer-Aided Design — designing on the computer.
2) CAM — Computer-Aided Manufacture — machining with computers.
3) CAD/CAM — Computer-Aided Design & Manufacture — links CAD & CAM.
4) CIM — Computer-Integrated Manufacturing — links many different stages.
5) CNC — Computer Numerical Control — runs computer-controlled machines.

Eeee — it were never like this when I were a lass...

Amazing, all this stuff they can do nowadays. Although probably not if you used to be a craftsman who no longer has a job because all this work's now being done by computers.

Section Six — Industrial Awareness

Advertising and Marketing

In industry, just making something isn't good enough — you've got to be able to sell it.

There are Five Key Roles in the Design Process

A product developed for industry not only needs to work, and fulfil its design purpose — it also needs to make a profit. Along the way, there are key people who have important roles to play:

1) Client — identifies a need, gives the designer a clear brief, carries out market research and raises money for the project.
2) Designer — develops the client's ideas, sets out a specification and produces detailed working drawings of the final design.
3) Manufacturer — plans and carries out manufacturing, safely and efficiently, to produce consistent results and make a profit.
4) Retailer — gives customers what they want, at an affordable price.
5) User — gets a high quality product that works, fulfils a need and is good value for money.

Legislation — BSI and ISO

1) BSI — the British Standards Institution is a quality control organisation. It sets out standards, testing procedures and quality assurance techniques.
2) Kitemark — any product meeting BSI standards is given a Kitemark, as long as the manufacturer can ensure all their products are of the same standard.
3) ISO 9000 — the ISO 9000 is an internationally agreed set of standards (see p41).
4) Drawing conventions — the ISO standards give specific ways of drawing things (e.g. circuit diagrams), so that anyone looking at a standardised drawing can read it in the same way.

There are Two Main Types of Marketing

You either need to find out what people want, or convince them that they want your product.

> Advertising Standards — the ASA (Advertising Standards Authority) regulates all advertising in the UK. It makes sure that adverts are legal, honest, responsible and fair.

1) **The Media** — advertising media include newspapers, magazines, mail, television, radio, cinema, posters, e-mail and the Internet. All advertising aims to influence people, and convince people to buy a product.

2) **Market Research** — this is often useful to find out who your customers are and what their needs are. It can be carried out using published statistics, surveys or questionnaires.

Designing Your Own Questionnaire

1) Write your questions carefully, so the answers give you information you can use.
2) Be brief, relevant, clear and inoffensive.
3) Multiple-choice questions are often a good idea.

According to my research, Birmingham Rag Market's the best...

Marketing's such a tricky thing that it's easy to see why companies are so fond of market research. Even if it's a pain in the neck for everyone else who ends up with a doormat covered in junk mail...

Section Six — Industrial Awareness

Good Working Practice

In school, good working practice is all about <u>forward planning</u> and <u>organisation</u>.
In industry it means pretty much the same thing — it's just done on a much larger scale.

Quality Control — Controlling the Quality of a Product

Nothing like stating the obvious, eh? (see p41 for more stuff on QC)
1) <u>Quality control</u> is easy to include and monitor in any project if you build it into a <u>flow chart</u>.
2) Many of the questions / decisions (diamond symbols) will form quality control points <u>automatically</u>.

Flow Charts — Project Planning Using Symbols

1) A <u>flow chart</u> is a simple diagram showing the <u>order</u> that things happen in (also see p8).
   It works just as well for a simple school project or a complex manufacturing process.
2) There are <u>standard symbols</u> used, so that once you know the basics you'll be able to read and understand any flow chart. All the shapes are linked with simple arrows, which guide the reader through the chart.

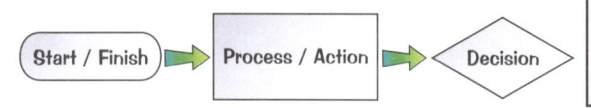

A <u>sausage shape</u> is used for the <u>start</u> and <u>finish</u> of a flow chart.
A <u>rectangle</u> is used to show a <u>process</u> or <u>action</u>.
A <u>diamond</u> is used for <u>decisions</u> or <u>questions</u>.

3) Often small sections of a project have their own flow chart, to avoid any single chart getting too complicated.
   A <u>summary chart</u> can be used to give an overview of the whole project, leaving the details of each section for the smaller charts. 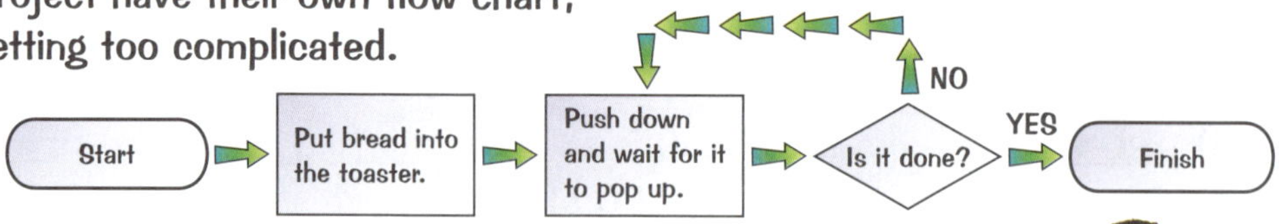
4) <u>Splits</u> or <u>loops</u> in a flow chart are important when <u>questions</u> need to be asked.
   If you're including a question, think about all the possible answers, and where these will lead you on the flow chart.

Time Planning Means Forward Thinking

1) <u>Good planning</u> is often just a question of <u>thinking ahead</u>.
   What will need to be done in a project and in what order?
2) One example of a planning tool is a <u>Gantt chart</u> (also see p8). This is a table where you <u>plot</u> <u>activities</u> or <u>stages</u> in a project against <u>time</u>.
3) If <u>realistic time limits</u> are set at the start, then you can use the chart to <u>monitor</u> your progress through a project. The marked out areas can be shaded in as they're completed.
4) Some stages on a Gantt chart will <u>overlap</u>, meaning that you can start one section before the previous section is finished. Others won't overlap, simply running one after another.

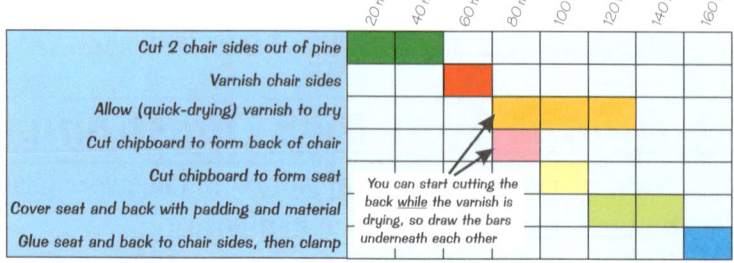

You can start cutting the back while the varnish is drying, so draw the bars underneath each other

I've told you once, I'm telling you again — always plan ahead

Well no one said D & T was going to be "fun fun fun all the way" — or if they did, they were lying.
This is pretty tedious, but presumably you do care what grade you get, so I suggest you learn it.

Section Six — Industrial Awareness

Jigs, Moulds and Templates

Jigs, moulds and templates are pretty handy things all round — they save you a lot of work. In industry they're used to increase the speed and efficiency of the production process.

Templates are Used to Make Repetitive Shapes

1) Templates are very easy to make and simple to use.
2) You can use them to reproduce any number of identical shapes from one original pattern (template). The original is used to draw, scribe or cut round.
3) Templates need to be strong and hard-wearing so that they can be used repetitively without wearing down.
4) Afterwards, the components can be checked against the templates for accuracy.

template

Jigs Help Manufacture Repetitive Components

1) A jig guides the tools that are working on a component.
2) Jigs come in many different shapes and sizes and can be specifically made for a particular job. 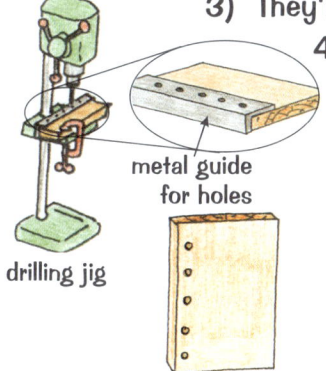
3) They're designed to speed up production and simplify the making process.
4) A drilling jig gets rid of the need for complex marking out. It can also help cut down on errors, and make sure every component is identical.
5) Some jigs are a standard size and shape and could be used on many different jobs. E.g. a dovetail jig enables complex dovetail joints (see p19) to be machined with a router, very quickly and easily, and with minimal measuring and marking out.

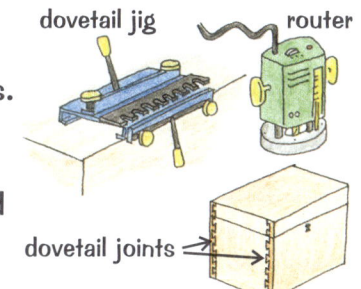

drilling jig — metal guide for holes — finished product

dovetail jig — router — dovetail joints

Moulds — Reproduce 3-D Shapes

1) Moulds are most commonly used in plastics manufacturing, in processes such as vacuum forming, compression moulding and blow moulding. See p14-15 for more on moulding.
2) Once an accurate mould has been made, detailed plastic shapes can be formed with it over and over again.
3) Industrial moulds are expensive to produce, so a manufacturer needs to be certain of their design, and needs to be able to make large numbers of their product to make it cost-effective.

mould — finished product

Design Your Own Jigs, Moulds and Templates...

As part of your GCSE project, you could design and make very simple jigs, moulds or templates to help you produce some of your components. By doing this you will also be able to illustrate how, in theory, you could put your product into small-scale batch production.

No — this page has nothing to do with Scottish dancing...

This is a pretty groovy section (compared with the rest of the book). It's got all those colourful little pictures and everything. Well, *I* like it anyway. You can suit yourself. But I suggest you learn how this stuff saves time in industry and how it could be used to improve *your* project.

Section Six — Industrial Awareness

Revision Summary for Section Six

Congratulations, you've made it through Section Six. There's a load of important stuff in this section, so you need to revise it well. You can be sure that there'll always be an exam question on some area of 'Industrial Awareness'. Try these questions again and again until you know all the important facts and details off by heart.

1) Give a simple definition of "scale of production". What are the 4 main types?
2) How many products would you make in jobbing production?
3) What type of production would you use to make a specific quantity of a product?
4) Why, in the above production method, do machinery and labour need to be flexible?
5) a) What is large-scale production (e.g. production of cars or electrical goods) called?
   b) How are the tasks broken down, and what skill level is needed of the workforce?
6) In continuous production, why do the machines have to run non-stop?
7) Describe cell production, and list 3 advantages of it.
8) Describe in-line assembly, and give one disadvantage of it.
9) What does FMS stand for? What does this approach see as the key to successful manufacturing?
10) Which manufacturing system needs good communication links between stages?
11) What does JIT stand for? What things does it eliminate?
12) Which of the manufacturing systems is best? Explain how you would choose.
13) What does CAD stand for, and what's it all about?
14) What does CAM stand for? What processes does it refer to?
15) Explain the process of CAD/CAM. What does it involve?
16) Describe CIM. What does it do, and what's the really clever bit?
17) List some of the advantages of using CIM.
18) What are the 5 key roles in the design process? Describe each in detail.
19) What does BSI stand for? Describe what it sets out to do.
20) Sketch a Kitemark and explain what it stands for.
21) What is the ISO 9000? What does it aim to do?
22) Why does part of the ISO outline specific drawing requirements?
23) Which authority regulates all British advertising?
24) Explain the role of the media in advertising? What's the main purpose of an advert?
25) Why is market research important?
26) If you were designing a questionnaire, how would you structure the questions?
27) What is a flow chart?
28) Sketch the standard symbols used in a flow chart, and explain what each one represents.
29) When would you use a split or loop in a flow chart?
30) What's the point of planning ahead in a project?
31) Sketch a simple example of a Gantt chart, and explain how to use it.
32) How can you build quality control into a flow chart? What would it be used for?
33) What are templates used for?
34) What is a jig? Why are drilling jigs useful?

SECTION SEVEN — PROJECT ADVICE

Tips on Getting Started

This section's got all the stuff people <u>don't</u> do that the exam boards get really annoyed about. Read this before you start your project to make sure you keep those markers happy.

Step 1 — Get your Idea

You can get ideas from <u>different</u> places — for example, your teacher might:
1) <u>tell</u> you exactly what your task is.
2) give you a <u>range</u> of tasks to choose from.
3) leave the project <u>choice</u> completely up to you.

Don't choose anything Too Easy or Too Boring

Choose a project that will:
1) <u>stretch</u> you and let you <u>demonstrate</u> just how <u>good</u> you are. If the project's too <u>easy</u>, or contains little scope for design, then you'll <u>lose</u> valuable marks.
2) be <u>interesting</u> and <u>challenging</u> enough to keep you <u>motivated</u>. Coursework's a <u>long</u> old process, and you need to stay <u>committed</u>.
3) give you the opportunity to produce a <u>wide range</u> of <u>research</u>, and demonstrate your <u>ICT</u> skills.
4) allow for a <u>variety</u> of solutions, resulting in a project which can be completed <u>before the deadline</u> (and this includes allowing time for <u>testing</u> and <u>evaluation</u>).

The Design Brief — Give Loads of Detail

See page 1 for more on the design brief.

1) Your idea needs to have "<u>real commercial potential</u>".
2) You need to describe <u>exactly</u> what you're trying to do.
3) <u>Explain all the factors</u> you need to consider — things like price, weight, market trends, etc.

Say Why your Research is Relevant

1) <u>DON'T</u> just <u>plonk</u> bits of paper in your research folder without any explanation.
2) <u>DON'T</u> just copy and paste stuff from the Internet either.
3) <u>DO</u> <u>write notes</u> on <u>every</u> piece of research to say <u>why</u> it's <u>relevant</u>, how it changed your thinking or how it backed up your existing ideas.
4) <u>DO</u> <u>refer back</u> to the research section <u>throughout the project</u> — that helps to show you've <u>used your research</u>.

See page 2 for more on research.

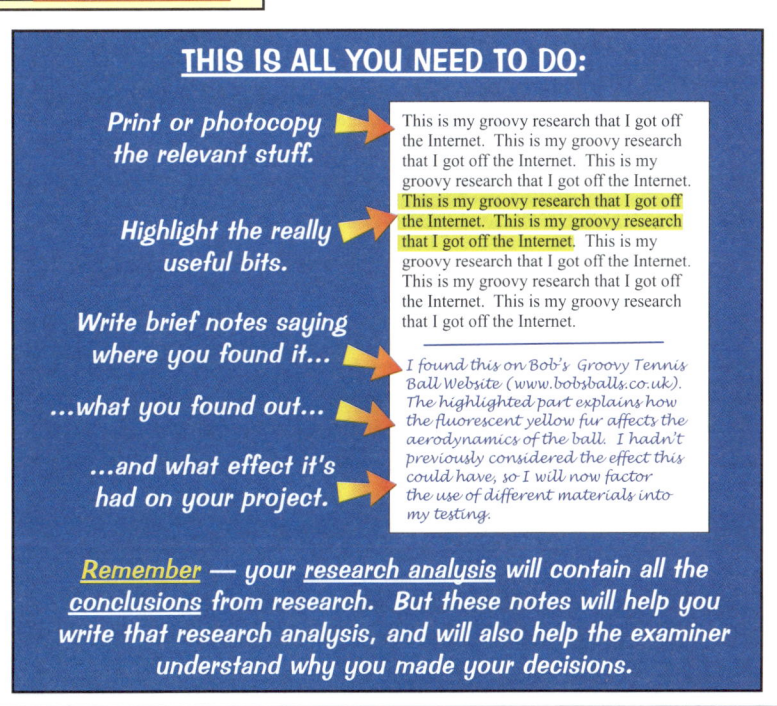

THIS IS ALL YOU NEED TO DO:

Print or photocopy the relevant stuff. → This is my groovy research that I got off the Internet. This is my groovy research that I got off the Internet. This is my groovy research that I got off the Internet. This is my groovy research that I got off the Internet.

Highlight the really useful bits. → This is my groovy research that I got off the Internet. This is my groovy research that I got off the Internet. This is my groovy research that I got off the Internet. This is my groovy research that I got off the Internet. This is my groovy research that I got off the Internet.

Write brief notes saying where you found it... → I found this on Bob's Groovy Tennis Ball Website (www.bobsballs.co.uk).

...what you found out... → The highlighted part explains how the fluorescent yellow fur affects the aerodynamics of the ball. I hadn't previously considered the effect this

...and what effect it's had on your project. → could have, so I will now factor the use of different materials into my testing.

<u>Remember</u> — your <u>research analysis</u> will contain all the <u>conclusions</u> from research. But these notes will help you write that research analysis, and will also help the examiner understand why you made your decisions.

Tips on Development

If you're smart you'll keep planning and evaluating throughout your project. If you're a buffoon you'll do a bit at the start, then forget about it and get a bad mark for your project.

You Need a Wide Range of Ideas — Be Creative

1) There's more than one way to skin a cat.
2) Consider plenty of different ways to solve the problem.
3) Don't just come up with one good idea and stick with it. You'll only be sure it's the best idea if you've thought about other ways of doing it.
4) The examiners do really get annoyed about this one — so get those creative juices flowing.

Developing your Ideas — Try Out a Few Alternatives

1) The same goes for developing ideas as for creating them.
2) There's still more than one way to skin a cat.
3) Once you've got the idea, there are still plenty of ways to turn that into an ace product.

Do Loads of Planning — and Not Just at the Start

Planning is for life, not just for... um... the start of your project.
These are the things you should do:

OVERALL PROJECT PLAN AT THE START:

1) to help you focus on the task
2) to make sure you know what stage you should have reached at any time — this way, if you fall behind schedule, you'll know about it as soon as possible, and can do something about it
3) to allow enough time for all the different stages of the design process — including testing, evaluation, and writing up your project

Remember to include testing and evaluating in your time plan — it's all too easy to forget them...

PLAN YOUR RESEARCH:

Work out what research you need to do, and how long you're going to allow yourself for each bit (e.g. questionnaires, disassembling a competing product, and so on).

DON'T GET BOGGED DOWN:

When you're generating proposals or developing your product, don't spend too long working on one little aspect of the product. There's a lot to do — so try to keep your project moving forward.

I have a cunning plan...

OK, repeat after me: "I will allow time for testing in my time plan. I will allow time for testing in my time plan. I will allow time for testing in my time plan. I will allow time for testing in my time plan..."

Section Seven — Project Advice

Tips on Evaluation

Evaluation means examining and judging your work (and you have to do this as part of your project — it's not just something for the examiner to do). If your product doesn't work, but you explain why, you can still get good marks.

Test and Evaluate your Product Throughout the Project

I quote:

> "To be achieving the highest marks in this section, candidates must show that they have used a clear and objective testing strategy."

That's from one of the Chief Examiners' Reports.
(In other words, it's important.)

Don't Wait until you're Finished to Evaluate your Work

1) Like any designer, it's a good idea to be thinking about evaluation from the moment you start working on your design brief.

2) Make notes on your designs and developments as you go along, explaining what was good and bad about each one.

3) When you're writing up your final evaluation, you can also think about whether you'd do anything differently if you were starting again. It's okay if you made some bad decisions during your project — everyone does. But you can get marks if you explain why they were bad decisions, and what you wish you'd done instead.

Check your Brief and Specification

You need to evaluate your product fully. Use these guidelines:

1) Compare your final product to your brief and specification. Does your product satisfy all the conditions it's supposed to? If not, why not?

2) Try to get a likely user (or an expert in this kind of product, maybe) to trial your product and give their honest opinions. This will give you a realistic view of whether it's fit for its purpose — e.g. does it do what it's meant to? And if it does, how well? They may also be able to give you ideas for improvements.

3) It's also dead important to think about things you could have done better, such as...

> 1) Time implications — did you spend too much time in one area, or rush to finish?
> 2) Practical work — were you completely satisfied with the quality of your final product?
> 3) Would you approach aspects of your design and development work in a different way?

Never forget to check your briefs...

Everyone makes mistakes (well, everyone except me, obviously). More specifically, everyone makes mistakes in their D & T projects. So don't worry too much when it happens to you. Just explain what went wrong and how you'd avoid it in the future. You can get marks for that.

Section Seven — Project Advice

Tips on Presentation

It's no use doing a stonking project if your presentation's naff. You've put a lot of time and effort into your project (probably) so it would be a shame for you to mess it up at the last stage.
IT REALLY IS WORTH PUTTING IN THOSE FEW EXTRA HOURS.

The Finished Product — Good Photographs are Ace

Your evaluation should be clearly presented and easy to read.

1) Include an introduction to give a bit of background information — e.g. how you came to think of the project.

2) Always take photos of any non-permanent work or intermediate stages in making the product. You can use either a normal or a digital camera and then either glue in the print or place the digital image into a word-processed document — whatever suits.

> Photos are the only way of getting a lasting record of your work — and the examiners *REALLY WANT* you to do it.

3) Use a mixture of media to present your project. It's always good to show off how nifty you are with CAD or that desktop publishing program, but don't forget about old-fashioned *words* to explain what you did, and sketches and prototypes to show how you did it.

4) Split up your evaluation into different sections to make it easy to read. Give each section a clear heading.

The sections could include:
a) how well your product satisfies the brief and specification
b) results from user trials
c) problems you encountered
d) improvements for the future

5) Think about how it fits together — your project needs to work as a whole. It should flow seamlessly from one bit to the next — don't just shove loads of separate bits in with no clue as to how they fit together.

Vocabulary — use the Right Technical Terms

BIG, FANCY WORDS:
1) Do yourself a favour — learn all the technical terms.
2) And how to spell them.
3) And don't worry if you sound poncy.
4) Using the right technical terms impresses the examiners. They say so in their reports.

GRAMMAR, SPELLING, PUNCTUATION:
1) Treat your project like an English essay.
2) Get your spellings right. Double-check any words you often get wrong.
3) Remember to use full stops and capital letters and write in proper sentences.
4) Short sentences make your work clearer. Long sentences, with loads of commas, can often get very confusing, because it's easy, once you get to the end of the sentence, to forget what you were reading right at the start.
5) Structure your work in paragraphs — a new paragraph for a new topic.

Santa cheats at presentation — he uses elves...

Of course your project has to look nice. I mean, what would you rather read... a beautifully presented folder of work, or something scribbled down on the back of a mucky paper towel...

Section Seven — Project Advice

Summary Checklist

This stuff can really make your project *sparkle*.
That's why I've given it a whole extra page — so you can't forget any of it.

Before you hand in your project, make sure you've covered all of these bits, and you'll be well on your way to D & T heaven. ☺

Sparkly Project Checklist

- [ ] 1) My design brief has loads of detail.
- [ ] 2) I've done plenty of research, and said why it's relevant.
- [ ] 3) I've made a detailed design specification.
- [ ] 4) I've come up with a wide range of project proposals.
- [ ] 5) I've included different ways of developing my product, and explained why I made my decisions.
- [ ] 6) I've tested my product on consumers.
-     7) I've done loads of planning, including:
  - [ ] a) a production plan (time plan),
  - [ ] b) planning for mass production.
- [ ] 8) I've evaluated my product throughout the project.
- [ ] 9) I've taken photos of intermediate stages and anything that won't last.
- [ ] 10) I've used a mixture of media to present my project.
- [ ] 11) I've checked my spelling and grammar.
- [ ] 12) I've used the right technical terms.

Section Seven — Project Advice

Index

A
acrylic cement 31
adhesives 18, 31
advantage — mechanical 34, 36-38
advertising 51
Advertising Standards Authority (ASA) 51
aesthetics 4, 40
all-body suits 45
Allen key 17
alloys 24, 29
animal glue 18
annealing 13, 25
annotate 4
anthropometrics 42
apron ties 45
Araldite 31
arc welder 20
assembly 16, 49
audits and assessments 44
auger bits 10
automated 49
axe to grind 42

B
backache 42
bandsaw 11
batch production 48, 49
behaving dangerously 45
bell crank 38
belt drive 36
bench grinder 12
bench plane 12
bevel-edged 10
bicycle 34
big, fancy words 58
biodegradable 40, 42
biological washing powders 44
black japan 17
blind rivet 18
block and tackle 36
blockboard 28
blocks 19
blow moulding 14, 53
blow torch 20
boards 28
body measurement data 42
bolts 17
braces 10
brackets 19
bradawls 10
brainstorm 4
brass spelter 20
brazing 20
briefs 1, 43, 57
Britain 44
British Electrotechnical Approvals Board (BEAB) 43
British Standards Institute (BSI) 43, 46, 51
British Standards Kitemark 43, 46, 51
British Toy and Hobby Manufacturers' Association 43
brittle 23, 25
bundle of laughs 23
butt hinge 30
butt joint 19
by-products 44

C
cabinet rasps 10
CAD (computer-aided design) 21, 50
CAD/CAM (computer-aided design & manufacture) 50
CAM (computer-aided manufacture) 21, 50
camera — digital camera 4
cams 37
carbon fibre 29
carrying tools safely 45
casting 15, 45
catches 30
cell production 49
central computer system 50
chain and sprocket 36
chemical 46
    chemical manufacture 48
child labour 42
chipboard 28
chisels 10
chocolate fireguard 32
chocolate teapot 32
choking hazard 46
chuck keys 45
CIM (computer-integrated manufacture) 50
cinema 51
circuit diagrams 51
circular cam 37
circular saw 11, 12
Citizens' Advice Bureau 43
clamping 45
clearance 17
client 51
CNC (computer numerical control) 21, 50
cold chisels 10
comfort 40
communication 49, 50
competition 40
components 34
composites 29
compression moulding 53
computers — see CAD, CAM and CIM
concurrent engineering 49
consumers 43, 46
    Consumer Safety Act 43
    Consumers' Advice Council 43
contact adhesive 18, 31
continuous production 48
continuous strips 15
coping saws 10
COSHH (Control Of Substances Hazardous to Health) 46
cost 40, 44
    cost-effective 44
    costings 7
countersink 10, 17
cranks 37
    crank and slider 37
    crankshaft 37
critical temperature 25
cross 17
cross-sections 4
cup of tea 30
customer research 1
customer satisfaction 41, 43
cutters — flame cutters 21
cutting metals 10

D
deburring metal 45
deciduous 27
decisions 52
deforming 13, 14
degreasing metal 45
design process 1
    design brief 1, 43
    design specification 3, 41
designer 51
destructive testing 41
detachable components 46
development 5, 40
deviation 41
digital camera 4
disassembly 2, 40
disposal of waste 42, 44, 45
dodgy products 43
dome 14
doughnuts 20
dovetail 19
    dovetail jig 53
    dovetail joints 53
dowel joint 19

down time 48
drawing conventions 51
drawing programs 21
drills 10
    drilling jig 53
    drilling machines 21, 45
driver gear 35
drums 44
ductile 23
durable 23
dust 45
    dust extraction equipment 45

E
edges 45
efficiency 49, 53
effort 38
electric arc welder 20
e-mail 51
emergency 45
emissions 44
employers' responsibility 46
end-use performance 41
energy efficiency 44
energy saving 44
engineers' lathes 11
environment 40, 42, 44
    environmental audits 44
    Environmental Health Department 43
    environmental responsibility 42
    environmentally friendly 44
    environmentally unfriendly 40
enzyme technology 44
epoxy resin 18, 31
ergonomics 40, 42
EU law 44
European neighbours 44
evaluation 5, 6, 8, 43, 57, 58
extrusion 15
eye strain 42

F
face masks and visors 45
factory siting 44
faults 41
ferrous 24
fibreboard — MDF 28
fingerprints 16
finishing 16
fire safety regulations 43
firmer 10
first class levers 38
flame cutters 21
flammable liquids 45
flat bits 10
flexibility
    flexible machinery and labour 48, 49
    flexible manufacturing systems 49
    lack of flexibility 49
flow charts 8, 52
fluidised powder 25
flush hinge 30
flux 20
follower 37
forged 13
form 40
formative evaluation 6
four-lobed cam 37
freehand sketching 4
fun fun fun 52
function 40
    functional requirements 32

G
Gantt charts 8, 52
gap in the market 1
gas brazing torch 20
gauges 41
gauntlets 45
gears 35
glass-reinforced plastic 29
gloves 45
glue 18, 31

go-faster stripes 40
goggles 45
grease 45
green 44
grinders 12

H
hacksaws 10
hair tied back 45
halving 19
Hammerite 25
hand tools 10
handles 26, 37
hardened threads 17
hardening 25
hardness 23
hardwood 27
harm 42
hazardous materials 45
health 42, 45, 46
Health and Safety at Work Act 46
heat treatments 25
hexagonal 17
high speed steel (HSS) 10
highly skilled workforce 48
hinges 30
honest advertising 51
horrific injury 45
housing 19
HSS (high speed steel) 10, 11
hydroelectricity 44

I
identifying faults 41
industrial washing machines 44
influence people
    how to make friends and... 51
injection moulding 15
injury 45
in-line assembly 49
input, process and output 34
Internet 51
introduction 58
iron 24
ISO 9000 41, 51
isometric projection 4

J
japan (the varnish, not the country) 17
jigs 53
jigsaw 12
JIT (just-in-time manufacturing) 49
jobbing production 48
joints 19
junk mail 51

K
kids 42
Kitemark 43, 46, 51
knock-down fittings 19

L
labels 43
labour intensive 48
lacquer 25
laminating 13
laminboard 28
landfill 44
lap joint 19
lathes 11, 17, 21, 45
laws 43, 44, 46, 51
lazy tongs 38
leg fastenings 30
legislation 43, 46, 51
levers 38
    double-acting levers 38
life cycle assessments 44
limbs
    loss of 42
limit gauges 41
linear motion 34
links 38

ICT 8 framework solutions

Stephen Doyle

OXFORD

OXFORD
UNIVERSITY PRESS

Great Clarendon Street, Oxford, OX2 6DP, United Kingdom

Oxford University Press is a department of the University of Oxford.
It furthers the University's objective of excellence in research, scholarship,
and education by publishing worldwide. Oxford is a registered trade mark of
Oxford University Press in the UK and in certain other countries

Text © Stephen Doyle 2004
Original illustrations © Oxford University Press 2004

The moral rights of the authors have been asserted

First published by Nelson Thornes Ltd in 2004
This edition published by Oxford University Press in 2014

All rights reserved. No part of this publication may be reproduced,
stored in a retrieval system, or transmitted, in any form or by any
means, without the prior permission in writing of Oxford University
Press, or as expressly permitted by law, by licence or under terms
agreed with the appropriate reprographics rights organization.
Enquiries concerning reproduction outside the scope of the above
should be sent to the Rights Department, Oxford University Press, at
the address above.

You must not circulate this work in any other form and you must
impose this same condition on any acquirer

British Library Cataloguing in Publication Data
Data available

978-0-7487-8085-3

20 19 18 17 16 15

Printed in India

Acknowledgements

Illustrations: Pantek Arts Ltd and Roger Fereday, Linda Rodgers Associates
Page make-up: Pantek Arts Ltd

Although we have made every effort to trace and contact all
copyright holders before publication this has not been possible in all
cases. If notified, the publisher will rectify any errors or omissions at
the earliest opportunity.

Links to third party websites are provided by Oxford in good faith
and for information only. Oxford disclaims any responsibility for
the materials contained in any third party website referenced in
this work.

Contents

Acknowledgements		v
Introduction		vi

1 Public information systems — 1

Lesson 1	Introduction to public information systems	1
Lesson 2	The sources of weather data	11
Lesson 3	Planning and creating a simple public information system	17
Lesson 4	Getting new data direct from a website	21
Lesson 5	Automating processes in a simple information processing system	34
Lesson 6	Evaluating a public information system	42
Lesson 7	Create your own public information system	45

2 Publishing on the web — 47

Lesson 1	Introduction to publishing on the web	47
Lesson 2	What to consider when creating a website	56
Lesson 3	Creating web pages using HTML	62
Lesson 4	Creating web pages using Microsoft Word	73
Lesson 5	Using FrontPage	80
Lesson 6	Creating a website using a wizard	86
Lesson 7	Completing the website for the bedding plants project	106
Lesson 8	Creating a feedback form and a table of contents for the bedding plants website project	110
Lesson 9	Checking and publishing the website	116
Lesson 10	Evaluating a website	119

3 Information: reliability, validity and bias — 122

Lesson 1	Introduction to information: reliability, validity and bias	122
Lesson 2	Using searches	135
Lesson 3	Using key words and Boolean operators for searching	144

Contents

Lesson 4 Using different search engines and searching for images — 150

Lesson 5 Learning and finding out — 154

4 Models and presenting numeric data — 158

Lesson 1 Introducing models and presenting numeric data — 158

Lesson 2 Turning the output into the input – using goal seek — 164

Lesson 3 Creating models to determine the break-even point — 172

Lesson 4 Two other models for finding the break-even point — 180

Lesson 5 Introducing randomness into a model — 184

5 Integrating applications to find solutions — 193

Lesson 1 Introduction: what is a system? — 193

Lesson 2 Understanding the problem and thinking about solutions — 202

Lesson 3 Developing a financial model for the bedding plants project — 207

Lesson 4 Keeping records — 213

Lesson 5 Sending letters to customers — 220

Lesson 6 Monitoring and controlling conditions in the greenhouse — 231

Lesson 7 Controlling more conditions in the greenhouse — 242

Lesson 8 Marketing the plants — 247

Lesson 9 Looking at the feasibility of the project — 252

Lesson 10 The final report — 253

Glossary — 256

Index — 257

Acknowledgements

The author would like to thank the following people for their valuable advice and assistance in the development of this resource: Sarah Robertson and Helen Kerindi at Nelson Thornes and Mandy Ridd and Robert Harries.

The author and publishers are grateful to the following for permission to reproduce material:

Weather reporter image and screenshot from The Advisory Unit: Computers in Education **www.advisory-unit.org** pp. 8, 12; Data Harvest Group Ltd **www.data-harvest.co.uk** and Rod Bowker © Flowol: Keep I.T. Easy (K.I.T.E) for screenshots on pp. 9, 236, 238, 239, 240, 241, 243, 244, 245; Thompson and Morgan for screenshot on p. 204; Onlineweather.com powered by Accuweather.com for screenshots on pp. 18, 19, 23, 24; Yahoo! Inc. for screenshots on pp. 130, 150, 151.

Microsoft screenshots are reproduced with permission from Microsoft Corporation. Microsoft and its products are registered trademarks of Microsoft Corporation in the United States and for other countries.

Photo credits:
BBC Picture Library p. 138; British Gas Plc p. 196; Corbis Images pp. 151, 184; La Crosse Technology pp. 9, 10; Ronald Grant Archive p. 157; Hozelock p. 196; Rowan McOnegal p. 205; National Meteorological Library and Archive p. 9; Kohler Mira Limited p. 196; Powerstock Photo Library p. 184; Martin Sookias pp. 96, 244, 245; Whirlpool pp. 10, 96. Wyevale Garden Centres **www.wyevale.co.uk** p. 96.

Archive images:
Corel 131 p. 232; Corel 219 (NT) p. 172, Ingram IL V2 CD5 p. 194; Photodisc 5B (NT) p. 34; Photodisc 17 (NT) p. 45; Photodisc 38 (NT) p. 207; Photodisc 67 (NT) p. 200; Photodisc 79 (NT) p. 154; Stockbyte 29 (NT) p. 52.

Every effort has been made to contact copyright holders and we apologise if any have been overlooked. Should copyright have been unwittingly infringed in this book, the owners should contact the publishers, who will make corrections at reprint.

Picture research by Sue Sharp.

Unit 1 Public information systems

- Flood warnings can be given so that homes can be evacuated.
- Fog warnings can be given so that motorway warning systems can forewarn motorists.

We are lucky in Britain because extreme weather conditions do not occur that often.

Weather affects what we do every day

STORMS PREDICTED ALL WEEK

FREEZING WEATHER PREDICTED – MINUS 10 DEGREES IN SOME PARTS!

Lesson 1 Introduction to public information systems

Ways of presenting weather data/information

There are many different ways that you can present the weather. The way the weather is presented depends on the audience and what the information will be used for. Here are some examples.

A website where you can search for the weather forecast for the area where you live

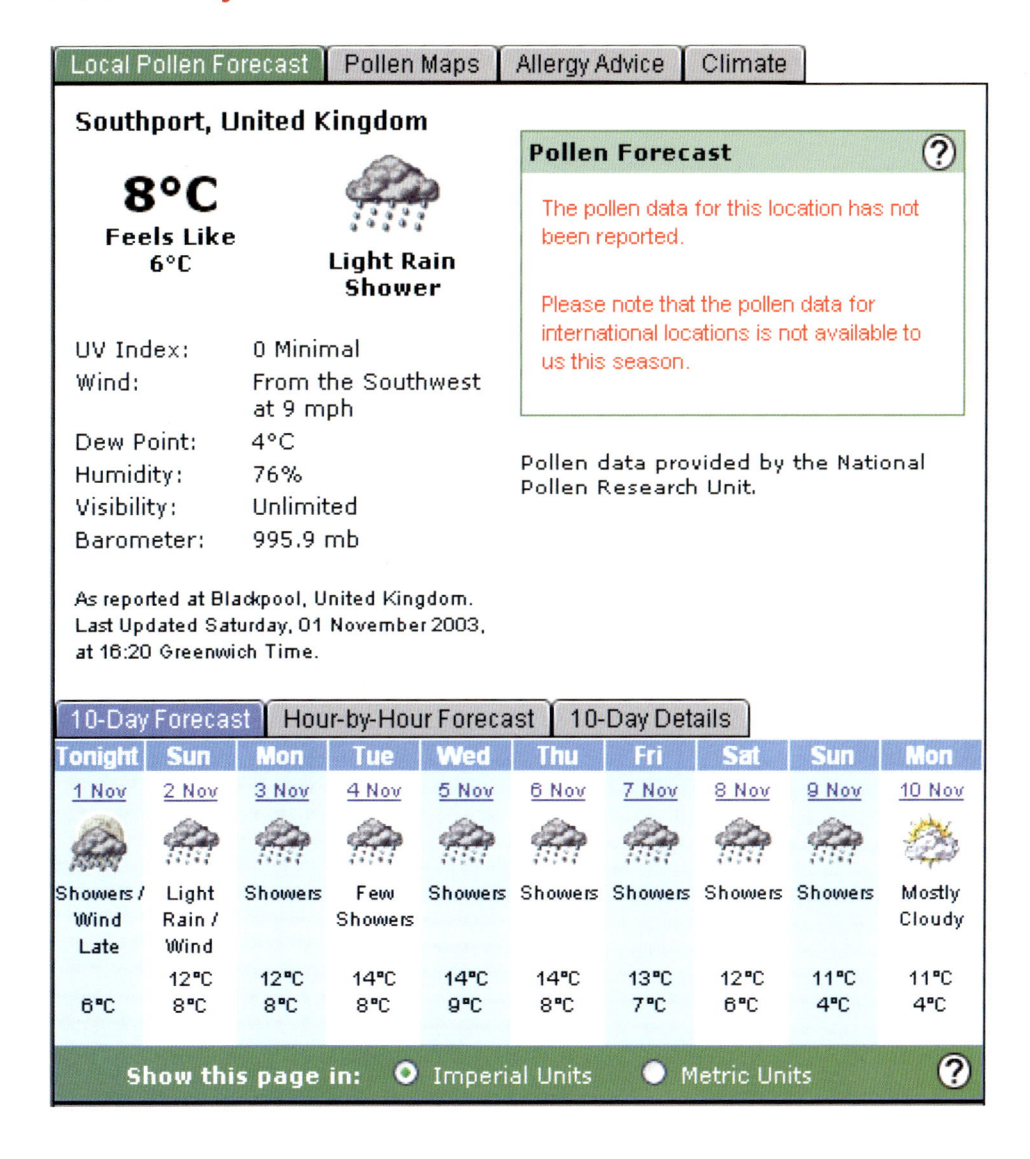

Presented as data (UV index, wind speed and direction, temperatures, etc.) and interpreted data (i.e. what the weather will do)

Source: www.weather.co.uk

Simple text without any data

Notice that this is a general forecast for the whole region. There is no data to support the forecast such as maximum and minimum temperatures.

Today
Showers will become restricted to eastern coastal Britain today, with the remainder of Britain being dry and sunny. Meanwhile thickening cloud will spread rain across Ireland.

A description of what the weather is forecast to do

Source: uk.weather.com/weather/local/UKXX0139?x=12&y=4

3

Unit 1 Public information systems

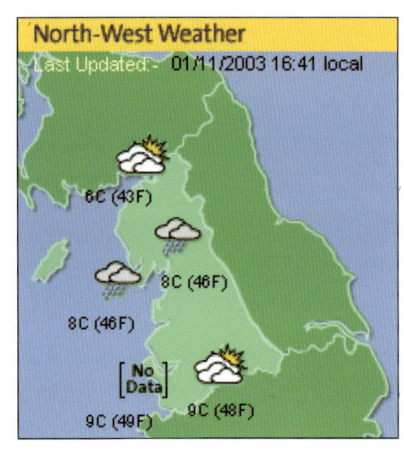

A weather map for the north-west

Source: www.aol.co.uk

A table of raw data from a weather forecasting station

Source: www.llansadwrn-wx.co.uk/monthly/m_wea2003.html#data

A weather map

A weather map is useful if you are going on a journey and want to see what the weather is like in different places.

Tables of weather data

These show the raw data collected from a weather station. The data needs to be interpreted before a weather forecast can be produced.

Monthly data 2003

```
           Llansadwrn (Anglesey): Monthly weather data for 2003.
                   (~ Based on the 1993-02 average)
           ------------------------------------------------------------
                   Jan   Feb   Mar   Apr   May   Jun   Jul   Aug   Sep   Oct    Year
           ------------------------------------------------------------
                              Air temperatures (C)

           Mean max   7.3   9.0  12.3  14.5  15.0  18.8  19.9  20.8  17.7  12.8   14.8
           Mean min   3.1   1.8   3.9   6.0   8.2  11.2  13.4  13.1  10.5   6.5    7.8
           Mean       5.2   5.4   8.1  10.3  11.6  15.0  16.7  17.0  14.1   9.7   11.3
           Anomaly~  -0.3  -0.4  +1.1  +1.6   0.0  +1.5  +1.2  +1.1  +0.3  -1.5     -
           High max  12.1  14.9  17.4  25.3  24.8  23.9  31.2  31.7  23.5  17.6   31.7
           Date        26    26    28    16    30    16    14     5  4,14    11     -
           Low max    1.7   4.6   8.1   8.4   9.5  14.1  14.9  15.0  13.1   6.8    1.7
           Date         7    14    12    10     2     4     4    31    27    21     -
           High min   8.8   7.7   8.0  10.3  14.0  14.4  18.9  17.7  15.0  11.7   18.9
           Date        27    26  9-11    15    30    27    16     9    18     9     -
           Low min   -2.9  -3.1  -1.5  -1.3   3.3   8.5   9.2   7.5     6   2.1   -3.1
           Date         8    15    14    10    10    20     1    31    23    30     -
           Grass min -7.3  -9.0  -7.0  -6.0  -0.4   5.3   6.8   5.0   2.7  -1.6   -9.0
           Date         5 15,18    14    10     3    20    12    31    23    30     -

                             Atmospheric moisture means

           RH (%)      88    83    80    78    83    80    84    83    84    86     83
           Dew point (C) 3.1  1.5   0.3   6.3   8.6  11.9  13.6  14.0  11.4   6.8    7.8
```

An animation

Weather changes throughout the day and these changes can be shown as an animation (i.e. a moving picture). Satellite pictures are often animated to show how the cloud is likely to move during the day.

ACTIVITIES

ACTIVITY 1: How much do you know about weather maps?

See if you can write down the meaning of each of the following weather symbols used on weather maps in newspapers, on TV and on the Internet. It is a good idea to look at all of the weather symbols shown below before writing your answer as some of the symbols and meanings are very similar.

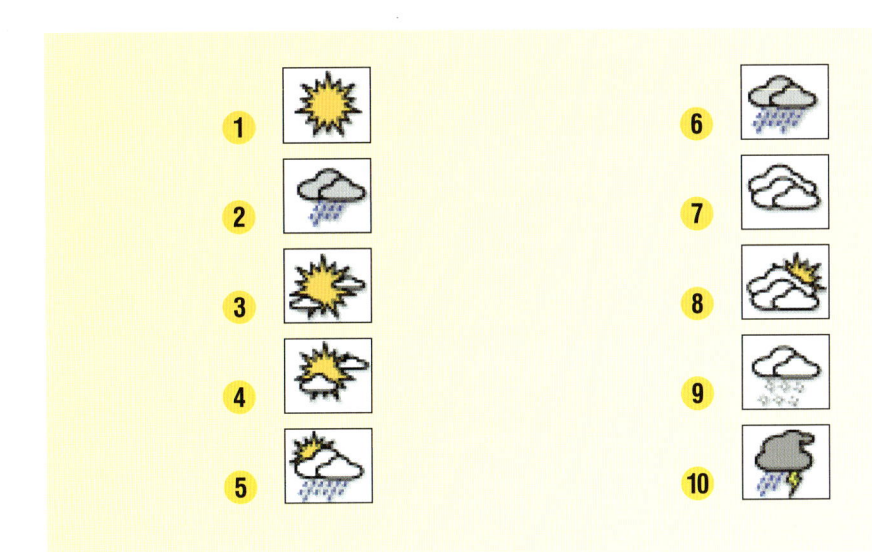

Lesson 1 Introduction to public information systems

1. ☀
2. 🌧
3. 🌤
4. ⛅
5. 🌦
6. 🌧
7. ☁
8. ⛅
9. 🌨
10. ⛈

Presenting weather statistics as graphs and charts

Suppose you want to head for the sun over Christmas. You need to find some weather statistics to check how hot it will be at your destination, whether it is likely to rain much and how many hours of sunshine you might expect. Most holiday brochures contain this information.

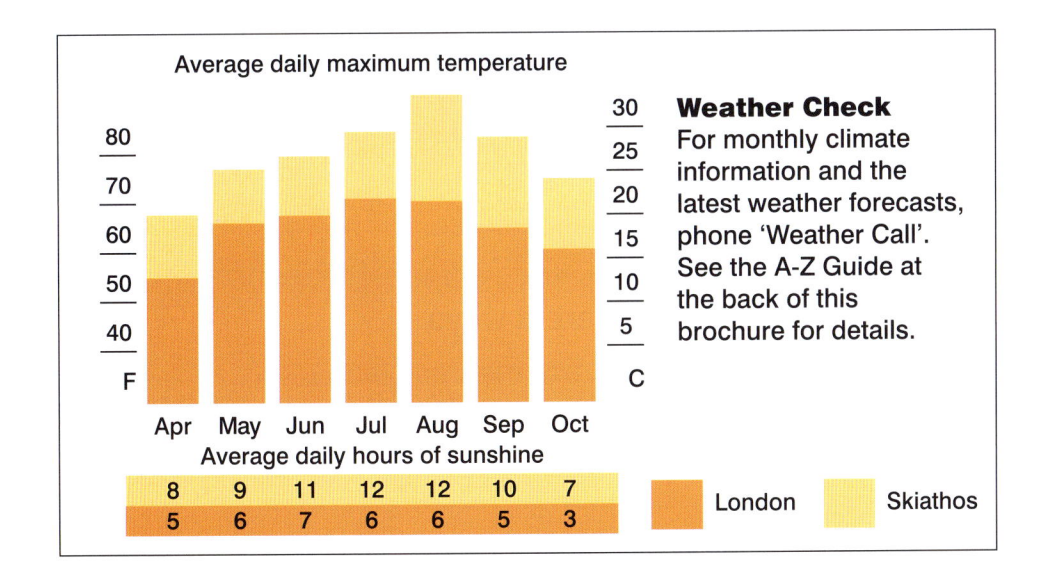

Average daily maximum temperature

	Apr	May	Jun	Jul	Aug	Sep	Oct
Average daily hours of sunshine	8	9	11	12	12	10	7
	5	6	7	6	6	5	3

London ▇ Skiathos ▇

Weather Check
For monthly climate information and the latest weather forecasts, phone 'Weather Call'. See the A–Z Guide at the back of this brochure for details.

Holiday brochures show the kind of weather to be expected in particular resorts

Unit 1 Public information systems

Weather maps and forecasts for a specialist audience

If you were an airline pilot or the captain of a ship, then the sort of weather map we are used to seeing in newspapers or on the television would not be detailed enough for your purposes. Meteorological maps use different symbols to those we are used to, but they are helpful for people who understand how to interpret them.

The figure shows the weather symbols used by specialists. You can see that such symbols give a lot of information without using many words.

How you present information such as the weather is extremely important. You always need to consider the way the information will be used by the audience. A holidaymaker will only want brief details that are easy to understand. If you presented them with the symbols shown in the figure (left), they would probably not be able to understand them. However, an airline pilot or captain of a ship would be able to understand the symbols.

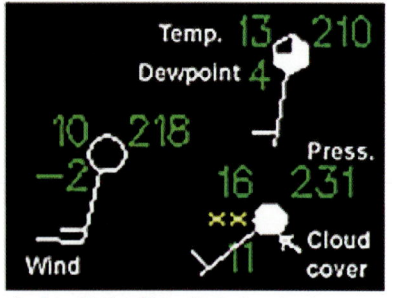

Surface Station Plots displaying cloud cover, temperature, dewpoint, wind speed and direction, pressure, and weather. The plot on the lower right indicates light snow as xx.

Source: www.nssl.noaa.gov/edu/lessons/lesson1.html

Websites

The Met Office website contains a huge amount of information and statistics about the weather and climate. See **www.met-office.gov.uk/education/links.html**. You can see the real-time weather in California, USA on the following website: **www.anegada.com/weather/wx.htm**. Notice how much information is given and how clearly the data is presented.

ACTIVITY 2: Presenting weather data in different ways

Here is some temperature data. It shows the average maximum and minimum temperatures recorded at a school weather station for the months January to September 2003.

	Temperature of the air (°C)								
	Jan	Feb	Mar	Apr	May	Jun	Jul	Aug	Sep
Mean max	7.3	9	12.3	14.5	15	18.8	19.9	20.8	17.7
Mean min	3.1	1.8	3.9	6	8.2	11.2	13.4	13.1	10.5

This data could be presented in different ways.

1. Describe three different ways of presenting this data.

2. Use suitable software and your knowledge and skills in ICT to present the above data in the ways you have described in question 1.

3. Save your work and produce printouts of the results.

Lesson 1 Introduction to public information systems

ACTIVITY 3: Produce a line graph showing maximum and minimum temperatures

In this activity you will produce two graphs (one for the maximum temperature and one for the minimum temperature) on the same set of axes.

1 Load the spreadsheet software Excel and enter the following data onto the spreadsheet.

	Temperature of the air (°C)								
	Jan	Feb	Mar	Apr	May	Jun	Jul	Aug	Sep
Mean max	7.3	9	12.3	14.5	15	18.8	19.9	20.8	17.7
Mean min	3.1	1.8	3.9	6	8.2	11.2	13.4	13.1	10.5

REMEMBER!
The legend is the box at the side of the graph.

!Note
To get the degree (°) sign, type it in as an ordinary 'o'. Then highlight it and click on Format then Cells. Now click on Superscript and then on the OK button.

2 The numbers in the spreadsheet would look better if they were all shown to one decimal place. Therefore, format the numbers like this:

	Temperature of the air (°C)								
	Jan	Feb	Mar	Apr	May	Jun	Jul	Aug	Sep
Mean max	7.3	9.0	12.3	14.5	15.0	18.8	19.9	20.8	17.7
Mean min	3.1	1.8	3.9	6.0	8.2	11.2	13.4	13.1	10.5

3 Highlight the months and the temperature readings and then click on the graph/chart icon. NB: Do not highlight anything else.

4 Now follow the instructions for producing a line graph and show how the monthly maximum and minimum temperatures vary. Produce your graph so that it is positioned on the same worksheet as the data.

5 Make sure that you give the graph a suitable title. Think about what the graph shows – if you can put it into words briefly, this can be your title.

Make sure that both the x and y axes are suitably labelled.

Check that the legend correctly identifies each line.

6 Save your worksheet using a suitable file name and then print out a copy of your work for your teacher.

A modern weather station

Modern electronic weather stations use sensors to take readings automatically and they store this data in a storage device called a data logger. These measurements can be transferred to a computer

Unit 1 Public information systems

for analysis and display. The data logger can either be attached to the computer to transfer the data, or the information can be transferred automatically using telecommunications, i.e. radio signals. Sometimes the data is transferred immediately so that the readings are in real time. Such data readings can be displayed on the Internet so that the weather readings are completely up to date.

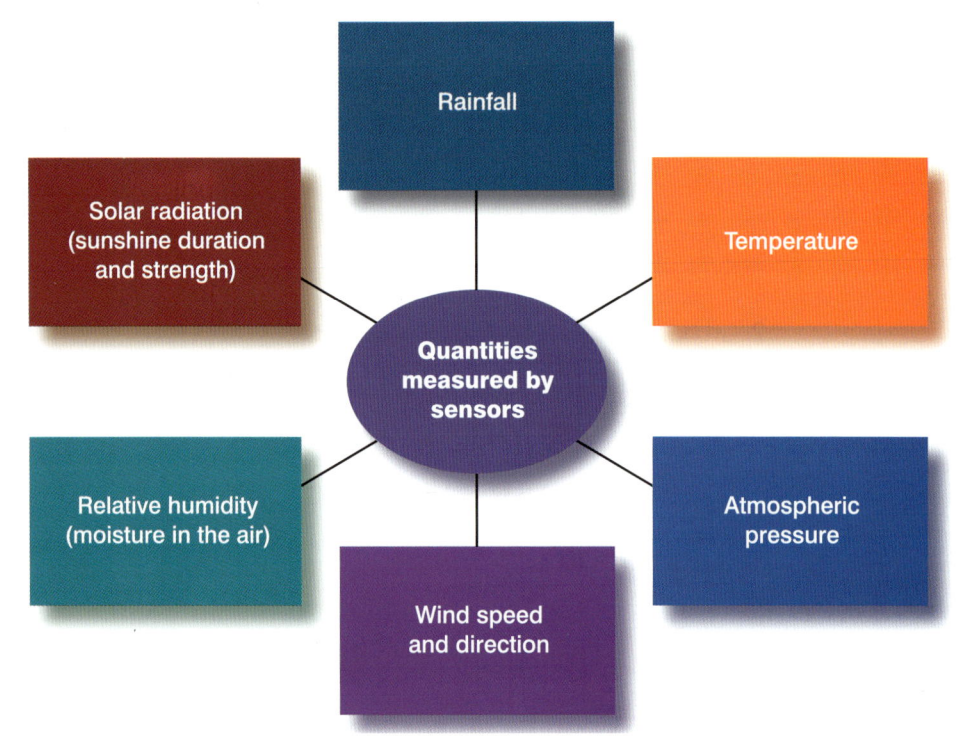

The Weather Reporter is a popular weather station used by schools

Source: www.advisory-unit.org.uk/

Quantities measured by sensors:
- Rainfall
- Temperature
- Atmospheric pressure
- Wind speed and direction
- Relative humidity (moisture in the air)
- Solar radiation (sunshine duration and strength)

The measurements needed in order that a weather forecast can be produced

WORKSHEET

WORKSHEET 8.1.1 How much can you remember about sensors and data logging?

You may be given a worksheet on which to write your answers or you may be asked to write your answers in your book. When you have finished, your teacher will either go through the answers or give you an answer sheet so that you can check the answers yourself.

Task 1

Environmental data was collected using a data logger. The conditions measured by the data logger were:

- Temperature
- Light
- Humidity
- Pressure

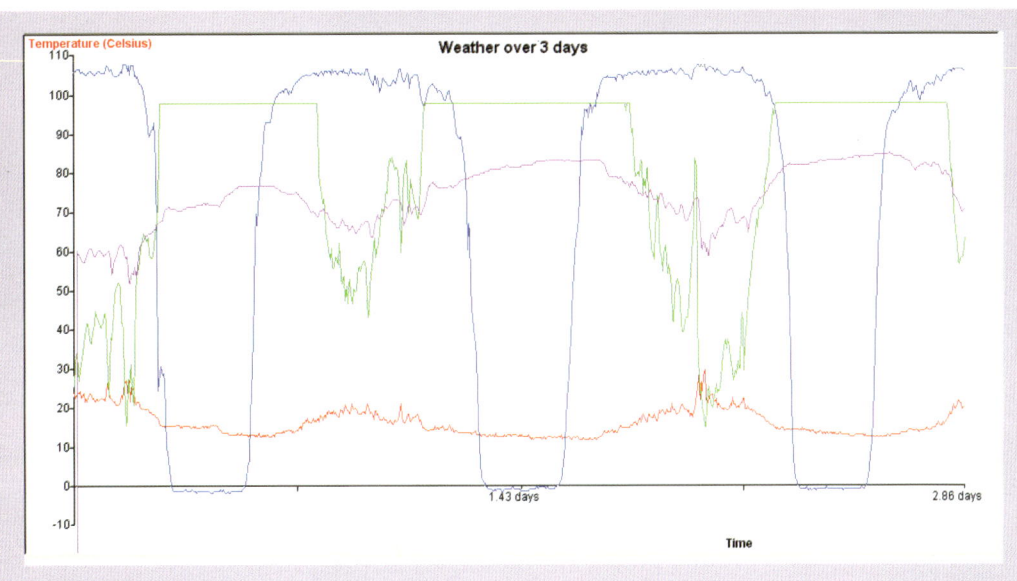

Lesson 1 Introduction to public information systems

Graph: Weather over 3 days, Temperature (Celsius) vs Time, showing values from -10 to 110, with markers at 1.43 days and 2.86 days.

Source: DataHarvest

Examine the graphs carefully and then answer the following questions.

1 (a) What is the logging period, in days, for the experiment?

(b) Give a reason for your answer to (a).

2 The red line shows how the temperature varies.

(a) Which colour line shows how the light intensity varies?

(b) Explain how you decided on your answer to (a).

3 The humidity graph varies a lot between the day and night values. Which colour line represents the humidity?

4 The pink line represents the pressure. Which one of the following describes the variation of the pressure?

(a) The pressure stays constant.

(b) The pressure varies but the general trend is upwards.

(c) The pressure varies but the general trend is downwards.

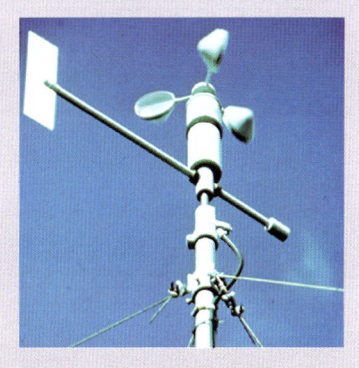

Part of a weather station

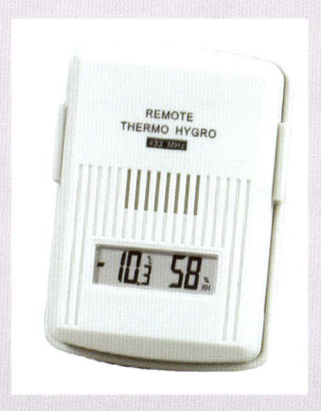

Task 2

Answer the following questions about sensors.

1 Here (right, above) is part of a weather station situated on the roof of a building.

Two sensors are used to measure the wind.

What two quantities are being measured by this sensor?

2 Here (right, below) is a remote temperature sensor. It measures the outside temperature.

A remote temperature sensor

Unit 1 Public information systems

The temperature appears indoors on a display like this (right):

(a) There are no wires between the sensor outside and the display inside. How do you think the data is sent?

(b) There is also a temperature sensor inside the building. Why is this needed?

(c) There is a pressure sensor inside the building. Explain why a sensor is not needed outside.

3 A washing machine contains a number of sensors.

Give the names of two sensors you would find in an automatic washing machine.

Describe the purpose of each of the sensors you have named.

An automatic washing machine contains many sensors

An indoor weather station with some internal sensors

QUESTIONS

1 'The way you present weather details depends on your audience.'

Write a brief explanation of what this sentence means.

2 A weather forecasting system is one example of a public information system.

Write down *two* different examples of public information systems.

3 Weather maps are often animated.

(a) Explain what the word 'animate' means.

(b) Briefly explain why animating a weather map is useful.

What you should already know

In this unit you will be extending your knowledge of spreadsheet software, so before carrying on make sure that you understand the basics covered in Year 7. You will need to know how to copy and paste data from the Internet.

You will build on the following, which you covered at Key Stage 2:

- Control and monitoring – What happens when?

Lesson 2 The sources of weather data

What you will learn

In this unit you will:
- Collect data from a range of sources.
- Prepare the information for processing.
- Design a public information system.
- Publish a public information system.

Lesson 2: THE SOURCES OF WEATHER DATA

Background: How do you get weather data?

REMEMBER!

Raw data is simply facts and figures without any interpretation. When you interpret raw data you get information.

To get weather data you can:
- Collect the data yourself.
- Use the raw data that others have collected.

Collecting data yourself provides primary data.

The data that someone else has collected provides what is called secondary data.

KEY WORDS

primary data – data you have collected yourself

secondary data – data collected by someone else

Make it happen

ACTIVITY 4: Different ways of presenting the weather

Weather details may be obtained from the following websites. Look at each website and state who the information is aimed at.

1. www.snoweye.com/
2. www.weather.gliderpilot.net/
3. www.bbc.co.uk/weather/features/gardening.shtml
4. www.meto.gov.uk/datafiles/offshore.html
5. www.meto.gov.uk/loutdoor/mountainsafety/brecon.html

Unit 1 Public information systems

WORKSHEET WORKSHEET WORKSHEET WORKSHEET WORKSHEET

WORKSHEET 8.1.2 Looking at weather data from a remote weather station

You may be given a worksheet on which to write your answers or you may be asked to write your answers in your book. When you have finished, your teacher will either go through the answers or give you an answer sheet so that you can check the answers yourself.

Below are some readings from the weather station called Weather Reporter.

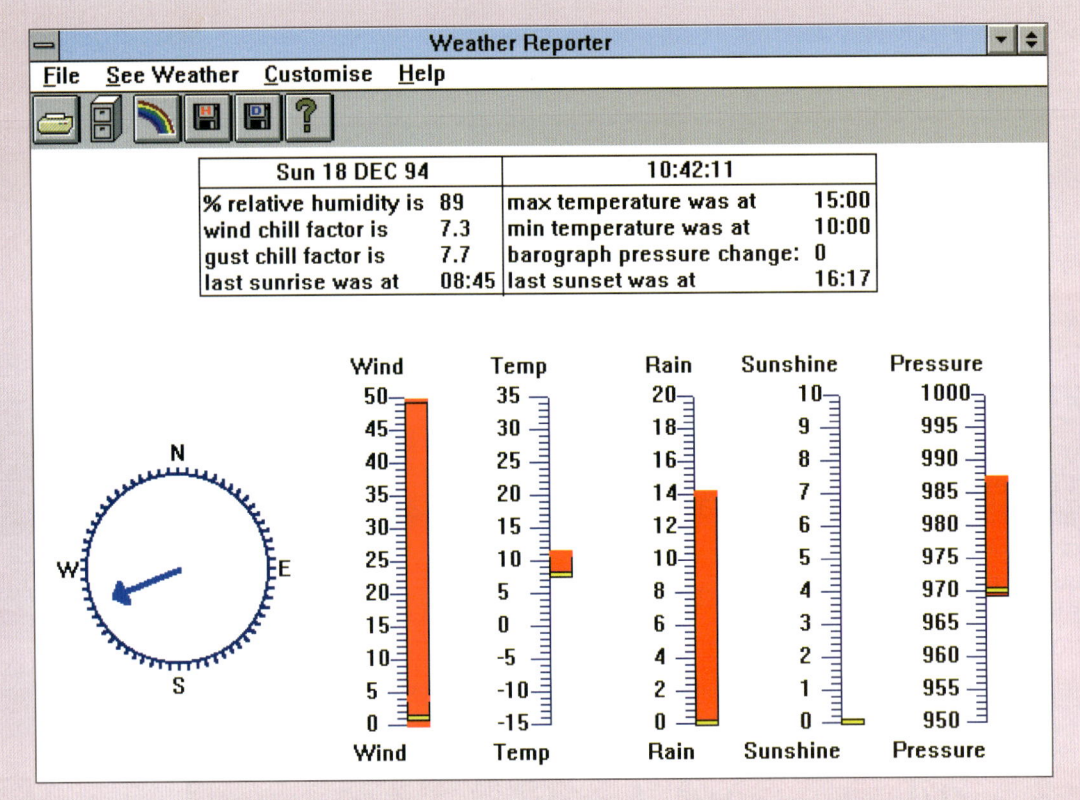

```
Weather Reporter
File  See Weather  Customise  Help
```

Sun 18 DEC 94		10:42:11	
% relative humidity is	89	max temperature was at	15:00
wind chill factor is	7.3	min temperature was at	10:00
gust chill factor is	7.7	barograph pressure change:	0
last sunrise was at	08:45	last sunset was at	16:17

Source: www.advisory-unit.org.uk/

Look at the information given by Weather Reporter and then answer the following questions.

1 Some weather stations are connected to a web cam. Why are web cams sometimes a feature of weather stations?

2 The date and time has been included on the screen. Explain why this is important.

3 Write a list of all the sensors that would be needed to give the readings as shown on the screen.

4 Fill in the following table to show how the data from the sensors is displayed.

12

Lesson 2 The sources of weather data

Type of display	Quantity/Quantities
Text in a table	
Dial	
Numbered scale	

5 By looking at the information on the screen you should be able to describe what the weather is like.

Write a few sentences to describe what you think the weather is like.

6 How might it be possible to find out if the weather, as shown by the weather readings, is typical or untypical for the time of year?

Public information systems

The weather station created by a school and available to users of the Internet is an example of a public information system. It is called a system because the data is obtained and input automatically into the computer where it is stored and processed so that it can be output onto the website. A computer system such as this can always be divided into the three stages: Input, Process and Output.

Importing a data file into a spreadsheet

A file created using one software package often needs to be used with a different package. For example, a data logger may store the data it collects as one type of file and you may want to analyse the data in that file using spreadsheet software such as Excel.

There are two ways to do this.

1. You could print out the file using the software in which it was created. Then you could type all of the data into the new package. The problem with this is that it takes a long time and typing errors may occur.

2. You could import (i.e. transfer) the data from the package in which it was created into the spreadsheet program.

People who produce software realise that files often need to be transferred from one piece of software to another. By using standard ways to store the file, they try to make it simple to import files. This makes it easy for other software to read the files.

KEY WORDS

import – to put the data created in one package into a different package

13

Unit 1 Public information systems

Make it happen

ACTIVITY 5: Importing weather data into Excel

The format of raw weather data may be different to the format you use for processing the data. In most cases it is possible to get the data into the software package that you are using without the need to re-type it.

In this activity you will learn how to import data from the Internet into the spreadsheet package Microsoft Excel.

1. Log on to the Internet and access the following site:
   www.firsthydro.co.uk/weather/current/llanberisdata.asp

2. You will see a set of weather data that has been collected as part of the Snowdonia Weather Stations Project. You are going to take this data and import it into Excel.

   Highlight all the data you see on the screen including the headings. How much data there is depends on the time you access the data as it is being added to throughout the day.

   Click on **Edit** and then on **Copy**.

3. Now load the spreadsheet package Excel and open a new worksheet.

Note

Your data will not be the same as this as it will relate to the day on which you perform this task.

	A	B	C	D	E	F	G	H	I	J	K	L
1	Year	Month	Date	Time (G.M.T.)	Air Temperature (C)	Temperature (inc. Wind chill effect)	Gust wind speed (Mph)	Average wind speed (Mph)	Average wind Direction (Degrees)	Sunlight (Watts/sq.m.)	Rain (mm/hour)	Humidity (%)
2	2004	Feb	28	15:30	3.2	-6.7	24	22	291	144	0	67
3	2004	Feb	28	15:15	3.2	-6.7	24	22	286	224	0	66
4	2004	Feb	28	15:00	3.1	-6.9	24	22	285	236	0	66
5	2004	Feb	28	14:45	3.2	-6.4	24	21	283	260	0	65
6	2004	Feb	28	14:30	3.3	-5.5	23	19	300	296	0	65
7	2004	Feb	28	14:15	4.1	-5.2	24	21	272	428	0	66
8	2004	Feb	28	14:00	3.6	-6.2	24	22	293	292	0	66
9	2004	Feb	28	13:45	3.7	-6.1	23	22	284	380	0	65
10	2004	Feb	28	13:30	4.7	-3.7	22	19	283	524	0	62
11	2004	Feb	28	13:15	4.3	-4.9	23	21	288	568	0	63
12	2004	Feb	28	13:00	3.3	-5.9	22	20	286	264	0	66
13	2004	Feb	28	12:45	4.6	-3.4	21	18	283	568	0	62
14	2004	Feb	28	12:30	5	-2.5	20	17	293	552	0	61
15	2004	Feb	28	12:15	4.6	-3.4	22	18	290	592	0	63
16	2004	Feb	28	12:00	4.7	-3.3	23	18	295	552	0	62
17	2004	Feb	28	11:45	4.2	-4.4	23	19	295	512	0	63
18	2004	Feb	28	11:30	3.5	-6	24	21	293	416	0	64
19	2004	Feb	28	11:15	4	-5.7	24	22	291	476	0	63
20	2004	Feb	28	11:00	3.7	-6.1	24	22	277	480	1.6	64
21	2004	Feb	28	10:45	3.2	-6.4	23	21	293	280	0	66

A sample of weather data imported into the spreadsheet package Excel

Source: www.firsthydro.co.uk/weather/current/llanberisdata.asp

Lesson 2 The sources of weather data

Click on cell A1 as this is where we want the data to start.

4 Click on **Edit** and then **Paste**.

Your data will now appear in the spreadsheet package as shown on the previous page.

5 You have now imported data that was created using one piece of software into a different piece of software.

Save this file using the file name 'Llanberis weather data'.

The data is now saved in a different format to the one it was created in. The file is an Excel spreadsheet file.

WORKSHEET WORKSHEETWORKSHEETWORKSHEETWORKSHEET

WORKSHEET 8.1.3 **Displaying data**

You may be given a worksheet on which to write your answers or you may be asked to write your answers in your book. When you have finished, your teacher will either go through the answers or give you an answer sheet so that you can check the answers yourself.

There are many different ways in which information can be displayed. The best way of presenting the data depends on the type of data and also the intended audience.

!Note
The examples do not need to be linked to the weather.

The following table gives examples of how information can be displayed. Complete the table by writing in three different examples.

How the information is displayed	Example 1	Example 2	Example 3
Using pictures			
Using dials			
Using numbers 70°F, 3 mm, 1035 mm			

15

Unit 1 Public information systems

How the information is displayed	Example 1	Example 2	Example 3
Using text			
Using charts			
Using sliding scales			
Using graphs			

WORKSHEET 8.1.4 **People use weather reports for different purposes**

You may be given a worksheet on which to write your answers or you may be asked to write your answers in your book. When you have finished, your teacher will either go through the answers or give you an answer sheet so that you can check the answers yourself.

You may need different weather details to those that someone else needs. It all depends on how the information is to be used.

Work in pairs to complete the following table by writing in the purpose of the information.

16

Lesson 3 Planning and creating a simple public information system

Target audience	Purpose of information
You	
Potholers (people who explore caves)	
Painter and decorator	
Yachtsman	
Ice-cream salesman	
Football supporter	
Airline pilot	
Skier	
Holidaymaker	
Rivers authority	
Coastguard	
Air traffic controller	
Farmer	
Local authority	
Surfer	
Groundsmen (people who look after football and rugby pitches etc.)	
Sun-cream manufacturer	
Formula 1 racing team	
Insurance company	
Manager of a supermarket	
Water utility company	
Hot-air balloonist	

Lesson 3: PLANNING AND CREATING A SIMPLE PUBLIC INFORMATION SYSTEM

Background

In this lesson you will learn how to make your own public information system. This public information system will take data

Unit 1 Public information systems

from a web page and put it into a spreadsheet which will then be used to process the data and output it as graphs/charts.

ACTIVITY 6: Investigating a public information system on the weather

In this activity you will look at a public information system that shows the weather.

Use the Internet and type in the following website address:
www.onlineweather.com/v4/uk/regional/index.html

Note that you can have:

- regional forecasts for the next 24 hours
- regional outlooks for the next four days.

Choose the region nearest to your school.

You will see the current regional forecast for the weather – split into two – one for the day and one for the night.

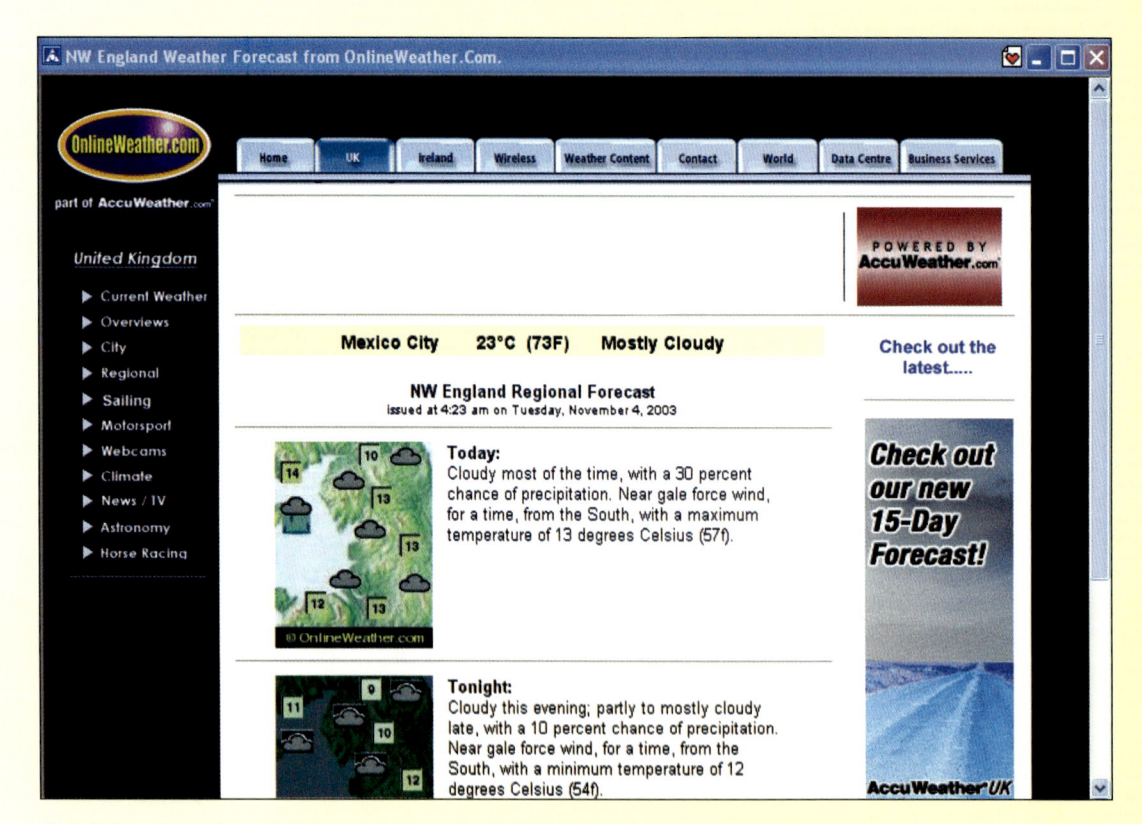

A 24-hour regional forecast

Source: www.onlineweather.com/v4/uk/regional/rfennw.html

Lesson 3 Planning and creating a simple public information system

North-West England Regional Outlook
Issued at: 4:23 am on Tuesday, November 4, 2003

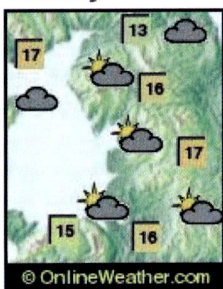

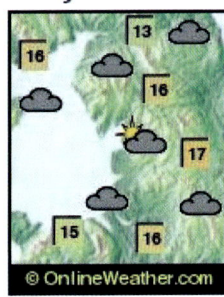

Wednesday

Partly sunny and pleasant, with a 10 percent chance of precipitation. Near gale force wind, for a time, from the South-South-East, with a maximum temperature of 16 degrees Celsius (61f). Wednesday night; Cloudy with rain, with a 70 percent chance of precipitation. Strong wind from the South-South-East, with a minimum temperature of 10 degrees Celsius (50f).

Thursday

Pleasantly warm with intervals of clouds and sunshine, with a 20 percent chance of precipitation. Strong wind from the South-South-East, with a maximum temperature of 17 degrees Celsius (63f). Thursday night; Partly to mostly cloudy, with a 20 percent chance of precipitation. Fresh wind from the South-East, with a minimum temperature of 13 degrees Celsius (56f).

Friday

Pleasantly warm with sunshine and patchy clouds, with a 20 percent chance of precipitation. Strong wind from the South-East, with a maximum temperature of 17 degrees Celsius (63f). Friday night; A moonlit sky,

Saturday

Several hours of sunshine, with a 10 percent chance of precipitation. Fresh wind from the East-South-East, with a maximum temperature of 12 degrees Celsius (55f). Saturday night; Partly to mostly cloudy, with a 10 percent

A four-day regional outlook

Source: www.onlineweather.com/v4/uk/regional/roennw.html

Use the information from the two web pages that you looked at to answer the following questions.

1 Two temperatures are always given. What is the significance of these temperatures?

2 How is the information displayed on each of these sites?

3 Weather maps are included as well as text. Why do you think both types of information are used?

4 Pictures are used to display the weather.

(a) Give one reason in favour of using pictures.

(b) Give one reason for not using pictures.

Unit 1 Public information systems

5 Pictures may be aimed at certain groups of people. Give the name of one group of people who would find the pictures easier to understand.

6 The weather shown in both web pages is aimed at a wide audience. More specialist weather is often needed by certain groups of people. Explain how the weather information might need to be changed for each of the following people:

(a) the pilot of a light aircraft

(b) a diving party

(c) a farmer.

> **KEY WORDS**
>
> **workbook** – a file that contains one or more worksheets
>
> **worksheet** – a single page showing the spreadsheet grid

ACTIVITY 7: Using ICT to set up a public information system

In the following activities you will create your own public information system in the form of a spreadsheet. The data you will use for your system will be obtained from a web page about the weather.

Workbooks and worksheets

In the following activities you will come across the terms 'workbook' and 'worksheet' and it is important that you understand the difference between these.

A workbook in the spreadsheet package Excel is a file that contains one or more worksheets. A worksheet is just like a page that contains a matrix of

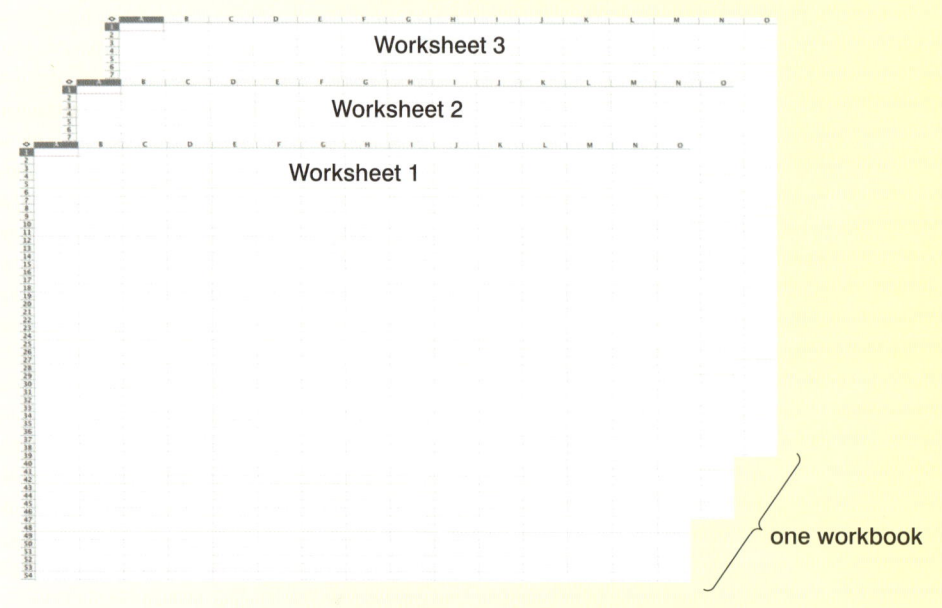

Worksheet 3
Worksheet 2
Worksheet 1

one workbook

Worksheets are the pages of a workbook

20

Lesson 4 Getting new data direct from a website

rows and columns where we can enter numbers, text, formulae, etc. Until now we have only used one worksheet in a workbook.

You have seen how graphs can be drawn and put on the same worksheet as the data. You can also put the graphs or charts on a different worksheet.

To move from one worksheet to another, you simply click on the tabs at the bottom of the worksheet window.

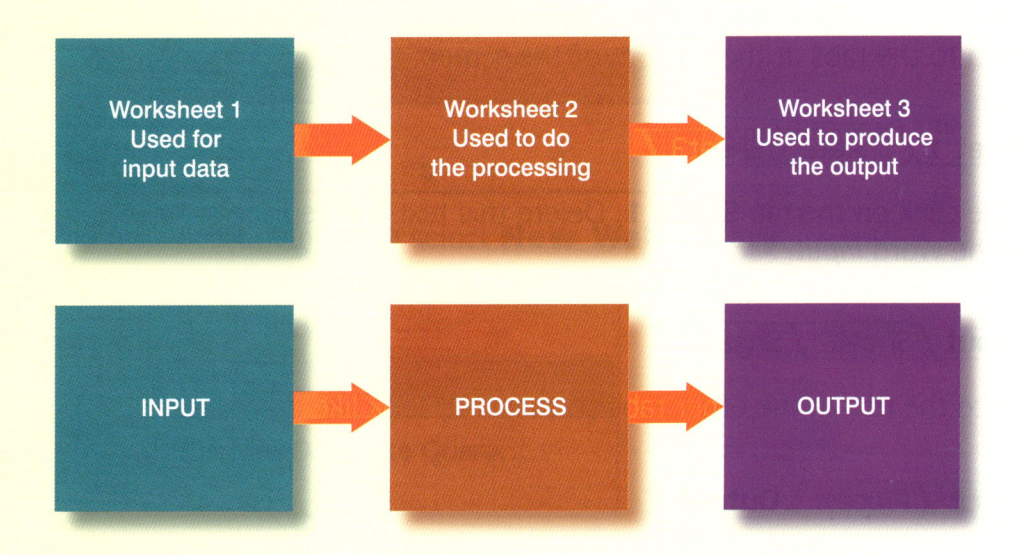

| Worksheet 1 Used for input data | → | Worksheet 2 Used to do the processing | → | Worksheet 3 Used to produce the output |

| INPUT | → | PROCESS | → | OUTPUT |

The three stages of computing: input, process and output. Each of the three stages can be carried out on a different worksheet

Lesson 4: GETTING NEW DATA DIRECT FROM A WEBSITE

Background: Taking data from a web page

A new public information system is to be set up which will automatically take the data from a website and put it into the input worksheet. As soon as this is done, the process worksheet will perform the processing and the output worksheet will contain the results such as graphs and charts.

KEY WORDS

URL – Uniform Resource Locator – the address that defines the route to a file on the Internet. This is the website or web page address that you type in (e.g. www.oxfordsecondary.co.uk)

web query – a query that gets data from the Internet. The data is usually in the form of a table

21

Unit 1 Public information systems

ACTIVITY 9: Creating the process worksheet

In this activity you will create the process worksheet and copy some of the data from the input worksheet. The data will be copied and a link will be provided back to the input worksheet so that if the data changes in the input worksheet, it will also change in the output worksheet.

1 Using the same worksheet as before, click on the tab for the process worksheet situated at the bottom of the screen ⟩Process⟨

A blank worksheet will appear.

This worksheet will eventually contain the data which will be processed to produce the graphs and charts on the output worksheet.

2 Go back to the input worksheet.

Widen column N so that the heading fits in.

Your worksheet will now look like this:

	A	B	C	D	E	F	G	H	I	J	K	L	M	N
1	Input worksheet into which weather data for Blackpool will be imported.
2	This worksheet contains a link to a webpage and will be updated whenever the data on the web page changes.
3														
4		Jan	Feb	Mar	Apr	May	Jun	Jul	Aug	Sep	Oct	Nov	Dec	Average/Total
5														
6	Mean(°C)	3.9	3.9	5.5	7.6	10.8	13.7	15.5	15.5	13.5	10.6	6.7	4.6	9.3
7	(°F)	39	39	42	46	51	57	60	60	56	51	44	40	49
8														
9	Sunshine (hours)	52.5	73	112.6	162.2	213.3	208.2	191.9	176.5	131.6	96.4	63	45.5	1526.7
10														
11	Rain(mm)	78	54	64	51	53	59	61	78	86	93	89	87	853
12	(in)	3.1	2.2	2.6	2	2.1	2.4	2.4	3.1	3.4	3.7	3.6	3.5	34

3 We are going to copy some of the data from this worksheet and put it into the process worksheet. We are only going to process certain rows of this data so we will need to copy and paste each row in turn.

Select the row from cell B4 to M4 containing the months.

Click on **Edit** and then **Copy**.

Now go to the process worksheet and make sure that the cursor is positioned on cell B4. This is the cell where the copying will start.

Click on **Edit** and then **Paste Special**.

The following window appears:

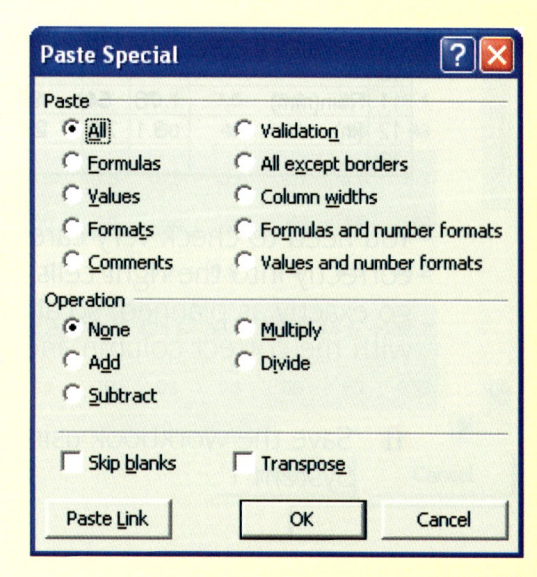

26

Lesson 4 Getting new data direct from a website

Check yours is the same as this and click on the **Paste Link** button.

Repeat these steps by selecting:

- Row from cell A6 to M6 containing the mean temperatures in degrees Celsius and then pasting it into the process worksheet from cell A5.

- Row from cell A11 to M11 containing the rainfall in mm and then pasting it into the process worksheet from cell A6.

- Row from cell A9 to M9 showing the total hours of sunshine in the month and then pasting it into the process worksheet from cell A7.

When you have completed the above the process worksheet will look like this:

	A	B	C	D	E	F	G	H	I	J	K	L	M
1													
2													
3													
4		Jan	Feb	Mar	Apr	May	Jun	Jul	Aug	Sep	Oct	Nov	Dec
5	Mean(°C)	3.9	3.9	5.5	7.6	10.8	13.7	15.5	15.5	13.5	10.6	6.7	4.6
6	Rain(mm)	78	54	64	51	53	59	61	78	86	93	89	87
7	Sunshine (	52.5	73	112.6	162.2	213.3	208.2	191.9	176.5	131.6	96.4	63	45.5
8													

9 Now widen column A so that all of the headings for the rows are shown.

	A	B	C	D	E	F	G	H	I	J	K	L	M
1													
2													
3													
4		Jan	Feb	Mar	Apr	May	Jun	Jul	Aug	Sep	Oct	Nov	Dec
5	Mean(°C)	3.9	3.9	5.5	7.6	10.8	13.7	15.5	15.5	13.5	10.6	6.7	4.6
6	Rain(mm)	78	54	64	51	53	59	61	78	86	93	89	87
7	Sunshine (hours)	52.5	73	112.6	162.2	213.3	208.2	191.9	176.5	131.6	96.4	63	45.5

10 You have now completed the process worksheet. Each row of data has links to the data in the input worksheet.

Click on cell B5 and you will see the following =Input!B6 in the Formula bar.

This shows you where in the linked worksheet it is getting the data from.

This means that if the data in the input worksheet changes, then any cells which are linked in the process worksheet will automatically change.

11 Save the workbook using the file name 'Public Information System 2'.

(Do not exit the activity as it is needed in the next activity.)

Unit 1 Public information systems

ACTIVITY 10: Creating the output worksheet

In this activity you will use the data in the process worksheet to produce graphs and charts in the output worksheet.

One line graph will be produced showing the mean temperature and the rainfall.

A bar chart will be drawn showing the total rainfall for each month.

1 Load the spreadsheet software Excel and open the workbook called Public Information System 2, if it is not already loaded.

2 Making sure that the Process tab is selected, select the months, temperature data and rainfall data by highlighting it like this:

	A	B	C	D	E	F	G	H	I	J	K	L	M
1													
2													
3													
4		Jan	Feb	Mar	Apr	May	Jun	Jul	Aug	Sep	Oct	Nov	Dec
5	Mean(°C)	3.9	3.9	5.5	7.6	10.8	13.7	15.5	15.5	13.5	10.6	6.7	4.6
6	Rain(mm)	78	54	64	51	53	59	61	78	86	93	89	87
7	Sunshine (hours)	52.5	73	112.6	162.2	213.3	208.2	191.9	176.5	131.6	96.4	63	45.5

3 Click on the chart wizard icon.

4 Select a line graph.

28

Lesson 4 Getting new data direct from a website

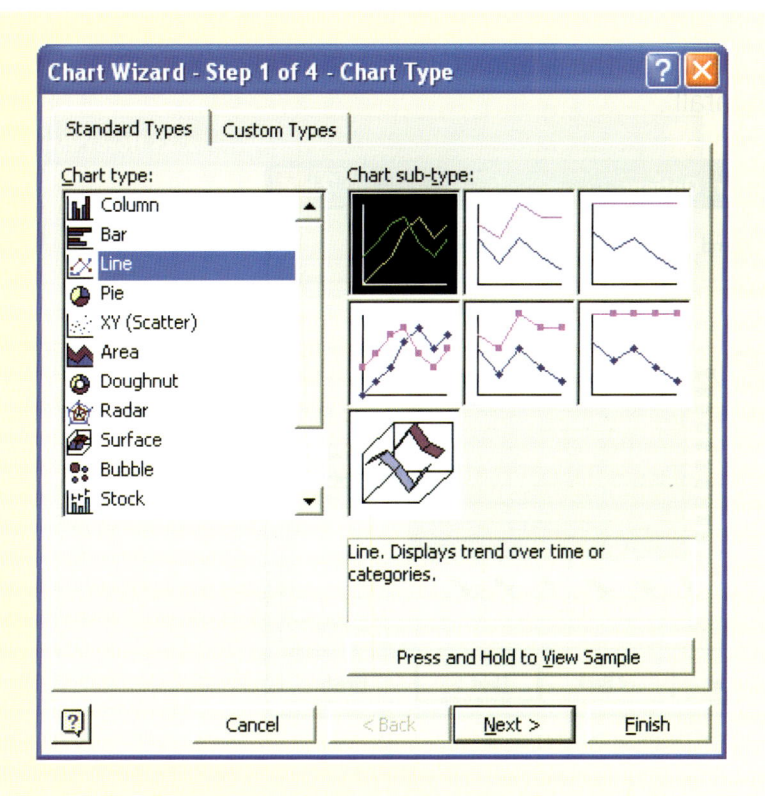

Click on **Next >**.

5 Check that the correct range of cells is being used to produce the graph.

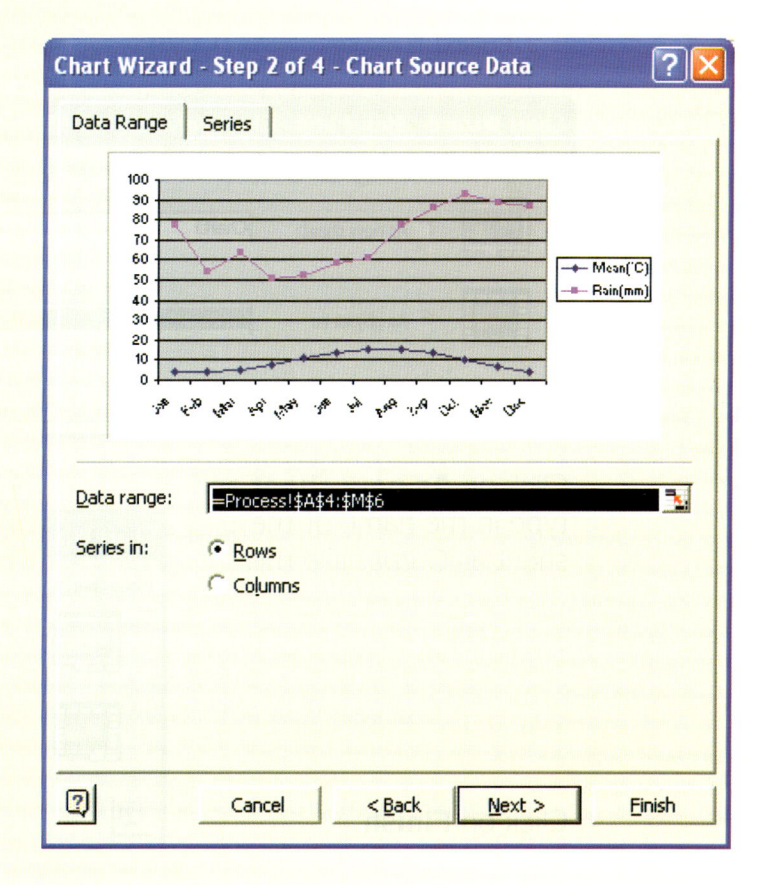

Click on **Next >**.

29

Unit 1 Public information systems

> **EXTENSION ACTIVITY**
>
> The workbook Public Information System 3 could have its appearance dramatically improved. For example, there are no proper titles for two of the worksheets and colour could be used to make the graphs and charts more eye-catching.
>
> Alter the workbook and play around with the design until you are happy with the results.
>
> Save a final copy of your workbook using the file name 'Public Information System 4' and print out copies of those worksheets you have altered.

> **QUESTIONS**
>
> 1 Data can be obtained from a website and put into a spreadsheet.
>
>   (a) Give one advantage of linking the spreadsheet to the web page.
>
>   (b) Give one disadvantage of linking the spreadsheet to the web page.
>
> 2 Give one reason why it is often better to present data in graphs and charts rather than as a table of numbers.

Lesson 5: AUTOMATING PROCESSES IN A SIMPLE INFORMATION PROCESSING SYSTEM

Background

In the following activities you will see how, by using a web query, you can build an information system that can be kept up to date and perform any processing automatically.

Gambling on shares

Many people buy shares as an investment. When you buy shares you are buying a stake in the company, i.e. you become a part owner of the company. Shares in companies are bought for a certain price on a certain day and this price can vary on a daily basis. Shares in the company can rise or fall, so the price you will get for them if you sell may change from day to day. This means that the value of your shares may change from day to day, but hopefully it will rise over a longer period.

People who own shares like to keep track of them to see which are doing well and which are not. This information is important because they may want to sell some of the shares and buy different ones.

34

Lesson 5 Automating processes in a simple information processing system

ACTIVITY 12: A public information system – share prices

Lots of people buy and sell shares. They like to keep track of the prices of the shares that they own. There are several public information systems that show the latest share prices and you can see them in banks, on Teletext or on websites on the Internet.

Use the Internet to access the following website:
www.moneyworld.co.uk/stocks/ftse100/.

This web page shows information about the shares of the 100 most successful UK companies. Look carefully at the information contained on this page.

Make it happen

ACTIVITY 13: Winners and losers

Amy has been left some money by her grandfather who died. Her mother has bought some shares on her behalf, as follows.

Company	Number of shares bought
Marks and Spencer	1000 shares
Tesco	500 shares
Sainsbury	1000 shares
Barclays Bank	500 shares

Amy would like to be able to keep track of these shares and be able to see how much they are worth from day to day.

We are now going to build an information system that will enable her to keep track of the value of her shares on a day-to-day basis.

1. Load the spreadsheet software Microsoft Excel and create a blank workbook.

2. Name the worksheets 'Input', 'Process' and 'Output' on the tabs likes this:

\ Input / Process / Output /

3. Go to the Input worksheet.

Position the cursor on cell A3.

Unit 1 Public information systems

4. Click on **Data** and then click on **Import External Data**, and click on **New Web Query**.

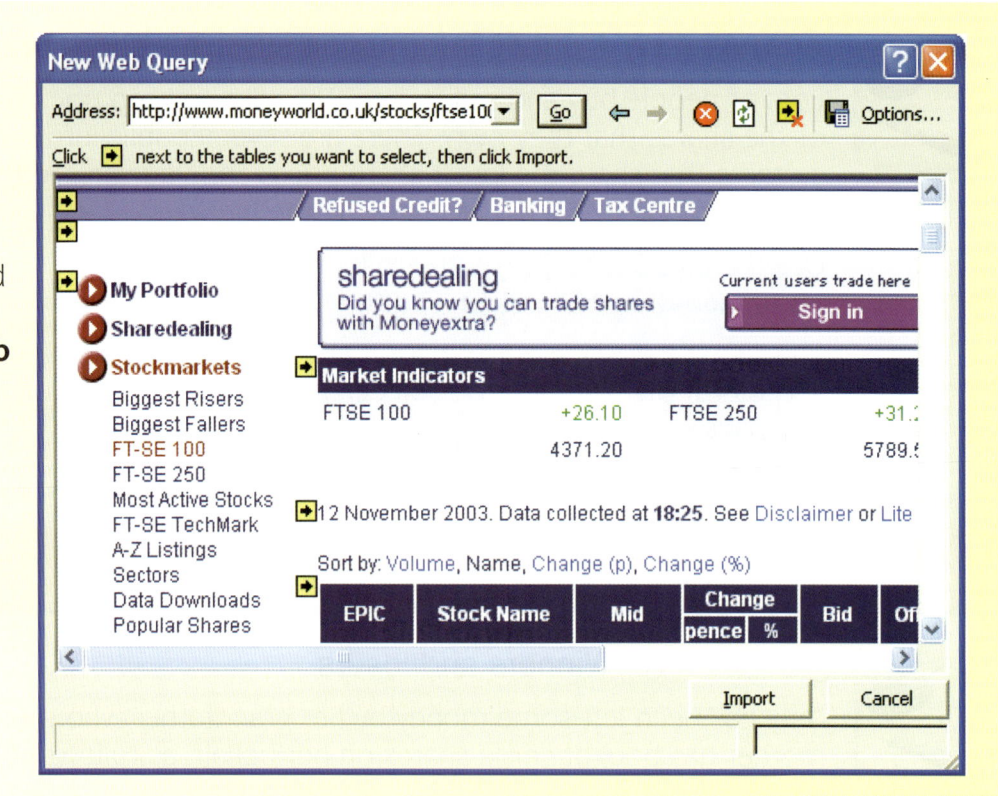

5. Type the web address **www.moneyworld.co.uk/stocks/ftse100/** in the space marked 'Address' on the New Web Query form. Click on **Go**.

Click on the main table of shares and their prices by clicking on the yellow square with a black arrow inside it

You will notice that it now turns into a tick like this:

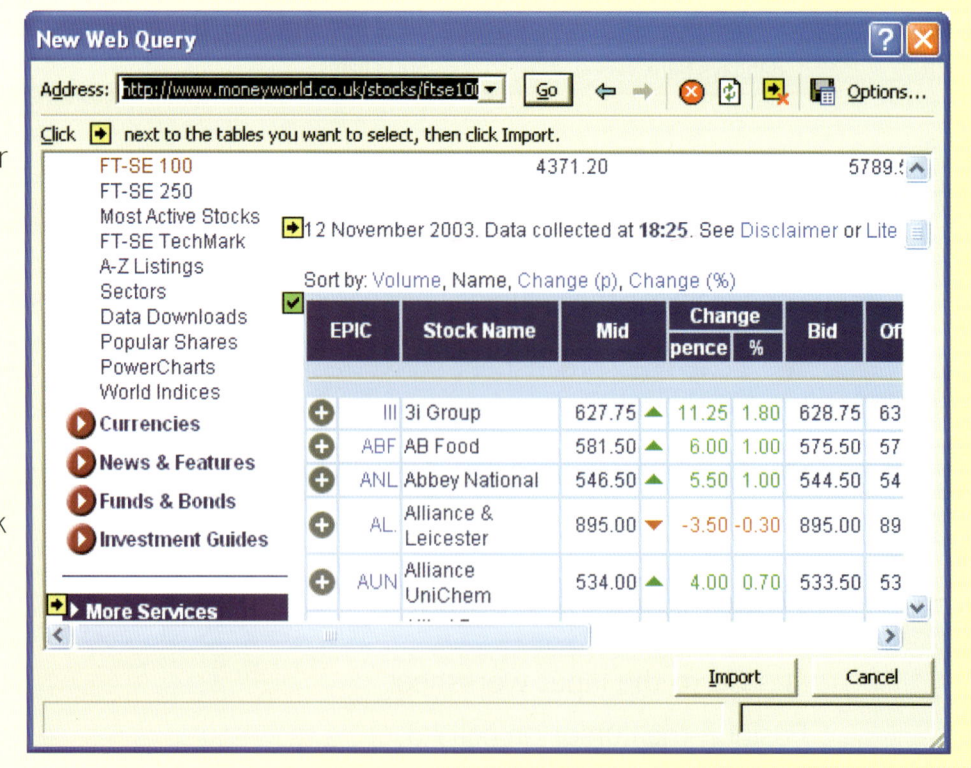

36

Lesson 5 Automating processes in a simple information processing system

You have now selected the data you want to import. To complete the process, click on the **Import** button.

6 The following screen appears and you can alter the cell reference where you want the imported data to be copied to.

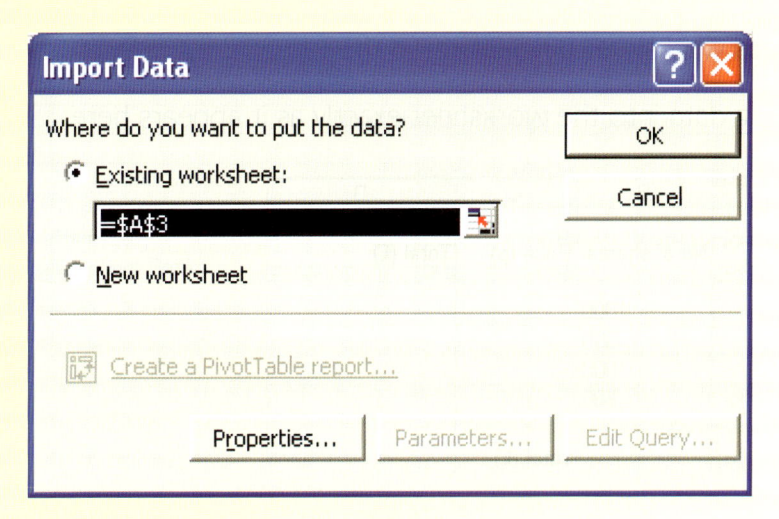

We do not need to alter this so click on the **OK** button.

7 The data now appears in the input workbook like this:

	A	B	C	D	E	F	G	H	I	J	K	L	M	N
1														
2														
3														
4	EPIC		Stock Name	Mid		Change		Bid	Offer	Trading Day				Volume
5						pence	%			Open	High	Low	Close	
6														
7														
8		III	3i Group	627.75	Up	11.25	1.8	628.75	630	619.25	629.75	617.25	627.75	5.19m
9		ABF	AB Food	581.5	Up	6	1	575.5	578	575	588.5	571.5	581.5	2.22m
10		ANL	Abbey National	546.5	Up	5.5	1	544.5	545	540	549.5	535.25	546.5	5.12m
11		AL.	Alliance & Leicester	895	Down	-3.5	-0.3	895	895	900	904.5	891	895	1.99m
12		AUN	Alliance UniChem	534	Up	4	0.7	533.5	536.5	539	539	526	534	0.89m
13		ALLD	Allied Domecq PLC	417.25	Up	5	1.2	415	416.5	412.5	418.5	408.75	417.25	3.07m
14		AHM	Amersham	738.5	Up	1.5	0.2	738.5	739	738.5	741.5	738	738.5	6.21m
15		AVZ	Amvescap	416	Up	3	0.7	416	417.5	409.5	422.5	409.5	416	8.43m
16		AAL	Anglo American PLC	1251	Up	20	1.6	1252	1254	1235	1255	1228	1251	2.64m
17		AZN	AstraZeneca	2727	Down	-9	-0.3	2728	2728	2726	2762	2721	2727	5.58m
18		AV.	Aviva	516	Up	13	2.5	516	516.5	504	522.5	499	516	20.29m
19		BAA	BAA	490.25	Down	-2	-0.4	489	489	489	491.25	482.75	490.25	7.01m
20		BA.	BAE Systems	180.75	Up	1.25	0.6	180	180.5	177.25	182.25	177	180.75	21.96m
21		BARC	Barclays	499	Up	3	0.6	498.5	499	496.25	499	491	499	23.76m
22		BG.	BG Group	278.25	Up	1.5	0.5	278.25	278.25	276.25	280.25	276.25	278.25	8.47m

8 Save this workbook using the file name 'FTSE 100 version 1'.

Do this and your worksheet will look similar to (but not the same as) this:

	A	B	C	D	E	F	G	H
1								
2		No of shares	Price (p)	Total (£)				
3								
4	Marks and Spencer	1000	283.25	2832.50			Marks and Spencer	2832.50
5	Tesco	500	239.00	1195.00			Tesco	1195.00
6	Sainsbury	1000	293.00	2930.00			Sainsbury	2930.00
7	Barclays Bank	500	496.00	2480.00			Barclays Bank	2480.00
8								
9			Total (£)	9437.50				

3 Now draw a pie chart using the data you have just copied to show the proportion of money that each share contributes to the whole amount.

Select the shares and their values in cells G4 to H7 by highlighting them.

Click on the chart wizard icon .

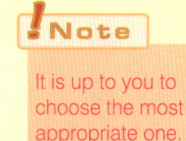

!Note
It is up to you to choose the most appropriate one.

4 Select a suitable pie chart.

5 Work through the steps in the chart wizard. The title of the pie chart should be: 'The proportion of money each holding of shares contributes to the total'. Also, place the pie chart in the output worksheet.

6 Your chart will look something like this:

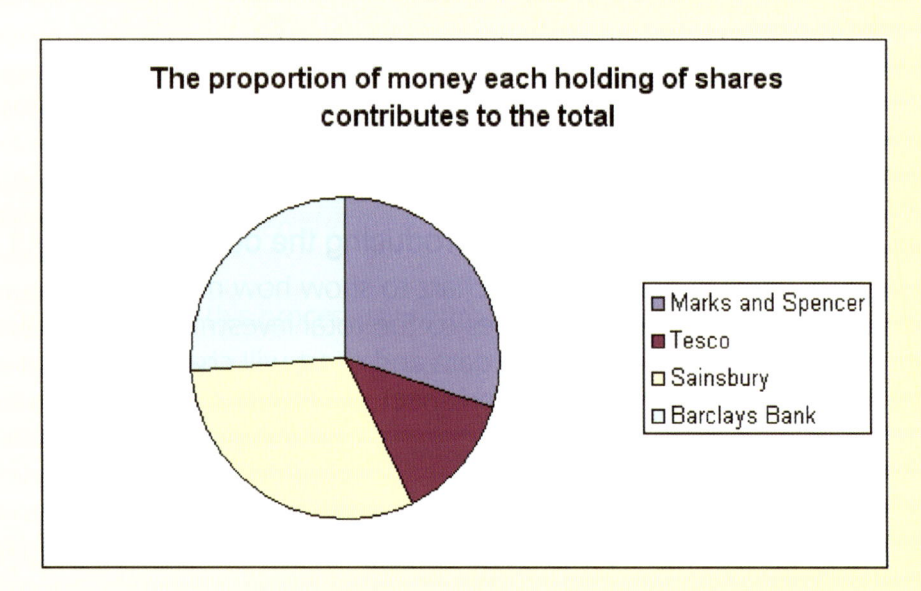

7 Save the workbook using the file name 'FTSE 100 version 2'.

Lesson 5 Automating processes in a simple information processing system

ACTIVITY 16: Updating the data on which the input, process and output worksheets are based

You have seen how data can be obtained from a website and put into a worksheet. This data will not be updated automatically. The user has to give an instruction to update.

REMEMBER!
Do not click on an empty cell.

1. Load Excel and open the workbook FTSE 100 version 2.

2. Make sure that you have the input worksheet on your screen.

3. Click on any of the data in the worksheet.

4. Click on **Data** and the following pull-down menu will be displayed:

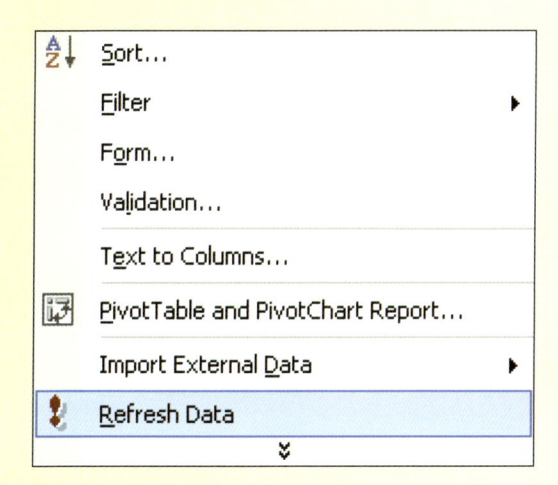

   - Sort...
   - Filter
   - Form...
   - Validation...
   - Text to Columns...
   - PivotTable and PivotChart Report...
   - Import External Data
   - Refresh Data

Click on **Refresh Data**.

The computer will connect to the Internet, locate the web page containing the share prices and then import them into your spreadsheet. If you are using broadband, this only takes a short time. You will notice that the prices on the input screen have changed.

5. Go to the process worksheet. You will see that the share prices have changed here and the total amount of money invested has changed.

Below, and on the next page, is part of the process worksheet on two different days. You can see that the prices and totals have changed.

	A	B	C	D
1				
2		No of shares	Price (p)	Total (£)
3				
4	Marks and Spencer	1000	283.25	2832.50
5	Tesco	500	239.00	1195.00
6	Sainsbury	1000	293.00	2930.00
7	Barclays Bank	500	496.00	2480.00
8				
9			Total (£)	9437.50

41

Unit 1 Public information systems

	A	B	C	D
1				
2		No of shares	Price (p)	Total (£)
3				
4	Marks and Spencer	1000	282.25	2822.50
5	Tesco	500	245.50	1227.50
6	Sainsbury	1000	289.50	2895.00
7	Barclays Bank	500	481.50	2407.50
8				
9			Total (£)	9352.50

6 Go to the output worksheet. Data from the process worksheet was used to create the pie chart so the chart may have changed slightly, although this is quite hard to spot.

7 Save the workbook using the file name FTSE 100 version 3.

Lesson 6: EVALUATING A PUBLIC INFORMATION SYSTEM

Background: What is evaluation?

If you evaluate something you make a judgement about it. You form an idea about the worth of the thing you are evaluating. Was it easy to use? Did it give you the information you required? Would you use it again?

When you draw a picture or paint a painting you will probably evaluate it yourself without thinking too much about it. You probably know whether it is any good or not. When you are making a judgement about the picture or painting you are evaluating it.

There are two types of evaluation:

- An evaluation of work that you have produced yourself.
- An evaluation of work produced by others.

In many ways evaluating work produced yourself is harder because people tend to be more critical of their own work.

Lesson 6 Evaluating a public information system

Criteria for evaluation

In order to produce a good evaluation it is a good idea to write a list of the criteria by which the work would be judged a success. Here is a list of criteria that could be used to evaluate a public information system.

- Was the system easy to use?
- Were all the items of information arranged in a logical order on the screen?
- Did the system give all of the information required by the user?
- Did the system meet the user's needs?
- Was the information given in the most appropriate way, e.g. text, tables, graphics, graphs and charts, etc.?
- Was the information updated regularly?

WORKSHEET

WORKSHEET 8.1.5 Evaluating a weather forecasting public information system

You may be given a worksheet on which to write your answers or you may be asked to write your answers in your book. When you have finished, your teacher will either go through the answers or give you an answer sheet so that you can check the answers yourself.

In Lesson 3 a public information system was developed that produced charts and graphs from weather data.

You have to evaluate this public information system using the following criteria.

Criteria for evaluation	Comments
How easy is the system to use?	
How easy is it to change so that the weather for a different town/city is displayed?	
Will the user know how to change the URL?	
Have appropriate graphs and charts been produced?	
Is it clear what the graphs/charts show?	
Is there any information that should have been included but was not?	
Has the graph been labelled properly?	
Is data organised clearly on the worksheets?	
Do you think the data is accurate?	

43

Unit 1 Public information systems

Criteria for evaluation	Comments
Is the data kept up to date?	
Would it be easy for someone inexperienced in spreadsheets to use the system?	
Could the graphs/charts be better presented?	
Are there headings on each worksheet to explain what they do?	
Is it clear to the user how the system works?	
Have colours been used to good effect?	
What impression does the output give?	

Make it happen

ACTIVITY 17: Evaluating the share price system

In Activities 13 to 16 you developed a public information system and tailored it to meet a user's needs. You will remember that the user wished to see how much her shares were worth each day, and the proportion that each share contributed to the total investment changed from day to day.

You now have to evaluate this system.

1. Write a list of the criteria you could use to evaluate this system.

2. Using those criteria as a guide, evaluate the system. One way to do this would be to assess, on a scale of one to five, whether each criteria was fully met.

3. Identify any improvements that could be made to the system and write a short sentence about each of them.

EXTENSION ACTIVITY

Using the evaluation in Activity 17 to help you, write a list of points to explain how you might modify the system to meet the needs of a user.

Lesson 7 Create your own public information system

Lesson 7: CREATE YOUR OWN PUBLIC INFORMATION SYSTEM

Background

In the following activity you will produce your own public information system. Your teacher will tell you whether you will work on your own or as a group to produce the system.

Make it happen

ACTIVITY 18: Public information system: A place in the sun

Many people want to live abroad in order to get away from the wind, rain and cold weather in the UK. You may have seen the popular TV programme *A Place in the Sun* where people are taken to lots of different places and shown properties in the sun.

You have been asked to develop a public information system in conjunction with this programme. The idea is that you will produce information that people can use to find out about the weather all year round in a number of popular European countries where people from the UK like to buy property.

Here are the steps you must take.

1. Decide on some popular places in Europe where people from the UK like to live. You may need to do some research on the Internet.

2. Think about those aspects of the weather that people who are considering moving abroad would want to know about.

3. Obtain data on the average monthly weather in each of these places. Decide which items of data you will use and how best to present the information.

4. You have to use a spreadsheet to present the data. Using the spreadsheet you can organise the data, do some processing, e.g. working out averages etc., and output the results usually in the form of graphs and charts.

5. Produce an evaluation of the system you have produced.

You need to produce the following as evidence:

- printouts of all the worksheets you have produced
- a word-processed evaluation.

Your teacher will tell you how your work is to be assessed.

2 Publishing on the web

Lesson 1: INTRODUCTION TO PUBLISHING ON THE WEB

In this unit you will learn about web pages and websites and how they are used to satisfy the needs of an audience. You will learn by constructing your own website containing appropriate material. After your website has been constructed you will look at it critically to see what improvements could be made.

Background theory and key information

Everyone seems to have a website nowadays and having a web presence is very important for businesses and organisations. Websites are quite easy to produce, as you will learn later in this unit. There are many different ways you can produce a website and we will look at a few of them here.

Brian the spider is not the only one to need a web presence these days!

What is the difference between a web page and a website?

A web page is an individual document that can be viewed by anyone connected to the Internet. A website is a collection of linked web pages and it consists of one or more web pages.

Web pages are the building blocks of websites. When you are accessing websites using a browser you are looking at a website one page at a time. You can jump from one web page to another by using the special navigational features that link pages together.

Unit 2 Publishing on the web

Types of site

Websites are created for lots of different reasons. The following figures show the main types of website.

E-tailers selling goods and services over the Internet

Source: www.amazon.co.uk

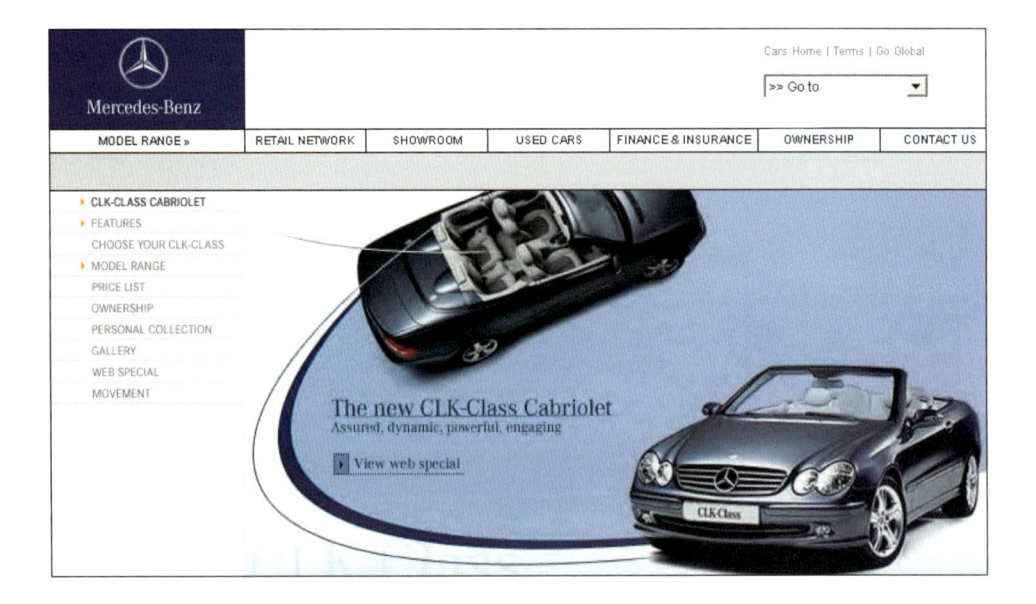

Large business sites promoting their services or products

Source: www.mercedes.co.uk

48

Lesson 1 Introduction to publishing on the web

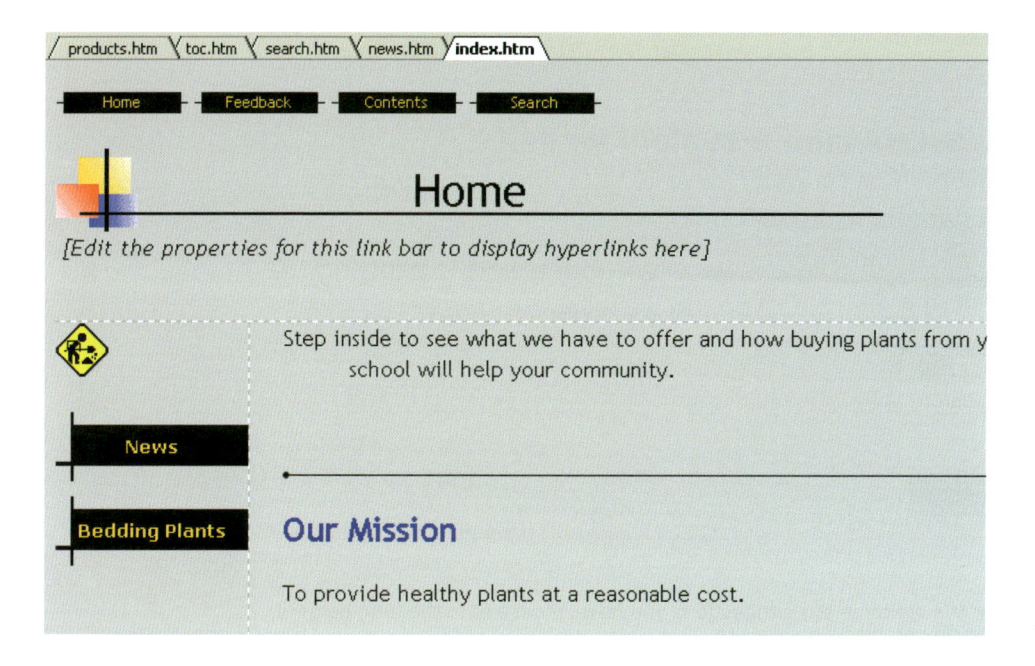

Small organisations' sites

Personal websites

Investigating the format of a website

The format of a website depends on its purpose and the intended audience. For example, a website for an e-tailer (an on-line retailer) needs to contain information about the products or services and it also needs to allow the shopper to select goods (usually by what is called a shopping cart) and to pay for those goods. A website for the BBC has a different purpose, for example you can listen to radio programmes that you missed or want to hear again, or you can find out about all the TV and radio programmes.

Unit 2 Publishing on the web

WORKSHEET WORKSHEET WORKSHEET WORKSHEET WORKSHEET

WORKSHEET 8.2.1 **Deconstructing a typical website**

You may be given a worksheet on which to write your answers or you may be asked to write your answers in your book.

Here are some bits taken from different websites. Your task is to explain what the bits are and why they are included on the websites.

1 Search [   ] Go
Advanced Search

2 Site Map

3 ▶ Links

4 **Send Feedback**

This website is new. We welcome any suggestions you have. Please fill in the form below if you are experiencing any problems on the site.

Please fill in the form if you want to send any comments about the content of the site, how it is presented or how it works. This will be sent to the Website Manager.

Only fill in your name and email address if you want a reply.
For details of how we process this information please see our Privacy Statement.

Name:
[   ]

Email address:
[   ]

Message:
[   ]

Submit

5 ▶ **Weather** for London
sunny intervals
min 10°C max 13°C
View the **5 day forecast**

6 Thursday 5th February 2004

7 Your Shopping Basket
You have 0 items in your Shopping Basket.

8 Last update: 02/02/04

9 035711

50

Lesson 1 Introduction to publishing on the web

⑩ Comments

ACTIVITIESACTIVITIESACTIVITIESACTIVITIESACTIVITIESACTIVITIES

ACTIVITY 1: Comparing a website with a book

In this activity you will compare using a website with using a book to find certain information.

① First look up the following words in a paper dictionary:
- Access
- Audience
- Evaluate.

Think about how you performed this task.

② Now look up the same words using an on-line dictionary at: **www.dictionary.cambridge.org/**.

Think about how you performed this task.

③ Write a few sentences to explain the difference in the two tasks. Which way was easier, and which did you prefer and why?

Ways of accessing information on the Internet

There are two main ways of accessing the Internet: by using a dial-up modem or by using a broadband connection.

Dial-up or broadband

You have probably heard a lot about broadband. Broadband is basically a very fast way of connecting to the Internet. It is always on, so there is no need to wait to connect. You need a special piece of equipment called a network card and some special software

Unit 2 Publishing on the web

installed in your computer. Broadband comes to you via your existing phone line or by using a cable through which you can also get cable TV.

Dial-up uses a modem. Modems come with all new computers and they simply connect to your ordinary phone line using a cable. When you log on to the Internet the modem dials the number of your Internet Service Provider (ISP for short) and this takes time. Surfing the Internet is quite slow especially at peak times.

Broadband is a lot faster and greater numbers of people are using it. You can do a lot more with broadband. For example, you can do the following, which would be very slow using a dial-up modem:

When Amy ordered Broadband she got more than she expected!

- Watch a video.
- Listen to the radio.
- Use web cams.
- Download games, music, software, videos, etc. quickly.
- Play on-line games.

How one website can serve more than one audience

Some websites have a special section for younger surfers. When they click on a picture they are sent to a part of the website that contains material aimed specifically at them.

FIND IT OUT

Access the Internet and then type in the following URL: www.bbc.co.uk.

Most of the material you see here is aimed at adults. However, if you click on the following picture you will be taken to an area especially for children.

Big Cook Little Cook — CBeebies

www.bbc.co.uk

Take a look at what a child (or adult!) can do on such a site.

Lesson 1 Introduction to publishing on the web

What can you do on a website?

What you can do on a website really depends on the type of website you are looking at. All websites serve a purpose and have a typical audience. What you can do with the website really depends on both of these.

If you look at the official site of a singer or group, then you might expect to see some videos, hear some music, download pictures and so on. If you want to use a website that shows train or plane timetables, getting fast and accurate information would be the main criteria and you would not be too worried about the appearance of the site.

Here is a list of some of the things you can do on websites:

- Search the site for information.
- Read advertisements.
- Follow links to other websites.
- Download files.
- Play music.
- Watch an animation.
- Watch a video.
- Play a game.

ACTIVITY 2: Investigating websites

For this activity you are required to investigate certain websites. For each website you have to answer the questions that follow.

- The NASA website: **www.nasa.gov/home/index.html**.
- The McLaren racing car website: **www.mclaren.co.uk/**.
- An unofficial website on the footballer David Beckham: **www.paulsworld.co.uk/beckham/**.
- The *Pop Idol* website: **www.itv.com/popidol/**.
- CD-WOW – a company that sells CDs on the Internet: **www.cd-wow.com**.

1. Who is the intended audience for this website?
2. How do you know?
3. What are the main features of this website?

Unit 2 Publishing on the web

It is hard to talk about a typical website as they all have different aims. For example, a website to sell CDs would be totally different from a website to promote a particular school and give information to parents.

One way to evaluate a website is to use a checklist. The checklist can be used to make sure that the website does not make some of the common mistakes.

Make it happen

ACTIVITY 4: Making an evaluation checklist

You have been asked to evaluate a website. Produce a checklist consisting of 20 things you should look for in a website.

There are two ways to evaluate your website:

- You could do it yourself.
- You could get someone else to do it for you.

It is often best to use both of these methods.

Some things to watch out for

When you look at websites, you get a feel for what works and what does not. Here are some things to watch out for when making your own websites.

GO EASY ON THE HIGH SPEED GRAPHICS!

Too many moving images

Moving images can be overpowering and distracting. It is best to give the person looking at your site some peace and quiet so they can read the text.

Long scrolling pages

Some pages go way past the screen length. Most users will not look beyond what they see on the screen, so they may not get to important information at the end. It is important to put any important information at the top of the screen.

Lesson 2 What to consider when creating a website

Information that is out of date

Many people create websites but do not keep them up to date. Keeping the existing content up to date is as important as adding new information to a website.

Long download times

If you put lots of animations or video into your websites it will take time to download the information. Users will get fed up after about 10 seconds and will generally click on something else.

Links that no longer work

When you click on a link it takes you to a different part of the web page or even a different website. If your links no longer work it is annoying for the user.

> **REMEMBER!**
> Not everyone has broadband.

Tips for building your own website

When you build your own website you should:

1. Keep it simple – do not fill it with clutter.
2. Do not put in music or sound files – people often work in rooms with others so it is distracting to hear music or sound blaring out.
3. Do not put slow-loading graphics on the page – people will get bored waiting for them to load.
4. Make it pleasing on the eye – no crazy fonts or colours.
5. Make sure that the important information is at the top of the screen – people need to be sure what your site is about.
6. Avoid the use of pop-ups – these annoy users because they have to click on them to get rid of them.

> **KEY WORDS**
> **navigate** – find your way around a website by making use of site maps and links
>
> **hits** – the number of times a particular page is visited. (It can also mean the number of matches from a search condition that you set)

Make it happen

ACTIVITY 5: Investigating the features of websites

Websites often contain a number of elements. When you design and create your own websites you too can include different elements.

59

Unit 2 Publishing on the web

In this activity you will look at the home page (i.e. the first page you come to) of an unofficial website about the footballer David Beckham.

The website address for this site is: **www.paulsworld.co.uk**

Look carefully at the home page of this site. Write down the names of as many elements on the home page as you can spot. For each of these elements, briefly describe why they have been included.

ACTIVITY 6: Investigating home pages

A home page is usually the first page a visitor will see when they access a website from the Internet. It is extremely important to have a good home page as it will prevent visitors from moving on to another more interesting or more professional-looking site.

REMEMBER!
You are only commenting on the first page even though you might want to investigate the site further.

In this activity you will list the features you liked on each of the following home pages.

- The Red Arrows: **www.raf.mod.uk/reds/**
- The official Harry Potter films website: **www.harrypotter.warnerbros.co.uk/home.html**
- Chester City Council – Visiting Chester: **www.chestercc.gov.uk/visitingindex.html**
- A personal home page from Cara: **www.hometown.aol.co.uk/carabubble/home.html**

KEY WORDS

home page – the page you normally start at when accessing a website

Planning the home page of a website

The home page of the website is the first page a person will see when they access your website. It is important to make an immediate impression with this page so that they want to stay and investigate the site further.

How to design your own web pages

As with all documents, you should make your pages appeal to the intended audience. Since there are no real rules regarding the design of web pages you can use your artistic talents.

Some points you might want to keep in mind are:

- Make sure that any text contrasts with the background. Dark text on a light background is best.

Lesson 2 What to consider when creating a website

- Use subheadings to break up large amounts of text.
- It is better if the text in a web page does not stretch right across the screen.
- Make sure that the design is consistent from one page to another.
- Do not use too many graphics on one page.

REMEMBER!

Big graphics take time to load and can therefore be annoying to users of your page, especially those who do not have broadband.

I THINK YOUR WEBSITE HAS OVERDONE THE WHITE SPACE!

The use of white space

Try not to cram too much information onto a page. The appearance of a web page is improved if it looks uncluttered. If you think of a web page as a paper document, then it is important to leave plenty of white space.

Make it happen

ACTIVITY 7: Designing a home page

You are going to produce the home page of your personal website.

A home page is the first page that someone who accesses your website will see.

Consider the following questions:

- What information would you put on your home page?
- How might you find out what should be included on a home page?
- What would your friends expect to see on your home page?

1. On paper plan a design for your home page. For your draft design simply arrange named boxes on the page.

2. Play around with the designs until you decide on a final arrangement. Copy out neatly your final home page design.

Unit 2 Publishing on the web

Putting images into websites

Images brighten up any web page. The images can be photographs, pictures, clip art, etc.

Images can take time to load so it is important to use compressed images. Compressing an image makes the file size smaller, which makes it quicker to upload or download.

Images put into web pages are normally either:

- GIF (Graphics Interchange Format) – this is a file format for compressed images.
- JPEG or JPG – these are other file formats for compressed images.

Web browsers (i.e. the programs you use to view web pages) are able to view both of the above types of images.

Remember, not everyone has Broadband.

KEY WORDS

Graphics Interchange Format (GIF) – a file format for saving pictures that can be sent and displayed easily on the Internet

Joint Photographic Experts Group (JPEG) – a file format mainly used for saving photographs

web browser – a program used to search and display web pages on the Internet

Lesson 3: CREATING WEB PAGES USING HTML

KEY WORDS

Hypertext Markup Language (HTML) – a series of instructions used to format and display text and images on the World Wide Web. You use it to specify the structure and layout of a web document.

tags – special markers used in HTML to tell the computer what to do with the text. A tag is needed at the start and end of each block of text to which the tag applies

Background

HTML is short for Hypertext Markup Language and it is the special code that is used for making web pages. HTML consists of special markers called tags that tell the computer what to do with the text that is entered. It could tell the computer to present the text in a certain way. For example, the tags could tell the computer that the text being entered is intended to be a heading, or to make a certain block of text bold.

Lesson 3 Creating web pages using HTML

HTML is a text file, just like Word except that it contains the special markers called tags. Tags basically tell the computer how to display the text or format the page.

> **!Note**
> HTML is not a programming language as such. It just tells the computer how to display text and pictures in web pages.

Make it happen

ACTIVITY 8: Looking at HTML

In this activity you will discover how you can view the source code (i.e. the set of instructions used to produce the website).

① Log onto the Internet and type in the following website address: **www.oxfordsecondary.co.uk**

This is the website for the publishers of this book.

② Rather than look at the content of this site, we are going to look at the HTML code used to produce the website.

To do this, position the cursor anywhere on the web page.

Right click the mouse button.

The following window appears:

```
Back
Forward

Save Background As...
Set as Background
Copy Background
Set as Desktop Item...

Select All
Paste

Create Shortcut
Add to Favorites...
View Source

Encoding           ▶

Print
Refresh

Export to Microsoft Excel

Properties
```

③ Select **View Source** by clicking on it, using the left mouse button.

63

The following window appears showing the HTML code.

```
www.nelsonthornes[1] - Notepad

<!DOCTYPE HTML PUBLIC "-//W3C//DTD HTML 4.01 Transitional//EN">
<html>
<head>
<TITLE>Nelson Thornes Education – Online lesson plans, Revision guides, Books for education<
<meta http-equiv="Content-Type" content="text/html; charset=iso-8859-1">
<META NAME="DESCRIPTION" CONTENT="Nelson Thornes is a leading publisher of educational resou
<META NAME="KEYWORDS" CONTENT="nelson thornes, educational publishers, educational resources
<META NAME="VERSION" CONTENT="March 2002">
<LINK REL="StyleSheet" HREF="common/styles/generic.css" TYPE="text/css">

<script language="JavaScript" TYPE="text/javascript">
<!--
<!-- hide

//function popup(){
        //window = window.open('temp_message2.htm', 'temp_message', 'width=400, height=430')

if (document.images){
edge_f1 = new Image
edge_f2 = new Image
edge_f1.src = "common/images/resource_edge.gif"
edge_f2.src = "common/images/resource_edge_f2.gif"
edge2_f1 = new Image
edge2_f2 = new Image
edge2_f1.src = "common/images/resource_edge2.gif"
edge2_f2.src = "common/images/resource_edge2_f2.gif"
}

function MM_swapImgRestore() { //v3.0
   var i,x,a=document.MM_sr; for(i=0;a&&i<a.length&&(x=a[i])&&x.oSrc;i++) x.src=x.oSrc;
}

function change(directory){
```

As you can see, it is very difficult to make sense of HTML, but luckily there are some easy ways to create web pages and websites.

How to create a website using HTML

There are two steps to create a website using HTML:

1. Use a program called an Editor or a word-processing package to produce your text with HTML code.
2. Put the pages on a web-server, which is a computer with a permanent connection to the Internet.

Simple HTML code

Here is a simple section of HTML:

<HTML>
<title> An example of HTML code </title>

```
<h1> This is a sample document </h1>
<p> This is a sample paragraph </p>
<p> This is another paragraph </p>
</HTML>
```

The tags are the words enclosed between the < and > signs. They are HTML instructions and they tell the computer how to display or format the text.

Look at the sample of code. We are now going to look at what each tag does.

<HTML> and </HTML> tells the computer that we are creating an HTML document.

The <HTML> tag tells the computer that the document is starting and </HTML> tells the computer that the document has ended.

The tags <title> and </title> tell the computer that you want the text between the tags to be shown as a title. The reason for the difference in the two tags is that the first one tells the computer where to start the title and the second one tells it where the title ends.

<h1> and </h1> says that you want the text to be a heading of type h1. There are other headings, h2, h3, etc. to choose from. Headings coded h1 are larger in size compared with h2 headings and so on.

The tags <p> and </p> mean start and end a new paragraph. A break of approximately two lines deep is inserted between the paragraphs.

Make it happen

ACTIVITY 9: Creating a web page using HTML

In this activity you will create a very simple web page using HTML.

1. From your operating system screen, click on the **Start** button **start** then click on **All Programs** and then **Accessories** and then on **Notepad**.

2. Notepad is an editor and you can use it to put the HTML together.

Unit 2 Publishing on the web

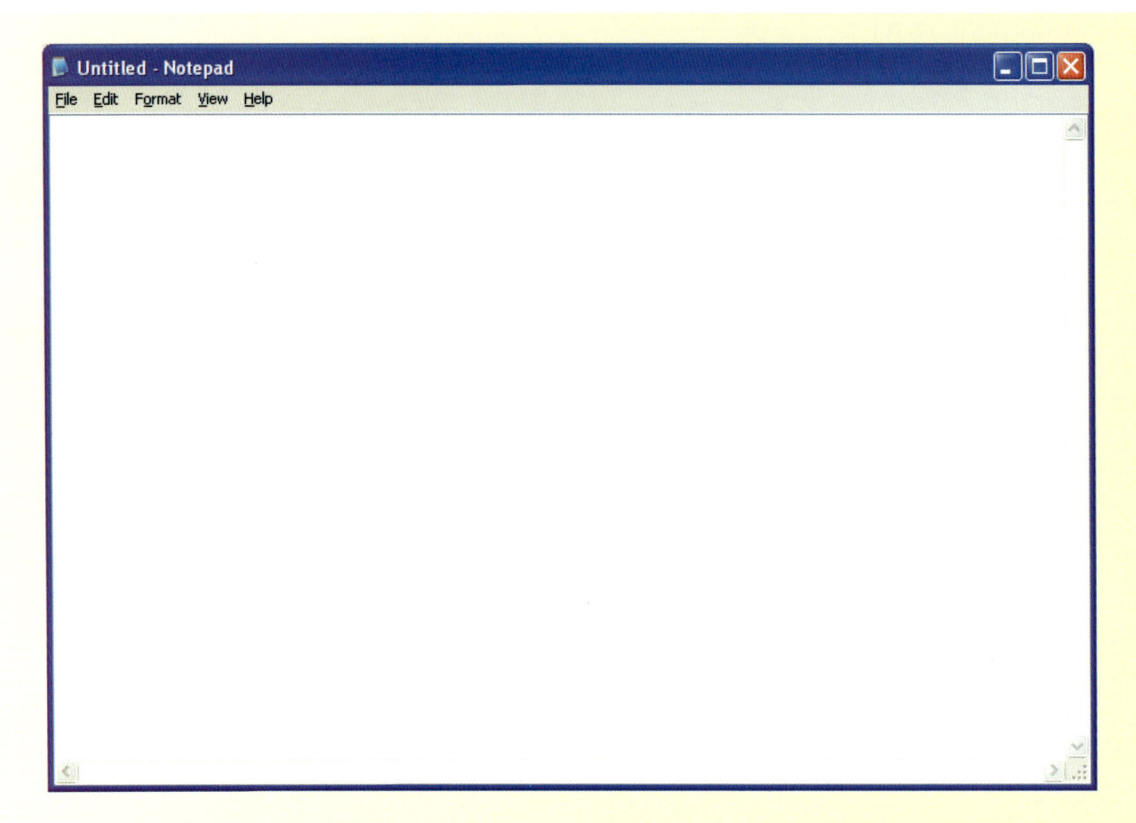

You can type the instructions straight onto this window.

3 Type in the following lines of HTML to create a simple web page:

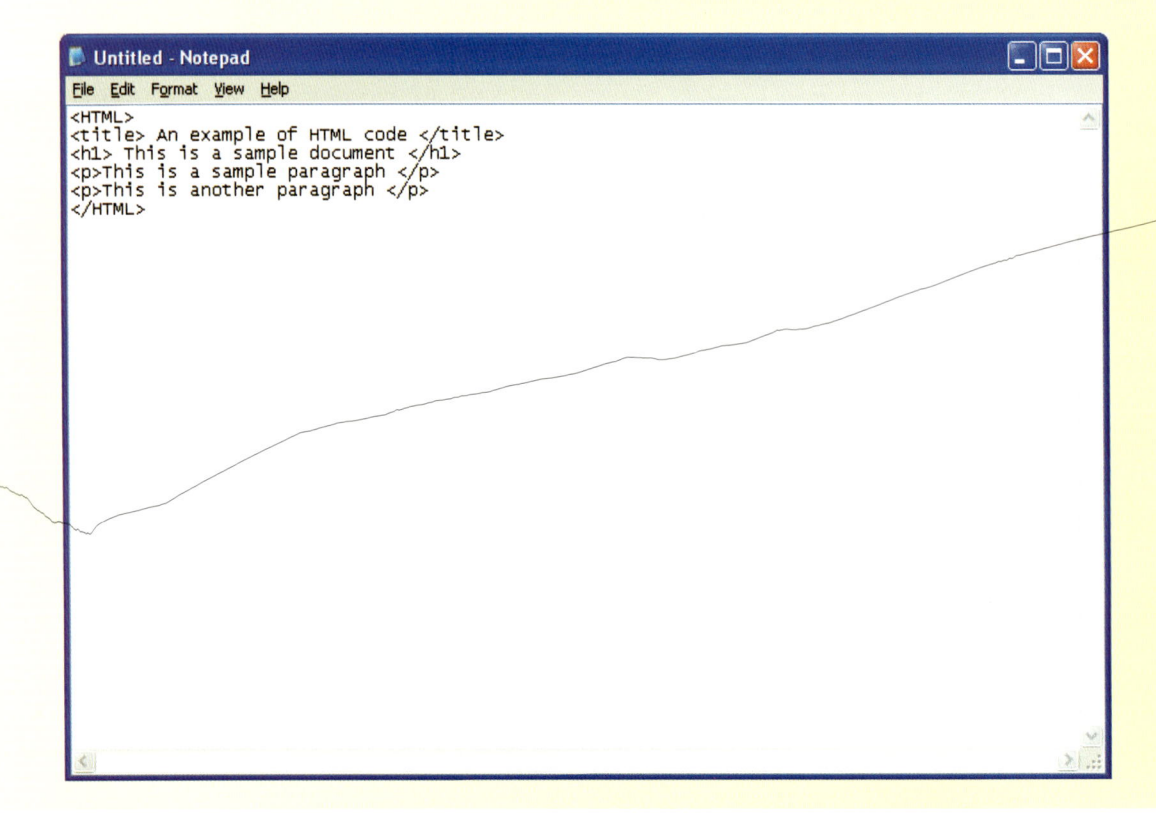

```
<HTML>
<title> An example of HTML code </title>
<h1> This is a sample document </h1>
<p>This is a sample paragraph </p>
<p>This is another paragraph </p>
</HTML>
```

Lesson 3 Creating web pages using HTML

4 Save this file as an HTM file. To do this click on **File** and then **Save As**.

The following window appears:

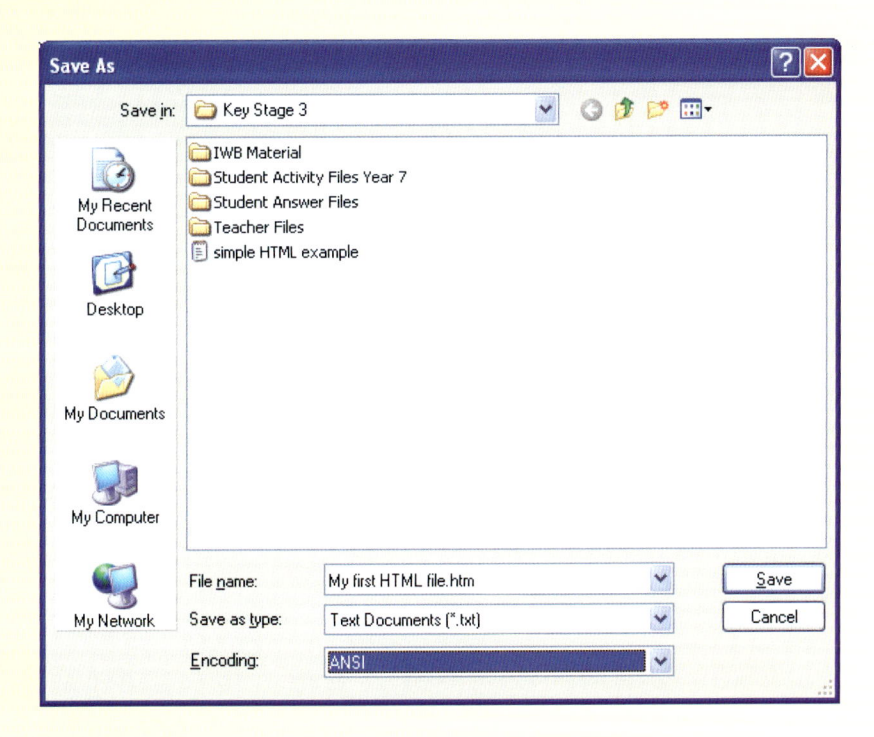

Your teacher will tell you where to save this file.

Enter 'My first HTML file.htm' for the file name and then click on the **Save** button.

Your first HTML file has now been saved.

5 To see what this web page looks like it is necessary to use a web browser program to open it in.

Load the web browser software you usually use.

6 Click on **File** and then **Open**.

A window similar to this will appear.

You now need to locate the file called My first HTML file.htm and then click on the **Open** button.

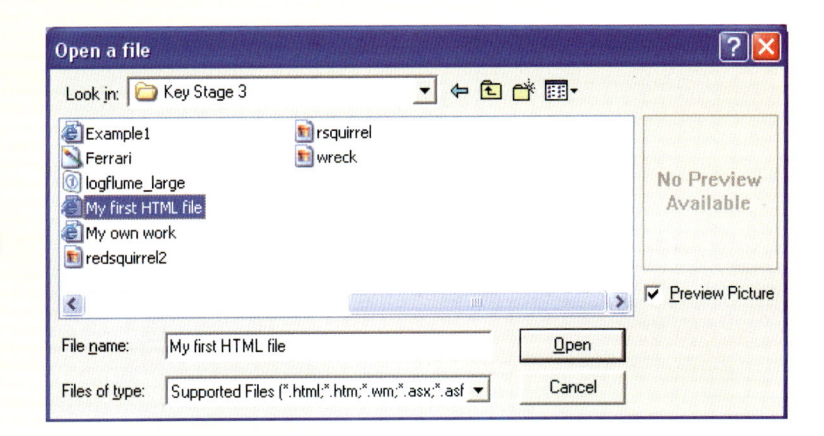

67

7 The web page will now open and you can see the results.

An example of HTML code

This is a sample document

This is a sample paragraph

This is another paragraph

Well done! You have created your first web page using HTML.

8 You can now close this file.

Some more tags and their meanings

<b> and </b> means start bold and stop bold.

<u> and </u> means start underline and stop underline.

<i> and </i> means start italics and stop italics.

Putting messages in the HTML code

If you look at a large section of HTML code, it is quite difficult to make sense of it. It is best if the code is divided up into sections with each section creating a different feature of the web page.

You can include comments in the code without them actually appearing on the web page. This is done by putting them into a special tag that starts with <!-- and ends with -->. For example:

<!-- This comment only appears in the HTML and not in my web page -->

<head> This comment only appears in the HTML and not on the web page </head>

Typing in the text

<body> and </body> are the tags used to say where the main body of the text starts and ends.

Lesson 3 Creating web pages using HTML

If you are typing in text using a word processor and you want to start a new line you just press the **Enter** key.

In HTML you have to give an instruction to tell the computer to start a new line.

 is used to produce a line break and this particular tag is only needed once. This means that there is no closing tag.

WORKSHEET

WORKSHEET 8.2.3 What does it do?

Before you start this worksheet you should re-read and check that you understand the material on the use of HTML tags.

Your teacher will either give you a worksheet on which to write your answers or will ask you to write your answers in your book.

For each of the following, you need to describe what the tags do.

1. <b> Hello my name is Amy </b>
2. <title> My Home page </title>
3. <HTML>
4. <h1> My Interests and Hobbies </h1>
5.
6. <i> My favourite music is rap </i>
7. <h4> My Favourite Groups </h4>
8. <u> Here is a list of some great websites </u>
9. <head> This section of HTML creates a table </head>
10. <p> Hello. My name is John and I am the developer of this site. If you have any problems with this site, then I am the person to contact for help. </p>

The steps to take when you make a web page using HTML

When you create a simple web page using HTML you normally carry out the following tasks in this order:

1. Instruct the package that you are creating a web page.
2. Add the title.
3. Add the text with the tags (i.e. the HTML code).
4. Add images (if required).
5. Add links.

Unit 2 Publishing on the web

KEY WORDS

hyperlink – a link from a place in one document to a different place in the same document or a completely different document. If you click on a hyperlink it takes you to a different place

Note

'Click here' is the instruction to the user.

Adding hyperlinks

When you click on certain words or pictures on a website you are taken to a different part of the same website or possibly a totally different website. These are called links or hyperlinks.

Hyperlinks make it easy for you to 'surf' the Internet.

Suppose we want to link in a website. Again tags are used.

<a href> and </a> are used for the start and end of a hyperlink.

Suppose we want to insert a hyperlink to the Nelson Thornes website (i.e. the publishers of this book). We could use the following:

<a href = **www.oxfordsecondary.co.uk**> Click here </a>

Inserting images

Images are not inserted directly into an HTML document. Instead an instruction is used to tell the browser where the image file is located. It is usually best to put the HTML file and the image file in the same folder.

Here is the line of HTML used to insert an image called Britney.jpg in a web page:

<img src="Britney.jpg">

QUESTIONS

1 What does the abbreviation HTML stand for?

2 HTML uses things called tags. What is the purpose of these tags?

3 (a) Files can be compressed. What is meant by the word 'compressed'?

(b) Image files used on websites are usually compressed. Give the main reason for this.

4 Websites make use of hyperlinks. What are hyperlinks and how do they make using the Internet easy?

5 When you use the Internet you can upload or download files. What is the difference between uploading and downloading? If you are stuck, use an on-line computer dictionary to find the meanings of these two terms.

6 A web page needs to contain a link to the following website: **www.bbc.co.uk**.

Write down the HTML to produce this link.

Lesson 3 Creating web pages using HTML

Make it happen

ACTIVITY 10: Looking at a school website

In this activity you will look at a website created by a junior school and you will see how it has been constructed.

1. Use your browser to type in the following URL:
   www.schools.hants.org.uk/gomerjunior/

2. Position your cursor on the web page and then right click.

3. A pull-down menu appears. Click on **View Source**.

A window, called the notepad, appears showing all the HTML tags and the text to which they apply.

Your screen will show the HTML code. This diagram shows some of the code from this website although yours may look different:

```
Welcome[1] - Notepad
File  Edit  Format  View  Help
<HTML>
<HEAD>
<TITLE>Gomerweb.   Welcome Page</TITLE>
</HEAD>
<BODY   BGCOLOR= "#8BB0E7">
<TABLE WIDTH=100% border="0">
<TR ALIGN= CENTER>
<TD BGCOLOR= "#8BB0E7"><IMG SRC="desk.jpg"></TD>
<TD BGCOLOR= "#8BB0E7"><IMG SRC= "welcome.jpg"></TD>
<TD BGCOLOR= "#8BB0E7"><IMG SRC= "desk.jpg"></TD>
</TR>
<TR><TD COLSPAN=3></TD></TR>
<TR ALIGN= LEFT>
    <TD BGCOLOR= "#8BB0E7" height="100"></TD>
    <TD BGCOLOR= "#001F66" height="100"> <FONT COLOR= "#8BB0E7">
      <H4 align="center"><font size="4">Welcome to the Gomer Junior School website!
       </font></H4>
     </font></TD>
    <TD BGCOLOR= "#8BB0E7" height="100"></TD>
  </TR>
<TR ALIGN= LEFT>
    <TD BGCOLOR= "#8BB0E7" height="131"></TD>
    <TD BGCOLOR= "#001F66" height="131"> <FONT COLOR= "#8BB0E7">
      <H4 align="center">Our aim is to be a school which has a friendly, caring
         and welcoming atmosphere. We hope to provide a wide range of balanced
         learning opportunities for all children and thus help them grow into independent
         and responsible people.</H4>
      <H4 align="center">If you wish to know more about the school, then a prospectus
         is available from the school office. </H4>
     </font></TD>    <TD BGCOLOR= "#8BB0E7" height="131"></TD>
</TR>
<TR ALIGN= CENTER>
<TD><IMG SRC= "letterblocks.jpg"></TD>
<TD BGCOLOR= "#8BB0E7"><IMG SRC= "AddressBar.jpg"></TD>
```

4. Look at the screen shown here. From your knowledge of HTML you should be able to spot certain tags and recognise what they do.

Write down three lines of code and explain what each line does.

71

Unit 2 Publishing on the web

5 A good way to learn about HTML is to look at the code and then the web page to which it refers. You can then try to spot which part of code does what. Look at the window on the previous page. Which of the lines of HTML shown in this diagram produces the following?

(a)

Welcome

(b)

Our aim is to be a school which has a friendly, caring and welcoming atmosphere. We hope to provide a wide range of balanced learning opportunities for all children and thus help them grow into independent and responsible people.

If you wish to know more about the school, then a prospectus is available from the school office.

6 With some bits of HTML you will have a fairly good idea what they do just by the names of the tags. See if you can make an educated guess as to what the following lines will do.

(a) <TITLE> GomerWeb. Welcome Page </TITLE>

(b) <H4 align="center"><font size="4"> Welcome to the Gomer Junior School website! </font></H4>

(c) <IMG SRC= "Welcome.jpg">

FIND IT OUT

If you want to learn more about HTML there are plenty of good on-line tutorials you can look at. Here are some sites you can look at:

- www.w3schools.com/html/default.asp
- www.cwru.edu/help/introHTML/toc.html

For your reference, a quick guide to all the tags that are used with HTML can be found at: www.cwru.edu/help/introHTML/toc.html

Lesson 4: CREATING WEB PAGES USING MICROSOFT WORD

Background

You can create simple web pages and websites using the word-processing package Microsoft Word. For more complex web pages and websites it is better to use a specialist package such as FrontPage.

Creating web pages

Word is fine for producing simple web pages. Provided you just want to use text, graphics and hyperlinks (these provide a method to move from one item to another), then Word is suitable.

To make things easy for you Word XP has a few templates you can use and also a Wizard to guide you through the steps involved in creating a web page.

Simple websites can be created using the word processing package Microsoft Word

Make it happen

ACTIVITY 11: Designing a web page

Step 1

Design your web page on paper first. Decide on the graphics you intend using (e.g. clip art, scanned-in photographs, photographs from a digital camera, etc.). Decide how you want the very first page, called the default page, to look. Also, decide what other pages you want to link to the default page.

Decide how the text is to look.

Step 2

1. Load the word-processing package Word.

REMEMBER!
You are free to use all the text enhancements that you have.

73

Unit 2 Publishing on the web

2 Click on **File** and then **New**. The following screen will appear (right):

Now click on **General Templates** in the **New from template** section.

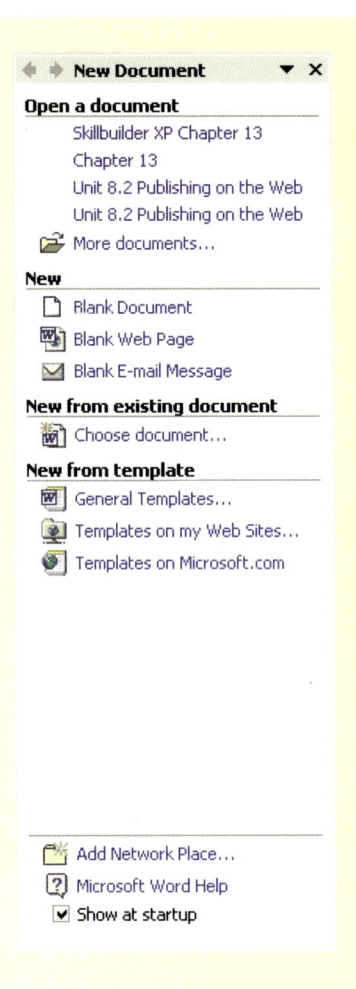

3 Click on the **Web Pages** tab. The following screen appears:

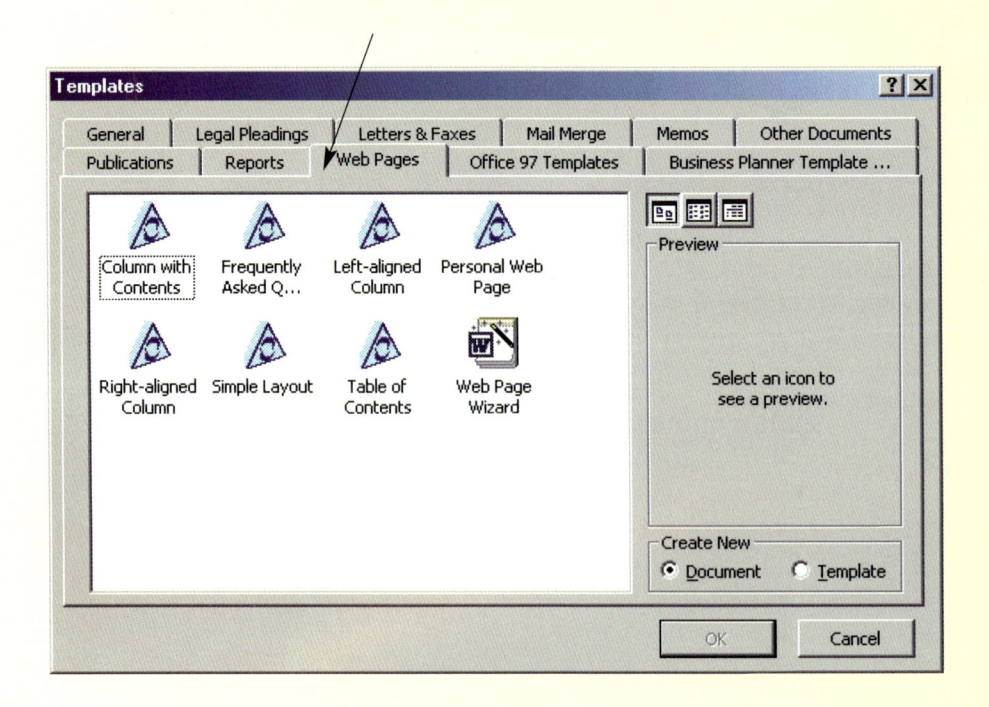

74

Lesson 4 Creating web pages using Microsoft Word

4 Double click on the **Web Page Wizard** icon on the above screen. The following screen will appear:

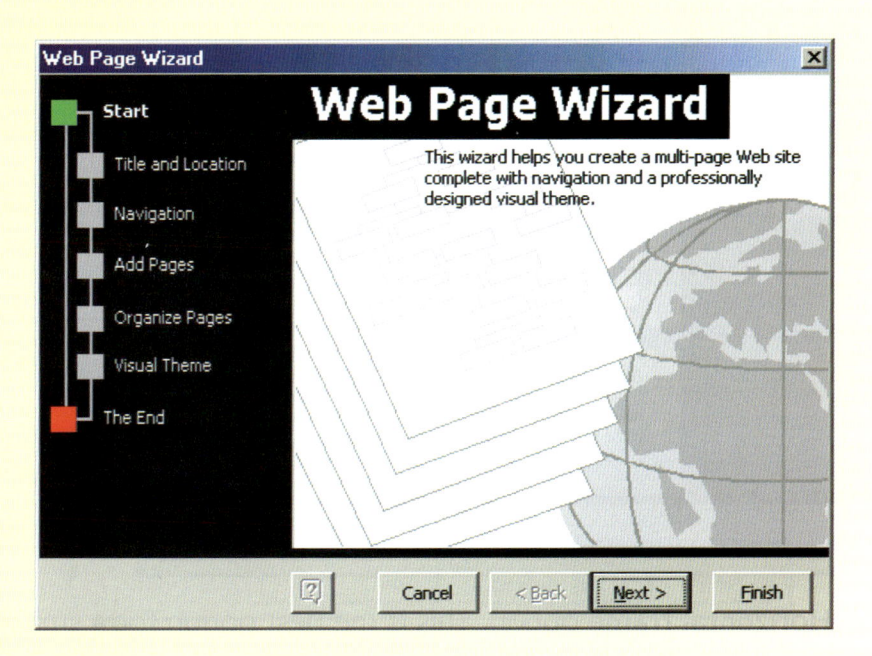

5 Look at the left-hand side of the screen. It shows stages in creating the web pages. Click on the **Next >** button to go to the next step.

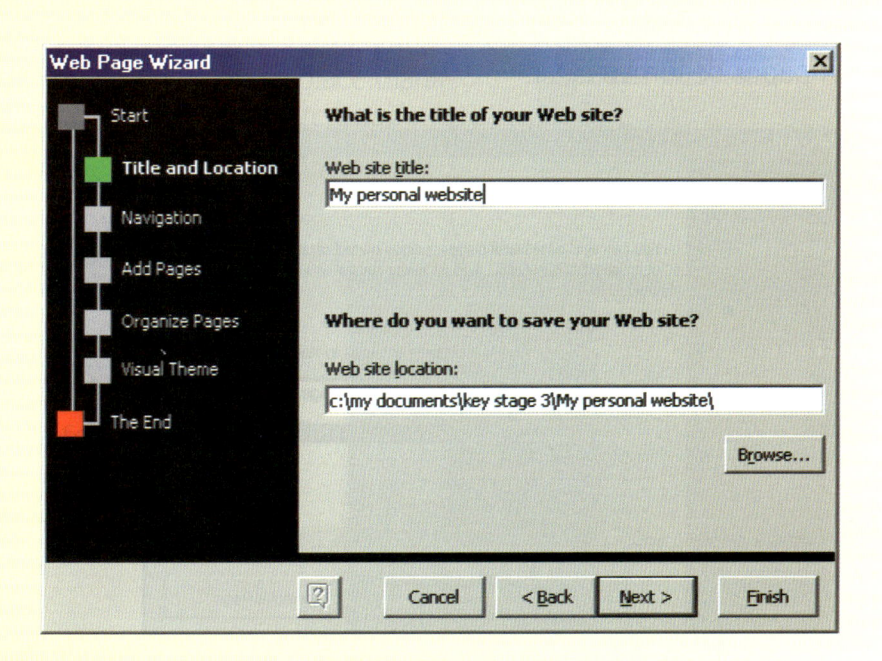

Type in the website title ('My personal website' in this case).

Notice the box below. Here you can specify where you want your website saved. Your teacher will tell you where to save your work.

Click on the **Next >** button to move to the next step.

75

Unit 2 Publishing on the web

Click **Next >** to go to the next step.

5 Here you can tick boxes to indicate that you want certain types of pages on your website.

You will use all of these pages so just click on **Next >**.

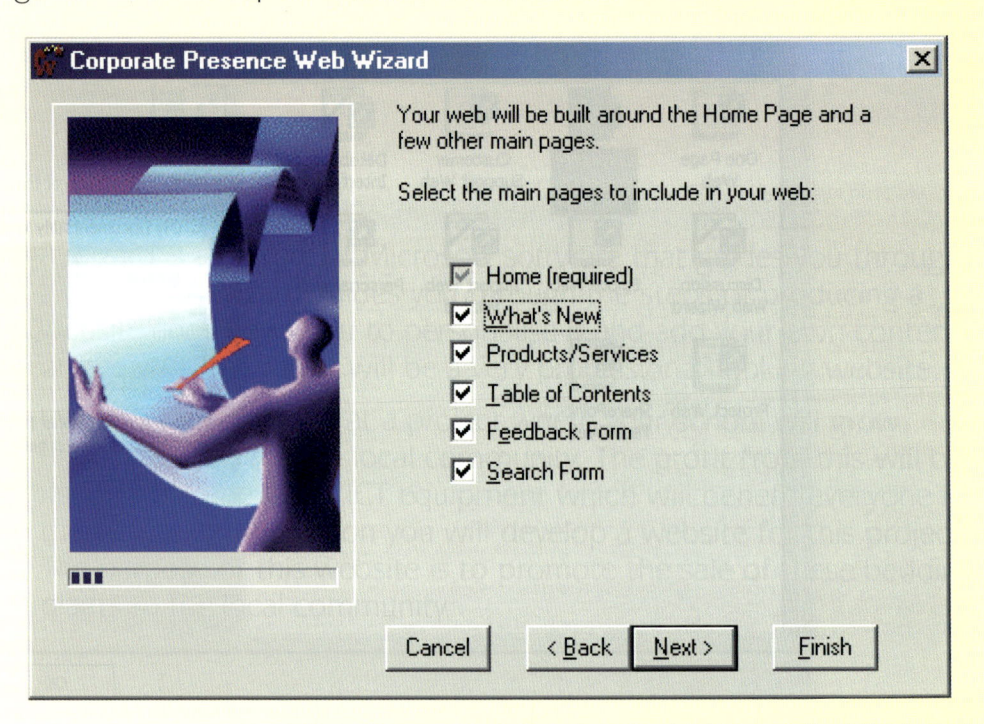

6 This page allows you to specify the topics you want to include on the home page. The home page is the most important page because it is the first page the audience will see.

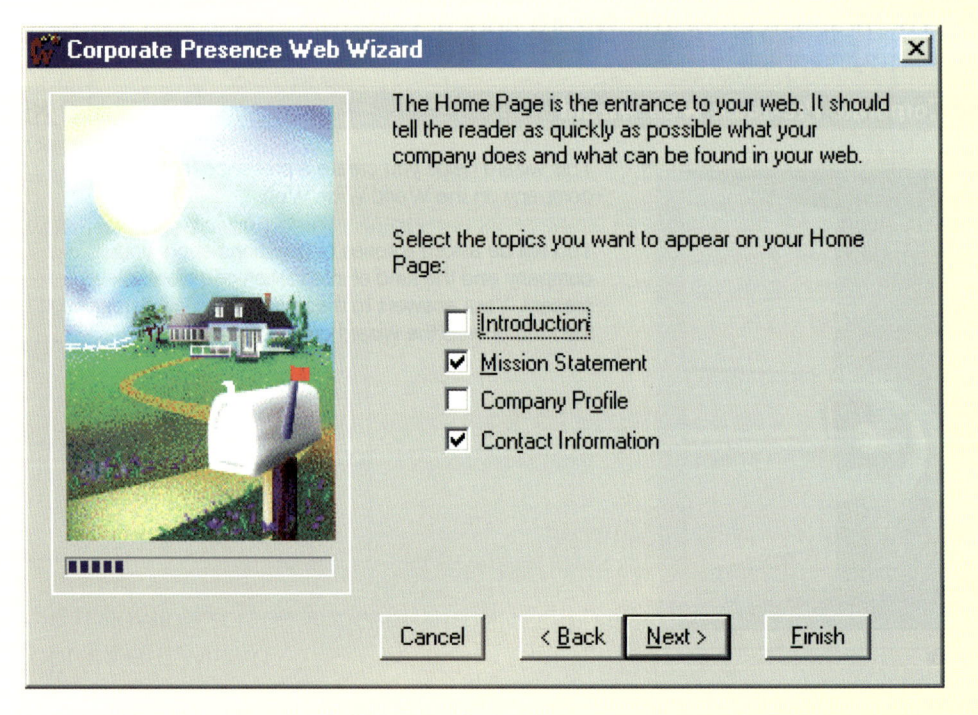

Check that the ticks appear as they are in the above screen and then click on **Next >**.

Lesson 6 Creating a website using a wizard

7 If people have visited your site before, they will go straight to the **What's New** page. Here you can specify what you want to include on this page.

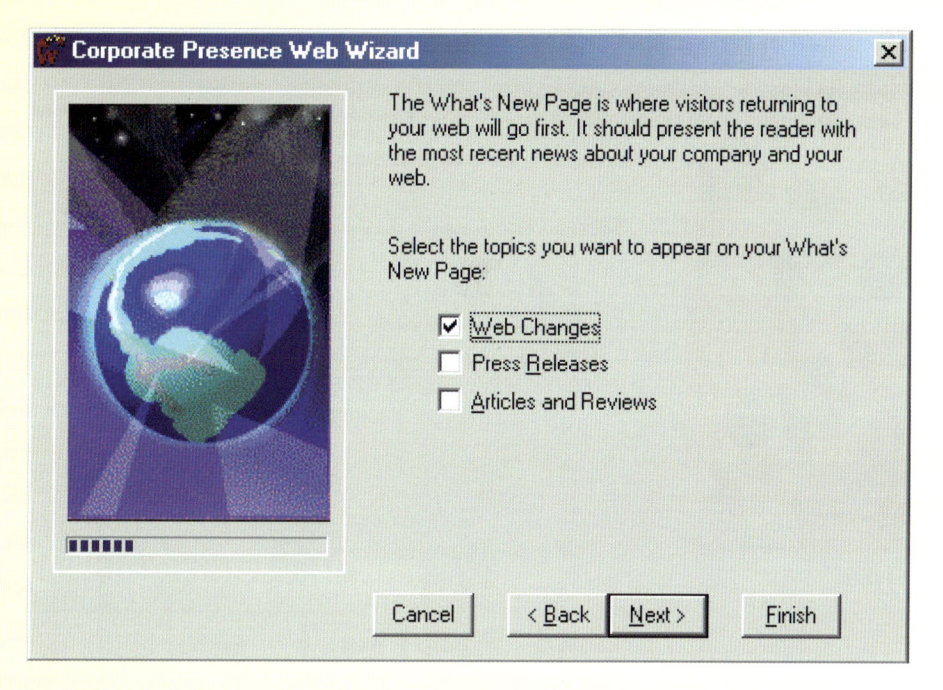

Check that you have a tick in the first box and then click on **Next >**.

8 In this screen you can have a page for each product or service being sold. As we are selling bedding plants and there are four varieties (Pansy, Lobelia, Marigold and Alyssum), it makes sense to have a page for each plant containing growing instructions etc.

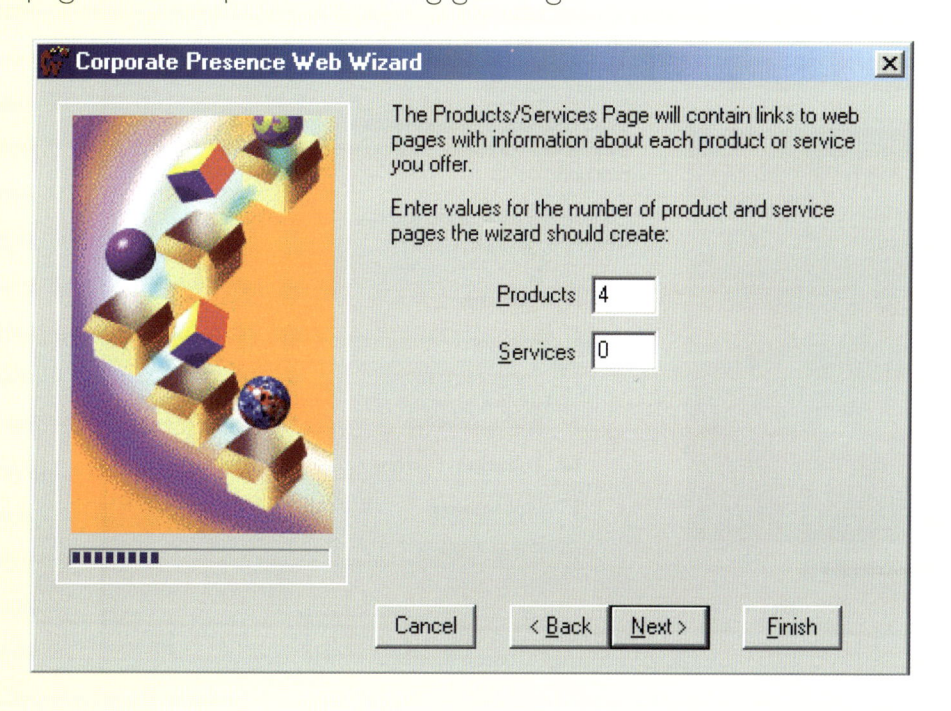

89

Alter the number in the Products box to **4** and the Services box to **0** and then click on **Next >**.

9 The following screen appears:

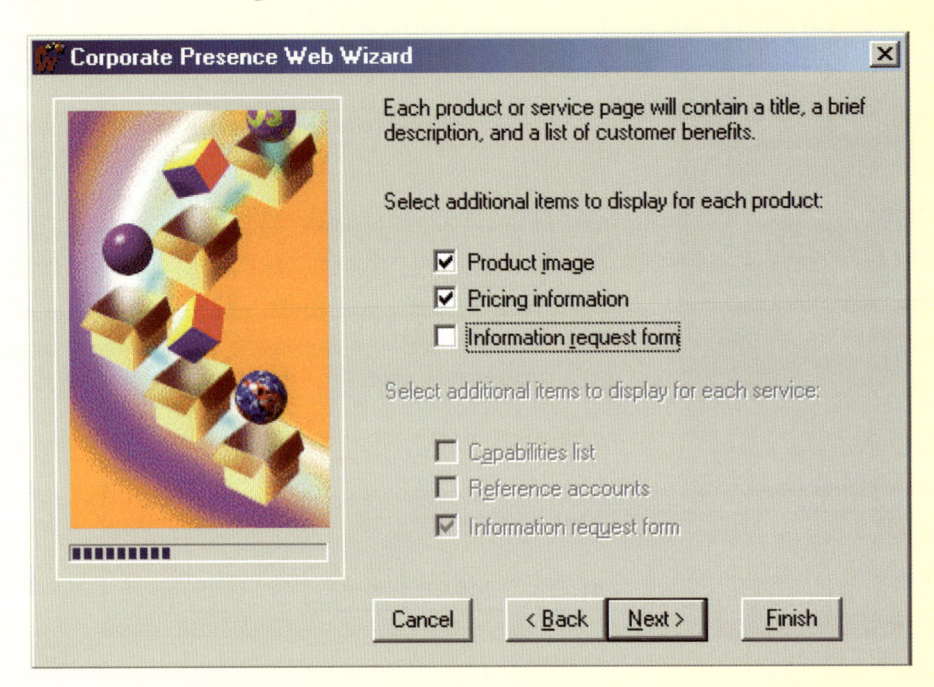

We want to include a photograph of each plant and also the price. Make sure you tick the boxes as shown here and then click on **Next >**.

10 The following screen appears. Here the customers or visitors can give you feedback.

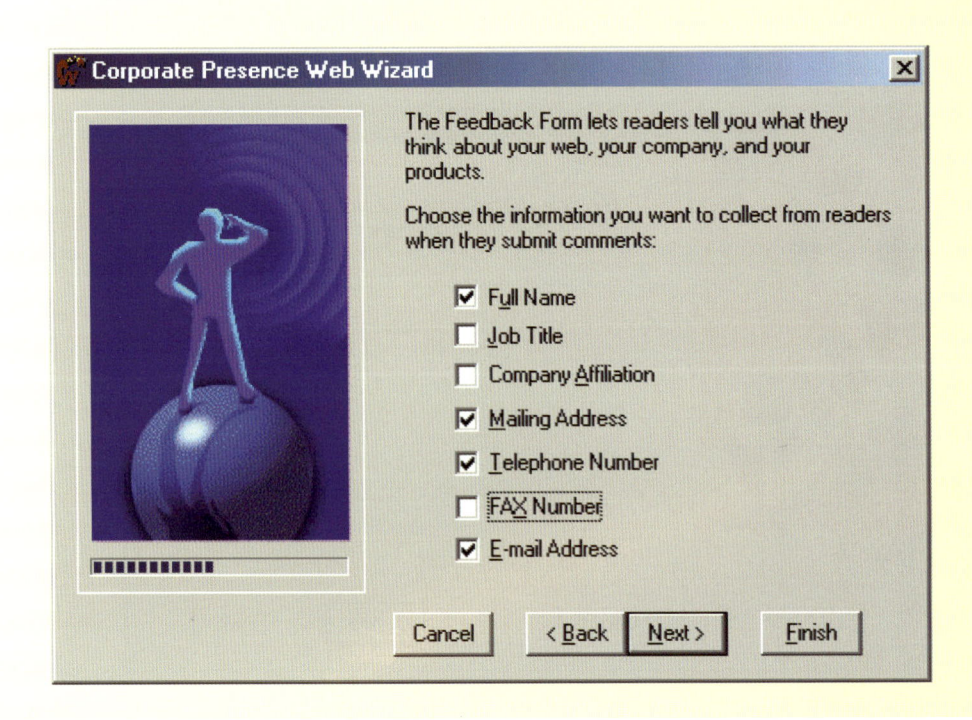

Lesson 6 Creating a website using a wizard

Make sure the boxes are ticked as shown above and then click on **Next >**.

11 The next screen is about how you want the file containing the feedback to be stored. You do not need to do anything here, just click on **Next>**.

12 This screen appears:

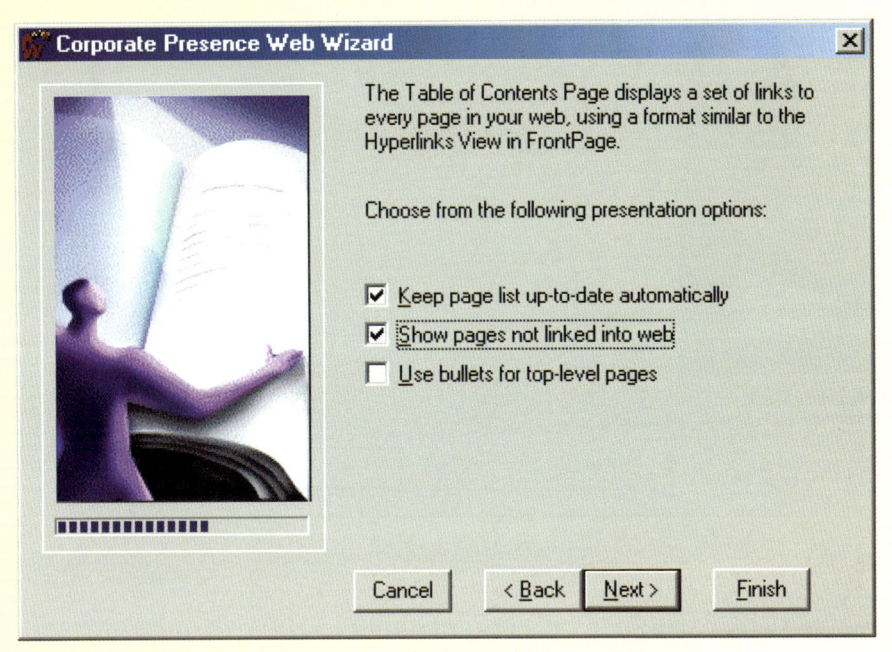

[Corporate Presence Web Wizard dialog:
The Table of Contents Page displays a set of links to every page in your web, using a format similar to the Hyperlinks View in FrontPage.

Choose from the following presentation options:
☑ Keep page list up-to-date automatically
☑ Show pages not linked into web
☐ Use bullets for top-level pages]

Click the boxes as shown and then click on **Next >**.

13 The following screen appears:

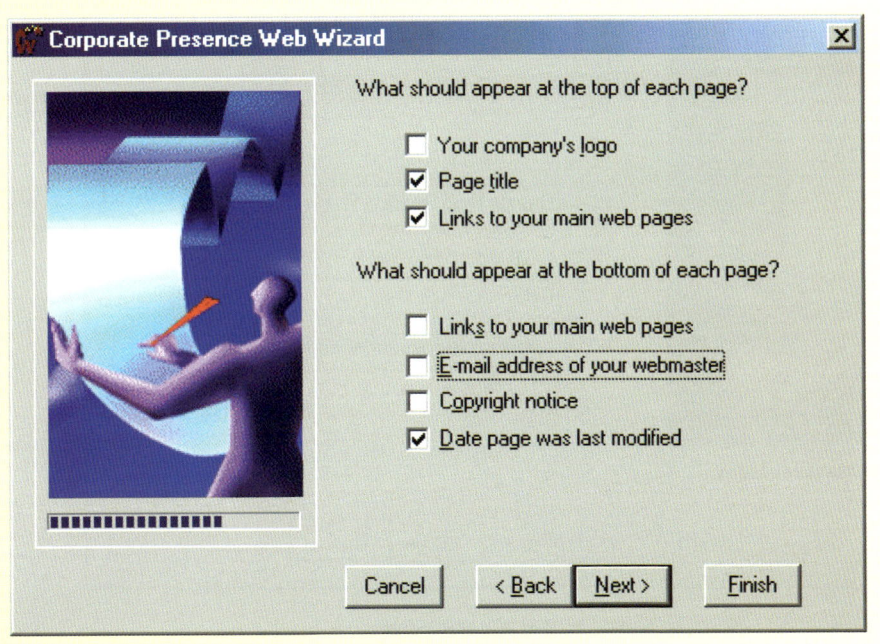

[Corporate Presence Web Wizard dialog:
What should appear at the top of each page?
☐ Your company's logo
☑ Page title
☑ Links to your main web pages

What should appear at the bottom of each page?
☐ Links to your main web pages
☐ E-mail address of your webmaster
☐ Copyright notice
☑ Date page was last modified]

Notice that you can alter what appears at the top and the bottom of each page. Put the ticks in the boxes as shown in the screenshot and click on **Next >**.

91

Unit 2 Publishing on the web

14 This screen appears:

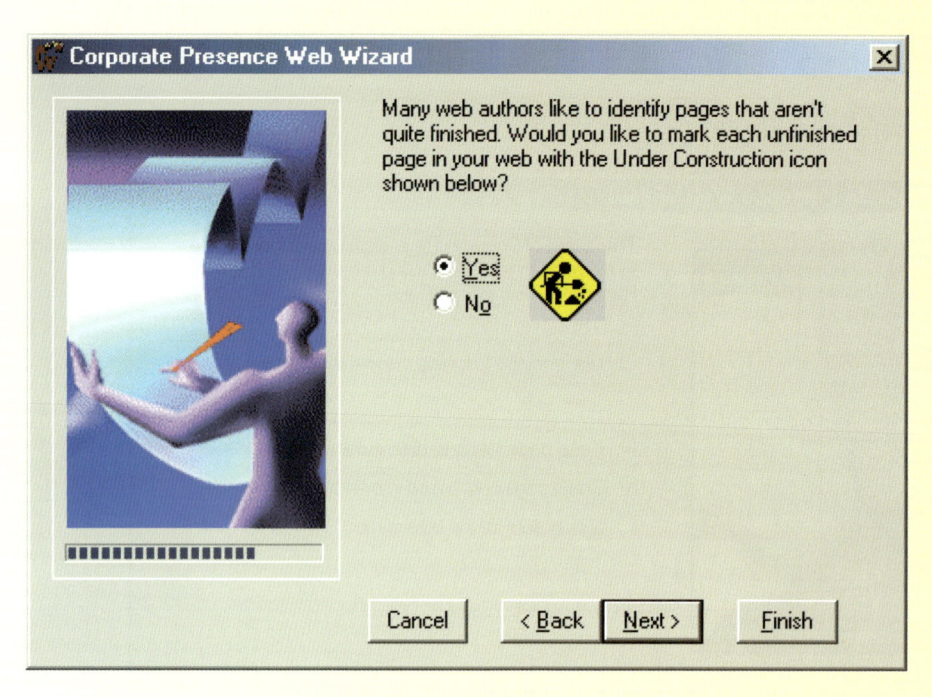

[Screenshot: Corporate Presence Web Wizard dialog asking "Many web authors like to identify pages that aren't quite finished. Would you like to mark each unfinished page in your web with the Under Construction icon shown below?" with Yes selected and No option, plus Cancel, Back, Next, Finish buttons.]

Click on **Next >**.

15 The following screen appears and you can delete the existing text and put your own in.

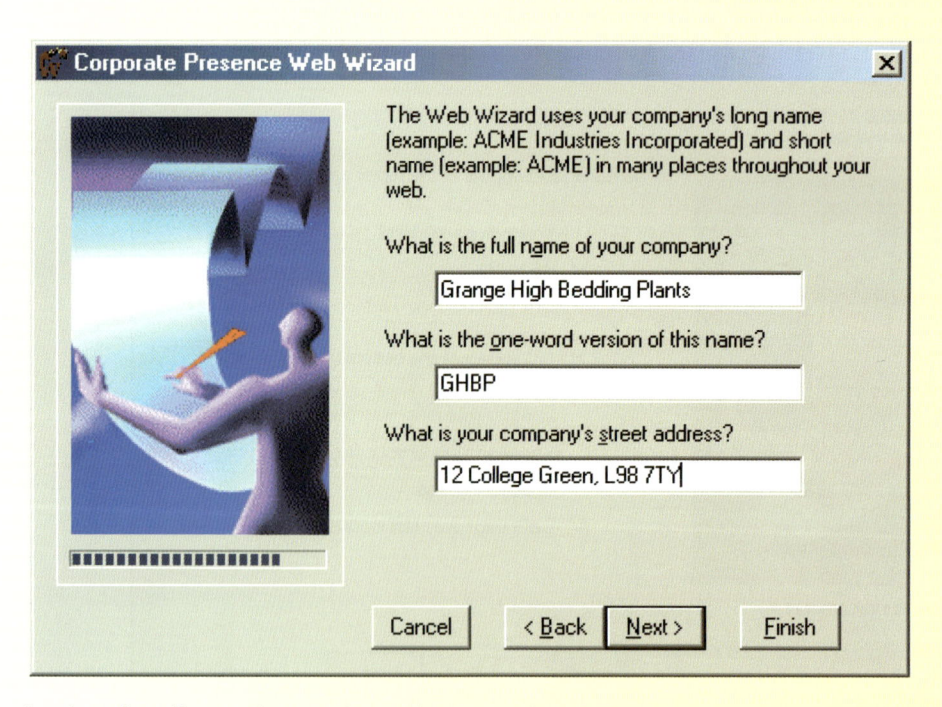

[Screenshot: Corporate Presence Web Wizard dialog with fields:
- What is the full name of your company? "Grange High Bedding Plants"
- What is the one-word version of this name? "GHBP"
- What is your company's street address? "12 College Green, L98 7TY"]

Put in the details as shown here (you could put in details of your own school instead).

Click on **Next >**.

Lesson 6 Creating a website using a wizard

16 The next screen asks for further contact details.

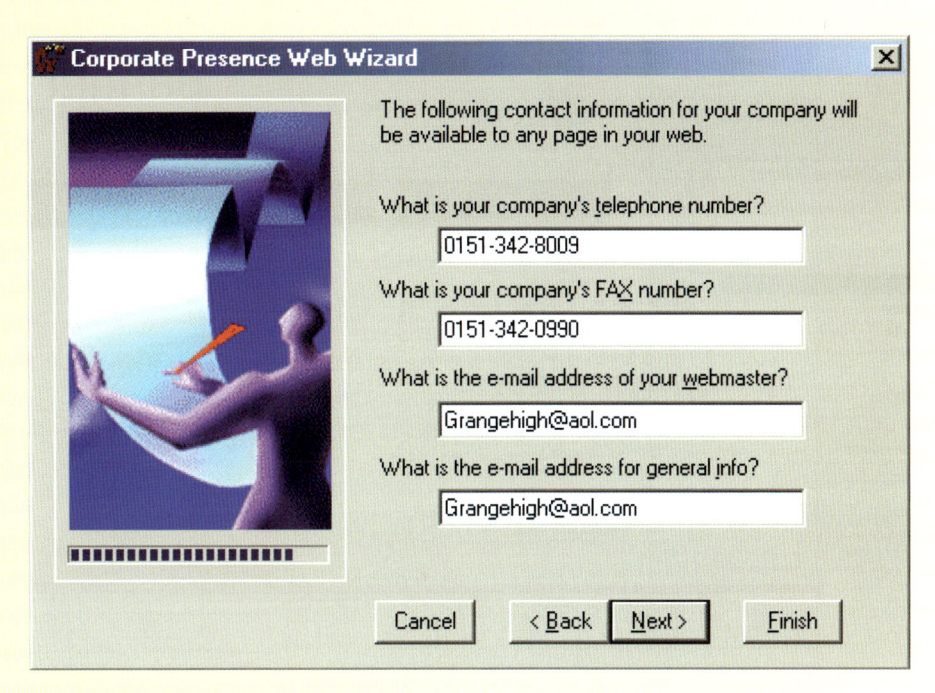

Corporate Presence Web Wizard

The following contact information for your company will be available to any page in your web.

What is your company's telephone number?
0151-342-8009

What is your company's FAX number?
0151-342-0990

What is the e-mail address of your webmaster?
Grangehigh@aol.com

What is the e-mail address for general info?
Grangehigh@aol.com

[Cancel] [< Back] [Next >] [Finish]

Enter the information shown or enter details of your own school.

17 The following screen appears:

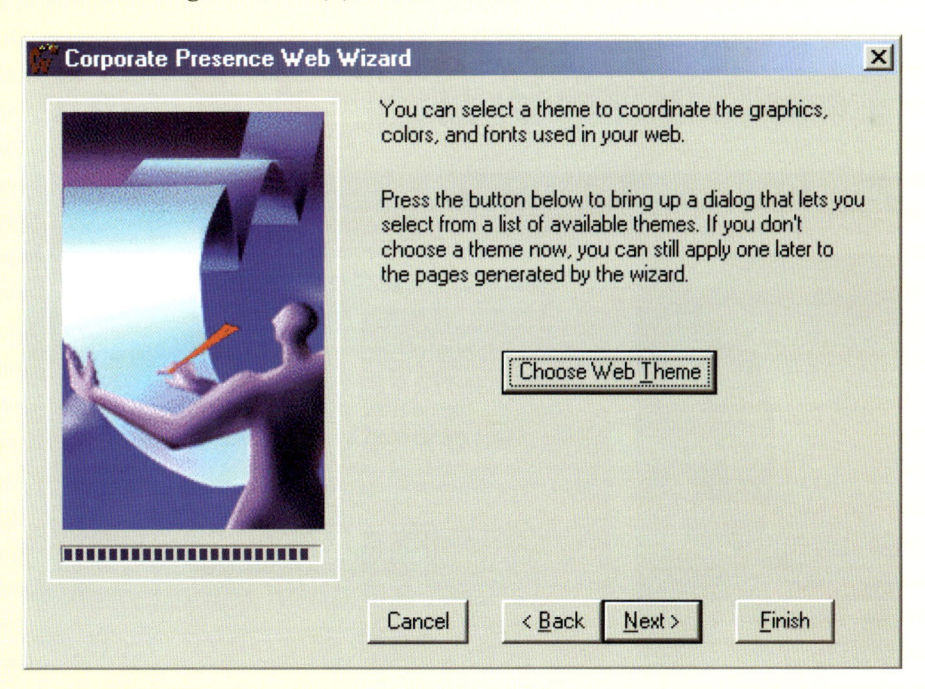

Corporate Presence Web Wizard

You can select a theme to coordinate the graphics, colors, and fonts used in your web.

Press the button below to bring up a dialog that lets you select from a list of available themes. If you don't choose a theme now, you can still apply one later to the pages generated by the wizard.

[Choose Web Theme]

[Cancel] [< Back] [Next >] [Finish]

Click on [Choose Web Theme].

18 The following screen appears. Here you can choose what you want your web pages to look like.

93

Unit 2 Publishing on the web

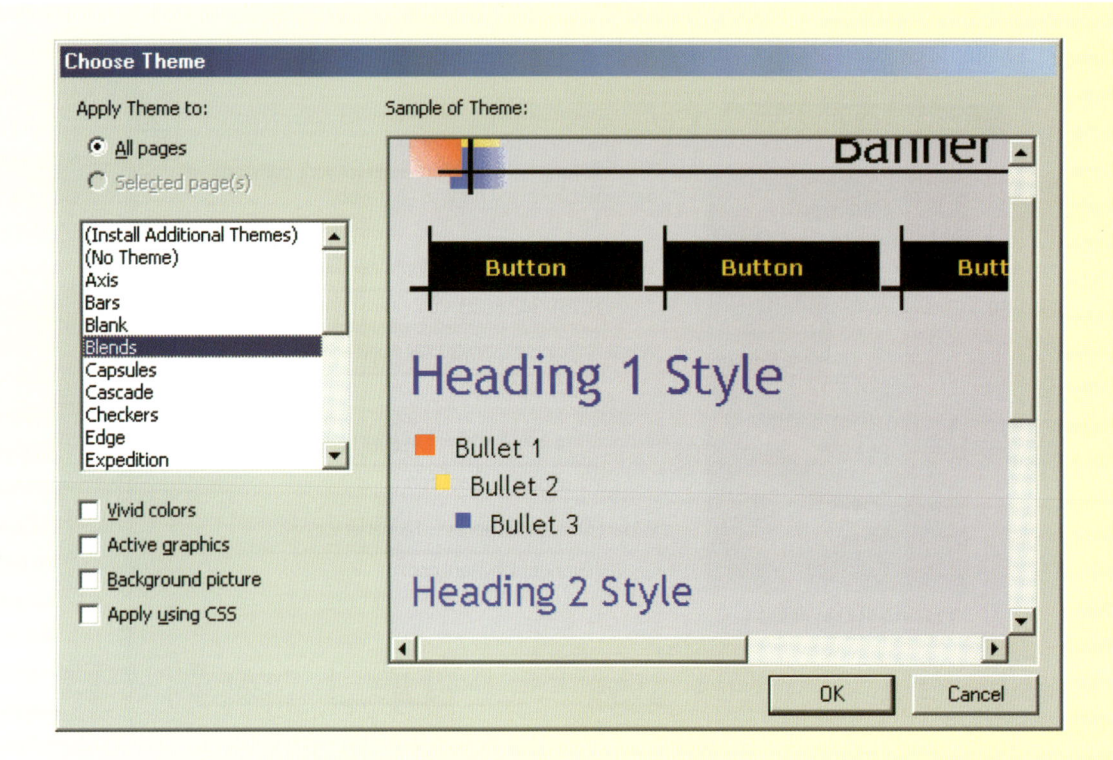

Look at each theme in the list on the left. Pick your own theme or use the one suggested here.

Click on the **OK** button.

19 The following screen reappears:

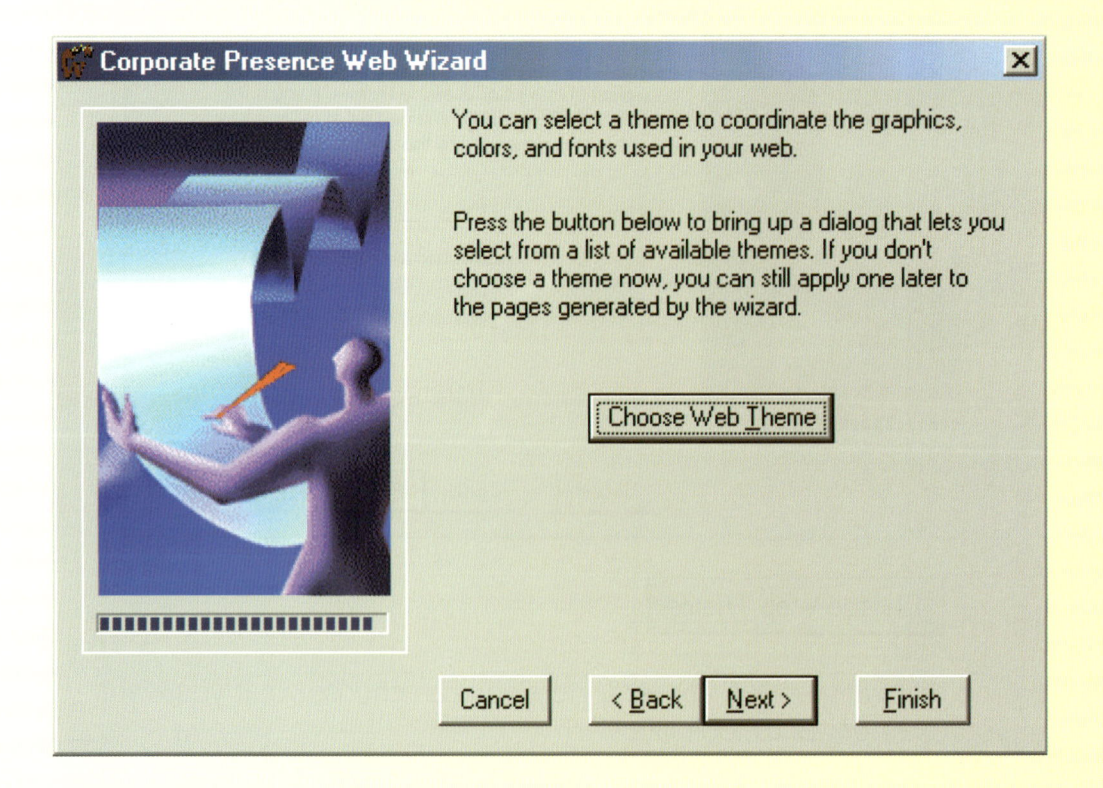

Lesson 6 Creating a website using a wizard

Click on **Next >**.

20 The following screen (right) appears showing that the Wizard has completed the structure of your website.

Click on the **Finish** button.

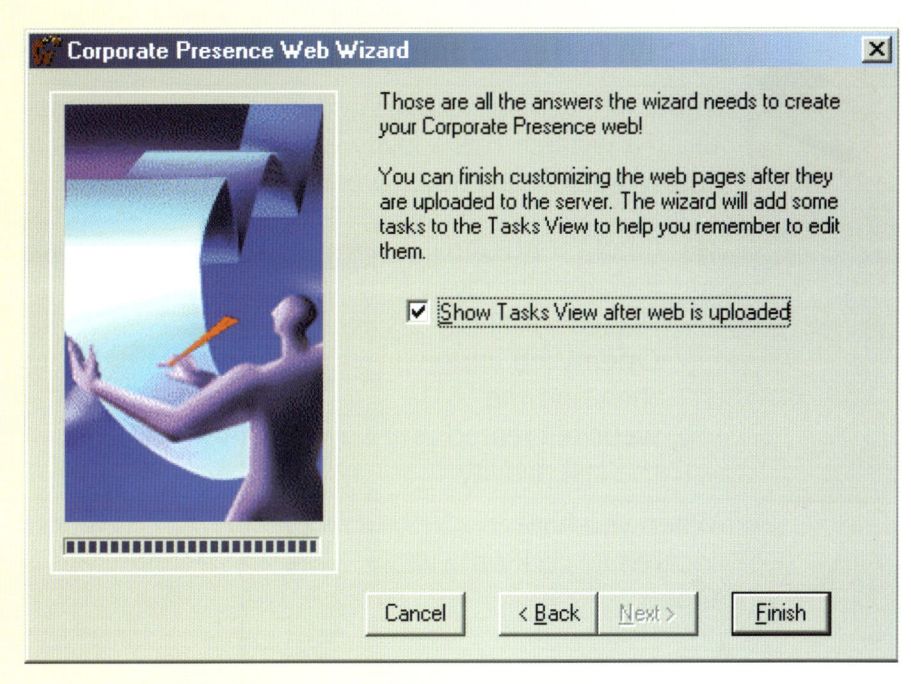

21 FrontPage creates the site structure and then lists the things that need to be done to complete the site.

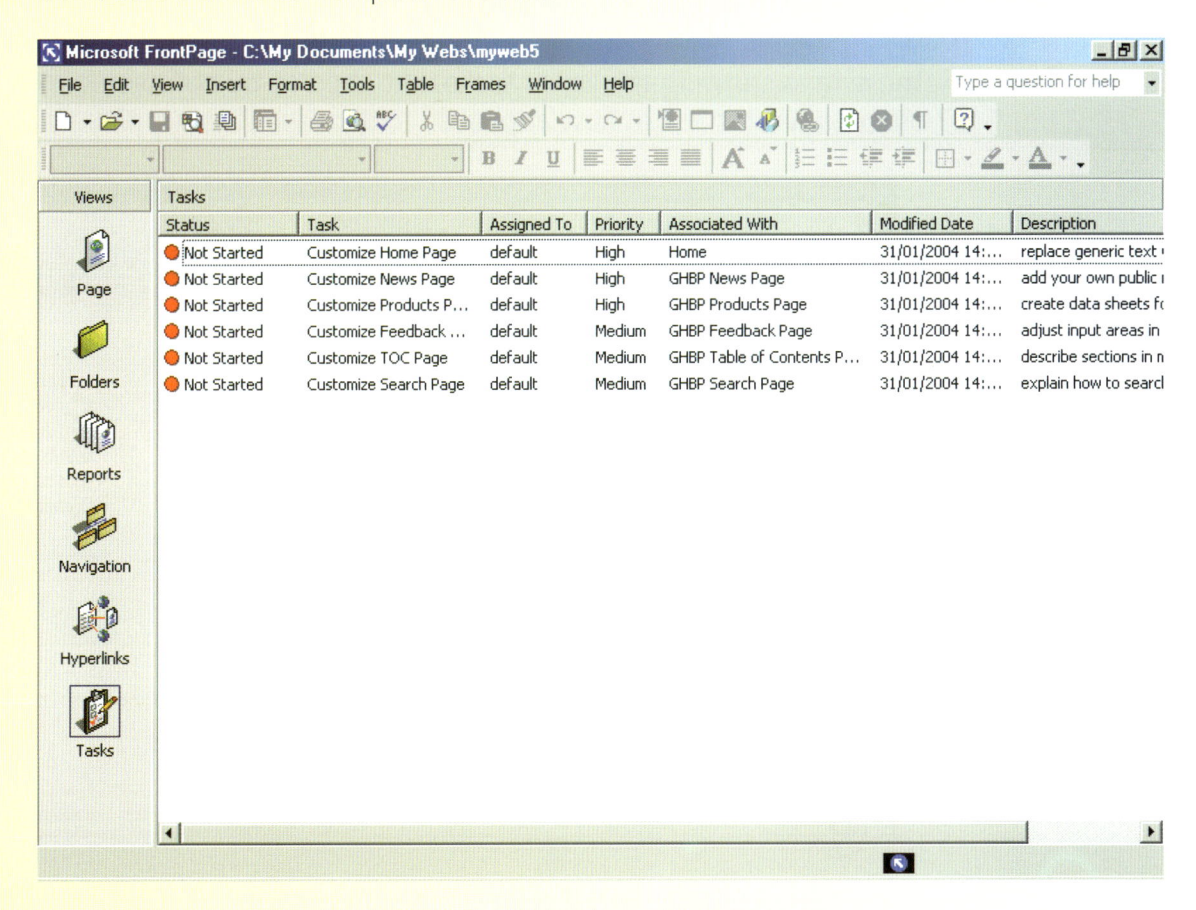

22 We will now close the file so it is saved.

Click **File** on the toolbar and then **Close Web**.

95

Unit 2 Publishing on the web

ACTIVITY 15: Adding your own text to the website

In the last activity you created a structure or framework for a website using a wizard. This activity will show you how to add to this structure. You will also learn how to edit the text.

1 Load FrontPage if it is not already loaded. Click on **Open Web** and then find the website created in the last activity.

When you have located it, click on **Open**.

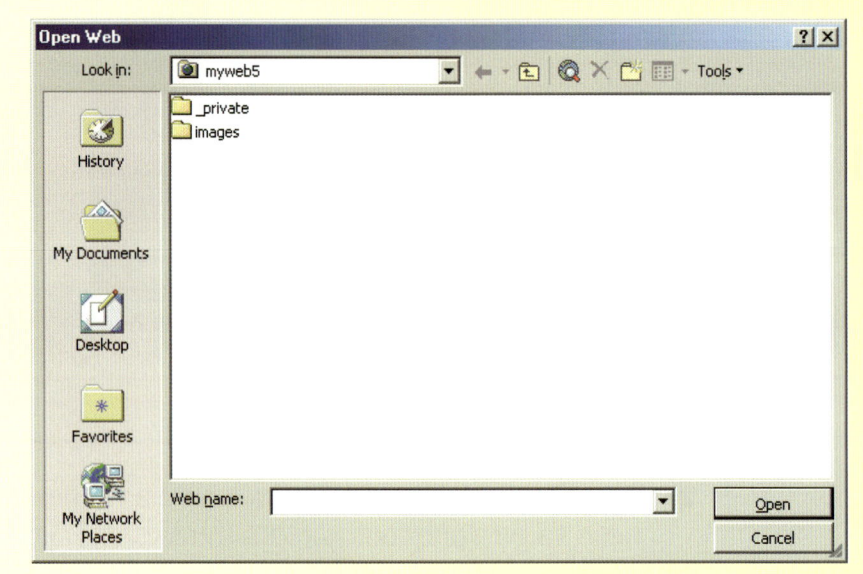

2 The screen showing the list of tasks that need to be completed in order to finish the site now appears.

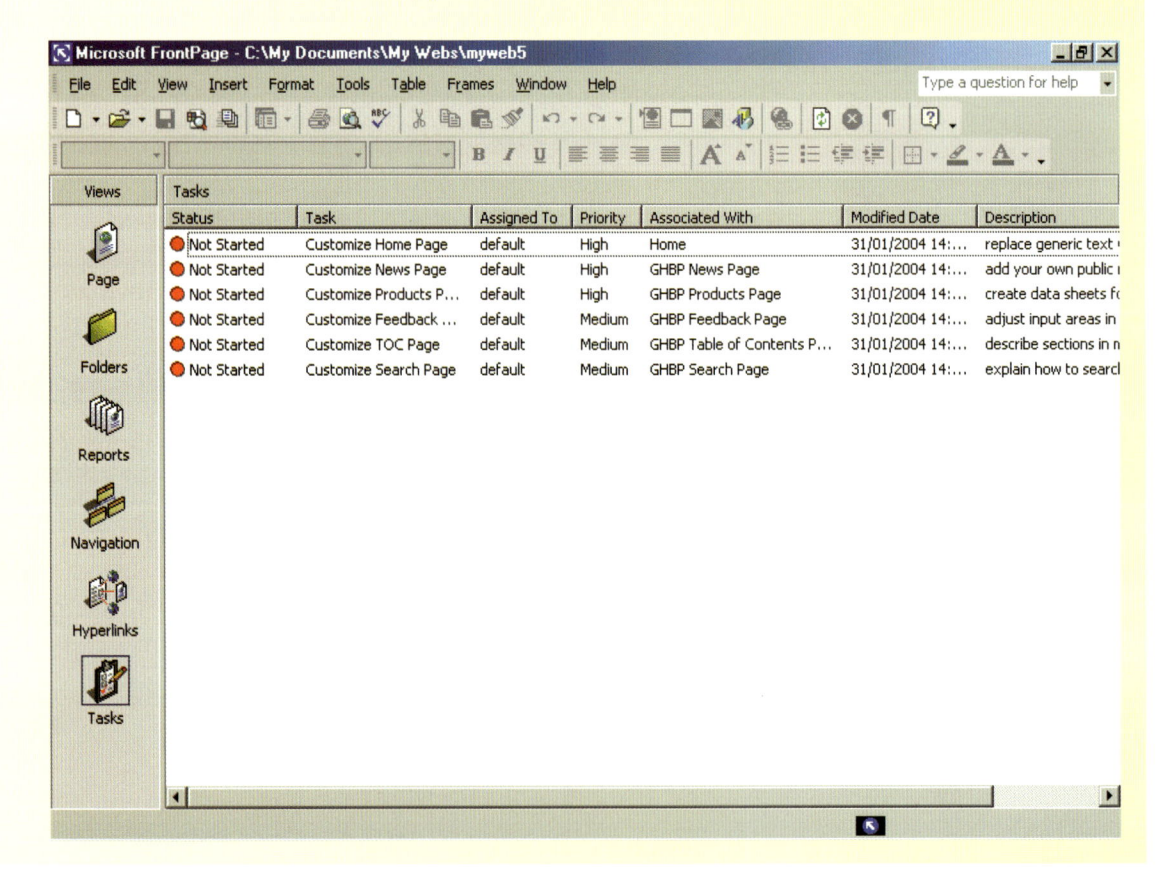

Lesson 6 Creating a website using a wizard

Double click on the first item in the list, **Customize Home Page**.

3 The following screen appears (right):

This screen tells you a little about what the task involves.

Click on **Start Task**.

4 The following screen now appears (below) and you can delete the existing text that tells you what to do (this is called 'placeholder text') and replace it with your own text.

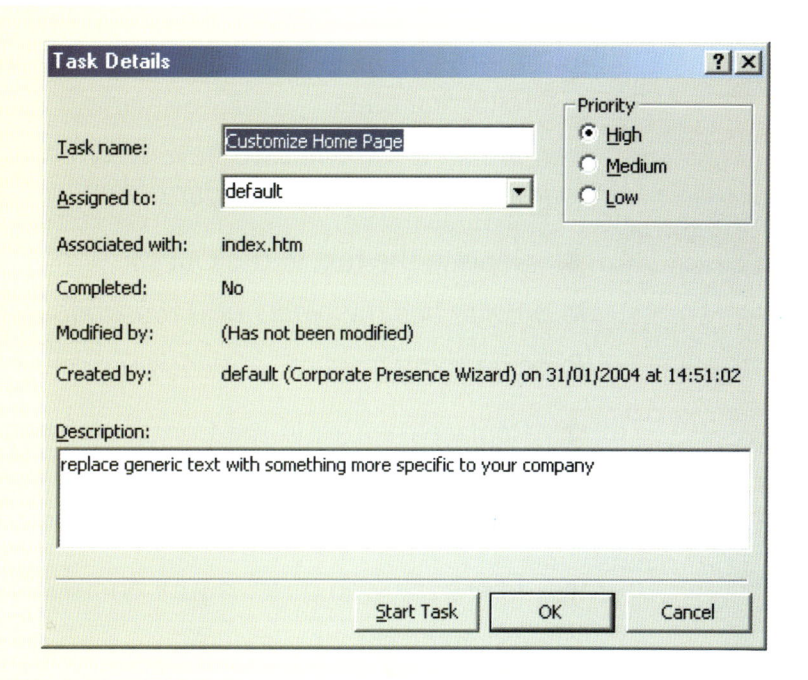

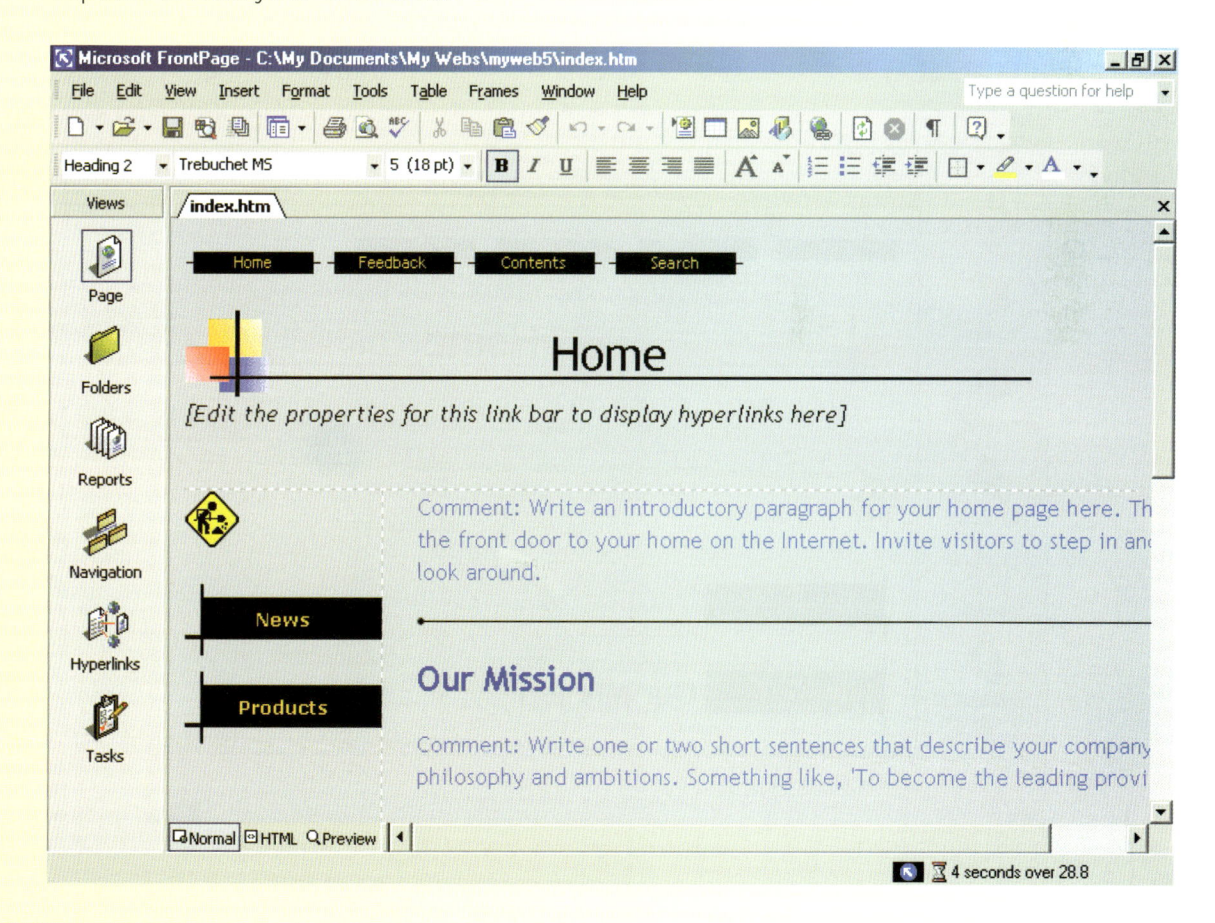

97

Unit 2 Publishing on the web

5 Replace the text in the comment part of the web page with the following text:

Step inside to see what we have to offer and how buying plants from your local school will help your community.

6 Replace the text in the Our Mission section with the following text:

To provide healthy plants at a reasonable cost.

To be your main source of bedding plants.

7 Replace the text in the Contact Information section with the following:

You can contact the project leaders using the following methods:

8 To see the web page as your audience will see it, click on **Preview**.

The following screen appears:

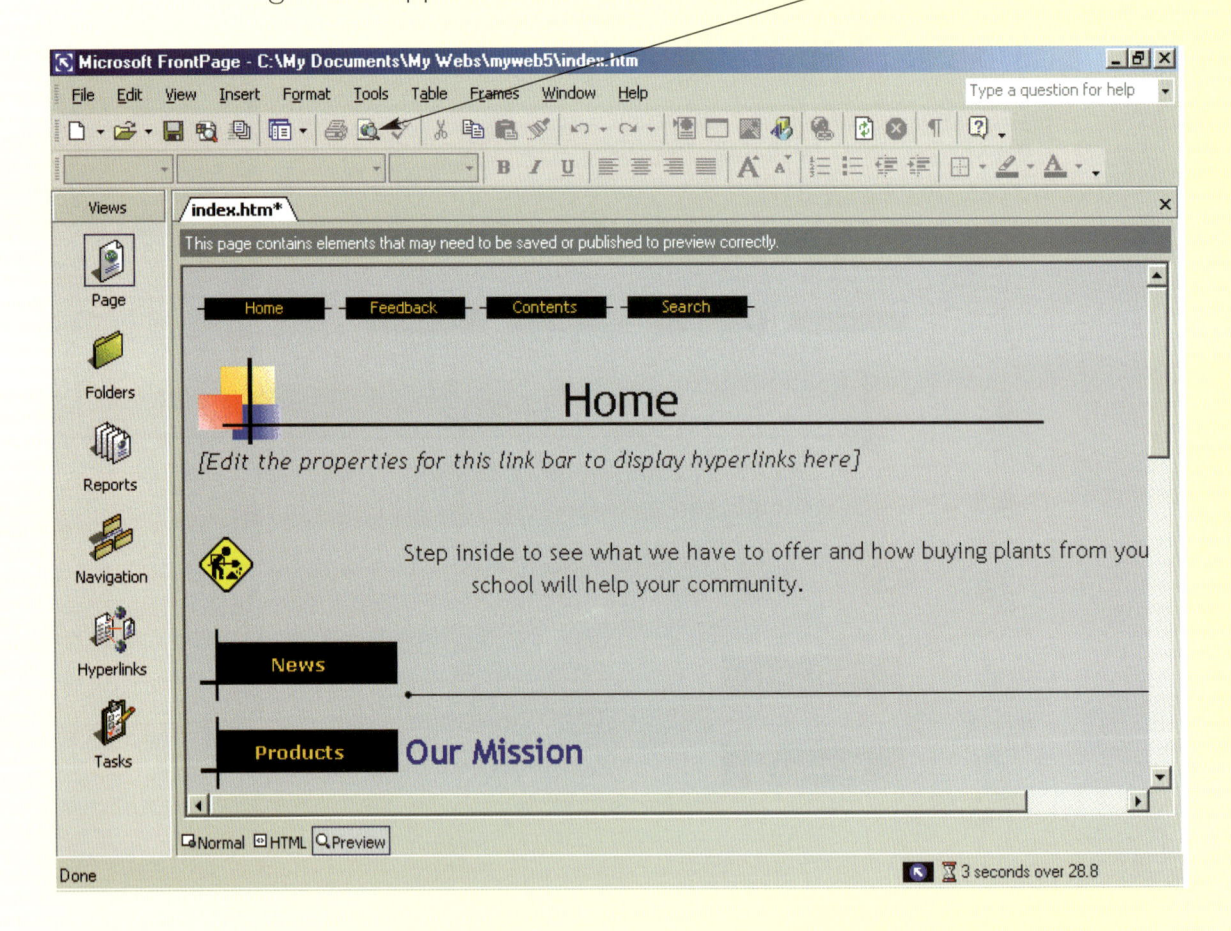

To continue building the website, click on **Normal**.

98

Lesson 6 Creating a website using a wizard

9 Save your web page by clicking on the save icon 💾 on the toolbar. If the following screen appears:

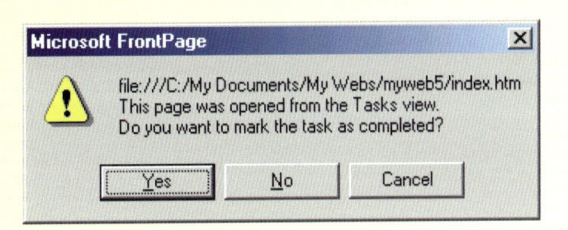

as we have completed the first task, just click on **Yes**.

10 You now need to complete the rest of the tasks.

In the Views part of the screen, click on the **Tasks** icon  .

The list of tasks now appears. Notice that the first task has been completed.

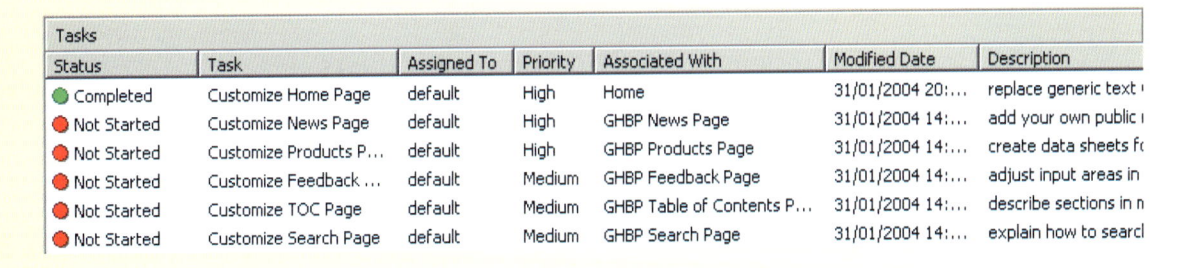

Status	Task	Assigned To	Priority	Associated With	Modified Date	Description
Completed	Customize Home Page	default	High	Home	31/01/2004 20:...	replace generic text
Not Started	Customize News Page	default	High	GHBP News Page	31/01/2004 14:...	add your own public
Not Started	Customize Products P...	default	High	GHBP Products Page	31/01/2004 14:...	create data sheets fo
Not Started	Customize Feedback ...	default	Medium	GHBP Feedback Page	31/01/2004 14:...	adjust input areas in
Not Started	Customize TOC Page	default	Medium	GHBP Table of Contents P...	31/01/2004 14:...	describe sections in
Not Started	Customize Search Page	default	Medium	GHBP Search Page	31/01/2004 14:...	explain how to searc

11 Double click on **Customize News Page** in the list of tasks.

The following window appears:

Click on the **Start Task** button.

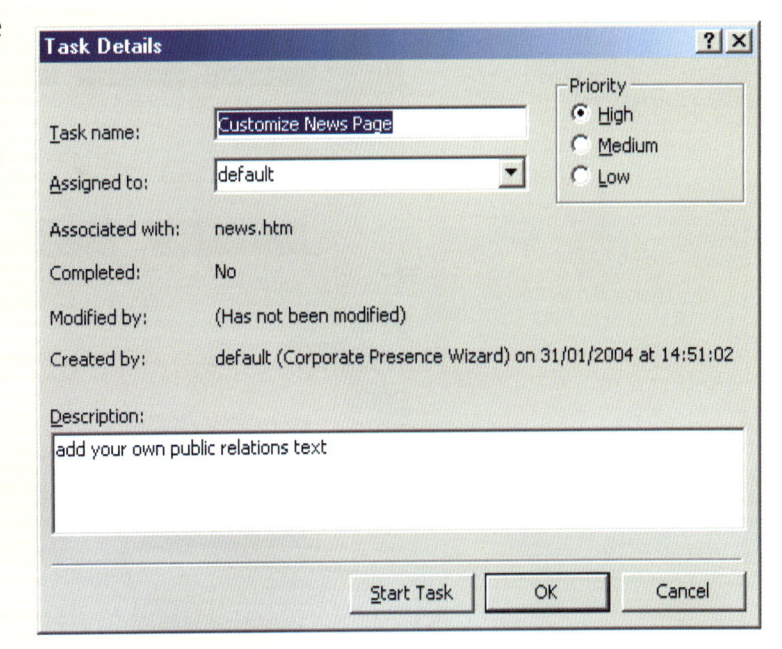

99

Unit 2 Publishing on the web

12 The following information with the placeholder text appears:

> **Web Changes**
>
> This is where we'll announce the most recent additions to our web site. If you've visited us before and want to know what's changed, take a look here first.
>
> Comment: Try to keep this material up to date; get rid of old items every few weeks.
> Each item below should link to the document that holds the new information.
> Enter new items at the top of the list, so the most recent information comes first.

As there are no web changes yet we can just delete the blue placeholder text below the heading Web Changes.

13 Save your web page, mark the task as complete and go onto the Tasks screen again to complete the next task in the list.

Status	Task	Assigned To	Priority	Associated With	Modified Date	Description
● Completed	Customize Home Page	default	High	Home	31/01/2004 20:...	replace generic text
● Completed	Customize News Page	default	High	GHBP News Page	31/01/2004 20:...	add your own public
● Not Started	Customize Products P...	default	High	GHBP Products Page	31/01/2004 14:...	create data sheets f
● Not Started	Customize Feedback ...	default	Medium	GHBP Feedback Page	31/01/2004 14:...	adjust input areas in
● Not Started	Customize TOC Page	default	Medium	GHBP Table of Contents P...	31/01/2004 14:...	describe sections in
● Not Started	Customize Search Page	default	Medium	GHBP Search Page	31/01/2004 14:...	explain how to searc

Click on the next task in the list, **Customize Products**.

Click on **Start Task** when the Task window appears.

14 The following screen appears and you can enter the names and details of the bedding plants.

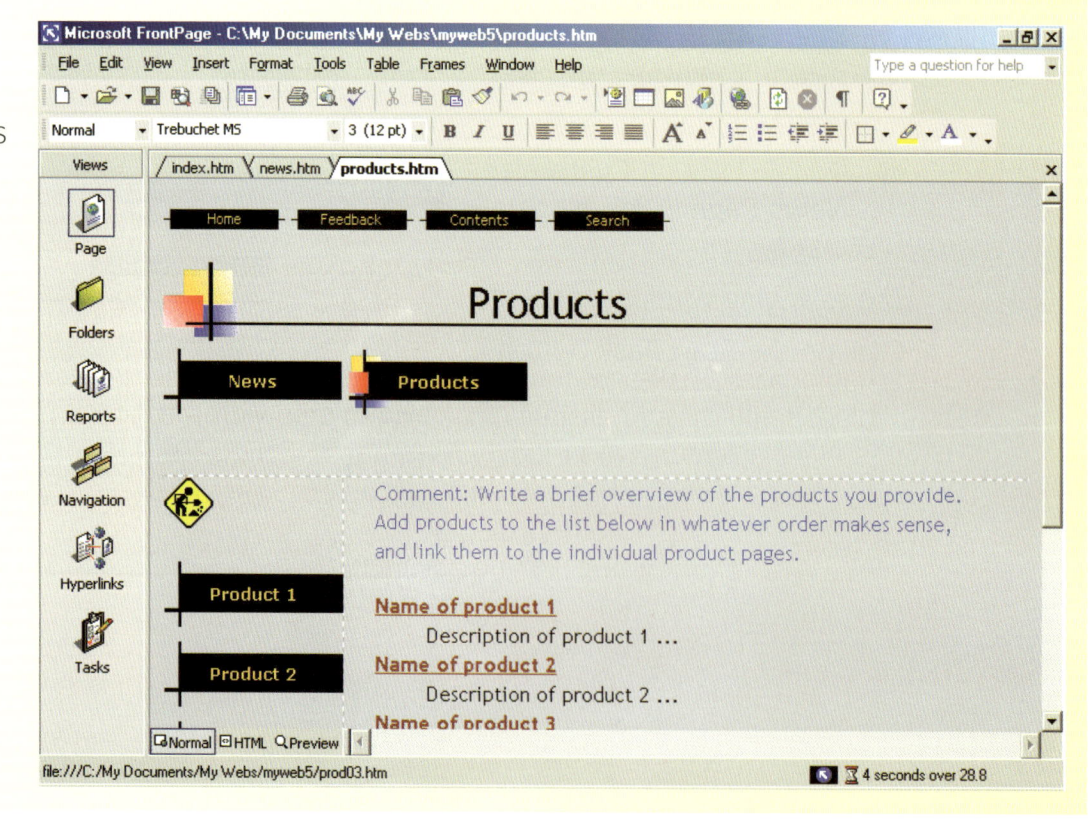

Lesson 6 Creating a website using a wizard

15 Delete the blue text in the comment section and replace with the following text:

Comment: As this is the first year of our project we will only be supplying four popular types of bedding plants. Next year we hope to increase our range.

16 Click on **Name of product 1**, delete it and replace it with the following text:

Pansy – Universal Mixed

Delete the placeholder text for the description **Description for product 1** ... and replace it with the following text:

Wonderful for summer bedding or if sown in summer will flower through the winter in mild spells. Compact and in a very wide range of blotched and clear colours. Height 6–9in.

17 Repeat step 16 for the other three products: delete the existing text and type in the new product names and descriptions.

The text you should type in is shown in the following screenshot.

> Comment: As this is the first year of our project we will only be supplying four popular types of bedding plants. Next year we hope to increase our range.
>
> **Pansy - Universal Mixed**
> Wonderful for summer bedding or if sown in summer will flower through the winter in mild spells. Compact and in a very wide range of blotched and clear colours. Height 6 - 9in.
>
> **Marigold - French: Bonita Mixed**
> A sparkling mixture of large carnation-sized blooms. Likes full sun and grows to height of 12in.
>
> **Lobelia - Cambridge Blue**
> Easy to grow plants, forming compact globes of clear sky-blue flowers. Superb for bedding and edging. Height 10cm.
>
> **Alyssum - Carpet of snow**
> A magnificent low-growing, widespread annual with a continuous display of massed white-flowers all summer through. Height 3-4in

18 Double click on the **Page banner** (this is the large heading at the top of the page).

Products

101

Unit 2 Publishing on the web

The following window will appear:

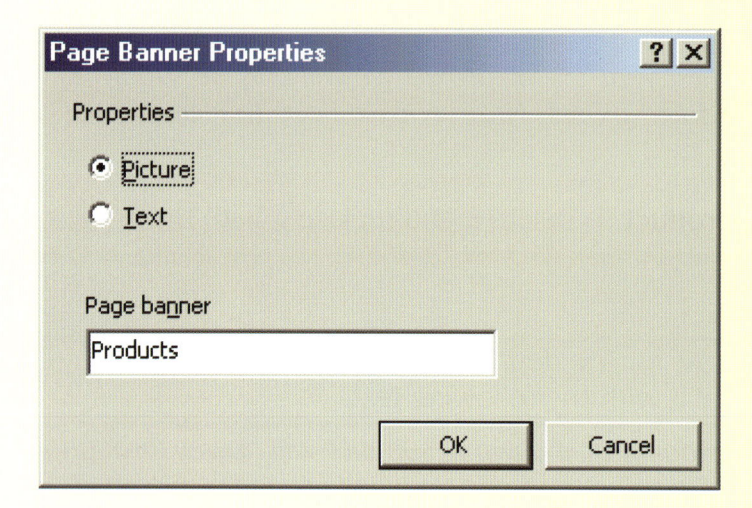

19 Change the word Products to *Bedding Plants* and then click on **OK**. Check that the top of your page now looks like this:

20 Now click on Folders in the Views section on the left of the screen.

All of the files to do with the website are listed here. Double click on **prod01.htm**.

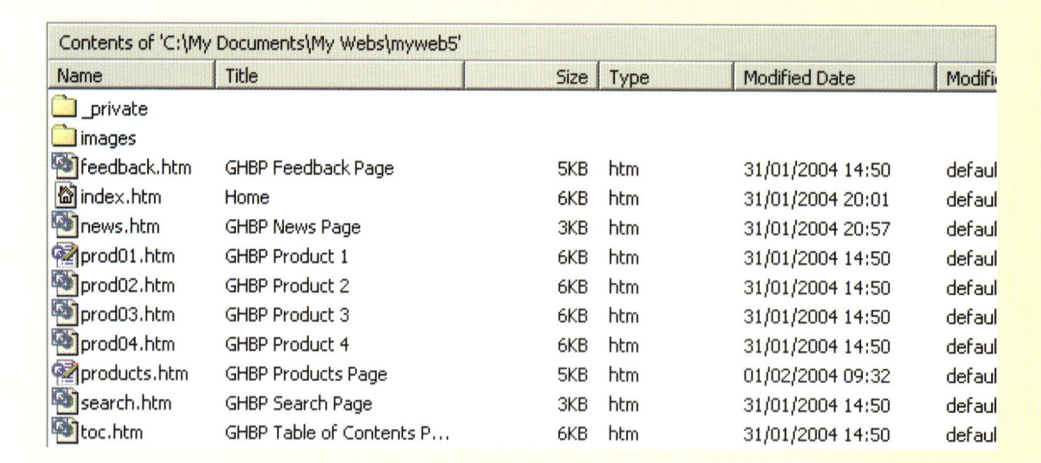

Lesson 6 Creating a website using a wizard

21 The following screen appears:

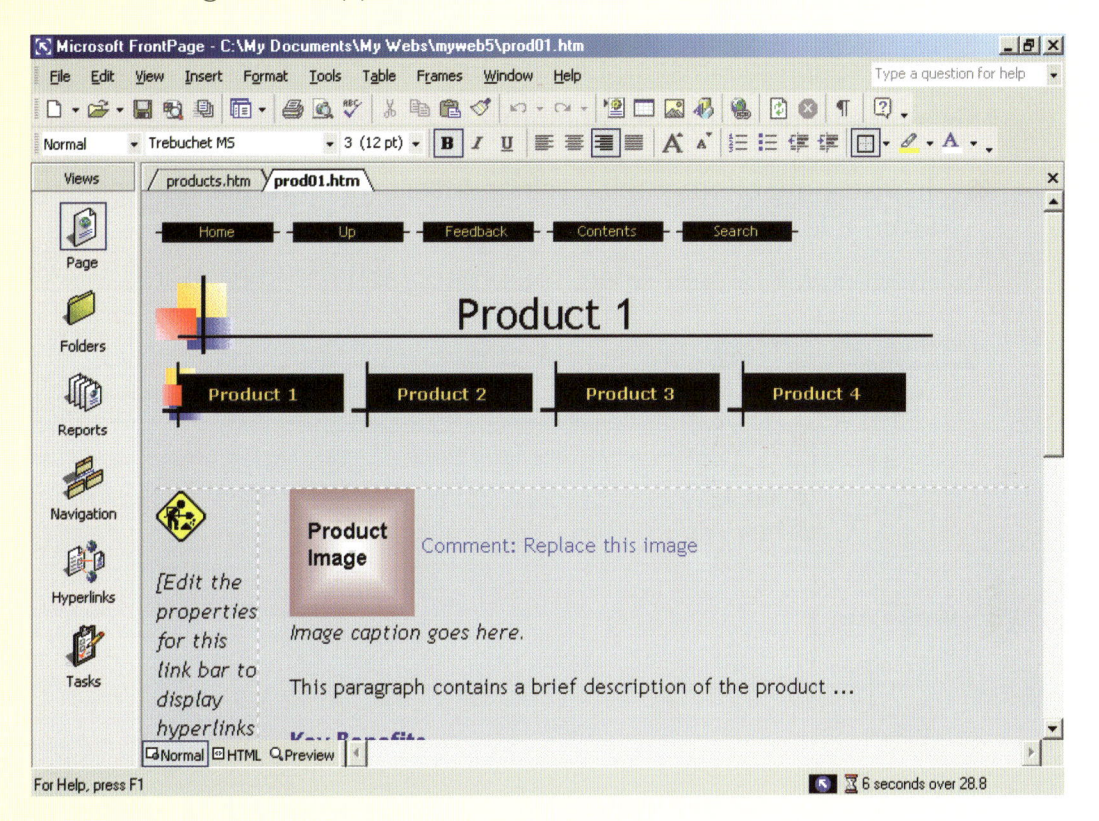

Click on the banner heading:

In the window which appears, change the words Product 1 to *Pansy*.

This part of the screen will now look like this:

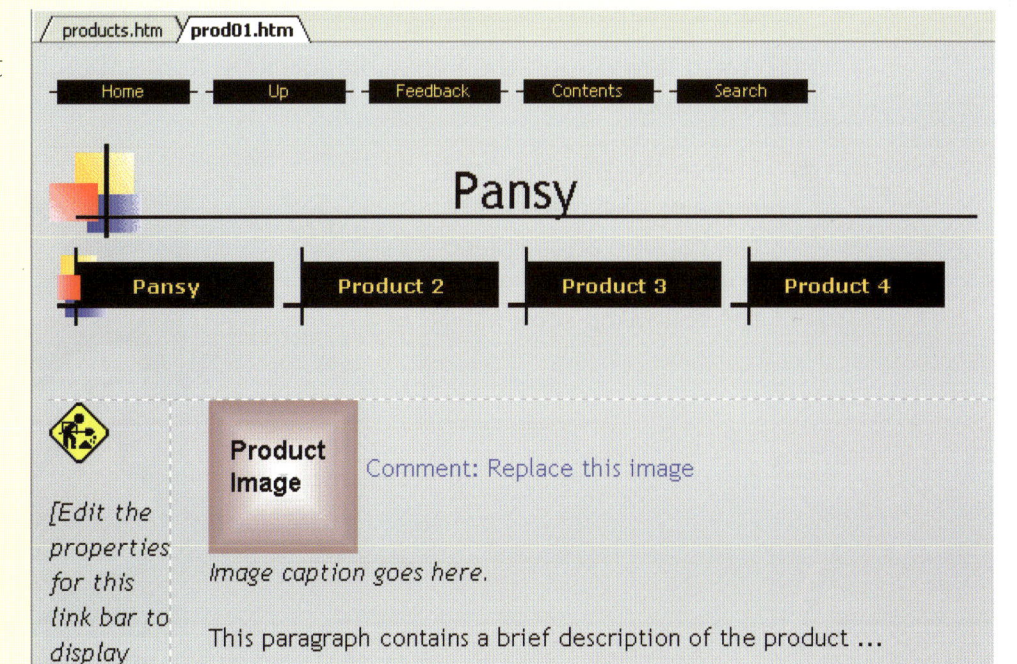

103

Unit 2 Publishing on the web

22 You are now going to add a photograph of the pansies.

Click on **Product Image** to select it (you will see the squares (called handles) around the image). Click on **Edit** and then **Cut**.

This removes the marker Product Image.

23 To insert the photograph, click on **Insert** then **Picture** and then **From File**.

Your teacher will tell you where the photograph has been stored.

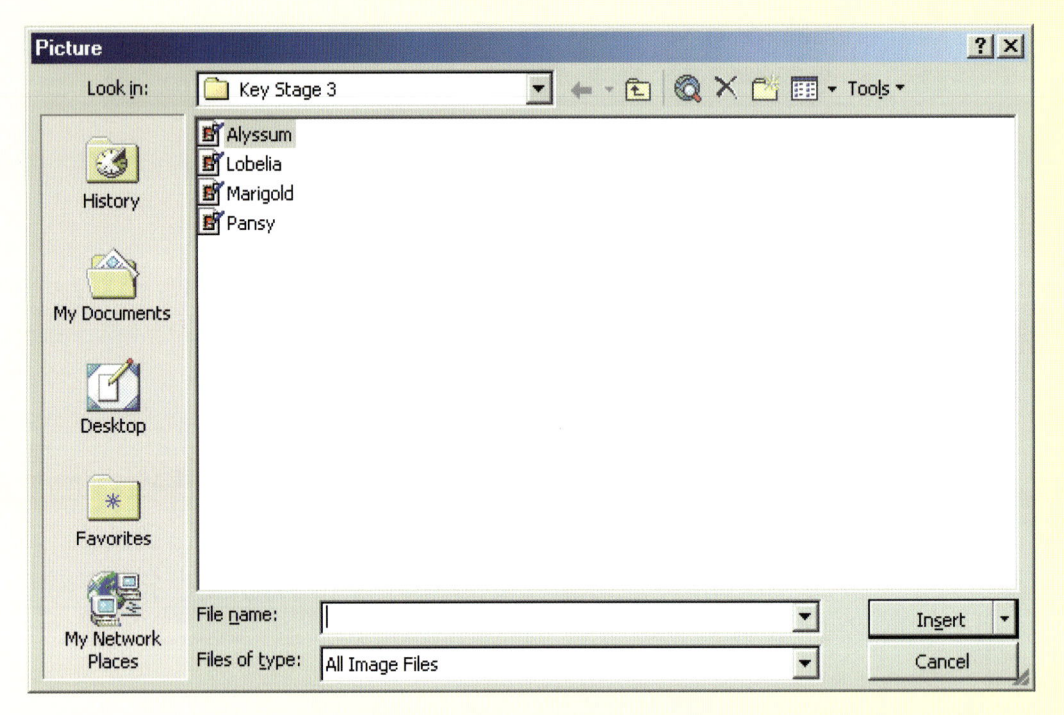

When you have found the Pansy file, click on it and then click on the **Insert** button.

24 Delete the blue text that remains and also delete the caption and replace it with the text shown in the following screenshot:

[Edit the properties for this link bar to display hyperlinks here]

Pansy - Universal Mixed

104

Lesson 6 Creating a website using a wizard

25 Delete the existing text and replace it with the text shown in the following screenshot:

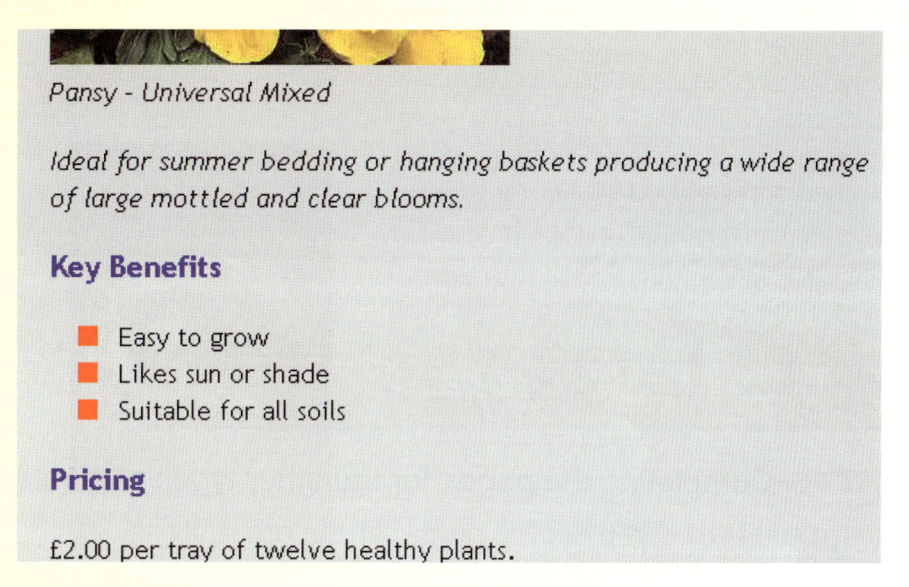

> *Pansy - Universal Mixed*
>
> *Ideal for summer bedding or hanging baskets producing a wide range of large mottled and clear blooms.*
>
> **Key Benefits**
>
> - Easy to grow
> - Likes sun or shade
> - Suitable for all soils
>
> **Pricing**
>
> *£2.00 per tray of twelve healthy plants.*

You will see a table as part of the placeholder material. You will not be using a table so you can delete this by using **Cut**.

26 You have now completed the web page for the Pansy plants.

Save your page. To do this click on **File** and then **Save**.

The following window appears:

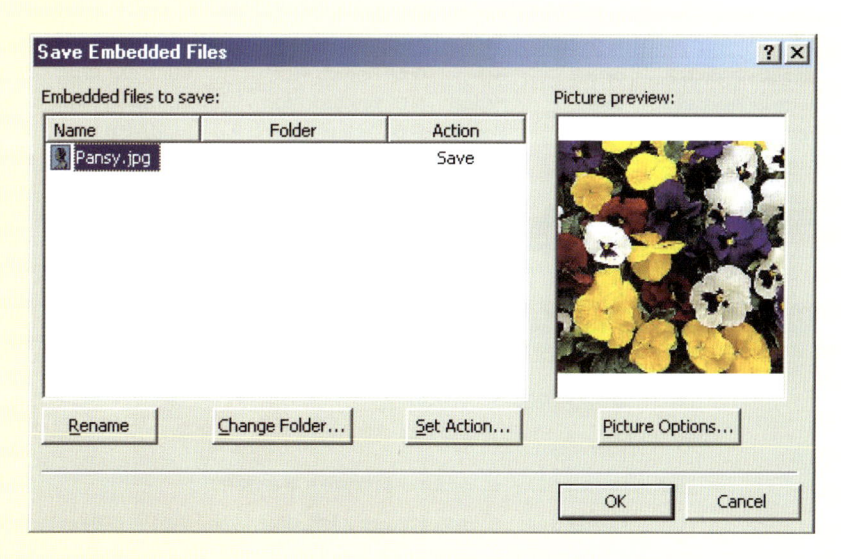

Image files can be stored separately even though they are part of the web page. Click on the **OK** button to save the photograph of the pansies.

27 Now click on **File** and then **Close Web**.

Unit 2 Publishing on the web

Lesson 7: COMPLETING THE WEBSITE FOR THE BEDDING PLANTS PROJECT

This lesson completes the website promoting the bedding plants that was created in Lesson 6. The next stage of the site development is to complete the pages for the other three types of plant.

Make it happen

ACTIVITY 16: Completing the pages for the other types of plants

In this activity you will complete the pages for the other plants.

1. Load the software FrontPage.

2. Click on **Tasks**. The following window shows the task that still needs to be completed (i.e. In Progress).

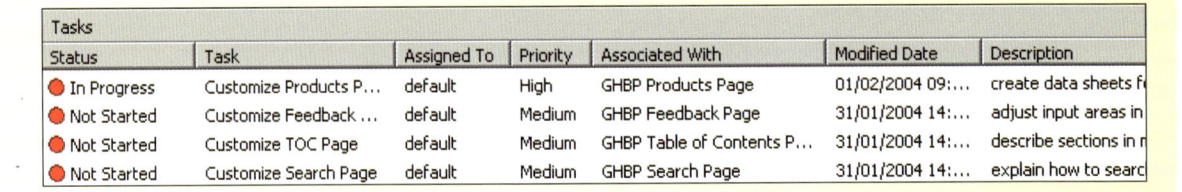

Tasks						
Status	Task	Assigned To	Priority	Associated With	Modified Date	Description
In Progress	Customize Products P…	default	High	GHBP Products Page	01/02/2004 09:…	create data sheets fo
Not Started	Customize Feedback …	default	Medium	GHBP Feedback Page	31/01/2004 14:…	adjust input areas in
Not Started	Customize TOC Page	default	Medium	GHBP Table of Contents P…	31/01/2004 14:…	describe sections in
Not Started	Customize Search Page	default	Medium	GHBP Search Page	31/01/2004 14:…	explain how to searc

3. Double click on the first task.

   When the following window appears, click on **Start Task**.

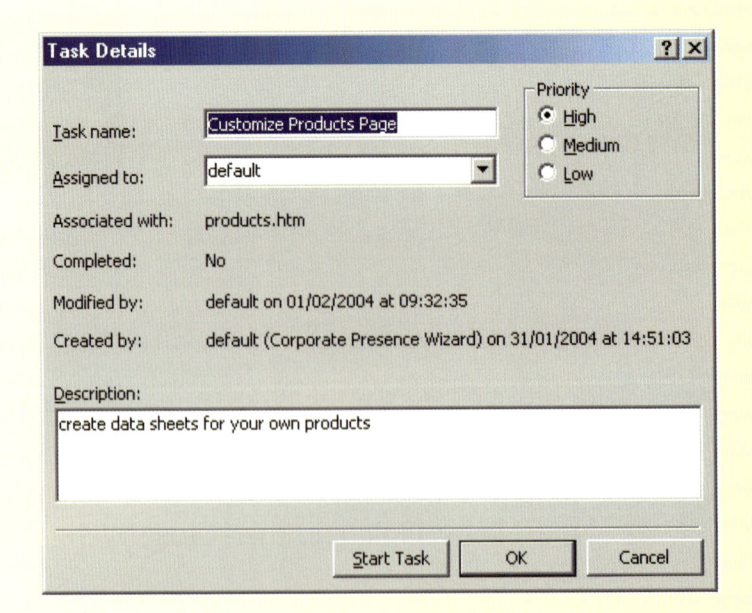

   Task Details

   Task name: Customize Products Page
   Assigned to: default
   Associated with: products.htm
   Completed: No
   Modified by: default on 01/02/2004 at 09:32:35
   Created by: default (Corporate Presence Wizard) on 31/01/2004 at 14:51:03
   Description: create data sheets for your own products
   Priority: High / Medium / Low

106

Lesson 7 Completing the website for the bedding plants project

4 Now click on *Folders* and the following screen appears:

Name	Title	Size	Type	Modified Date	Modifi
_private					
images					
feedback.htm	GHBP Feedback Page	5KB	htm	31/01/2004 14:50	defau
index.htm	Home	6KB	htm	03/02/2004 15:53	defau
news.htm	GHBP News Page	3KB	htm	31/01/2004 20:57	defau
Pansy.jpg	Pansy.jpg	20KB	jpg	01/02/2004 23:28	defau
prod01.htm	GHBP Product 1	5KB	htm	01/02/2004 23:28	defau
prod02.htm	GHBP Product 2	6KB	htm	31/01/2004 14:50	defau
prod03.htm	GHBP Product 3	6KB	htm	31/01/2004 14:50	defau
prod04.htm	GHBP Product 4	6KB	htm	31/01/2004 14:50	defau
products.htm	GHBP Products Page	5KB	htm	01/02/2004 09:32	defau
search.htm	GHBP Search Page	3KB	htm	31/01/2004 14:50	defau
toc.htm	GHBP Table of Contents P...	6KB	htm	31/01/2004 14:50	defau

5 You will need to complete the details for Product 2. Double click on **prod02.htm** to select it.

The web page for Product 2 appears and you can input the product details.

6 Click on the banner heading:

Product 2

7 In the window which appears, change Product 2 to *Marigold: French*.

This part of the screen will now look like this:

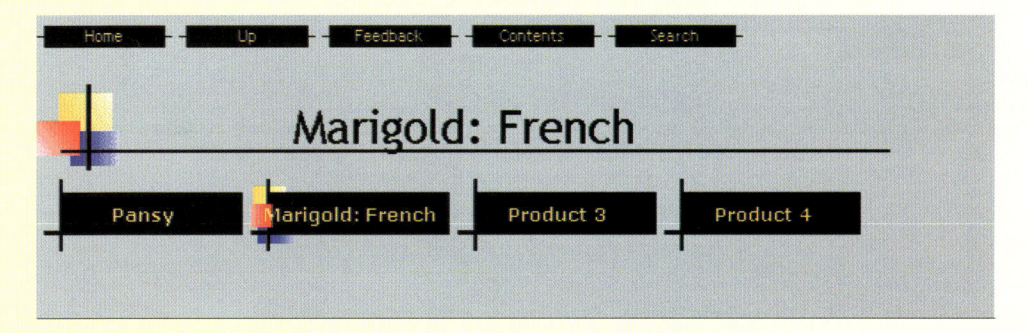

Marigold: French

8 You are now going to insert a photograph of a Marigold.

Click on **Product Image** to select it (you will see the squares (called handles) around the image). Click on **Edit** and then **Cut**.

This removes the marker Product Image.

To insert the photograph, click on **Insert** then **Picture** and then **From File**.

107

Unit 2 Publishing on the web

Your teacher will tell you where the photograph has been stored. The file you need to insert is called Marigold.

9 Delete the existing text and replace it with the text shown in the following screenshot:

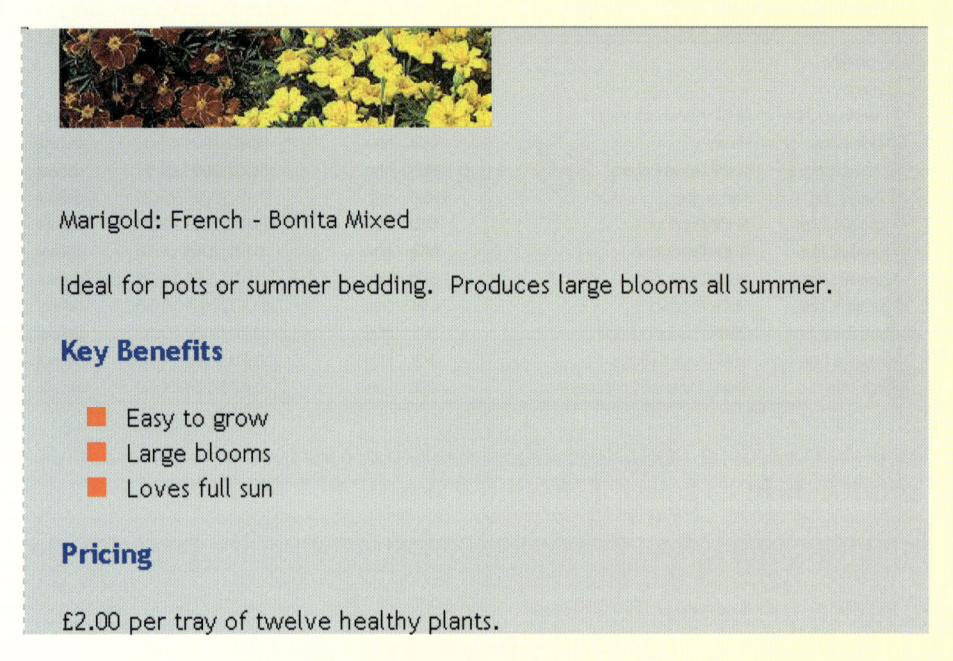

Marigold: French - Bonita Mixed

Ideal for pots or summer bedding. Produces large blooms all summer.

Key Benefits

- Easy to grow
- Large blooms
- Loves full sun

Pricing

£2.00 per tray of twelve healthy plants.

10 You have now completed the web page for the Marigold plants.

Save your page. To do this click on **File** and then **Save**.

The following window appears:

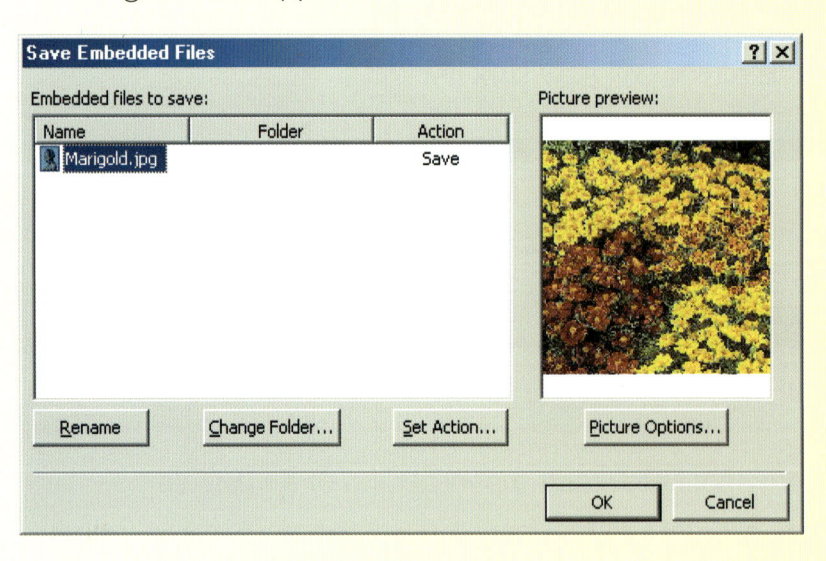

Click on the **OK** button.

11 Now click on **File** and then **Close Web**.

108

Lesson 7 Completing the website for the bedding plants project

ACTIVITY 17: Adding the product details for the Lobelia and the Alyssum

You now have to repeat the processes to build the web pages for the other two types of plant (i.e. Lobelia and Alyssum). Just follow the steps in Activity 16, remembering that the Lobelia is prod03.htm and the Alyssum is prod04.htm.

You will find the images for the Lobelia and the Alyssum in the same place as the other plants.

Here are the details you will need to include for each plant:

Banner heading: Lobelia

Caption: Lobelia – Cambridge Blue

Easy to grow plants for tubs, pots or hanging baskets.

Key Benefits

Easy to grow

Likes sun or shade

Lots of sky-blue flowers

Pricing

£2.00 per tray of twelve healthy plants.

Banner Heading: Alyssum

Caption: Alyssum

Great for edging borders. Produces a carpet of white flowers throughout the summer.

Key Benefits

Very easy to grow

Good for exposed sites

Continuous white flowers all summer

Pricing

£2.00 per tray of twelve healthy plants.

When you have completed this your web pages will look like these:

Lobelia - Cambridge Blue

Easy to grow plants for tubs, pots or hanging baskets.

Key Benefits

- Easy to grow
- Likes sun or shade
- Lots of sky blue flowers

Pricing

£2.00 per tray of twelve healthy plants.

Unit 2 Publishing on the web

Alyssum

Great for edging borders. Produces a carpet of white flowers throughout the summer.

Key Benefits

- Very easy to grow
- Good for exposed sites
- Continuous white flowers all summer

Pricing

£2.00 per tray of twelve healthy plants.

You have now completed the products section of your website.

You can see all of the pages for the products.

```
products.htm  prod02.htm  prod03.htm  prod04.htm  prod01.htm
```

Remember to save these web pages.

If you click on **Tasks**, you will see that the window has changed and it now shows that the task of customising the products has been completed.

Status	Task	Assigned To	Priority	Associated With	Modified Date	Description
● Completed	Customize Products P…	default	High	GHBP Products Page	06/02/2004 10:…	create data sheets fo
● Not Started	Customize Feedback …	default	Medium	GHBP Feedback Page	31/01/2004 14:…	adjust input areas in
● Not Started	Customize TOC Page	default	Medium	GHBP Table of Contents P…	31/01/2004 14:…	describe sections in r
● Not Started	Customize Search Page	default	Medium	GHBP Search Page	31/01/2004 14:…	explain how to searcl

Lesson 8: CREATING A FEEDBACK FORM AND A TABLE OF CONTENTS FOR THE BEDDING PLANTS WEBSITE PROJECT

Background

In this lesson you will be adding further features to the website you created in the previous two lessons. You will create a form where

Lesson 8 Creating a feedback form and a table of contents

visitors to the site can leave comments as well as contact details for more information. You will also create a table of contents.

Make it happen

ACTIVITY 18: Creating a form where customers and other visitors to the website can leave comments

In this activity you will continue building the website using FrontPage to create a feedback page where customers and other visitors to the site can leave comments.

1 Double click on the next task in the list of tasks:

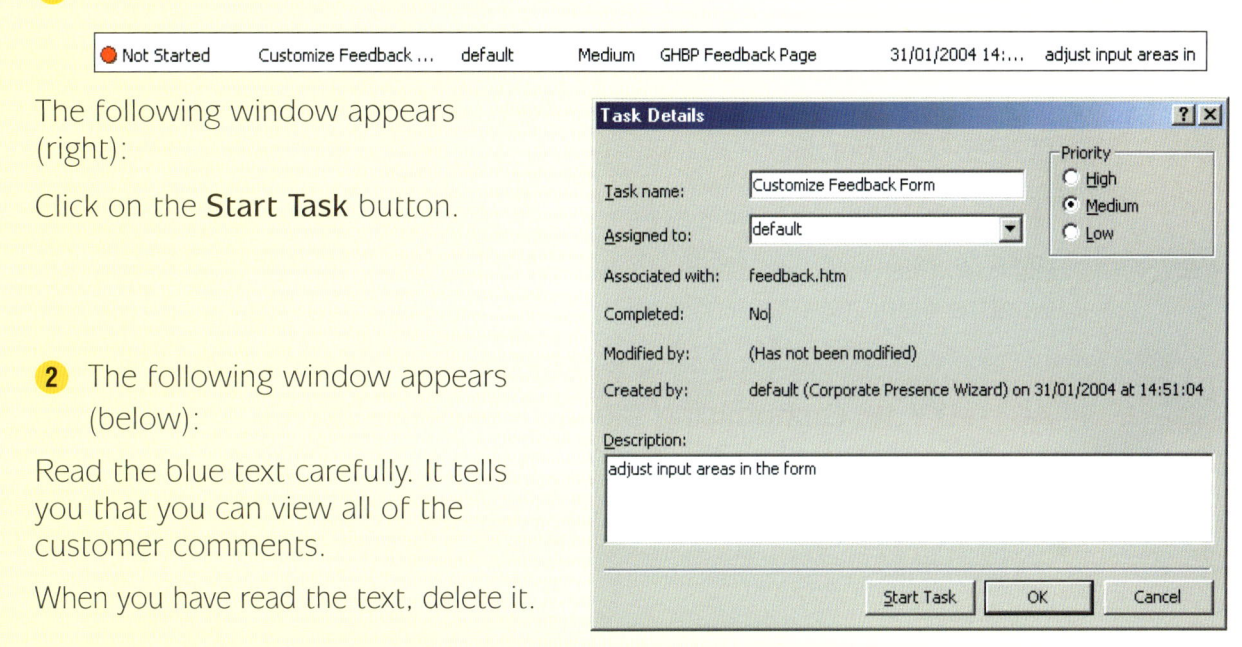

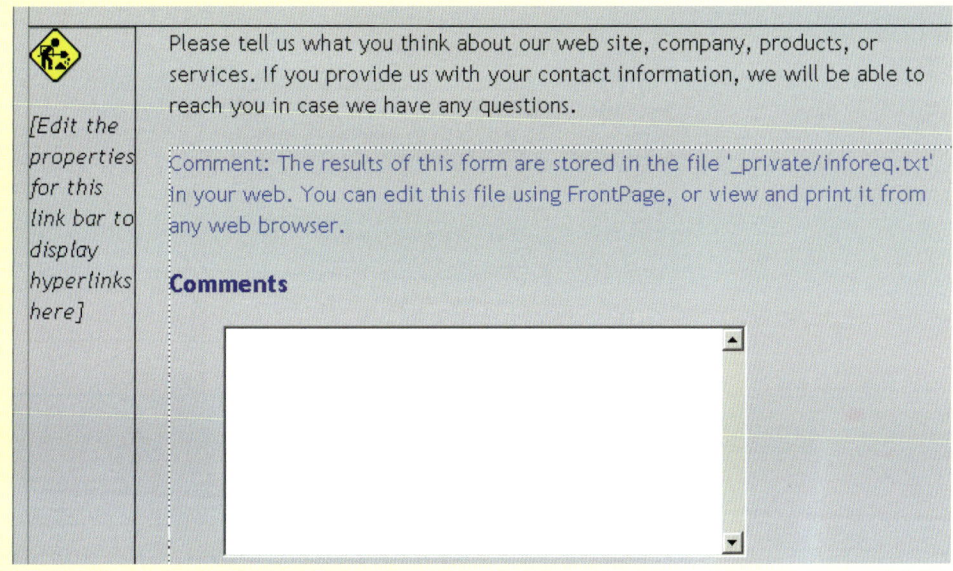

| ● Not Started | Customize Feedback ... | default | Medium | GHBP Feedback Page | 31/01/2004 14:... | adjust input areas in |

The following window appears (right):

Click on the **Start Task** button.

Task Details dialog:
- Task name: Customize Feedback Form
- Assigned to: default
- Associated with: feedback.htm
- Completed: No
- Modified by: (Has not been modified)
- Created by: default (Corporate Presence Wizard) on 31/01/2004 at 14:51:04
- Description: adjust input areas in the form
- Priority: Medium

2 The following window appears (below):

Read the blue text carefully. It tells you that you can view all of the customer comments.

When you have read the text, delete it.

[Edit the properties for this link bar to display hyperlinks here]

Please tell us what you think about our web site, company, products, or services. If you provide us with your contact information, we will be able to reach you in case we have any questions.

Comment: The results of this form are stored in the file '_private/inforeq.txt' in your web. You can edit this file using FrontPage, or view and print it from any web browser.

Comments

111

Unit 2 Publishing on the web

3 Scroll down the screen and you will see the boxes where the customers can put their comments.

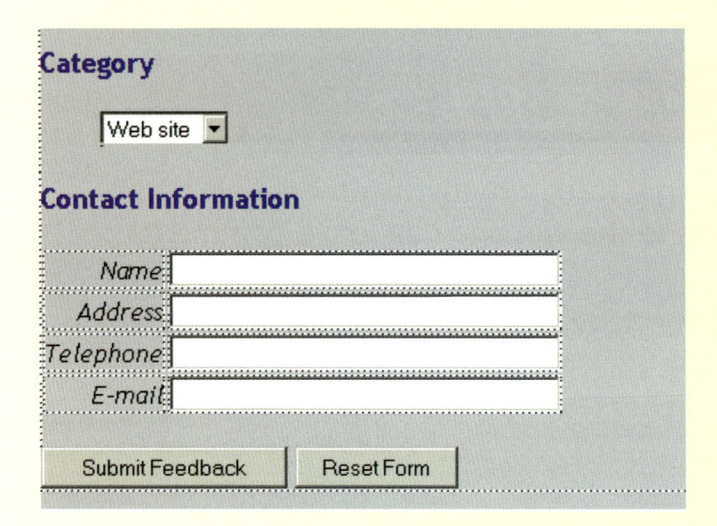

Notice that as well as making comments, the customers can also leave their contact details.

4 There are no more changes to the feedback page.

Click on **File** and then **Save** to save the page. If you are asked if you want to mark the task as being completed, just click on **Yes**.

ACTIVITY 19: Customising the table of contents

1 If you need to, load FrontPage and open the file used to store your website.

Click on **Tasks** to see what is left to do in order to complete your website.

2 Double click on **Customize TOC** in the list of tasks. The following window will appear:

Now click on **Start Task**.

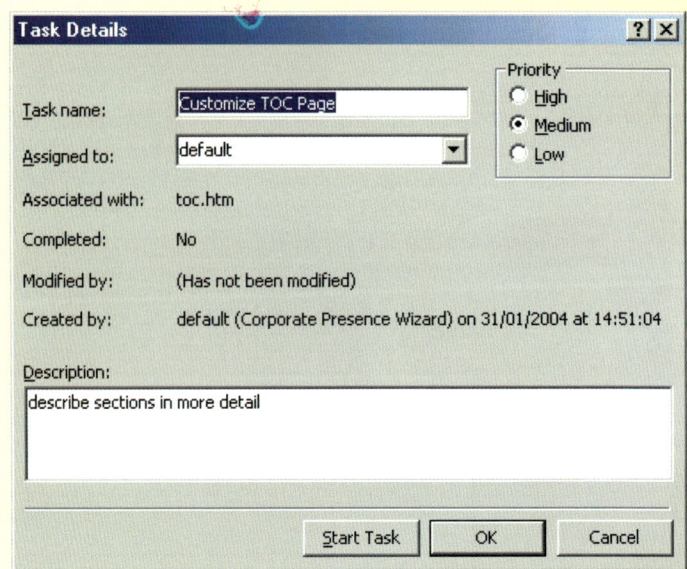

Lesson 8 Creating a feedback form and a table of contents

3 Click on the following text and then delete it.

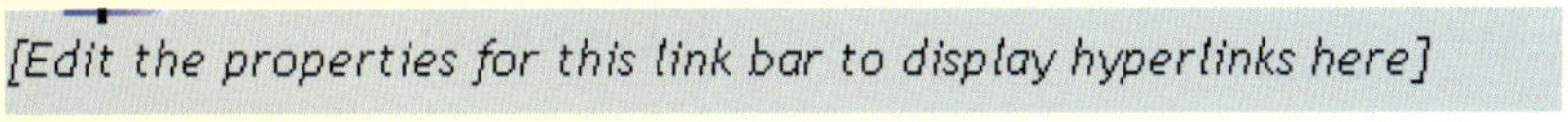

[Edit the properties for this link bar to display hyperlinks here]

4 Double click on the following:

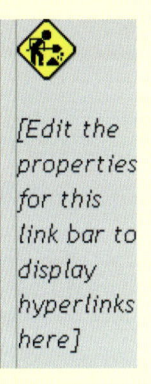

[Edit the properties for this link bar to display hyperlinks here]

The following window will open:

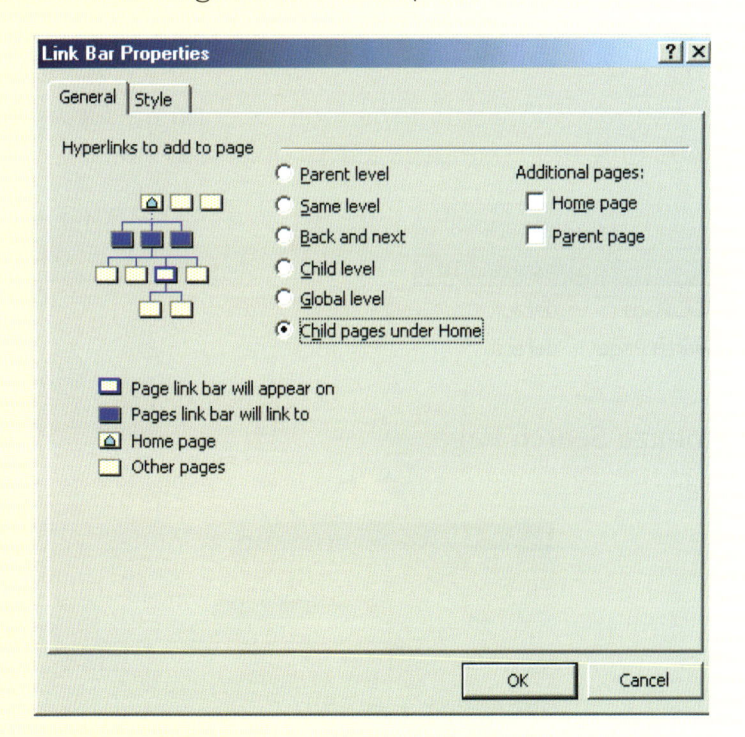

Select **Child pages under Home** by clicking it, and then click on the **OK** button.

Hyperlinks have now been established to the two web pages News and Home.

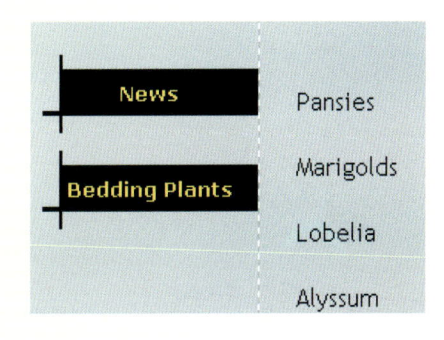

113

Unit 2 Publishing on the web

5 To see how this table of contents web page will appear when a user looks at it, click on the preview button **Preview**.

6 Click on the Normal button: **Normal** to go back to the page where you can edit the web page.

7 You have now completed the table of contents page.

Save this page by clicking on 💾.

The following window (right) appears asking if you want to mark the task as complete:

Click on the **Yes** button.

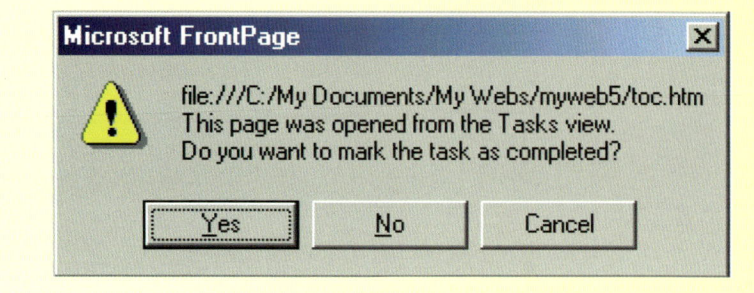

> **Microsoft FrontPage**
> file:///C:/My Documents/My Webs/myweb5/toc.htm
> This page was opened from the Tasks view.
> Do you want to mark the task as completed?
> [Yes] [No] [Cancel]

8 Click on **Tasks**.

The following information is shown. Notice that the table of contents has been completed and that you only have one page left to finish the site.

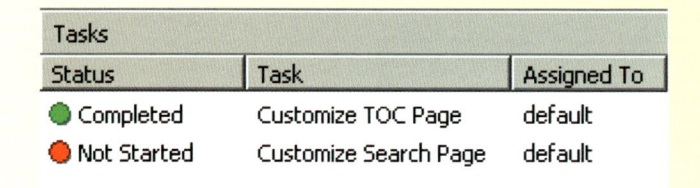

Tasks		
Status	Task	Assigned To
● Completed	Customize TOC Page	default
● Not Started	Customize Search Page	default

9 Double click on **Customize Search Page**.

The following window opens explaining what this task involves:

Click on the **Start Task** button.

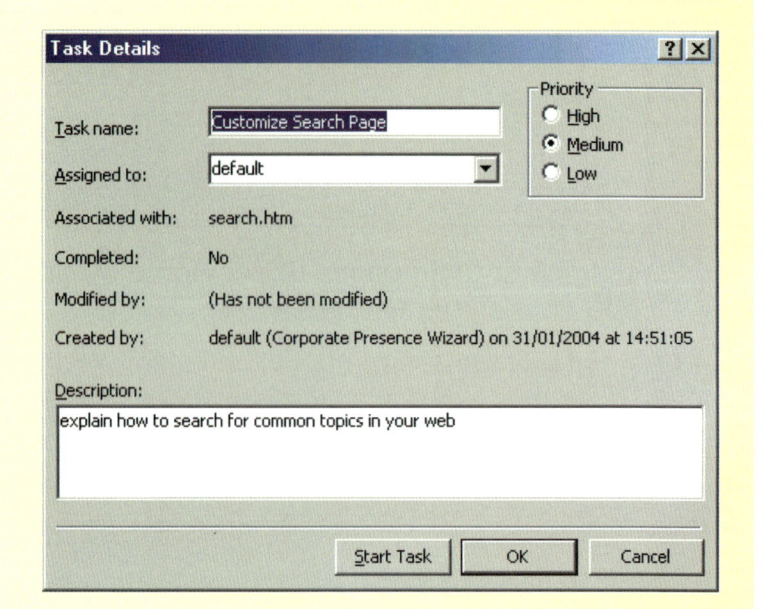

> **Task Details**
> Priority: ○ High ● Medium ○ Low
> Task name: Customize Search Page
> Assigned to: default
> Associated with: search.htm
> Completed: No
> Modified by: (Has not been modified)
> Created by: default (Corporate Presence Wizard) on 31/01/2004 at 14:51:05
> Description:
> explain how to search for common topics in your web
> [Start Task] [OK] [Cancel]

Lesson 8 Creating a feedback form and a table of contents

10 The following web page appears. Visitors to your site will be able to search for specific terms using this page.

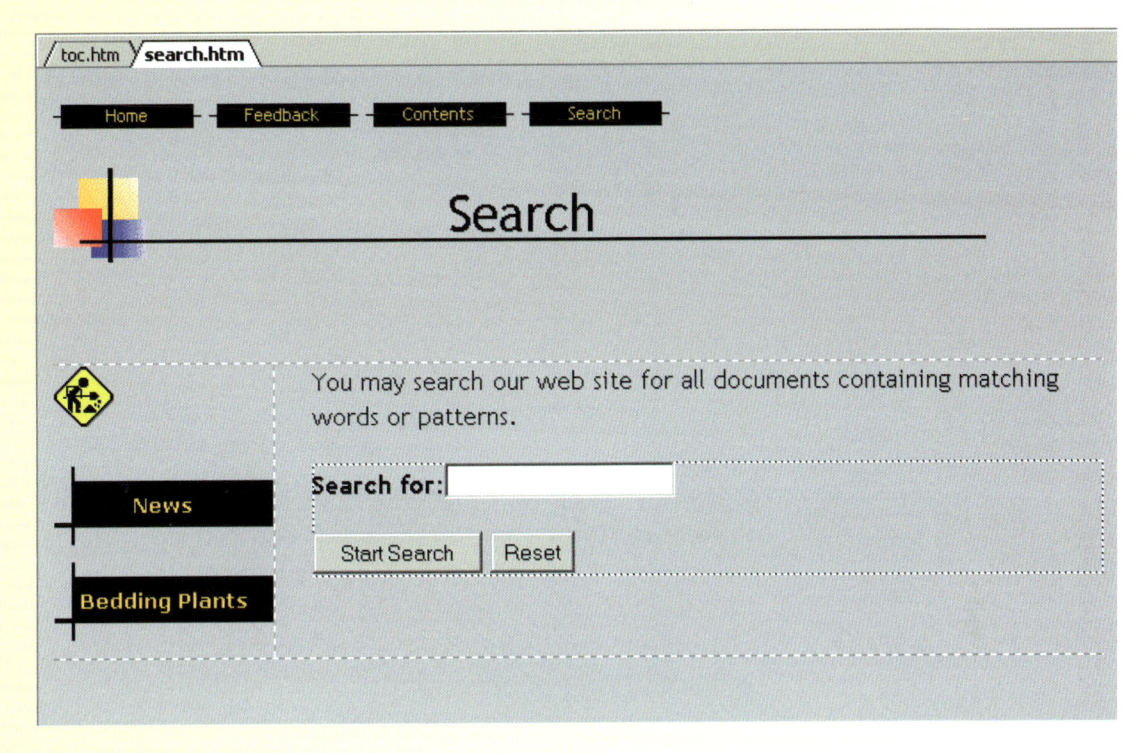

You do not need to add anything to this page.

11 You have now completed the Search page.

Save this page by clicking on ▣.

The following window appears asking if you want to mark the task as complete.

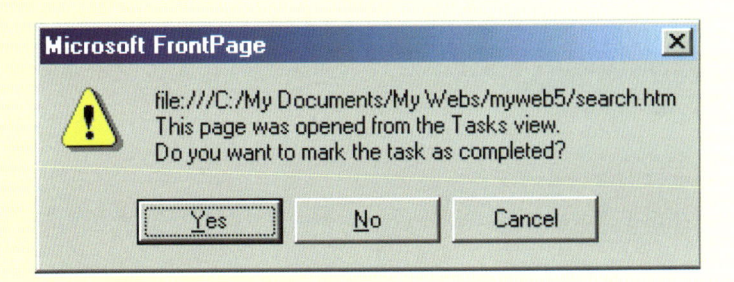

Click on the **Yes** button.

12 Click on **Tasks** Tasks .

Notice that the Search page has been completed.

13 Close down the software.

115

Unit 2 Publishing on the web

QUESTIONS

1. Why do most websites contain a search facility?

2. Give two ways that the customer feedback form might be used with the bedding plants project website.

3. Do you think this site could be used by customers to place their orders for trays of bedding plants? Explain your answer.

Lesson 9: CHECKING AND PUBLISHING THE WEBSITE

You have now completed the website for the bedding plants project. It is important that you check it carefully before putting it onto a web server (i.e. a computer that is permanently connected to the Internet). In many cases the web server will be provided by your Internet Service Provider (i.e. the company that you use to provide your Internet connection).

Make it happen

ACTIVITY 20: Checking the website

1. Load FrontPage and your bedding plant website.

2. Click on **Navigation** in the **Views** section of the screen.

!Note
Your view may look different as it depends on the files that are open.

3. Navigation lets you see how each of the pages is navigated. The following screen shows the first layer.

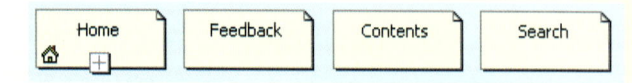

You can see that there is a home page and three other pages. The other pages are actually separate sites.

116

Lesson 9 Checking and publishing the website

4 The cross on the home page tells you that you can expand this to show other pages in lower levels.

Click on the cross and the following view appears:

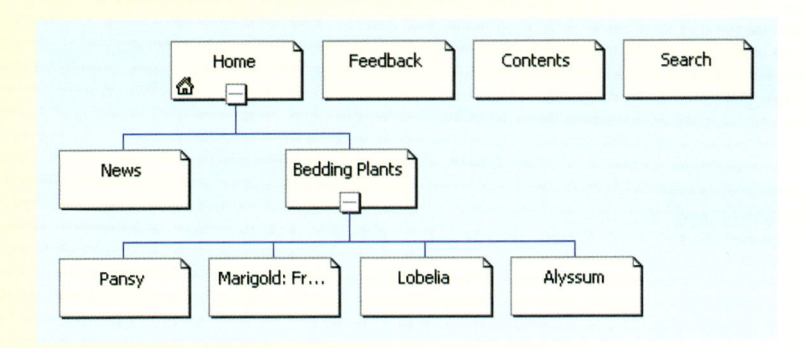

You can now see all of the web pages in this site and also the other sites included in the project. Notice that the separate sites, Feedback, Contents and Search, are at the same level as the Home page.

5 If you click on the minus sign on **Bedding Plants** you can collapse the lower layer and move to the layer one up as shown here:

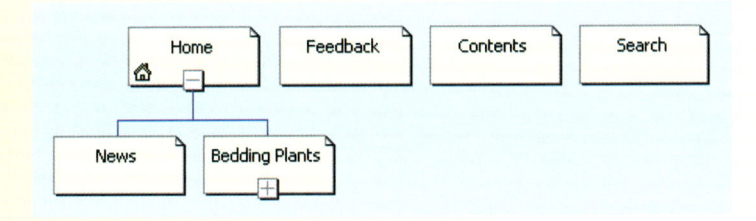

6 Now click on **Folders** in the View section of the screen.

The following screen shows the files associated with this project.

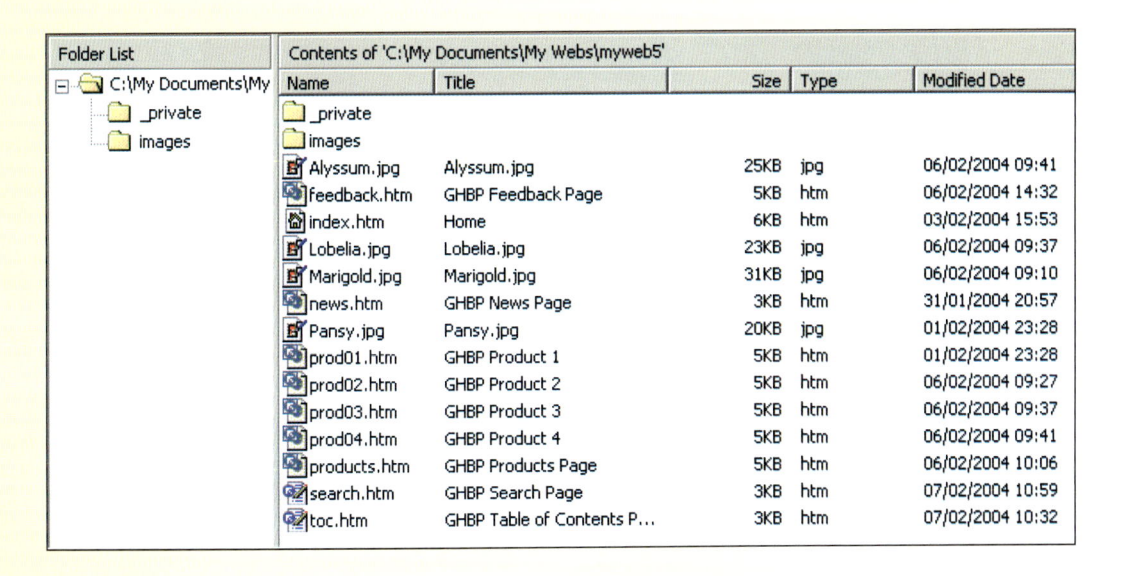

Name	Title	Size	Type	Modified Date
_private				
images				
Alyssum.jpg	Alyssum.jpg	25KB	jpg	06/02/2004 09:41
feedback.htm	GHBP Feedback Page	5KB	htm	06/02/2004 14:32
index.htm	Home	6KB	htm	03/02/2004 15:53
Lobelia.jpg	Lobelia.jpg	23KB	jpg	06/02/2004 09:37
Marigold.jpg	Marigold.jpg	31KB	jpg	06/02/2004 09:10
news.htm	GHBP News Page	3KB	htm	31/01/2004 20:57
Pansy.jpg	Pansy.jpg	20KB	jpg	01/02/2004 23:28
prod01.htm	GHBP Product 1	5KB	htm	01/02/2004 23:28
prod02.htm	GHBP Product 2	5KB	htm	06/02/2004 09:27
prod03.htm	GHBP Product 3	5KB	htm	06/02/2004 09:37
prod04.htm	GHBP Product 4	5KB	htm	06/02/2004 09:41
products.htm	GHBP Products Page	5KB	htm	06/02/2004 10:06
search.htm	GHBP Search Page	3KB	htm	07/02/2004 10:59
toc.htm	GHBP Table of Contents P...	3KB	htm	07/02/2004 10:32

Unit 2 Publishing on the web

7. You need to go through each of the web pages in turn and check the spelling and grammar and at the same time make sure that any of the stray placeholder text has been deleted.

As the project is now complete you can remove all the 'under construction' signs .

To do this, click on the picture and then **Edit** and **Cut**.

8. Now click on **Preview**. You can check the structure of the website by clicking on the links and check that each one takes you to the right place.

If you need to make any changes, then these cannot be made in the Preview view and you will need to click on **Normal**.

9. You have now completed this project and have created a proper website with lots of advanced features. Well done!

Publishing your site

Publishing a website means making the website available to the outside world by publishing it on the Internet. In order to publish a website on the Internet it is necessary to copy all of the website files to a web server.

Make it happen

ACTIVITY 21: Publishing the website

To publish your website, follow these instructions.

1. Connect to the Internet.

2. Load FrontPage.

3. Open the website you wish to publish.

4. Click on **File** and then **Publish Web**.

Lesson 10 Evaluating a website

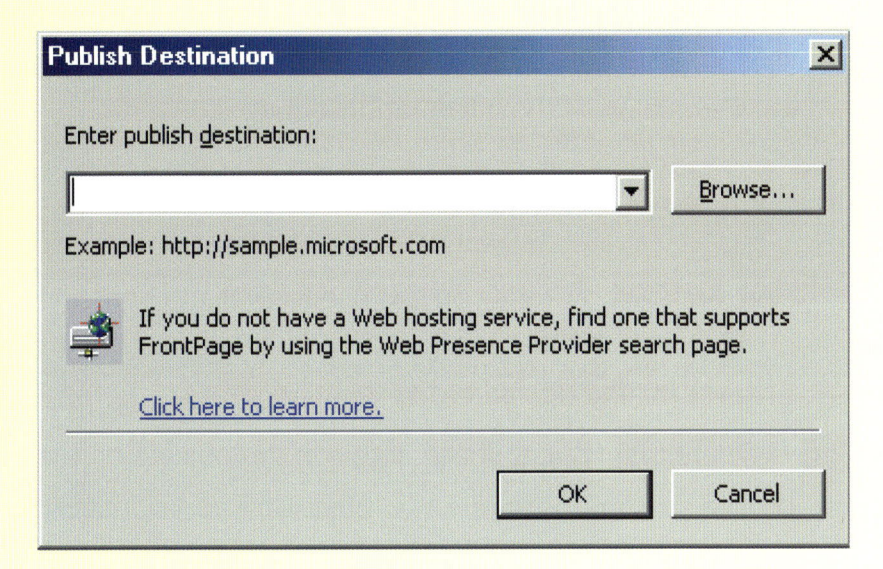

In the box that appears you need to type the web address of the site on which you intend to publish the pages. Your teacher will give you more information on this.

When you have entered the website address, click on the **OK** button.

5. You will be prompted for your user ID and password and your teacher will tell you what to enter.

6. Your pages will now be copied to the server.

7. You can use a browser to open your own website and view it in the same way as a user would view it.

Lesson 10: EVALUATING A WEBSITE

Background

In the first lesson you looked at what makes a good website. After you have made your website you need to be as critical of your own work as you would be of others'.

In evaluating your website you need to think about the following aspects of the site:

- The structure of the site.
- The design of the pages.
- The quality of the information included.

Criteria for evaluating websites

Here are some criteria you can use to evaluate your website.

Criteria for the design of the website pages

- There is sufficient space between the objects on the page.
- The size and position of an object are appropriate for its relative importance.
- The images and any sounds selected for the page are relevant.
- The layout and use of colour would be attractive to an adult.

Criteria for the structure of the site

- It is easy to navigate and find your way around.
- Menus and hyperlinks help you to find the information that you want.

Criteria for the quality of information

Some features of a good website

Lesson 10 Evaluating a website

- The information is comprehensive, up to date and clear.
- The language used is easy to understand.
- The information matches the needs of the intended audience.

Make it happen

ACTIVITY 22: Evaluating the bedding plants project website

Although you did not produce the bedding plants project website on your own, it is still useful to be able to evaluate it.

Use the headings in the section 'Criteria for evaluating websites' above to evaluate this website. Make sure that you consider all of the criteria under the headings given.

ACTIVITY 23: Evaluating the work you did for this unit

In this activity you are required to evaluate how well you did the work in this unit. Being able to evaluate your learning is important because you can learn from the mistakes you made and you can set personal targets on how you will improve your work in future.

You need to write your evaluation under each of the following headings:

- What I learnt.
- My confidence in being able to create a web page or website.
- What I found easy.
- What I found hard.
- The method I would use when creating websites in the future.
- How I can improve on my future work.

3 Information: reliability, validity and bias

Lesson 1: INTRODUCTION TO INFORMATION: RELIABILITY, VALIDITY AND BIAS

Data and information sources

In the first part of this unit you will be using data and information sources. You will look closely at the information to see whether it is fact or opinion or a mixture of both. You will look at the information to see whose viewpoint it represents and to decide if the information is clear, easy to understand and plausible.

The unit will show you how well the information that you are collecting supports the task you are doing. It teaches you how to select the best information for the job. You will learn how to justify the use of a particular information source as part of your information gathering.

The unit suggests the various ways you might check information on CD-ROMs and websites for reliability, validity and bias.

In the second part of the unit your knowledge of how to conduct searches using the Internet (covered in Year 7 Unit 2) will be expanded on. This material will enable you to search for relevant and accurate information as quickly as possible.

Background theory and key information

You use information sources all the time – weather reports in the paper, TV guides, football match reports, railway timetables, etc. Some sources are based on fact, some are based on opinion and some are a mixture of the two. It is important to know the difference between fact and opinion. Some people say things that they believe are fact but they are merely opinions.

Facts, opinions or a combination of both?

To be a skilled user of information you need to be able to distinguish between fact and opinion.

Lesson 1 Introduction to information: reliability, validity and bias

In the newspaper industry there is a saying, 'Never let the truth get in the way of a good story'

What are facts?

Here is some information about facts:

- Facts are statements that can be checked by others.
- Facts are usually presented as simple statements.
- Facts can be supported by evidence.
- Facts are based on direct evidence, actual experience or observation.
- Facts do not depend on the person making the statement.

If a fact is debatable, the words 'possibly' and 'probably' are often included in the sentence.

Facts can be proved:

- Your date of birth – this can be proved by your birth certificate or hospital records.
- The speed of light is 300 000 000 metres per second – this can be proved by experiment.
- England won the Rugby World Cup in 2003 – I watched them win it on TV.

What is an opinion?

Here is some information about opinions:

- An opinion is a statement of belief or feeling (i.e. a personal point of view).

Unit 3 Information: reliability, validity and bias

- An opinion is a statement that cannot be proven to be true or false.
- An opinion is what one person thinks or believes.
- An opinion will vary depending on the person making the statement.

Opinions express personal judgement about something. Look out for the following words. If they appear in a sentence, then it is probably an opinion.

- Best
- Worst
- Better
- Worse
- Lovely
- Disgusting
- Good
- Bad
- Beautiful
- Wonderful
- Terrible
- Great
- Probably

All of these words depend on the person saying them. A bad meal to one person may be a good meal to another.

A statement of opinion may be presented as if it was a fact if there is evidence to support it. The quality of the evidence may be debatable. Advertisers use this technique to persuade us to buy their products or services.

It is not always easy to separate facts from opinions.

- The best car is a Ferrari – the word 'best' can mean different things to different people.
- Burgers are better than pizza – this statement sounds like a fact. What it probably should say is, 'I prefer burgers to pizza'.

Lesson 1 Introduction to information: reliability, validity and bias

ACTIVITIESACTIVITIESACTIVITIESACTIVITIESACTIVITIESACTIVITIES

ACTIVITY 1: Spot the word

1. Certain words often change a statement from a fact to an opinion. Write down the word or words that make you think the following are opinions rather than facts.

    (a) Carlsberg lager is probably the best lager in the world.

    (b) Researchers seem to agree that a moderate consumption of alcohol, of about one to three units a day, is beneficial to health.

    (c) Switzerland possibly has the most stunning scenery in the whole of Europe.

    (d) I think that crime is getting worse in our cities.

    (e) Taking vitamin C tablets will probably not prevent you from getting a cold.

    (f) Liver is disgusting and I never eat it.

    (g) Justin Timberlake is the best singer in the world.

    (h) Go to the new bar in town. You will have a great evening, like we did on Saturday.

    (i) We had a terrible holiday. Our room was near a disco and we were woken up by the noise.

    (j) The dress is lovely, even if my mum and dad don't like it.

2. Read the following:

    I have just bought a new car. It is silver with twin exhausts and a great music system. I have put neon lights under the car so it looks really cool in the dark. I can cruise along the high street with my music blasting and everyone can see how cool I am. All the girls will fancy me now and the car will be worth all the money I have spent on it.

    (a) Write down two facts about the car.

    (b) Write down two opinions that the owner has about the car.

3. Read the following:

    I went to see Justin Timberlake in Manchester's MEN Arena last Monday. It was the best concert

REMEMBER!

Opinions are often masked as facts particularly in advertisements.

Facts can change as time goes on.

The world is flat – this was once a 'fact' but we now know that it was actually an opinion. We can now say that people once thought the earth was flat.

A fact that is a fact now may well turn out to be an opinion.

Unit 3 Information: reliability, validity and bias

ever. He sang all his hits and some new material. I went with three friends and they all thought he was cool. Afterwards we went to McDonald's for Big Mac and chips.

KEY WORDS

fact – truth or reality as distinct from mere statement or belief

opinion – a belief or judgement that is likely to be true but is not based on proof

(a) Write down two facts in the above passage.

(b) Write down two opinions in the passage.

WORKSHEET

WORKSHEET 8.3.1 Fact or opinion?

You may be given a worksheet on which to write your answers or you may be asked to write your answers in your book. When you have finished, your teacher will either go through the answers or give you an answer sheet so that you can check the answers yourself.

Decide whether each of the following statements is fact or opinion.

Statement	Fact	Opinion
Coronation Street is better than *EastEnders*.		
Jupiter is the largest planet in our solar system.		
There are 12 months in the year.		
Monday always follows Sunday.		
Will Young became famous through a TV programme called *Pop Idol*.		
Football is a better game than rugby.		
Mobile phones are dangerous to use because of the harmful radiation they give out.		
Liverpool is 197 miles from London.		
Taking vitamin C can help prevent colds.		
A low-fat diet is a more healthy one.		
Smoking is dangerous for your health.		
Water boils at 100°C at sea level.		
Athens is the capital of Greece.		

If you compare your answers with those of other students in your group you will see that they may differ. This shows that separating fact from opinion is not easy.

Lesson 1 Introduction to information: reliability, validity and bias

Some quotes from the past

If someone who is a world expert in their field says something, then you would normally think that it is a fact. However, even experts can get it wrong, especially if they try to predict the future. Here are some examples:

- In 1977 Ken Olsen, the founder of DEC (a large computer company), said, 'There is no reason for any individual to have a computer in their home.'
- In 1943 Thomas Watson, the chairman of IBM, said, 'I think there is a world market for maybe five computers.'
- In 1895 Lord Kelvin, the president of the Royal Society, said, 'Heavier-than-air flying machines are impossible.'
- In 1962 a spokesperson for the record company Decca Recording Co. said when rejecting the Beatles, 'We don't like their sound, and guitar music is on the way out.'
- In 1981 Bill Gates, the main person behind the computer company Microsoft, said, '640K ought to be enough for anybody.' (This refers to the amount of memory needed by a computer and most computers now have around 512 000K of memory.)

It is easy to look back and laugh at these statements. At the time, would they have been facts or opinions? In their day, how accurate and reliable would these statements have been? As all of the people concerned were authorities in their field, the statements would have been considered accurate and reliable. The individuals would have had all the information needed on which to base their statements. The main problem is that all of these statements try to predict the future and the future is almost impossible to predict.

Bogus information

Bogus information is false information and its purpose is to misinform or deceive. When looking at any website you should ask if the information it contains is plausible. Plausible information is information that is reasonable or likely to be true. Using your experience and knowledge of the world you can usually spot bogus information.

You came across bogus information and bogus sites last year.

REMEMBER

If you have a quote and you want to find out who said it and when you can simply type the exact quote enclosed between quotation marks into a search engine. Exact matches will be found and normally this will give you the required information.

Note

Bogus information is not necessarily given as a joke to catch you out. Some bogus information deliberately sets out to tell you lies.

KEY WORDS

plausible – the information is reasonable or likely to be true

Unit 3 Information: reliability, validity and bias

ACTIVITY 2: Spot the bogus information

You had some practice at spotting bogus websites last year. In this activity you have to look carefully at two sites and say which one is the real site and which is the bogus site.

Genetics is an important branch of biology. Which of these two sites will give real and accurate information about genetics?

- Site 1: **http://gslc.genetics.utah.edu/**
- Site 2: **www.genochoice.com/**

When you have decided, you should write down a few reasons for your choice.

Here are some more sites. Which of them are genuine and why?

- Site 1: **www.zapatopi.net/afdb.html#WHAT**
- Site 2: **www.birdfood.co.uk/**
- Site 3: **www.petsorfood.com/**

Reliability of information

Reliable information is information that you can trust and rely on.

To get reliable information you need to look at a reliable source. It is easier to get reliable information from books as these are normally written by experts in their field and lots of people check the material. If information is obtained from the World Wide Web, i.e. the Internet, then you need to check its reliability.

One way of ensuring that information is reliable is to use a reliable website. You can use the URL as an indicator of a website's reliability.

The URL is often referred to as the website address. It is what you type in to locate the website.

A website's URL is like a telephone number is to a telephone or a postal address is to a house. URLs can be quite long and if you think you might need to use a site again, it is worth saving the location in your Favourites. You can compile a list of your favourite websites and simply click on the name rather than type in the URL.

KEY WORDS

reliable – the information is dependable or trustworthy

web page – a single document on the World Wide Web, usually containing links to other web pages

website – a site on the Internet containing information. It consists of one or more web pages

World Wide Web (www) – a huge collection of web pages and other material, such as files for downloading, that you can access. This material is held on millions of computers all around the world

Lesson 1 Introduction to information: reliability, validity and bias

IT IS THE NEW POLICE INTERNET CRIME UNIT...

REMEMBER!

URL is another name for the website or web page address. Look at the glossary at the back of the book for a comprehensive definition.

Making sense of the URL

Look at the following URL: **www.edgehill.ac.uk**.

- edgehill is the domain name and basically it identifies the host computer or service on the Internet;
- ac tells you that it is an academic website (this part is called the domain type);
- uk tells you that the website is situated in the UK.

Domain types may be any of the following:

- .org is a non-profit organisation such as a charity.
- .ac is an academic institution such as a college or university.
- .gov is a government website.
- .sch is a school website.
- .com is a company or commercial organisation (usually an international one).
- .co.uk is a company or commercial organisation in the UK.

ACTIVITY 3: Predicting URLs

What would you expect the URLs to be for the following? Write down the URL you would expect to see and check it by typing it on the Internet to see if you were right. If you were wrong, use a search engine such as Yahoo to find the correct URL.

129

Unit 3 Information: reliability, validity and bias

WORKSHEET WORKSHEET WORKSHEET WORKSHEET WORKSHEET

WORKSHEET 8.3.2 **How accurate and reliable is the information on these sites?**

You may be given a worksheet on which to write your answers or you may be asked to write your answers in your book. When you have finished, your teacher will either go through the answers or give you an answer sheet so that you can check the answers yourself.

Access each of the following websites. Ask yourself how accurate and reliable the information on each of them is and score them according to the following scale:

Reliability				
Most				Least
1	2	3	4	5

Accuracy				
Most				Least
1	2	3	4	5

Site 1: www.flat-earth.org/

Accuracy score: ....

Reliability score: ....

Site 2: www.upmystreet.com

Accuracy score: ....

Reliability score: ....

Site 3: www.realaroma.com/

Accuracy score: ....

Reliability score: ....

Site 4: www.bbc.co.uk/

Accuracy score: ....

Reliability score: ....

Site 5: www.ovaprima.org/mission.html

Accuracy score: ....

Reliability score: ....

Site 6: www.amazon.co.uk

Accuracy score: ....

Reliability score: ....

Lesson 1 Introduction to information: reliability, validity and bias

Discussion points

When you have completed the worksheet your teacher will discuss the following points with you:

- Which website did you judge to be the least accurate and why?

Put your websites in order according to the total score for accuracy and then compare this with others in your class. If you have totally different scores, discuss the reasons why.

- The things you looked for when assessing the accuracy of a website.
- Whether the scores for accuracy and reliability were the same.
- The things you looked for when deciding on the scores.
- Which websites were commercial ones advertising goods to buy?

Biased information

Biased information favours a particular viewpoint and you need to be able to spot it. A lot of information is biased and is based on opinion rather than fact.

When you are reading information you should ask yourself whose viewpoint is being put forward and whether this viewpoint shows any bias.

KEY WORDS

biased – not balanced; favouring one side more than the other

viewpoint – an opinion or point of view

Is this website biased in some way?
Source: www.furshame.com

Unit 3 Information: reliability, validity and bias

KEY WORDS

accessible – easy to get at and understand

appraise – to decide on the quality or value of something such as information

precise – exact, clear and detailed

The validity of information

If you are researching a topic you need to make sure that the information you collect is both accurate and reliable. Information that is both accurate and reliable is said to be valid information.

Evaluating or appraising information

If information is valid, you can then evaluate or appraise it to look at its qualities. For example, you can check if the information is easy to get at and understand, i.e. the accessibility of the information. You can also look at how precise the information is.

QUESTIONS

1. Explain the difference between a fact and an opinion.

2. You are looking at a website. You suspect that the information on the site is bogus. State two things that you could look for to determine if the site is bogus or genuine.

3. You can often tell a genuine site from the URL.
   (a) Explain what is meant by 'URL'.
   (b) Explain one way you that could tell from the URL whether the site is a genuine one.

What you should already know

Much of the material in this unit relies on a good knowledge of the material in Unit 2 on Information and Presentation that you covered in Year 7. To a lesser extent, the unit also builds on the material in Year 7 Unit 8 on Public Information Systems.

Before starting this unit it will be helpful if you are able to:

- Search the Internet, CD-ROMs and other sources to find answers to simple queries.
- Cut, paste and save information from a number of sources to word processing, desktop publishing or presentation software packages.
- Export data from one package to another.

What you will learn

In this unit you will:

- Find and use a number of sources to select relevant information.
- Refine the information and use it to make informed judgements about the content and the messages websites want to give an intended audience.
- Understand how to learn and find things out for yourself.

Lesson 2: USING SEARCHES

Background

When you are looking for information on the Internet you are searching the largest collection of information in the world. Finding specific and useful information amongst all this is difficult. Luckily there are free programs available to help us; these are called search engines.

Sometimes you will have to perform searches for information in databases and these searches are often called queries. A query is a request for information from a database.

You will already have used search engines to find information on the Internet. Search engines were also mentioned in the Year 7 book.

As a reminder, here are some of the most popular search engines with their web addresses (URLs):

- www.yahoo.com or www.yahoo.co.uk
- www.google.com
- www.lycos.com
- www.ask.com

Search engines allow you to search the contents of millions of web pages at the same time. You are probably wondering why it takes so little time to do this. The answer is that you are searching a database of all the web pages on the computer of the search engine.

KEY WORDS

query – a request for information from a database

REMEMBER!

Use **www.yahoo.co.uk** if you want UK sites and **www.yahoo.com** if you want worldwide sites.

www.ask.com is the same as the AskJeeves search engine.

Getting at the information quicker

General searches using a single word will usually reveal lots of websites unless the word is obscure. The number of websites or web pages found in the search is sometimes referred to as the number of hits.

You need to be as specific as possible when searching. Understanding the way search engines work will enable you to carry out fast searches. Most people use several search engines, but unfortunately they do not all work in the same way. The search engine help screens will give you useful searching tips.

Unit 3 Information: reliability, validity and bias

Make it happen

ACTIVITY 4: Looking for alternative meanings using the thesaurus

Look for alternative meanings for each of the key words used in this unit.

FETCH THE THESAURUS

NO, NOT HIM! A THESAURUS IS A BOOK TO LOOK UP WORDS THAT HAVE SIMILAR MEANINGS

Use the thesaurus in Word to list synonyms, i.e. words with a meaning similar to the word that you are looking up.

By looking for alternative meanings for words you will understand the subtle differences in some of their meanings.

1. Load the word-processing software Word.

2. Create a new document and type in the following list of words as they appear here:

   Provenance   Authentic

   Reliability   Bias

   Relevant   Plausible

   Appraise   Viewpoint

KEY WORDS

synonym – a word that has the same meaning or almost the same meaning as another

3 Move the cursor so that it is on the first letter of the first word in the list.

4 Click **Tools** and then select **Language** and then **Thesaurus**.

5 The following window appears:

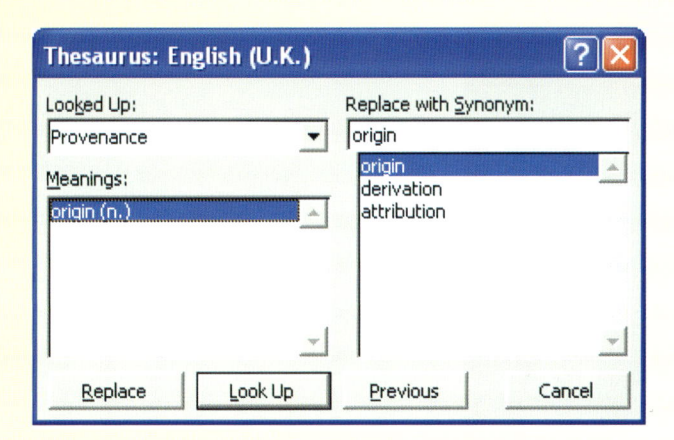

The words in the right-hand box are the synonyms (i.e. alternative words which have similar meanings).

6 Repeat this process with the other words and copy and complete the following table. The first answer has been inserted for you.

Original word	Synonym 1	Synonym 2
Provenance	Origin	Derivation
Reliability		
Relevant		
Appraise		
Authentic		
Bias		
Plausible		
Viewpoint		

Unit 3 Information: reliability, validity and bias

ACTIVITY 5: Narrowing down searches

Suppose you want to find out about the TV show *Dr Who*.

The eighth Doctor Who played by Paul McGann

You will be using the search engine Google to find suitable information. You could type in *TV show*, but this would be too general and would result in a huge number of websites to sift through.

1. Access the search engine Google by typing in its URL: **www.google.com**.

2. In the Google search box type in *Dr Who*.

3.

The words 'Dr Who' are typed into the search box
Source: **www.google.com**

When you press the Google Search button the search is performed.

The results are surprising. Google leaves out of the search any common words, and 'who' is one of the words excluded. Therefore, we have only searched for 'Dr'.

Words such as 'who', 'why', 'where', etc. are left out because they slow down the search and do not really improve the results.

Lesson 2 Using searches

4 Try the search again, this time putting quotation marks around the two words like this:

| "Dr Who" | Google Search |

By including quotation marks like this the common words are still included in the search. You are now searching for the exact phrase or combination of words.

You can see there are lots of sites so we need to narrow down the search and be more specific.

5 Suppose you want a list of all the actors who have played Dr Who over the years. How might we do this?

Try typing in this:

| "Actors who played Dr Who" | Google Search |

6 You can see there are lots of promising sites to check out.

The search results enable you to click on websites that look promising

Source: www.google.com

7 Look through the list of sites and pick one that looks promising. Click on it and see if it gives the required information, but be mindful of the reliability and accuracy. It is best to look at the information on another site to see if it is the same.

8 Write a list of the names of actors who have played Dr Who.

Unit 3 Information: reliability, validity and bias

ACTIVITY 6: Using the advanced search

1. Access the opening screen of Google.

2. Look at the opening screen. It tells you how many web pages the search engine can look through. This changes from day to day as more websites are added. Make a note of the current number.

   Click on the **Advanced Search** option.

The opening screen of the Google search engine. Notice the advanced search facility on the right of this screen

Source: www.google.com

3. Look at the first part of the screen. This is the part shown in the following diagram:

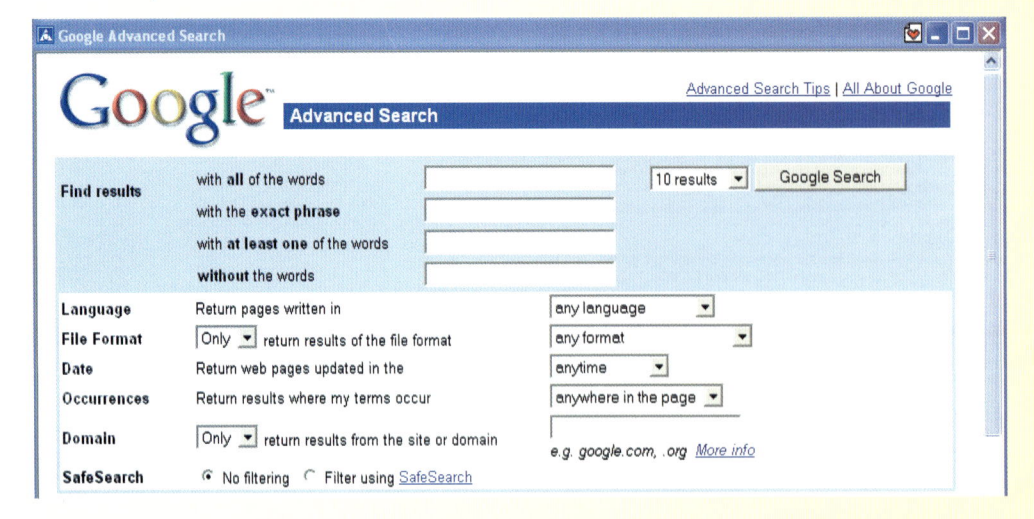

The Advanced Search in Google can be used to make the search more specific

Source: www.google.com

Notice the **Find results** section. By putting words into this section you can get relevant information quickly.

Lesson 2 Using searches

4 Suppose you wanted to go on a trip to Liverpool.

Type *Liverpool* into the first box and then click on the search button.

| with **all** of the words | Liverpool | 10 results ▼ | Google Search |

With Liverpool typed in the search box you will find lots of websites containing the word Liverpool

Source: www.google.com

5 There are lots of pages of information. Much of this relates to Liverpool Football Club. We can eliminate most of these pages by filling in the 'without the words' box. You need to list all of the words that you want to remove from the search. Here are some words to eliminate: football, soccer, FC and club.

| **without** the words | football soccer FC club |

Here you can enter words you want to exclude from the search

Source: www.yahoo.com

6 You need to include more words than just 'Liverpool'.

Type in *Liverpool tourist attractions*, like this:

Find results	with **all** of the words	Liverpool	10 results ▼	Google Search
	with the **exact phrase**	Liverpool tourist attractions		
	with **at least one** of the words			
	without the words	football soccer FC club		

You can now enter an exact phrase that you want to appear in all of the search results

Source: www.google.com

Now click on **Google Search**.

You will see plenty of relevant sites to check for suitable information.

Notice that the exact phrase 'Liverpool tourist attractions' is present in all of these sites

Source: www.google.com

Tourist Attractions
Liverpool Tourist Attractions. You've never toured **Liverpool** on anything like TheYellowDuckmarine. Nothing comes close! It's a trip you'll never forget! ...
www.liverpool-wirral.com/Tourism/Tourism3.html - 8k - Cached - Similar pages

Liverpool Attractions Hotels Flights Car Rental.com
... attractions. **Liverpool** Attractions: **Liverpool tourist attractions** & **Liverpool** information from Hotels Flights Car Rental.com. Online ...
www.hotelsflightscarrental.com/ index.asp?page=attractions&area=Liverpool - 15k - Cached - Similar pages

Cheap Hotels in **Liverpool**
... Click on this link to book sightseeing tours in **Liverpool** > **Tourist attractions** in **Liverpool**. Book Hotels in **Liverpool** online: There ...
www.cheap-uk-hotels.co.uk/liverpool.php - 22k - Cached - Similar pages

Merseyide Jazz Festival
... the high standard of accommodation and the wide range of facilities that are available - all within a stone's throw of most of **Liverpool's tourist attractions.** ...
www.jazzworld.btinternet.co.uk/mersfest.htm - 13k - Dec 12, 2003 - Cached - Similar pages

Open Roads Guide to the North West
... By Road Throughout Merseyside, there are numerous bus services, including the SMART Bus that operates between **Liverpool's tourist attractions.** ...
www.openroads.net/editorials/ENG/region_0003_03.php3 - 26k - Cached - Similar pages

Liverpool Tourist Attractions
Return to the Front Page, Click here to show the Area Covered by Locallife in **Liverpool**, Back to Entertainment Back to Days Out. Move ...
www.locallife.co.uk/liverpool/touristattractions3.asp - 12k - Supplemental Result - Cached - Similar pages

141

Unit 3 Information: reliability, validity and bias

7 Always think of other ways of writing the main words in your search phrase. For example, 'Liverpool tourist attractions' could be changed to 'tourist attractions in Liverpool'. Try this and see if the search reveals any different sites.

8 Sometimes you need to rephrase the sentence to get the information you want.

Type *Places to visit in Liverpool* in the exact phrase box.

You will see that this search did not reveal as many sites as the previous search.

9 If you want the latest information on the attractions you may wish to eliminate sites created a long time ago which have not been kept up to date. Most official sites will be updated regularly.

Use the Google advanced search to search for websites that have been updated in the last three months. Use the following to do this:

When you click on **search** it will only find sites updated in the last three months.

Date	Return web pages updated in the	past 3 months ▼

FIND IT OUT

1. A synonym is a word which has the same or a similar meaning to another word. Write as many synonyms as you can for each of the following words:
   - Soccer
   - Computer games
   - Make-up
   - Animation
   - Graphics.

2. Perform searches against the clock and get the required information as quickly as possible for the following:
   - You are going on a short break with your parents and you want the website for the Travel Inn (a good but cheap place to stay).
   Write down the web address of the site on which you can find a list of Travel Inn locations and can book rooms.
   - The date of the next solar eclipse in Britain (the last one was in 1999).
   Write down the date of the next eclipse and also the website address where you found the information.
   - Can you find a table of the latest premiership football results? Write down the website address where this can be found.

Lesson 2 Using searches

- I want to go sea fishing. I need a website which tells me where the best places for sea fishing are.
Write down the web address of a suitable site.
- I would like to attend the British Grand Prix. I need to find out when it is.
Write down the web address of the page where this information can be found.
- I would like to find the official government site on the Data Protection Act 1988.
Write down the web address of the site.

WORKSHEET

WORKSHEET 8.3.3 **Searching for information**

You may be given a worksheet on which to write your answers or you may be asked to write your answers in your book. When you have finished, your teacher will either go through the answers or give you an answer sheet so that you can check the answers yourself.

Information needed	The exact query you would type into the search engine	Notes on how you would narrow down your search
The films that are on at your nearest cinema		
The exact mileage between your home and your school. Use the post codes of each for this search		
The date of the Russian Revolution		
Information about keeping a tank of marine fish in the home		
Information about the manned landings on the moon		
Information about the prophet Nostradamus		
Information on which MP3 player is the best one to buy		
What CD album is number one in the charts?		

QUESTIONS

1. Explain the meaning of the word query.
2. Give the website addresses of two popular search engines.

Unit 3 Information: reliability, validity and bias

Lesson 3: USING KEY WORDS AND BOOLEAN OPERATORS FOR SEARCHING

Background

It is important to understand the different ways of searching for information using the Internet. The better your knowledge of the search methods, the faster you will be able to get relevant information that fits your needs perfectly.

In this lesson you will learn about using key words to find relevant information on a subject and also about Boolean operators that can be used to widen or limit the results from a search.

Using key words

KEY WORDS

key words – words that can be searched on to find more information on a topic

Key words are words that can be searched on to find more information on a topic.

Here is a sentence:

Software piracy involves the illegal copying of computer software.

The key words in this sentence are:

- Software
- Piracy
- Illegal
- Computer.

Searching using the key words individually would find too much information and most of it would be irrelevant. It is better to search using combinations of these words, thus making the search more specific.

Suitable combinations are:

- Software piracy.
- Illegal copying of computer software.
- Illegal computer software.

Lesson 3 Using key words and Boolean operators for searching

Make it happen

ACTIVITY 7: Spotting the key words in an article

Key words are words that you could type into a search engine to obtain more information. It is important to be able to spot these key words.

Below is an article on the unpleasant subject of leeches and maggots being used to treat patients.

Make a list of as many key words as you can spot in this article.

Maggots and leeches on the NHS?

If you seriously injured yourself hundreds of years ago, there were no antibiotics to stop your wound going septic. If it went septic, millions of flesh-eating bacteria would start to eat your dead tissue and when they finished they would go on to eat your live tissue. You would have what is called gangrene. If left, this process would carry on and you would be eaten away and a painful death would be inevitable.

Luckily there were some useful things in the medieval medicine cabinet – these were leeches and maggots! These leeches and maggots would be unleashed on the wound where they would eat the dead tissue and clean up the open wound.

You are probably wondering what the doctors of the day were thinking of, releasing these horrible creatures on someone's

145

Unit 3 Information: reliability, validity and bias

Lesson 5: LEARNING AND FINDING OUT

KEY WORDS

intended audience – the people who will be looking at and reading the information on the web page or other document

Background

Often you will be asked to explore a subject or topic that is completely new to you. You will have to use information sources such as CD-ROMs and the Internet to help you gather information. You will then have to sift through the information and evaluate how well it helps you with the task you have to do. You may be asked to summarise the information you have found and put it in writing as a report or deliver it as a presentation. Alternatively, you may be asked to do some research for someone else.

Consider the audience for the information

If you were asked to research a topic that you know nothing about for a local newspaper, but not to write an article, you would need to investigate and understand the topic yourself. You should ensure that the information you collect will be suitable for the intended audience.

If the material is for a local newspaper, the audience will be a complete cross-section of people. The information you collect will need to be informative and interesting. The person who is writing the material will then find it easy to grab the readers' attention. Even when doing research you must always consider the audience and only collect material that is appropriate for their needs. Any artwork collected must also be appropriate; so an upbeat image may be suitable for a teenage audience but not so fitting for a general audience.

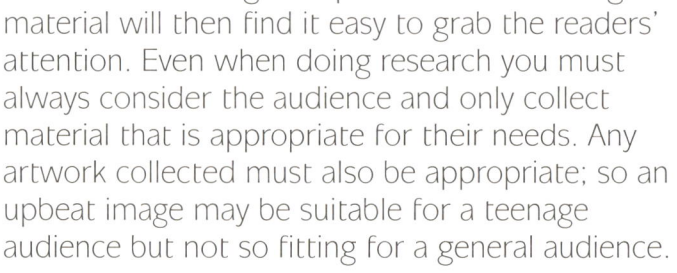

Below is a summary of the things you need to consider when collecting information:

- Make sure you have an appropriate level of detail.
- When there is a large amount of information, select the right data to suit the needs and interests of the audience.
- Choose appropriate images (pictures, clip, art etc.).

154

Lesson 5 Learning and finding out

Make it happen

ACTIVITY 12: Consider the audience when doing research

In this activity you have to answer questions about considering the audience when doing research.

1 A story is to be produced about the current Chelsea Football Club.

Explain how the level of detail in your research would need to be different for:

(a) A story in a Chelsea fan club magazine.

(b) A story to be published in a national newspaper.

2 You have to select some images to do with Chelsea Football Club. Explain how the choice of image depends on each of these:

(a) The age of the readership.

(b) The time of year when the article is to be published.

(c) Whether the article is aimed at a general reader (i.e. everybody who has an interest in football) or a more specialist reader (i.e. a Chelsea FC fan).

The appropriateness of information

Some information would be unsuitable for very young children and other information may shock a much older audience. It is important to make sure that the information you are collecting is appropriate.

Appropriate material also means well-chosen or well-timed material. For example, an article on the history of the Christmas tree would be appropriate in the run-up to Christmas but would be less appropriate in the summer.

KEY WORDS

appropriate – suitable or proper

Evaluating the accuracy, validity and reliability of the information you have collected

In this unit you have seen that there is bogus information on the Internet.

You have to make sure that the information you use is accurate, valid and reliable.

You also need to check the material's fitness for purpose.

KEY WORDS

fitness for purpose – how well the information obtained matches the purpose to which it is to be put

Unit 3 Information: reliability, validity and bias

REMEMBER!

Anyone with access to the Internet can produce a website. The information on the website could be searched for using search engines. Do not just accept the information you are given. Make sure you question it and verify it using other sources.

To test the accuracy of the information you can:

- Compare different sources of the same story (these could be on the Internet, in books, newspapers, radio programmes, TV programmes and interviews).
- Make your own judgement based on common sense and your own knowledge.
- Consider the publisher of the information – is it a source such as Britannica, the BBC, a government department, etc. or is it a site that someone with a basic knowledge of the topic has developed?
- Determine how many other people have used the site by looking at the counter.
- Check the URL of the publisher to see if it is the kind of web address you would expect.
- Determine when the site was last updated so that you can assess the accuracy of the information.

BBC website homepage

Acknowledging the sources of information

Information comes from lots of sources and when you use the information you need to mention these sources. This is called acknowledging your sources of information.

The reasons for acknowledging your sources are as follows:

- Out of courtesy (people usually do not mind you using their work if you mention that it is their work).
- So that readers know where to find further information.
- To convince your readers that your material is well researched and accurate.
- Some people allow you to use copyright work if you give a suitable acknowledgement.

Lesson 5 Learning and finding out

FIND IT OUT

The two main fish in the Disney film **Finding Nemo**

1 After watching the film *Finding Nemo*, John would like to know more about the types of fish in the film.

He knows:

- that both the fish are marine fish (i.e. they live in saltwater)
- that both fish are difficult to keep in an aquarium.

Use the Internet to find out:

- the names of the characters in the film (i.e. not the names of the types of fish) shown in the picture above
- the full name of the blue-and-yellow fish
- the Latin name of the two types of fish
- names of some countries where these fish can be found
- three interesting facts about each fish
- a summary of what makes these fish so hard to keep in an aquarium at home.

2 Find out about the history of the area where you live.

You are not required to present the information as you have been asked by someone else just to do the research. You will need to produce some interesting facts and also some artwork such as maps and photographs that could be used in an article for a local newspaper.

As the material must be accurate, try to verify the sites and use more than one website.

4 Models and presenting numeric data

Lesson 1: INTRODUCING MODELS AND PRESENTING NUMERIC DATA

Powerful techniques and the analysis of complex models

You came across the use of spreadsheets for modelling last year in Unit 4. This unit will take modelling further and you will learn new and powerful techniques to give answers to 'what if …?' questions. You will also learn about more complex models and how to interrogate and analyse them. After you have completed this unit you will be well placed to create your own models in lots of different subject areas.

REMEMBER!

A 'what if …?' query is a question you ask the spreadsheet. For example, 'What if the price of petrol goes up? How much more will it cost me to get to work?'

When Chloe's teacher told the class that they would be modelling in the next lesson, Chloe got hold of the wrong end of the stick

KEY WORDS

model – the process of representing a real-world object or phenomenon as a set of mathematical equations

simulation – seeing how the model behaves under different circumstances by altering the variables

Background theory and key information

Modelling basically means mimicking reality. One way of doing this is by producing a series of rules expressed as mathematical equations that parallel the real situation.

Lesson 1 Introducing models and presenting numeric data

Models and simulations

When you alter the variable numbers in the model to see what happens, you are said to be performing a simulation. The simulation will mimic how the real situation alters under the changed conditions.

The benefits of using a spreadsheet to create a model

In Year 7 Unit 4 you learnt about modelling. To recap, here are the main benefits of using spreadsheet software to create models:

- Speed: a model to simulate the total scores obtained when a pair of dice is thrown a large number of times (say 1000 times) can produce the results instantly, whilst doing this manually would take a long time.
- Accuracy: models use formulae and, provided the correct formulae have been used, there will be no mistakes in the calculations. It is easier to make mistakes doing calculations in your head or using a calculator.
- Automatic calculations: the rules of the model are expressed as calculations. By changing the quantity in a cell, all other cells that are linked to it will change automatically.

Make sure you know what the terms row, column and cell mean!

Unit 4 Models and presenting numeric data

- Data can be changed easily: the variable data is changed easily and the whole spreadsheet can be recalculated. This makes asking 'what if …?' questions very easy.

ACTIVITIES ACTIVITIES ACTIVITIES ACTIVITIES ACTIVITIES ACTIVITIES

ACTIVITY 1: Do you know the meaning of terms used in modelling?

A lot of specialist terms or key words are used when talking or writing about spreadsheets and modelling. It is important that you know what they mean. If you do not understand a term you should find out its meaning for yourself. Look for the key words in this chapter or in the glossary at the back of this book. Failing that, you can ask a friend or look it up by using the online help in the spreadsheet software Excel or by using the Internet to access computer glossaries.

Check that you understand the meaning of all these terms. Your teacher will ask you questions to check.

1. Cell
2. Cell reference
3. Column
4. Row
5. Cell format
6. Chart
7. Chart wizard
8. Model
9. Simulation
10. Sort
11. Worksheet
12. Drag
13. Copy
14. Paste
15. Label
16. Formula
17. Rule
18. Variable
19. 'What if …?' query
20. Assumption.

WORKSHEET WORKSHEET WORKSHEET WORKSHEET WORKSHEET

WORKSHEET 8.4.1 How much can you remember about models?

You may be given a worksheet on which to write your answers or you may be asked to write your answers in your book. When you have finished, your teacher will either go through the answers or give you an answer sheet so that you can check the answers yourself.

Lesson 1 Introducing models and presenting numeric data

Here is a model of the takings from an Indian takeaway. It has been produced to give the owner some idea of the takings he might expect on a typical day.

	A	B	C	D
1	Dish	Price	Qty Sold	Takings
2	Chicken Madras	£5.95	12	£71.40
3	Prawn Korma	£5.50	8	£44.00
4	Chicken Tandoori	£6.25	10	£62.50
5	Pilau Rice	£1.50	25	£37.50
6	Boiled Rice	£1.30	9	£11.70
7	Poppadom	£0.40	14	£5.60
8	Shish Kebab	£2.10	8	£16.80
9	Onion Bhaji	£1.90	15	£28.50
10				
11			Total Takings =	£278.00

1 Write down the contents of cell B2.

2 Write down the contents of cell A6.

3 Write down a cell that contains a label.

4 Write down a cell that contains a formula.

5 Models consist of rules and variables.

(a) Write down the cell reference of a cell containing a rule.

(b) Write down the cell reference of a cell containing a variable.

6 Write down the formula in cell D2 that would work out the takings for the sales of Chicken Madras.

7 The numbers in column D have been formatted. Which one of the following best describes the format?

(a) A number to two decimal places.

(b) Text.

(c) Date.

(d) Currency to two decimal places.

8 Once the formula to work out the takings has been entered into cell D2 it can be copied down the column as far as cell D9. Explain clearly how this would be done.

9 The price of Chicken Madras is to increase to £6.20.

(a) Which cell needs to be altered?

(b) Write down the cell references that will change automatically on making this amendment.

Unit 4 Models and presenting numeric data

10 Which of the following formulae would correctly work out the total takings in cell D11?

(a) =D2+D3+D4+D5+D6+D7+D8+D9

(b) =D2:D9

(c) =sum(d2:d9)

(d) =SUM(D1:D9).

11 Spreadsheets should always be checked to make sure that they are producing the correct results. Explain how you might check this spreadsheet.

12 State two advantages of the owner of the takeaway using a spreadsheet to model the takings from the shop.

13 Models are used to ask 'What if …?' questions. Write down two different 'What if …?' questions that could be asked of the model.

WORKSHEET 8.4.2 Using a model – performing a simulation

You may be given a worksheet on which to write your answers or you may be asked to write your answers in your book. When you have finished, your teacher will either go through the answers or give you an answer sheet so that you can check the answers yourself.

Do you remember the school disco model created in Year 7 Unit 4? A model was created to show how much money might be raised by holding a disco for all 220 Year 7 students.

You will need to have this model on the screen before answering the questions in this worksheet.

Load the spreadsheet software Excel and the file called Disco Model For Year 7.

Check that your worksheet is the same as this (right):

	A	B
1	Name: Stephen Doyle	Class: 7E
2	A Model to show the profit or loss for a disco	
3		
4	Price for printing one ticket	£0.01
5	Number of tickets sold	300
6	Ticket price	£2.50
7	Cost of one can of soft drink	£0.23
8	Cost of one packet of crisps	£0.14
9	Selling price of one can of soft drink	£0.40
10	Selling price of one packet of crisps	£0.30
11		
12	Income	
13	Money from ticket sales	£750.00
14	Income from the sale of **all** the soft drinks	£120.00
15	Income from the sale of **all** the crisps	£90.00
16	Total income	£960.00
17		
18	Costs	
19	Hire of disco and DJ	£60.00
20	Cost of printing all tickets	£3.00
21	Cost of buying all the cans of soft drink	£69.00
22	Cost of buying all the packets of crisps	£42.00
23	Cost of caretaker	£48.00
24	Total costs	£222.00
25		
26	Profit/Loss	£738.00

You now have to make the following changes to the worksheet and answer the questions.

1 The night of the school disco coincides with a big local football match. This might affect the number of tickets sold.

Lesson 1 Introducing models and presenting numeric data

Reduce the number of tickets sold to 240 and write down the new profit/loss.

2 When the number of tickets sold is reduced, write down the cell references of four cells that will automatically change.

3 A parent who is the sales manager of a large soft-drinks company has said that he will get the drinks much cheaper than buying them from the wholesalers. Each can is now acquired for 15p. Make this change.

!Note
Important: You need to make the changes in questions 3 and 4 one after the other.

Write down the new profit/loss.

4 The teacher says that £500 is enough profit to make and that the price of the tickets should be reduced so that the profit is as near to £500 as possible.

By altering the ticket price (i.e. by trial and error), see how near to £500 you can get.

Write down the ticket price and profit/loss.

5 Save your work using a suitable file name.

6 Print out a copy of your final worksheet. Your printout should show all the text, data, etc. and should contain the gridlines and also the column and row headings.

QUESTIONS

1 Explain one difference between a model and a simulation.

2 Financial models (i.e. models concerned with money) are very useful.

A young person who has just started work and has moved away from home decides to construct a model to show the money coming in and going out of her bank account.

(a) State one reason why this model would be useful for her.

(b) Name a piece of software that she could use to build this model.

(c) Give one advantage that a computer-based model has over working things out on paper.

(d) Write a sentence to explain how the model could be used to simulate her finances.

(e) Models have inputs and outputs. State one input to this financial model and one output.

3 Briefly describe three different models you have seen or used.

What you should already know

You will need to be familiar with the basics of using spreadsheets before starting this unit. You may need to revise material on models that you did in Year 7 Unit 4.

Unit 4 Models and presenting numeric data

You will be building on the following material that you covered in Year 7:

- Entering text, numeric data and formulae into a spreadsheet.
- Formatting cells.
- Creating simple charts using the chart wizard.
- Exploring a basic model.
- Selecting print areas.

What you will learn

In this unit you will:

- Use a spreadsheet to generate models.
- Ask questions of the models in order to analyse and present data.
- Use techniques to generate more effective models.
- Understand the relationship between input and output values in a model.
- Introduce randomness into models.

Lesson 2: TURNING THE OUTPUT INTO THE INPUT – USING GOAL SEEK

I THINK I'LL GET DAVID BECKHAM TO DO MY GOAL SEEK FOR ME

Background

In previous models we always put input values in to determine the output. In this lesson you will learn that a model can work both ways. In other words you can specify the desired output value and ask the model to determine an input value that will give this.

Lesson 2 Turning the output into the input – using goal seek

Input and output values in a model

You will be familiar with the three stages of computing:

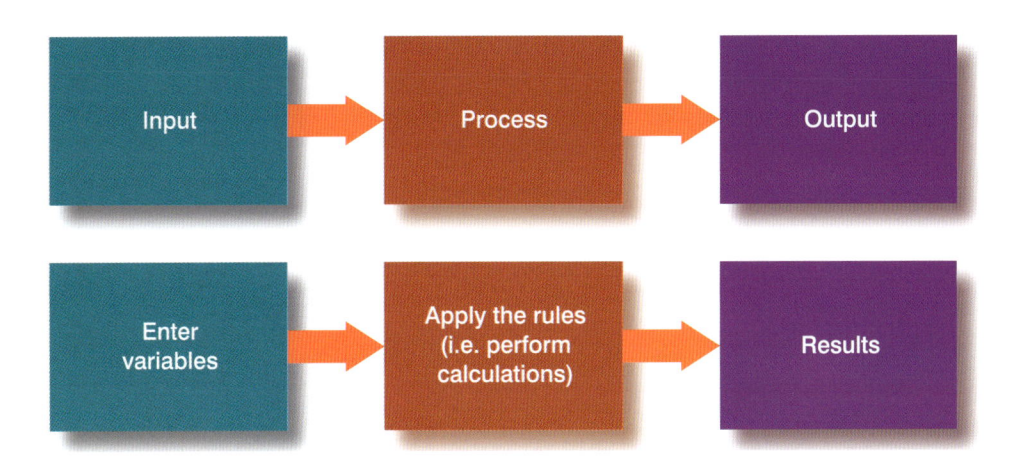

Input → Process → Output

Enter variables → Apply the rules (i.e. perform calculations) → Results

Going through the three stages in the usual direction

The bottom diagram shows these three stages as they apply to computer models.

Normally we go through these diagrams from left to right so that the output or results are obtained last.

It is possible using a model to go the other way. In other words you start with the output or results you would like (called the target value) and then find the input you could have to give the result. Usually, if there is more than one variable then we simply select the variable we would like to change to give the output.

This is shown in the following diagrams.

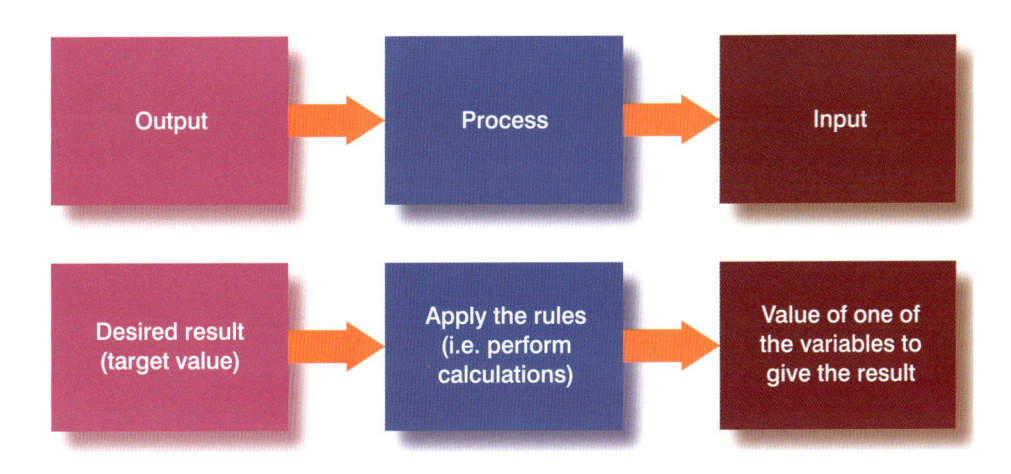

Output → Process → Input

Desired result (target value) → Apply the rules (i.e. perform calculations) → Value of one of the variables to give the result

Starting from the output value and determining the input value

Unit 4 Models and presenting numeric data

KEY WORDS

goal seek – allows you to achieve the figure required by altering another figure

target value – this is the value you would like the output to be

Goal seek

The concept of goal seek is explained in the set of diagrams above.

Goal seek is a very useful tool in spreadsheets. Goal seek allows you to set what you want the output to be and it then automatically varies one of the inputs until it gets as near to the output as it can. It then tells you the best input value and how near to the target value it got.

Make it happen

ACTIVITY 2: Commission in a clothes shop

At the weekends Chloe works in a clothes shop selling the latest fashions.

To encourage her to sell more, her wages are commission based. The more she sells the more money she earns. This suits Chloe as she is good at selling.

1. Load Excel and open a new workbook.

2. Type in the first two months in the following way:

	A	B	C
1			
2			
3			
4	Jan		
5	Feb		
6			
7			
8			

3. Rather than type all the months in yourself you can get the computer to do it.

The computer will complete a series provided that you put the first two terms in.

166

Lesson 2 Turning the output into the input – using goal seek

Select the two months (Jan and Feb) by highlighting them.

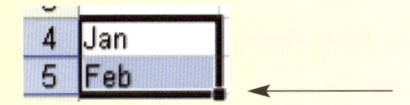

4	Jan
5	Feb

Click on the fill handle (this is the small square at the bottom right of the cell).

Click on the left mouse button and drag it down the column. You will see the months of the year change in the label. Stop when you reach Dec.

4 Type in the title of the worksheet starting in cell A1: *Chloe's commissions for the year 2003*.

Enlarge the text in the heading.

5 Enter the rest of the data exactly as it appears here.

	A	B	C	D
1	Chloe's commissions for the year 2003			
2				
3		Value of sales (£)	Commission (£)	
4	Jan	£12,890		
5	Feb	£6,578		
6	Mar	£5,900		
7	Apr	£6,519		
8	May	£7,089		
9	Jun	£8,560		
10	Jul	£9,005		
11	Aug	£10,098		
12	Sep	£9,087		
13	Oct	£7,812		
14	Nov	£6,089		
15	Dec	£15,687		
16				
17				
18				
19		Commission rate	3.00%	

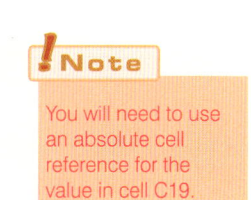

!Note
You will need to use an absolute cell reference for the value in cell C19.

6 Chloe is paid 3% commission on the value of the goods she sells. Using the value for the commission rate in cell C19 and the value of the goods sold in cell B4, put in a formula to work out the commission in cell C4.

7 Copy the formula in cell C4 down the column as far as cell C15.

Your worksheet should look like this:

	A	B	C	D
1	Chloe's commissions for the year 2003			
2				
3		Value of sales (£)	Commission (£)	
4	Jan	£12,890	£386.70	
5	Feb	£6,578	£197.34	
6	Mar	£5,900	£177.00	
7	Apr	£6,519	£195.57	
8	May	£7,089	£212.67	
9	Jun	£8,560	£256.80	
10	Jul	£9,005	£270.15	
11	Aug	£10,098	£302.94	
12	Sep	£9,087	£272.61	
13	Oct	£7,812	£234.36	
14	Nov	£6,089	£182.67	
15	Dec	£15,687	£470.61	
16				
17				
18				
19		Commission rate	3.00%	

8 It is the end of November and Chloe has put the sales figures from December 2002 into the worksheet so that she can see how much she should earn.

December is the busiest month in the shop. Chloe sells a lot more that month and she hopes to be able to pay for a skiing trip she has booked with some friends after Christmas.

The skiing trip will cost £567 and Chloe would like to find out the value of the sales she would need to make in December 2003 to pay for it. You could of course work this out manually but we will get the spreadsheet to work it out.

We use a tool called 'goal seek' to do this.

Click on cell C15 (this is the cell we want to set to a certain value which in this case is the cost of the holiday).

Click on **Tools** and then on **Goal Seek**.

The following Goal Seek window appears. We need to set the cell C15 to the value 567 (i.e. the cost of the holiday) by varying cell B15 (i.e. the value of sales).

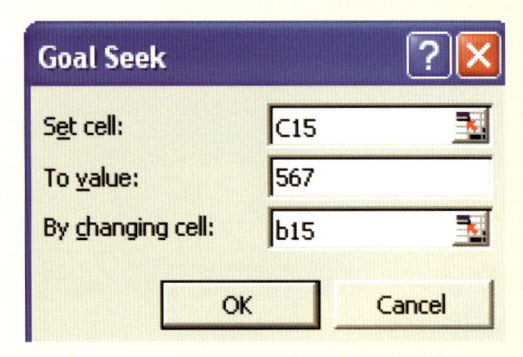

Lesson 2 Turning the output into the input – using goal seek

When you have entered the data as shown here, click on the **OK** button.

9 The following window appears. It is telling us that we asked for it to find a value of 567 (i.e. the target value) and that it has found the current value of 567 (i.e. an exact match in this case).

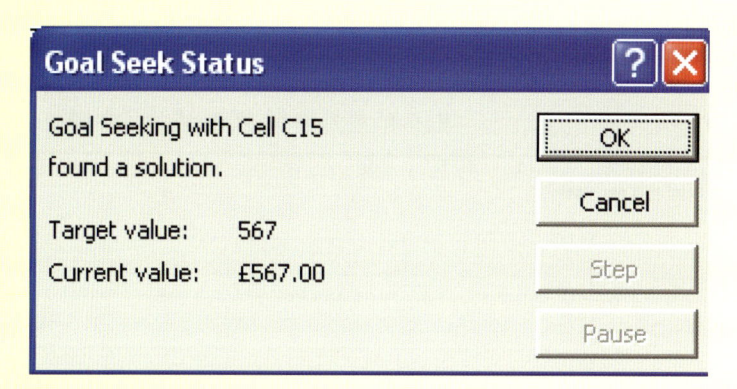

```
Goal Seek Status

Goal Seeking with Cell C15
found a solution.

Target value:    567
Current value:   £567.00

[ OK ]  [ Cancel ]  [ Step ]  [ Pause ]
```

Click on the **OK** button.

10 The values are now inserted in the spreadsheet like this:

| 15 | Dec | £18,900 | £567.00 |

Chloe now knows that she needs to sell at least £18,900 worth of goods to get enough commission to pay for her skiing holiday.

11 Save the workbook using the file name 'Chloe commission workbook'.

ACTIVITY 3: Can you describe what to do?

When you are an experienced user of spreadsheets people often ask you for help. Imagine someone was asking you to help them with each of the following. Describe clearly the answer you would give.

1 I would like to move the contents of one cell into a completely different cell. How do I do this?

2 What is the difference between a label and a formula?

3 I want to put the numbers from 1 to 1000 into a column of cells. I do not want to spend time typing them. Is there a quick way to do this and if so what is it?

Unit 4 Models and presenting numeric data

WORKSHEET WORKSHEET WORKSHEET WORKSHEET WORKSHEET

WORKSHEET 8.4.3 **A simple model**

Here is screenshot of a financial model for the costs of keeping pets.

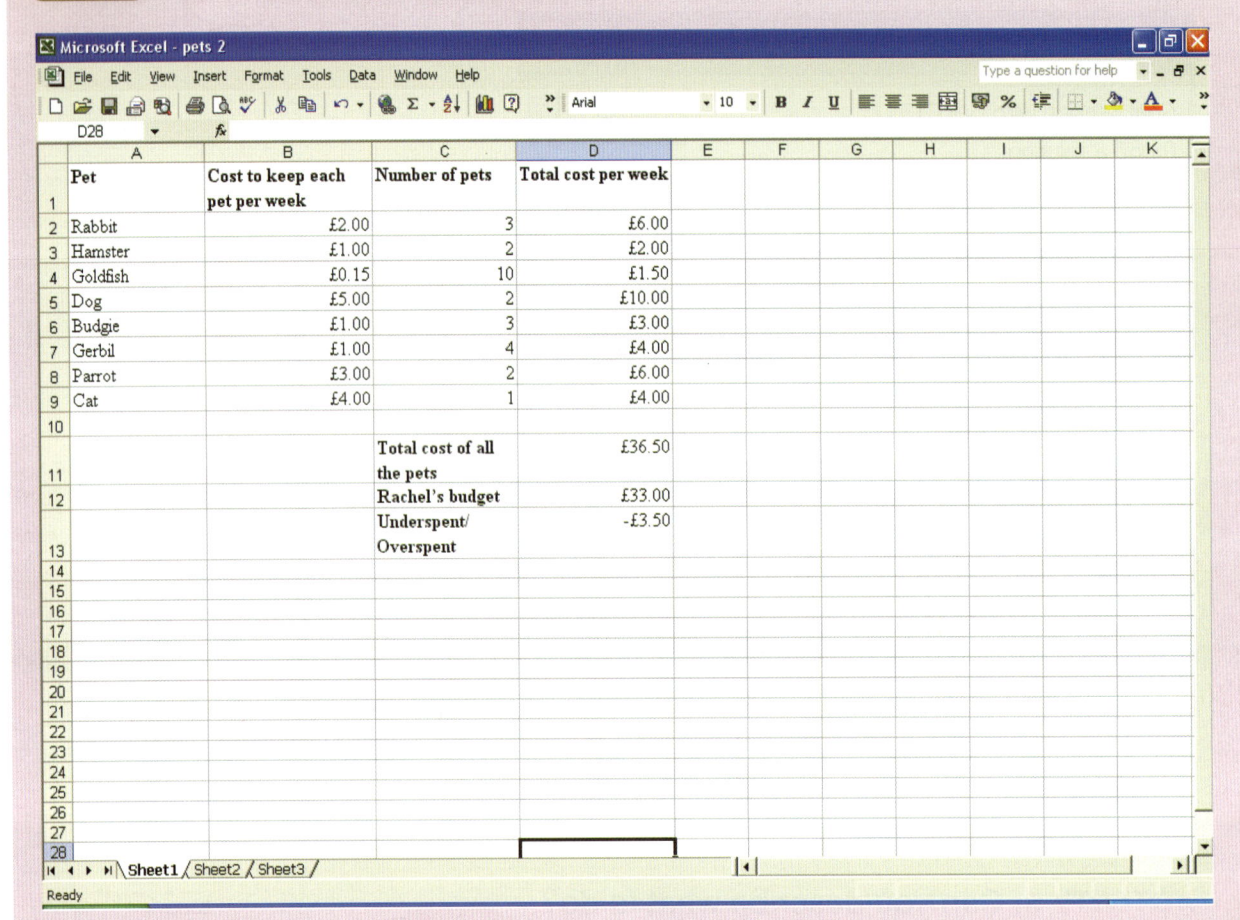

	A	B	C	D
1	Pet	Cost to keep each pet per week	Number of pets	Total cost per week
2	Rabbit	£2.00	3	£6.00
3	Hamster	£1.00	2	£2.00
4	Goldfish	£0.15	10	£1.50
5	Dog	£5.00	2	£10.00
6	Budgie	£1.00	3	£3.00
7	Gerbil	£1.00	4	£4.00
8	Parrot	£3.00	2	£6.00
9	Cat	£4.00	1	£4.00
10				
11			Total cost of all the pets	£36.50
12			Rachel's budget	£33.00
13			Underspent/ Overspent	-£3.50

1 Look at this screenshot and use it to answer the following questions.

(a) How much does it cost to feed one gerbil?

(b) What is the total cost of feeding the animals per week?

(c) Is Rachel overspending or underspending?

2 Load the spreadsheet called 'Rachel's pet-feeding model'.

Print out an entire copy of the screen (this is called a screenshot).

To do a screenshot press the **Alt** key and keep it pressed down. Then press the **Prt Sc** key. This will paste a copy of the screen into the clipboard (i.e. a temporary storage area).

170

Lesson 2 Turning the output into the input – using goal seek

Now leave Excel and load the word processor, Word. Open a new document and click on Edit and then Paste. A copy of the Excel screen will appear in the document. You can now print this document out.

3 Using the copy of the screenshot you have printed out, mark clearly the following:

(a) A cell.
(b) A column.
(c) A row.
(d) A label.
(e) A variable.
(f) The Chart Wizard button.
(g) The save button.
(h) The print button.
(i) A cell with a currency format.
(j) Numeric data containing no decimal places.
(k) The AutoSum button.

4 This worksheet contains formulae. Here are some reasons why formulae are put into spreadsheets. Which of these reasons are correct?

(a) If a cell changes, then all those cells that depend on it will also change.
(b) A more accurate answer is produced than with a calculator.
(c) Formulae make the spreadsheet look better.
(d) The formulae in the spreadsheet need to be kept secret.

5 A spreadsheet may not always be the best tool to use for a particular job. Look at the table below and tick the box which best applies to each activity.

(NB: If you are not using a worksheet, you will need to copy this table out before completing it.)

Spreadsheets are the best tools for:	True	False	Not sure
Answering 'what if …?' questions			
Writing an essay			
Making a poster			
Performing calculations			
Drawing a picture			
Creating a complex database			
Drawing graphs and charts			

Unit 4 Models and presenting numeric data

Lesson 3: CREATING MODELS TO DETERMINE THE BREAK-EVEN POINT

Background

When a new business starts up, money has to be paid out for premises, heating, lighting, etc. before the business starts to make any money. Money goes out of the business without any coming in. Once the business starts to sell things, money starts to come in. Eventually, when the business has sold a certain number of products, the money going out will equal the money coming in. This means that the business neither makes a profit or a loss. This is called the break-even point.

You will see that there are a number of alternative models that can be built to determine the break-even point.

KEY WORDS

break even – when the money coming into and going out of the business are the same

AromaBar coffee bar

John is thinking of opening a new coffee bar in his town. He has seen some premises in a good place and needs to convince the bank manager that the business is a good one so that she will lend him some money.

John wants to produce a break-even analysis so that he can find out how many cups of coffee he would need to sell in a week to cover the costs.

Before he produces the model for this using a spreadsheet, John needs to divide the costs into two: fixed costs and variable costs.

Here are the definitions for each of these:

- Variable costs are costs that go up or down depending on the number of cups of coffee sold.
- Fixed costs are costs that do not change with the number of cups of coffee sold. Fixed costs have to be paid whether you sell one cup or thousands of cups.

It is important to know that fixed costs do not stay fixed forever but are fixed for the short term.

The total costs that John has to pay out each month are made up of fixed and variable costs.

So, we have the rule:

Total costs = Fixed costs + Variable costs

Lesson 3 Creating models to determine the break-even point

Make it happen

ACTIVITY 4: Which costs are fixed and which are variable?

Decide which of the following are variable and which are fixed costs.

- Coffee filter papers.
- Coffee.
- Rent of premises.
- Staff wages.
- Milk or cream.
- Rates (money you have to pay the council).
- Interest payments on a loan from the bank.

REMEMBER!

Ask yourself, 'Does the cost depend on the number of cups of coffee sold?'

ACTIVITY 5: Producing the model to find the break-even point

John has to determine the number of cups of coffee he will need to sell in a month in order to break even. In other words, he has to find the number of cups he needs to sell so that the money coming into the business (called the sales revenue) is equal to the money going out of the business (called the total costs).

The break-even point is the number of cups of coffee sold when:

Sales revenue – Total costs = 0 (i.e. John is not making a profit or a loss).

When this happens, John is just covering his expenses. If he sells more than this number he will make a profit and he can experiment with the model to see what this might be.

1. Load Excel and open a new workbook.

2. Type the following labels and data into the worksheet exactly as it appears here:

	A	B	C	D	E	F
1	**AromaBar model to find the break-even point**					
2	All of the following figures are monthly figures					
3						
4	Selling price of a cup of coffee	£1.50				
5						
6	**Fixed costs**					
7	Rent of premises	£750				
8	Staff wages	£4,200				
9	Rates	£557				
10	Interest on loan	£345				
11	Total fixed costs	£5,852				
12						
13						
14	**Variable costs (per cup)**					
15	Coffee	£0.13				
16	Filter papers	£0.02				
17	Milk/Cream	£0.05				
18	Total variable costs (per cup)	£0.20				
19						
20						
21						
22	**Number of cups of coffee sold**	**Variable costs (£)**	**Fixed costs (£)**	**Total costs (£)**	**Sales revenue (£)**	

173

Unit 4 Models and presenting numeric data

3 Create a series of numbers starting from 200 in cell A23 and going up in steps of 200 until the number 6000 is reached. Remember the quick way of doing this?

4 In cell B23 you need a formula to work out the variable costs. This formula will need to multiply the total variable costs (per cup) in cell B18 by the number of cups of coffee sold in cell A23.

One of these cell references will need to be absolute and the other relative. Can you work out which one needs to be which and why?

Put the formula into cell B23.

5 Copy the formula in cell B23 down the column as far as cell B52. Check that this has been done correctly by working out some of the figures manually or by using a calculator.

6 Rather than enter the total fixed cost £5892 into cell C23 it is better to enter the formula =B11 in case we need to alter any of the fixed costs in the future. This provides a link back to the original figure in cell B11. Always try to use formulae rather than copy numbers.

7 Copy this formula down the column. The value will stay the same as the fixed costs do not vary with the number of cups of coffee being sold.

8 In cell D23 put a formula that will add the variable and fixed costs together. When this has been done, copy the formula down the column.

9 Calculate the column for the sales revenue. These figures are obtained by multiplying the selling price of a cup of coffee by the number of cups of coffee sold. Again, one cell needs a relative reference and the other an absolute cell reference.

Put the formula with the correct cell references in cell E23.

Copy this formula down the column.

REMEMBER!

Absolute reference in this type of reference, a particular cell is used in a formula, and when this formula is copied to a new address, the cell address does not change.

REMEMBER!

Relative reference when a cell is used in a formula and the formula is copied to a new address, the cell address changes to take account of the formula's new position.

Lesson 3 Creating models to determine the break-even point

10 Check that the part of the worksheet you have just completed is the same as this one:

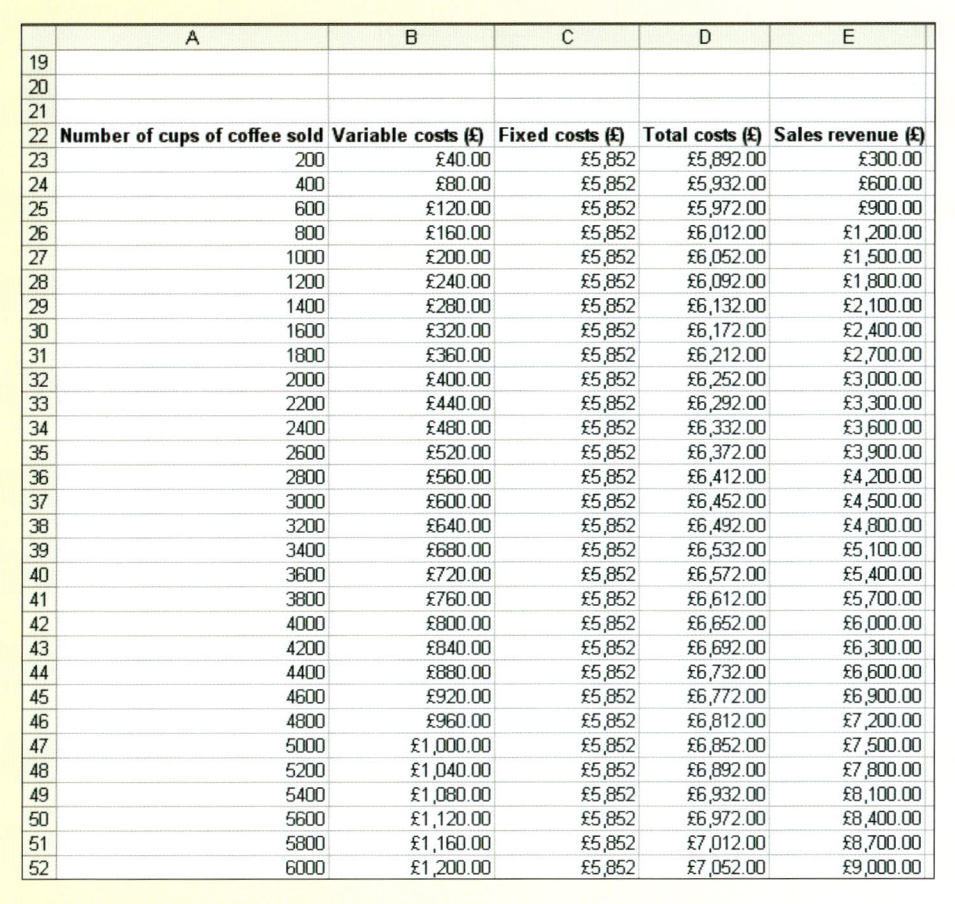

	A	B	C	D	E
19					
20					
21					
22	Number of cups of coffee sold	Variable costs (£)	Fixed costs (£)	Total costs (£)	Sales revenue (£)
23	200	£40.00	£5,852	£5,892.00	£300.00
24	400	£80.00	£5,852	£5,932.00	£600.00
25	600	£120.00	£5,852	£5,972.00	£900.00
26	800	£160.00	£5,852	£6,012.00	£1,200.00
27	1000	£200.00	£5,852	£6,052.00	£1,500.00
28	1200	£240.00	£5,852	£6,092.00	£1,800.00
29	1400	£280.00	£5,852	£6,132.00	£2,100.00
30	1600	£320.00	£5,852	£6,172.00	£2,400.00
31	1800	£360.00	£5,852	£6,212.00	£2,700.00
32	2000	£400.00	£5,852	£6,252.00	£3,000.00
33	2200	£440.00	£5,852	£6,292.00	£3,300.00
34	2400	£480.00	£5,852	£6,332.00	£3,600.00
35	2600	£520.00	£5,852	£6,372.00	£3,900.00
36	2800	£560.00	£5,852	£6,412.00	£4,200.00
37	3000	£600.00	£5,852	£6,452.00	£4,500.00
38	3200	£640.00	£5,852	£6,492.00	£4,800.00
39	3400	£680.00	£5,852	£6,532.00	£5,100.00
40	3600	£720.00	£5,852	£6,572.00	£5,400.00
41	3800	£760.00	£5,852	£6,612.00	£5,700.00
42	4000	£800.00	£5,852	£6,652.00	£6,000.00
43	4200	£840.00	£5,852	£6,692.00	£6,300.00
44	4400	£880.00	£5,852	£6,732.00	£6,600.00
45	4600	£920.00	£5,852	£6,772.00	£6,900.00
46	4800	£960.00	£5,852	£6,812.00	£7,200.00
47	5000	£1,000.00	£5,852	£6,852.00	£7,500.00
48	5200	£1,040.00	£5,852	£6,892.00	£7,800.00
49	5400	£1,080.00	£5,852	£6,932.00	£8,100.00
50	5600	£1,120.00	£5,852	£6,972.00	£8,400.00
51	5800	£1,160.00	£5,852	£7,012.00	£8,700.00
52	6000	£1,200.00	£5,852	£7,052.00	£9,000.00

11 Save your workbook using the file name 'AromaBar Break-Model v1'.

12 Print out a copy of your model on a single page and including the gridlines and the column and row headings.

To do this click on **File** and then **Page Setup**.

Select **Portrait** and then **Fit to 1** page width by clicking on the spots.

13 Click on the **Sheet** tab

In the window that appears, you should click on **Gridlines** and **Row and column headings**.

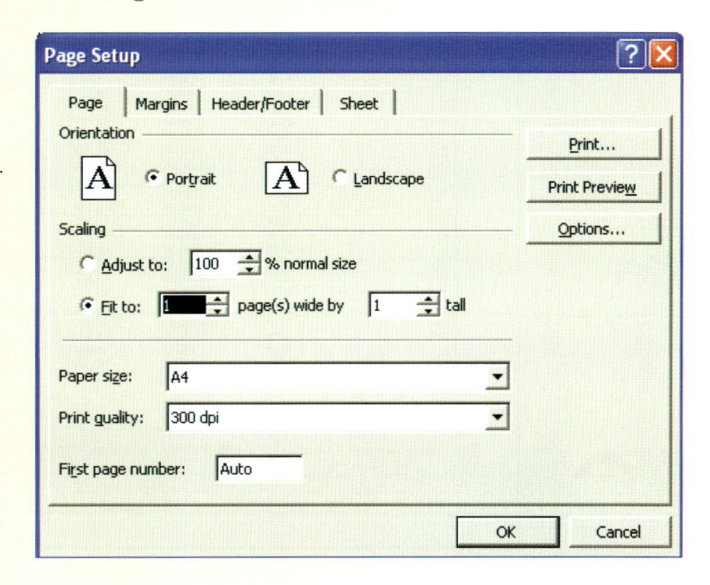

175

Unit 4 Models and presenting numeric data

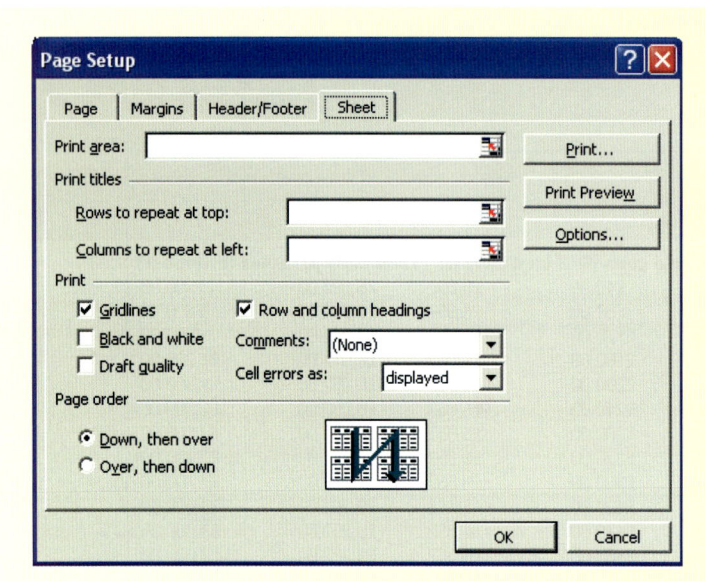

Click on **OK**.

It is always a good idea to use the **Print Preview** button to see if the page setup is ok.

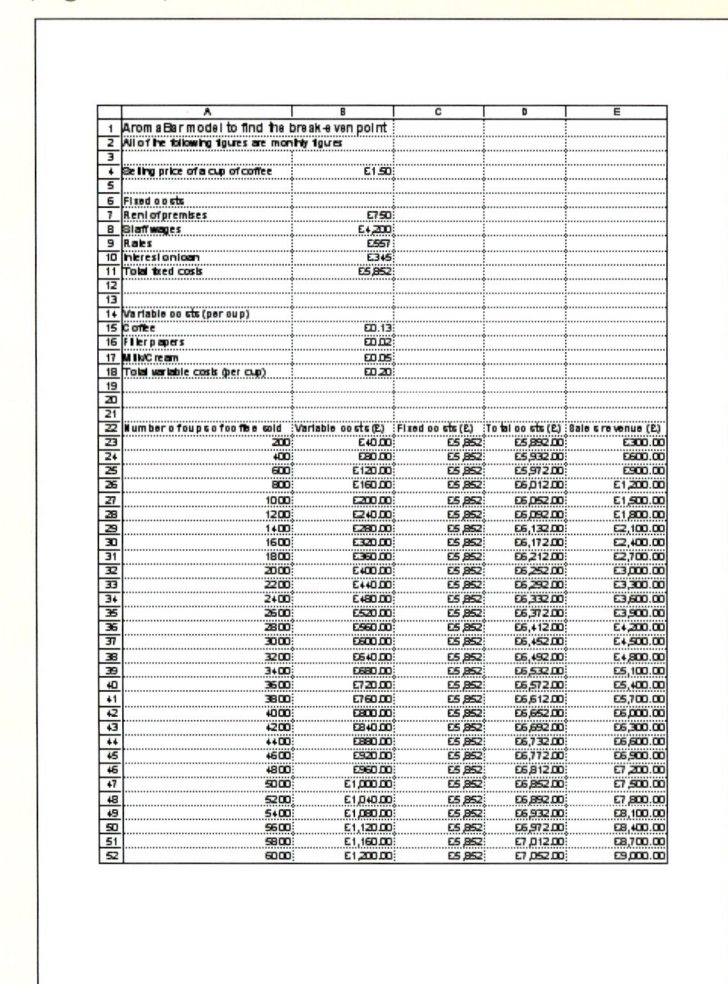

Do this to check if everything is laid out in the correct way and click on the **Close** button.

Click on **Print** to print the worksheet out.

176

Lesson 3 Creating models to determine the break-even point

ACTIVITY 6: Finding the break-even point

Look at the printout obtained from the last activity. Look down the Total costs (£) and Sales revenue (£) columns. We want to find the point where the numbers in the two columns are equal. A quick look reveals that there is no such point in the table. We therefore need to see where the sales revenue goes from being smaller than the total costs to being greater.

This is the section of the worksheet that we are interested in:

| 44 | 4400 | £880.00 | £5,852 | £6,732.00 | £6,600.00 |
| 45 | 4600 | £920.00 | £5,852 | £6,772.00 | £6,900.00 |

You can see that the break-even point occurs between sales of 4400 and 4600 cups of coffee a month. We need to investigate this area closely to get a more accurate picture. We therefore need to produce a spreadsheet covering just this area.

1. Load Excel (if it is not already loaded) and open the workbook AromaBar Break-Model v1.

2. It will be easier to spot the break-even point if we use another column called Profit/Loss. Put the column heading *Profit/Loss (£)* in cell F22 and make it bold.

3. Put a formula in cell F23 to work out the Profit/Loss by subtracting the Total costs from the Sales Revenue (i.e. Profit/Loss = Sales Revenue minus Total Costs).

Copy this formula down the column.

It is now easy to spot where break even occurs somewhere between 4400 and 4600 cups because this is where the loss (shown in red) changes to a profit (shown in black).

4. Now the loss of £132 changes to a profit of £128. These figures are similar (except one is positive and the other is negative). This means that the break-even point will probably lie almost exactly between 4400 and 4600 cups.

Working this out will save some time.

We will investigate starting at 4490 cups of coffee going up in steps of one.

!Note
You can tell negative numbers by the minus sign, but to make them stand out they are in red.

5. Rather than start a worksheet or a new section on the same worksheet, it is quicker to adapt the one we have.

Delete the existing numbers in cells A23 and A24 and replace with the numbers 4490 and 4491 like this:

	A
20	
21	
22	**Number of cups of coffee sold**
23	4490
24	4491

Unit 4 Models and presenting numeric data

(b) The selling price of a cup of coffee if (cell B4) changes to £1.60.

   (i) Write down the cell references (besides cell B4) that will change as a result.

   (ii) Due to this increase, would you expect the break-even point to go up or down? Give a reason for your answer.

Lesson 4: TWO OTHER MODELS FOR FINDING THE BREAK-EVEN POINT

Background

In the last lesson you learnt how to find the break-even point using trial and error. Using this method you tried different values until you got as near to the point at which the costs equalled the sales revenue. Trial and error takes time and the two methods in the activities here offer a quicker method.

Make it happen

ACTIVITY 7: Obtaining the break-even point by plotting graphs

1. Load the workbook AromaBar Break-Even Model v2.

2. In previous worksheets we moved data so that the columns were next to each other and a graph could be drawn. In this worksheet we will simply select columns that are not next to each other (i.e. not adjacent to each other).

Select the column heading and all the data in column A. Now hold down the **CTRL** key and select column D. Hold the **CTRL** key down and select column E.

You have now selected non-adjacent columns so that a graph/chart can be drawn.

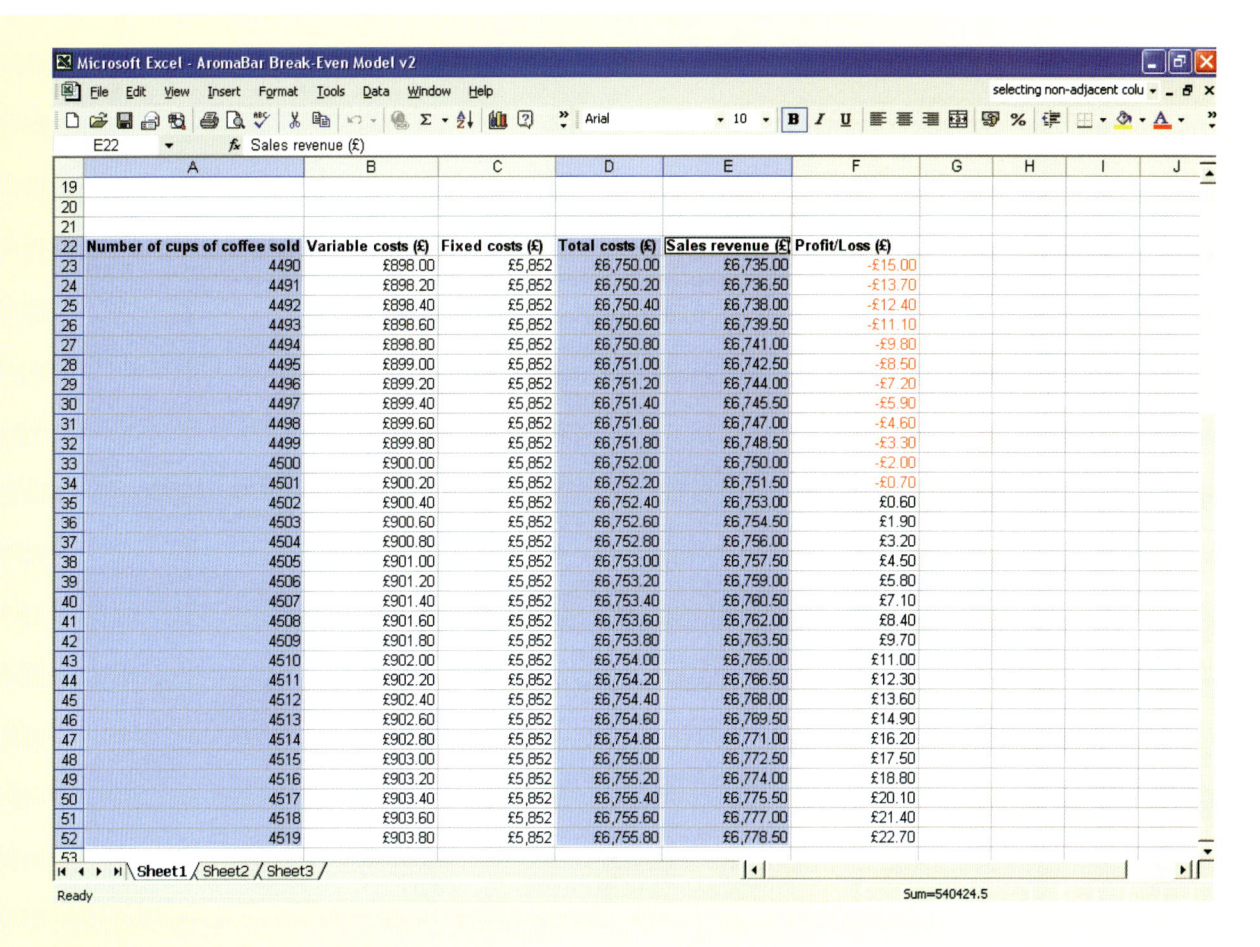

Lesson 4 Two other models for finding the break-even point

Number of cups of coffee sold	Variable costs (£)	Fixed costs (£)	Total costs (£)	Sales revenue (£)	Profit/Loss (£)
4490	£898.00	£5,852	£6,750.00	£6,735.00	-£15.00
4491	£898.20	£5,852	£6,750.20	£6,736.50	-£13.70
4492	£898.40	£5,852	£6,750.40	£6,738.00	-£12.40
4493	£898.60	£5,852	£6,750.60	£6,739.50	-£11.10
4494	£898.80	£5,852	£6,750.80	£6,741.00	-£9.80
4495	£899.00	£5,852	£6,751.00	£6,742.50	-£8.50
4496	£899.20	£5,852	£6,751.20	£6,744.00	-£7.20
4497	£899.40	£5,852	£6,751.40	£6,745.50	-£5.90
4498	£899.60	£5,852	£6,751.60	£6,747.00	-£4.60
4499	£899.80	£5,852	£6,751.80	£6,748.50	-£3.30
4500	£900.00	£5,852	£6,752.00	£6,750.00	-£2.00
4501	£900.20	£5,852	£6,752.20	£6,751.50	-£0.70
4502	£900.40	£5,852	£6,752.40	£6,753.00	£0.60
4503	£900.60	£5,852	£6,752.60	£6,754.50	£1.90
4504	£900.80	£5,852	£6,752.80	£6,756.00	£3.20
4505	£901.00	£5,852	£6,753.00	£6,757.50	£4.50
4506	£901.20	£5,852	£6,753.20	£6,759.00	£5.80
4507	£901.40	£5,852	£6,753.40	£6,760.50	£7.10
4508	£901.60	£5,852	£6,753.60	£6,762.00	£8.40
4509	£901.80	£5,852	£6,753.80	£6,763.50	£9.70
4510	£902.00	£5,852	£6,754.00	£6,765.00	£11.00
4511	£902.20	£5,852	£6,754.20	£6,766.50	£12.30
4512	£902.40	£5,852	£6,754.40	£6,768.00	£13.60
4513	£902.60	£5,852	£6,754.60	£6,769.50	£14.90
4514	£902.80	£5,852	£6,754.80	£6,771.00	£16.20
4515	£903.00	£5,852	£6,755.00	£6,772.50	£17.50
4516	£903.20	£5,852	£6,755.20	£6,774.00	£18.80
4517	£903.40	£5,852	£6,755.40	£6,775.50	£20.10
4518	£903.60	£5,852	£6,755.60	£6,777.00	£21.40
4519	£903.80	£5,852	£6,755.80	£6,778.50	£22.70

3 Click on the **graph/chart** icon. You need to choose xy (scatter) and a graph joined by straight lines.

You now need to work through the steps in the Chart Wizard to produce a graph similar to the graph shown on page 182, which can be used to determine the break-even point.

You may find it better to put the graph on a different worksheet to the data.

Make sure the graph is properly labelled.

The break-even point is the number of cups of coffee sold where the two lines cross. Even without gridlines (which you can always put on the graph if you want to), it is easy to find this. All you do is move the cursor (i.e. the arrow) onto the point where the two lines cross.

A label appears to tell you the x and the y value at this point. The break-even point is the x value which is 4502 cups of coffee.

4 Save this workbook (which contains both worksheets) using the file name 'AromaBar Break-Even Model v3'.

Print out a copy of the worksheet containing the graph and then close the worksheet.

Unit 4 Models and presenting numeric data

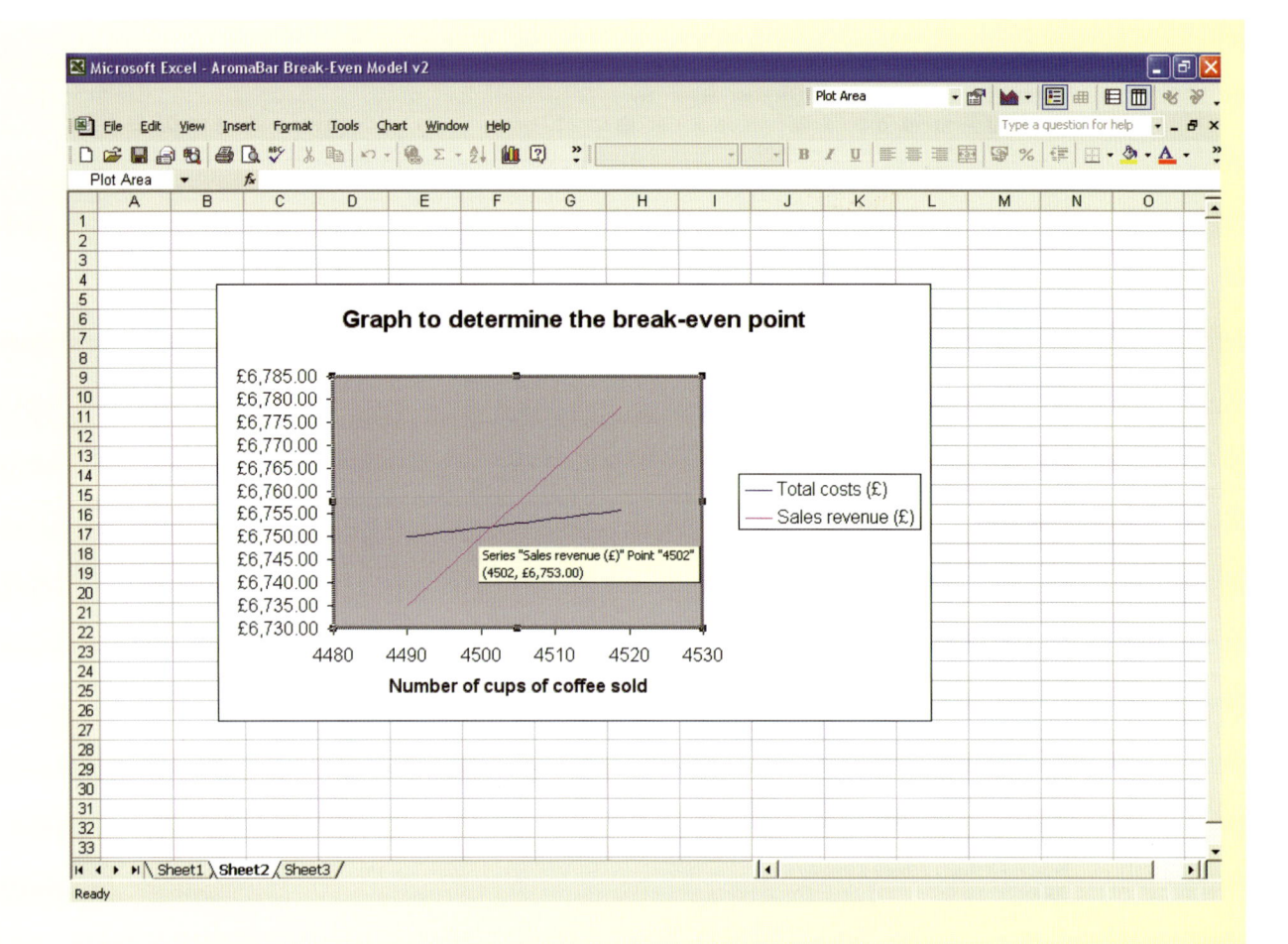

ACTIVITY 8: Using goal seek to determine the break-even point

The break-even point occurs when the profit/loss is zero. We can therefore use the goal seek tool to determine the break-even point.

1. Start Excel and load the workbook AromaBar Break-Even Model v3.

2. Click on cell F23. This is the cell we shall set to zero by altering cell A23 which contains the number of cups of coffee sold.

	A	B	C	D	E	F
19						
20						
21						
22	Number of cups of coffee sold	Variable costs (£)	Fixed costs (£)	Total costs (£)	Sales revenue (£)	Profit/Loss (£)
23	4490	£898.00	£5,852	£6,750.00	£6,735.00	-£15.00

3. Click on **Tools** and then on **Goal Seek**.

When the goal seek window appears, type in the values (yes, you have to think about what you need to type in!).

Lesson 4 Two other models for finding the break-even point

4 The following numbers will then appear in this row of the spreadsheet:

	A	B	C	D	E	F
19						
20						
21						
22	Number of cups of coffee sold	Variable costs (£)	Fixed costs (£)	Total costs (£)	Sales revenue (£)	Profit/Loss (£)
23	4501.538462	£900.31	£5,852	£6,752.31	£6,752.31	£0.00

4501.538462 needs to be rounded up to 4502 cups of coffee, which is the break-even point. You can see that goal seek provides a quick way of arriving at the break-even point, although the other methods are still useful.

5 Save this file as AromaBar Break-Even Model V4 or exit the program.

What makes a good computer model?

When a computer model is first built it is often much simpler than the real situation it is trying to represent. Real life is generally quite complicated.

A good model is one that behaves in an identical way to the real thing.

Take the AromaBar as an example. We only considered some of the costs. For example, no account was taken of electricity and gas charges or water rates. The more you think about the model, the more complicated it needs to become. Often the first model you produce is very rough and needs to be refined. The more refining you do, the better the model becomes.

So, what makes a good computer model? Here are some answers:

- It is easy to use.
- It is accurate (the formulae/rules are all correct and the model has been thoroughly tested).
- It accurately simulates a real situation.

Make it happen

ACTIVITY 9: How might you improve the AromaBar model?

For this activity you have to think about ways that this model could be improved.

Think about the following.

- Are there any fixed or variable costs that should have been included?
- If so what are they?

Unit 4 Models and presenting numeric data

- How easy is it to use the model?
- If it is not easy to use, how might it be improved?
- How accurate is the model?
- Do you trust the results from the model? If not, why not?

Lesson 5: INTRODUCING RANDOMNESS INTO A MODEL

KEY WORDS

random number – a number that is impossible to predict

random number generator – a spreadsheet function that produces random numbers automatically

Background

Lots of things in real life happen randomly. Spreadsheets have a random number generator to generate random numbers. In this lesson you will learn how to use the random number generator.

Randomness is present in lots of situations

The winning number in a raffle

The number of people at a supermarket checkout

The winning number on a roulette wheel

Lesson 5 Introducing randomness into a model

Modelling throwing a single dice

When a dice is thrown fairly, obtaining any one number from one to six is equally likely. The probability of getting any number from one to six is 1/6 because there is one way to get the number you want out of a total of six ways.

This is called theoretical probability. You will now see how a spreadsheet model can be produced to simulate throwing a dice a set number of times. By varying the number of times the dice is thrown we can see how the experimental probability compares with the theoretical probability.

The RAND function in Excel

The RAND function in Excel generates a random number between zero and one. This is not much use on its own because we usually want whole random numbers larger than this. Whole numbers are called integers.

To model the score obtained when a dice is thrown you would need to generate an integer from one to six.

To do this you would use the following function:

=ROUND((RAND()*(6−1)+1),0)

The ROUND part makes sure that a whole number is produced. It rounds the number produced by the RAND function to the nearest whole number. The six is the highest random number you want and one is the lowest. The zero tells the ROUND function that no decimal places are needed.

QUESTIONS

Write down how you would adapt the RAND function to generate each of the following random numbers.

1 A whole number from 1 to 10.

2 A whole number from 5 to 10.

3 A random number from 0 to 1.

4 A whole number from 20 to 100.

The RANDBETWEEN function in Excel

There is another function which is easier to use. However, it may not have been installed on your computers. If the function is available then it is used in the following way:

To generate a random number from one to six you would use:

=RANDBETWEEN(1,6)

185

Unit 4 Models and presenting numeric data

Make it happen

ACTIVITY 10: Modelling throwing a dice

1. Load Excel and start a new workbook.

2. Set up the following labels on your workbook in the positions shown here.

	A	B	C	D	E
1	A model to simulate throwing a dice				
2					
3					
4	Throw	Score			
5					
6					
7					
8					
9					

3. Starting from cell A5 enter the numbers from one to six into the cell like this:

	A	B	C	D	E
1	A model to simulate throwing a dice				
2					
3					
4	Throw	Score			
5	1				
6	2				
7	3				
8	4				
9	5				
10	6				

This shows the throws. As you can see, this model will use six throws of the dice.

4. In cell B5, enter the following formula which puts a random whole number from one to six into the cell.

=ROUND((RAND()*(6−1)+1),0)

You will see a whole number from one to six appear when the formula is entered.

5. Press the button **F9** in the top row of keys on the keyboard. This is the recalculate key. It will recalculate a new random number. Keep pressing this key and watch the random number change.

186

Lesson 5 Introducing randomness into a model

6 Position the cursor on cell B5. Now copy this formula down the column as far as cell B10.

> **Note**
> Your random numbers will be different.

You worksheet will look like this:

	A	B	C	D
1	**A model to throw a dice**			
2				
3				
4	Throw	Score		
5	1	2		
6	2	1		
7	3	5		
8	4	4		
9	5	3		
10	6	4		

7 Press the **F9** key and watch the spreadsheet software obtain another set of numbers for the scores. Notice the randomness of these numbers. Remember, in theory and over a very large number of throws, you would expect each score to appear the same number of times. Clearly six throws is not many and this is why you get the wide variations.

8 Save your model using the file name 'A model to throw a dice'.

ACTIVITY 11: Changing the model to throw the dice a larger number of times

In this activity you will alter the model created in the last activity so that the dice is thrown a large number of times. You will also add a feature which produces a breakdown of the number of scores obtained. This will make it easy to see how many ones, twos, etc. have been thrown.

1 Load Excel and the file called 'A model to throw a dice', which you created in the previous activity (if they are not already loaded).

2 We will now simulate throwing a dice 36 times, so you will need to add the extra numbers down column A. Put the numbers into this column so that they go from 1 to 36.

3 Click on the formula on cell B5 and copy it down the column so that it appears in all 36 cells next to the throw numbers in column A.

You do not need to delete the existing data as the new data will replace it.

Unit 4 Models and presenting numeric data

4 Rather than look at all the scores and count them up from one to six, it is easy to get the spreadsheet to do it using the COUNTIF function. You have already come across this function in Year 7 Unit 5.

Enter the labels in the cells as shown here:

	A	B
43	Total 1s	
44	Total 2s	
45	Total 3s	
46	Total 4s	
47	Total 5s	
48	Total 6s	
49		

5 Enter the following COUNTIF function in cell B43.

=COUNTIF(B5:B40,1)

This tells the spreadsheet to count the number of cells in the cell range from B5 to B40 containing the number one. Look carefully at the above formula to see how it may be adapted to count the other numbers (i.e. two to six).

Now enter similar formulas for cells B44 to B48 to count up the occurrences of the other scores.

When that is done, this part of the worksheet looks like this:

	A	B
43	Total 1s	9
44	Total 2s	6
45	Total 3s	6
46	Total 4s	9
47	Total 5s	3
48	Total 6s	3

!Note
If you try to copy this formula it may not copy in the way you expect. When the formula is copied into cell B44 it changes to =COUNTIF(B6:B41,1) which is not what you want. It is probably easier to type the formula in each time.

REMEMBER!
Your numbers will be different.

6 Whenever you add a formula you must always check that it is producing the required answer. One way to check this would be to recalculate by pressing F9 and check that the totals always give 36 when added together. You can also add up the scores manually to check the individual totals.

!Note
Always check any calculation manually. Do not assume it will be right.

ACTIVITY 12: Adding a bar chart to the model

Rather than have a table containing the totals for each score, these could be displayed using a bar chart.

Your task is to produce a bar chart situated next to the totals.

Each time you use the F9 key to recalculate, the simulation throws the dice 36 times, records the scores and totals, and re-draws a new bar chart.

Lesson 5 Introducing randomness into a model

Your graph will look something like this:

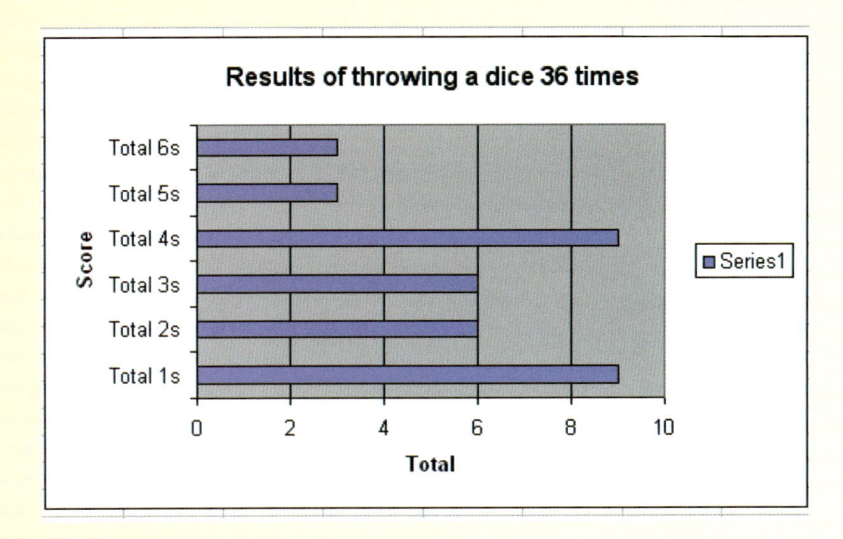

Results of throwing a dice 36 times

> **Note**
> You do not need to print the entire worksheet to do this.

Save your work using a suitable file name and print out a copy of the bar chart.

QUESTIONS

Using the above bar chart, answer the following questions:

1 John looks at the graph and says, 'These scores are not random because there would be equal totals for each score.' Explain why John is wrong.

2 How might you convince John using the model you have just produced?

Make it happen

ACTIVITY 13: Throwing the dice a large number of times

In this activity you will be required to produce a simulation to show a dice being thrown 360 times. Display the totals for the scores in the same way as last time and also produce a bar chart to display the results.

Save your work using a suitable file name and print out a copy of the bar chart (again you do not need to print the entire worksheet).

Unit 4 Models and presenting numeric data

ACTIVITY 14: The results of the two simulations

You will need the printouts for Activities 11 and 13.

In this activity you will compare the results of throwing a dice 36 times (i.e. a fairly small number of times) with those when the dice is thrown 360 times (i.e. a large number of times).

You now have to work out the best way to produce a model.

When the model is produced, press F9 to simulate the dice being thrown 360 times. Look carefully at how the total scores change.

Produce a bar chart that is a typical result and print this out.

Write a short paragraph discussing the simulation results from throwing the dice 36 times compared with throwing it 360 times. How did the results vary and were the scores more evenly distributed when the dice was thrown a greater number of times?

REMEMBER!

Theoretical probability predicts that there is a one in six chance of getting a certain score and that all the scores have the same probability. This would only apply to a very large number of throws.

WORKSHEET WORKSHEET WORKSHEET WORKSHEET WORKSHEET

WORKSHEET 8.4.5 Throwing two dice

You may be given a worksheet on which to write your answers or you may be asked to write your answers in your book. When you have finished, your teacher will either go through the answers or give you an answer sheet so that you can check the answers yourself.

There are lots of board games such as Monopoly, where you have to throw two dice and add the spots together to give the score.

Complete the following table showing all the combinations of throwing two dice.

I CAN'T BELIEVE HOW UNLUCKY I AM – 70 THROWS OF THE DICE AND NO DOUBLE!

Lesson 5 Introducing randomness into a model

Also, complete the total score column by adding the spots of each dice together. The first row has been filled in for you.

When you have completed the table, answer the questions that follow.

Score on dice 1	Score on dice 2	Total score
1	1	2

QUESTIONS

The following questions are based on the table you have just filled in.

1 How many different combinations are there when throwing two dice?

2 What is the probability of throwing a double six?

3 If you had to bet on a certain total score, which score would you choose and why?

4 Explain what the term 'unbiased' means.

Make it happen

ACTIVITY 15: Modelling throwing two dice

In this activity you will produce a model to simulate the throwing of two dice. You will be given a series of overall steps, although you will have to do a lot of work on your own.

1 Set up the title and labels as follows on a blank worksheet.

	A	B	C	D	E	F	G	H	I
1	Simulation to show the results when a pair of dice are thrown 360 times								
2									
3	Score on 1st dice	Score on 2nd dice	Total score						
4									
5									
6									
7									
8									
9									
10									

2 In cell A4 put in a formula to work out a random whole number between one and six.

3 Copy this formula down column A. As we want to simulate throwing 360 times, this will need to be copied down as far as cell A364.

4 Repeat step 3, but this time for column B (to throw the second dice).

5 In cell C3 put a formula to add together the numbers in cells A4 and B4 and then copy this formula down the column to add up the totals for all the pairs of throws.

6 At the end of the data put the following labels:
- Total Score of 2
- Total Score of 3
- Total Score of 4
- Total Score of 5
- Total Score of 6
- Total Score of 7
- Total Score of 8
- Total Score of 9
- Total Score of 10
- Total Score of 11
- Total Score of 12

7 In the column next to these labels use the COUNTIF function to work out the total scores.

8 Produce a bar chart using the total score, labels and the data.

9 Save your file using a suitable file name and print out a copy of the totals and the bar chart.

10 Put your name on the printout and hand it in to your teacher for marking.

5 Integrating applications to find solutions

Lesson 1:
INTRODUCTION: WHAT IS A SYSTEM?

In this unit you will learn about systems and how to use more than one piece of software to build a system. In order to build a system you will need to have a clear idea of what it must be capable of doing. You should consider carefully what needs to be done so that you fully understand the problem and can pick the best solution. Often there is more than one way of solving a problem, so it is important to be able to select the best solution.

This unit will show you how to solve ICT problems and you will use the skills and techniques learnt to solve your own ICT problems using a range of software.

Background theory and key information

KEY WORDS

system – a set of interconnected parts that work together to perform an overall task

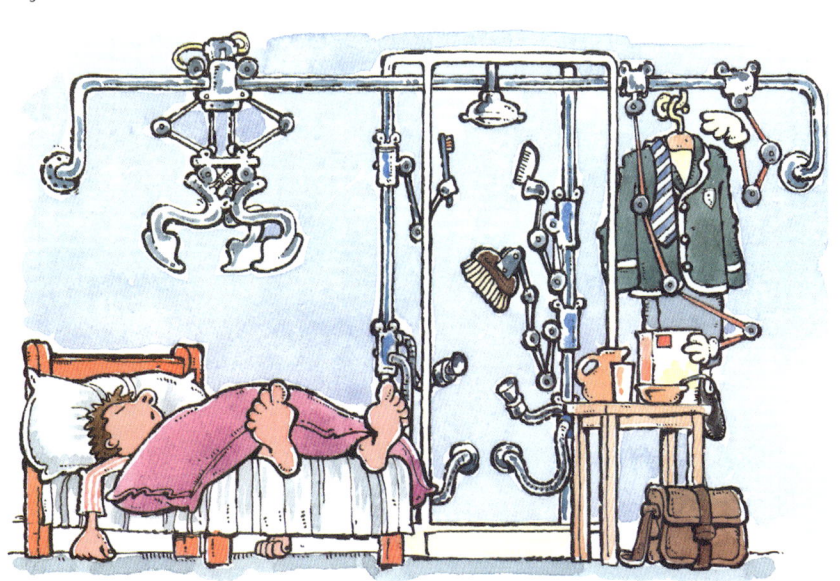

What is a system?

'System' is a simple word but it is quite hard to describe. The following is an explanation of the word 'system':

A system is a set of interconnected parts that work together to perform an overall task.

Here are some common systems:

- The digestive system.
- A car braking system.
- An air-conditioning system.
- A motorway warning sign system.

All of the above are general systems. We are more concerned with computer or information systems.

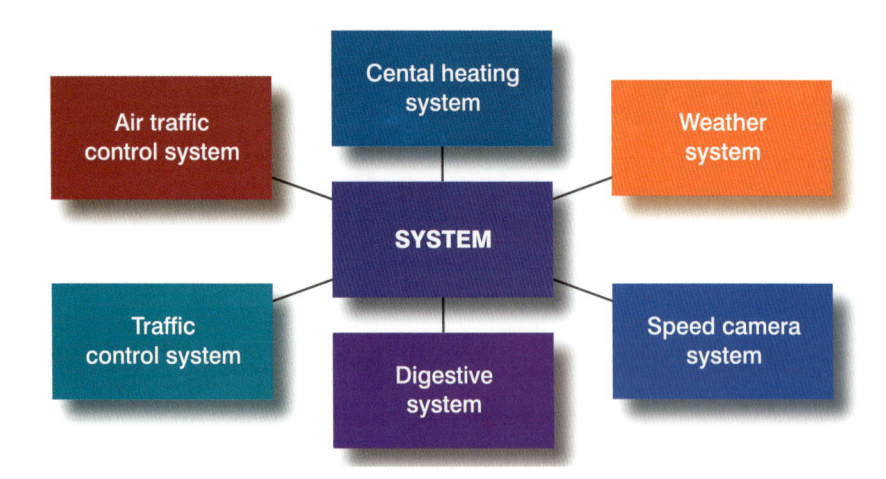

Unit 5 Integrating applications to find solutions

Here are some example of systems

Examples of information systems include:

- Holiday booking systems using the Internet.
- Order processing systems (e.g. buying goods via the Internet).
- Mail merge systems (used to produce individualised letters to lots of different people).
- Weather forecasting systems.
- Desktop publishing systems.
- A payroll system used to work out wages.

Basically, a system is a set of ways of putting something in, doing something to the input (i.e. what goes into the system) and producing the final version or answer. In the case of an information system, the input would be data. What causes the change is called the process. What comes out of the system is called the output.

Many simple systems are used in everyday life. A toaster converts bread into toast. The input is the bread and the setting on the toaster (e.g. how brown you want the toast). The process is the heating of the bread and the output is the toast itself.

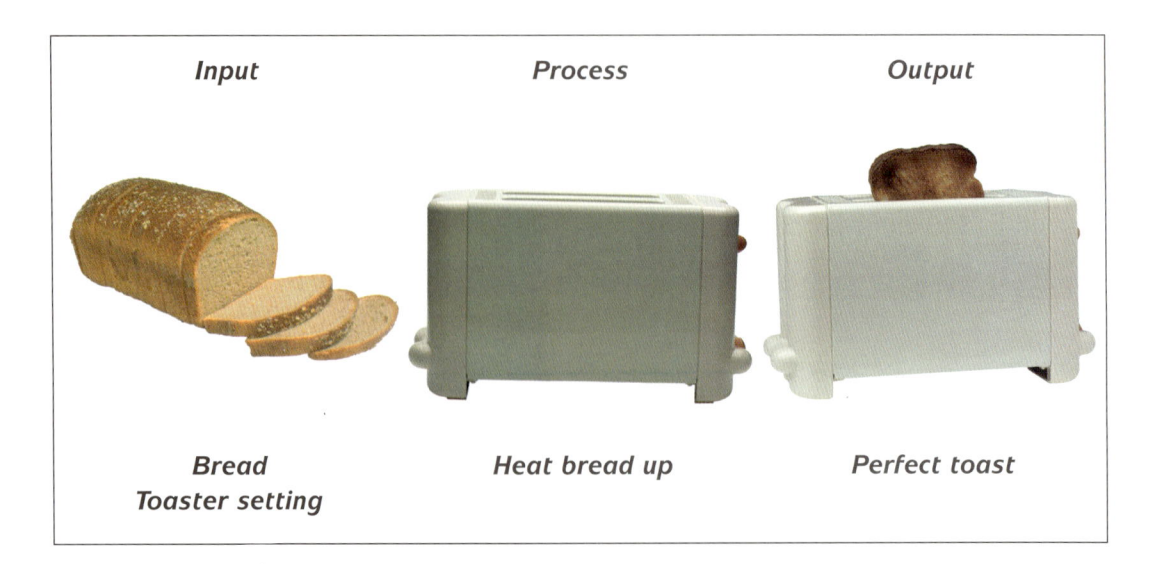

Input	Process	Output
Bread Toaster setting	Heat bread up	Perfect toast

Input, process and output for making toast

194

Lesson 1 Introduction: what is a system?

ACTIVITIESACTIVITIESACTIVITIESACTIVITIESACTIVITIESACTIVITIES

ACTIVITY 1: Identifying systems

This activity will test your understanding of systems.

1. Write down the names of three ordinary systems (i.e. ones not specifically concerned with ICT) that are not in the list above.

2. Write down the names of three information/computer systems that are not in the above list.

Identifying input, process and output in systems

It is important to be able to recognise the input, process and output in a system.

Take a weather forecasting system as an example. Such a system has the following inputs, process and output:

- Input: measurements are made automatically by sensors (e.g. temperature, pressure, humidity, rainfall, etc.).
- Process: the data is placed into a model where calculations are performed and the data is put into a form that enables ease of use.
- Output: the weather forecast for the next 24 hours. This could be in the form of text and a weather map.

In Unit 1 several systems where produced. One system used information on share prices obtained from the Internet and put that into a spreadsheet where the total value of the shares was calculated. Then a graph was drawn to show how the value of each of the shares contributed to the total.

In the system described above, the input, process and output steps (the three parts of the information system) have been put into different worksheets:

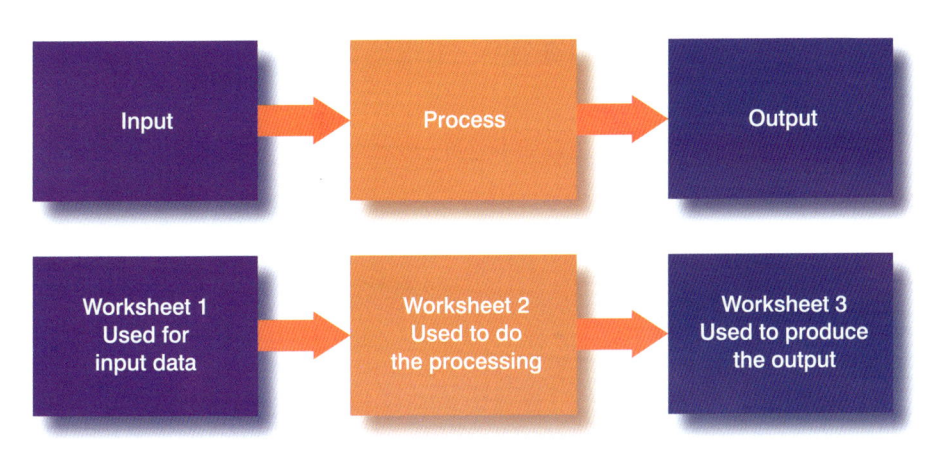

Input → Process → Output

Worksheet 1 Used for input data → Worksheet 2 Used to do the processing → Worksheet 3 Used to produce the output

The share price system in Unit 1 used three worksheets to represent the stages – input, process and output

All ICT systems have the three steps: input, process and output.

195

Unit 5 Integrating applications to find solutions

WORKSHEET WORKSHEET WORKSHEET WORKSHEET WORKSHEET

WORKSHEET 8.5.1 List the inputs, processes and outputs for each of the following systems

You may be given a worksheet on which to write your answers or you may be asked to write your answers in your book.

Overleaf are pictures that represent familiar systems. Decide on the inputs, processes and outputs needed for each system and then write them down.

- System 1: A security light outside a house.

- System 2: An automatic washing machine.

- System 3: An electric shower.

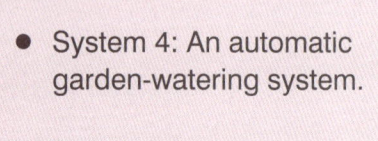

- System 4: An automatic garden-watering system.

- System 5: A pelican-crossing system.

- System 6: A central-heating system.

Lesson 1 Introduction: what is a system?

What does an ICT system consist of?

Most ICT systems consist of:

- Hardware
- Software
- Manual procedures.

The system life cycle

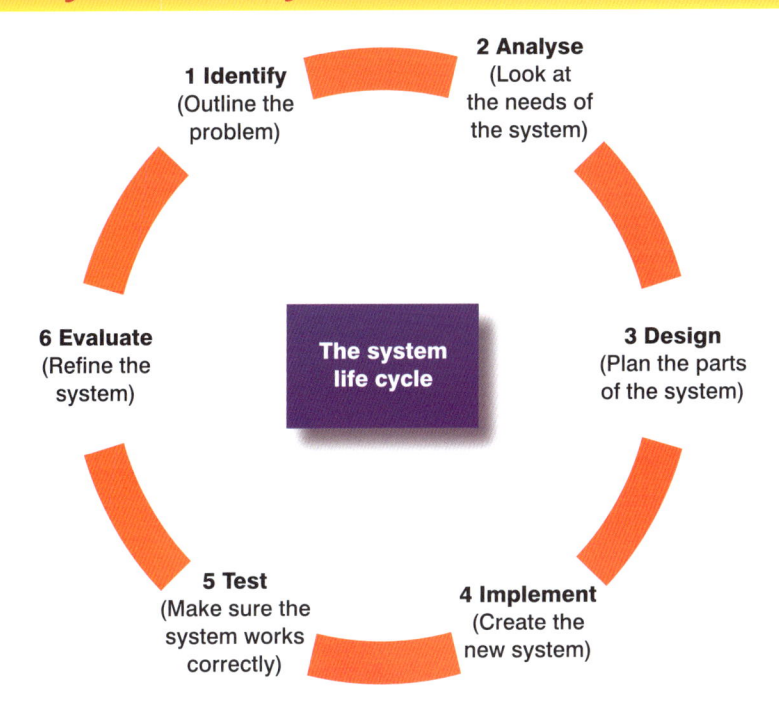

1 Identify (Outline the problem)

2 Analyse (Look at the needs of the system)

3 Design (Plan the parts of the system)

4 Implement (Create the new system)

5 Test (Make sure the system works correctly)

6 Evaluate (Refine the system)

The steps in the system life cycle

KEY WORDS

system life cycle – the series of steps carried out during the creation of a new system

The system life cycle comprises the stages that are worked through when a new ICT system is being developed. If you were to create an ICT system from scratch you would start at the identify stage and then carry out all of the steps up to step six. At step six you would look at the system you had developed, and if it was correct you would stop there. If it was not correct, you would look at the part causing the problem and go through all of the steps again.

What do these steps mean?

Here is what you would do for each step:

1. Identify: outline the problem.
2. Analyse: investigate the problem in detail and make sure you understand what needs to be done.
3. Design: plan each part of the system.
4. Implement: create the working version of the system.
5. Test: make sure that all parts of the system work and that the whole system works when the parts are put together.

Unit 5 Integrating applications to find solutions

6 Evaluate: consider if improvements are needed to the system.

When producing part of a system or the complete system, it is always best to follow the steps in the system life cycle.

Completing a project on time

A time is normally set for completion of a project. Often, projects are late because they have not been managed properly.

Putting events into order

A task can be broken down into lots of smaller jobs. To ensure that the overall task is carried out successfully, these smaller jobs need to be carried out in the correct order.

ACTIVITY 2: Sequencing events

This activity looks at the task of making a cup of coffee with milk and sugar.

1. Here are some events. Put them into the order in which they would normally be carried out.

    Add milk
    Stir
    Add coffee to cup
    Pour hot water into cup
    Add sugar
    Fill kettle with water

2. Are all of the necessary events in the above list? Write down any events that you think are missing from this list.

3. Combine the two lists from points 1 and 2 and then sort the items into the correct order.

4. Compare your list with those of your friends. Were your lists the same and if not how did they differ?

5. Are there any events in the list which could be swapped around? Write down which ones they are and give a reason why they could be swapped.

Thinking about the order of doing tasks is important particularly if it is possible to do more than one task at the same time. For example, while you were waiting for the water in the kettle to boil, you could add the coffee, milk and sugar to the cup to save time.

Lesson 1 Introduction: what is a system?

ACTIVITY 3: Preparing a roast dinner

In this activity you will work in a small group. Each member of the group should contribute to this group task.

The overall task of preparing a roast dinner can be broken down into lots of smaller activities or events such as peeling and preparing the potatoes, setting the table, etc.

Here are some of these activities:

Cook turkey	Set table
Cook carrots	Peel and prepare the potatoes
Serve meal	Peel and prepare sprouts
Make gravy	Slice turkey
Prepare turkey	Put food onto plates
Cook sprouts	Peel and prepare carrots
Heat plates	Cook potatoes

1 Your teacher will discuss these activities with you. Your task, along with the other members of your group, is to put these activities into a logical order.

2 The duration for each of these activities is shown in the following table.

Activity	Duration
Cook turkey	3 hours
Cook carrots	30 minutes
Serve meal	5 minutes
Make gravy	10 minutes
Prepare turkey	10 minutes
Cook sprouts	20 minutes
Heat plates	5 minutes
Set table	5 minutes
Peel and prepare the potatoes	15 minutes
Peel and prepare sprouts	10 minutes
Slice turkey	5 minutes
Put food onto plates	5 minutes
Peel and prepare carrots	10 minutes
Cook potatoes	1 hour

Unit 5 Integrating applications to find solutions

(a) Add up the time taken for each activity and write down your answer.

(b) Why would you not find the total time that it takes to make the meal by adding up all of the durations?

(c) What do you consider to be the minimum time needed to cook the dinner? Think about the problem carefully and discuss it with other members of your group. Write your answer down.

Managing a task

All of the activities need to be completed at a certain time; this is called the deadline. In the case of a roast meal, this would be the time when the meal has to be ready. In order that the whole task (i.e. the meal) will be ready on time it is necessary to manage the activities. You can do this using a time grid. The time grid can be used to mark the start and end time of all the activities. The length of the lines on this grid will show the duration of the activity.

Think about the following points:

1. Suppose the meal has to be ready at 3.00 pm. At what time should it be started?

2. Suppose just one person is preparing the meal. Which activities can be carried out at the same time as others?

3. If more than one person was available, could the meal be completed any quicker?

4. Which activities are fixed in position on the time line and which have a position that could be easily altered without changing the time needed to make the meal?

A time grid like this is called a Gantt chart. Gantt charts are used to schedule activities and help ensure that a task is completed on time.

KEY WORDS

Gantt chart – a horizontal time line used to plan and schedule activities

Lesson 1 Introduction: what is a system?

WORSHEET WORKSHEET WORKSHEET WORKSHEET WORKSHEET

WORKSHEET 8.5.2 **Complete the Gantt chart**

Your teacher will give you a copy of a table showing the answer for Activity 3 part 1, where you had to list the activities for creating a roast dinner into the correct order. Do not worry if your list is not the same as this; it could still be right. There are lots of different ways this could be ordered and still be correct.

Use the table containing the activities and their times to complete a Gantt chart.

Your teacher will give you the structure of the Gantt chart and you have to position and shade in the bars (or time lines).

Here is the Gantt chart. If you are using a worksheet, you will have to complete the other bars. If you are not using a worksheet, you will have to copy and complete the one shown below.

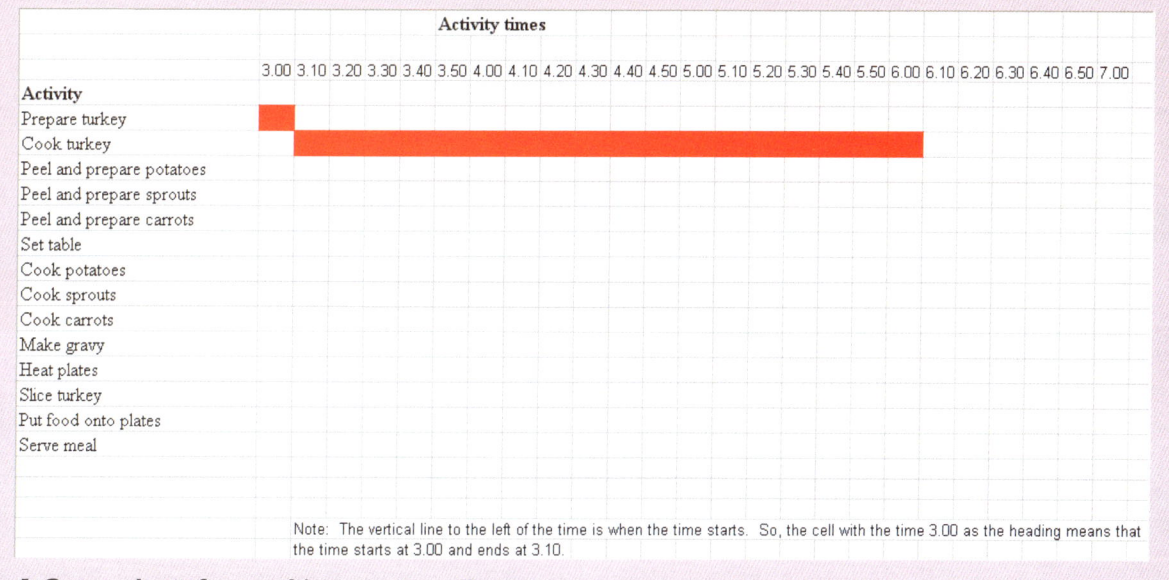

Activity	Activity times (3.00 – 7.00)
Prepare turkey	▮
Cook turkey	▬▬▬▬▬▬▬▬▬▬▬▬▬▬▬▬▬▬
Peel and prepare potatoes	
Peel and prepare sprouts	
Peel and prepare carrots	
Set table	
Cook potatoes	
Cook sprouts	
Cook carrots	
Make gravy	
Heat plates	
Slice turkey	
Put food onto plates	
Serve meal	

Note: The vertical line to the left of the time is when the time starts. So, the cell with the time 3.00 as the heading means that the time starts at 3.00 and ends at 3.10.

A Gantt chart for cooking a roast dinner

If you compare your Gantt chart with those of your friends it will probably be different because although some activities such as prepare turkey, cook turkey etc. are fixed, other activities can be slotted in various times.

What you should already know

As this unit requires you to use lots of different types of software, you will need a good knowledge of using word-processing, spreadsheet, desktop publishing and graphics software. You will also be using some database terms such as field and record, so you may need to refresh your memory on these. You may need to look back at previous work or help each other if you come across something you cannot do.

Unit 5 Integrating applications to find solutions

What you will learn

In this unit you will:

- Learn how to investigate and understand a problem.
- Schedule activities.
- Model a project's finances so that you can be sure it will make a profit.
- Design and create materials to market the project.
- Set up and perform a mail merge.
- Understand how to create customer records.
- Design and create control programs to control the conditions in a greenhouse.

Lesson 2: UNDERSTANDING THE PROBLEM AND THINKING ABOUT SOLUTIONS

Background

Each of your classmates has been given the following memo from the head teacher of your school.

A MEMO FROM YOUR HEAD TEACHER

To all year 8 students

You may have heard that we would like to improve the school ICT facilities so that we will be the most up-to-date secondary school in the authority. You will benefit from this as you will be using all the latest ICT equipment and this will make learning much more fun.

Buying all of this equipment will cost a lot of money. This is where you come in.

All of the students in the school will be given year projects. You will learn about the projects in your subject areas and particularly in your ICT lessons.

The project for year 8 pupils is to grow popular bedding plants from seed and then to sell them to the local community. Whilst doing this you will learn how to work as a team, how to use ICT to help with this project, how to run and manage a simple business and so on. The aim is to learn something useful and at the same time have fun and raise money for the school to buy new equipment.

Your ICT teacher will give you a project sheet explaining what you have to do.

After reading the above memo your ICT teacher gives you the following Project Sheet.

Lesson 2 Understanding the problem and thinking about solutions

> **PROJECT SHEET: USING ICT TO HELP WITH THE PROJECT**
>
> The overall aim of the project is to grow popular bedding plants from seed in a greenhouse and then sell them to the local community at a cheap price. The profit from the sale of the plants will be used to help buy the latest ICT equipment for the school.
>
> In this unit you will be looking at how ICT can support this project and you will develop ICT solutions to the problems of managing and running the scheme.
>
> A similar project was started several years ago but was abandoned despite making a reasonable profit after the first year. The main problem was that neither the staff nor the pupils wanted to come in to school to water the plants over the weekends or during the school holidays, which was understandable. This is not a problem any more as ICT can be used to monitor and control the conditions in the greenhouse. The plants will be watered automatically and neither staff nor students will need to give up time at the weekends or holidays to do this.
>
> The only information we still have from the last project is a database that was created using spreadsheet software. It shows the customers' names and addresses and their orders. This spreadsheet will be made available to you.

Using computer control in the greenhouse will mean that everything is taken care of

Finding out about the purchasing and growing of bedding plants from seed

There are many different companies that supply seed for plants. Thompson & Morgan is a well-known seed supplier and its seeds can be found for sale in most garden centres. It also supplies larger quantities of seed wholesale, which will make it cheaper.

Unit 5 Integrating applications to find solutions

Use the Internet to access the Thompson & Morgan website at **www.thompson-morgan.com/uk/en**.

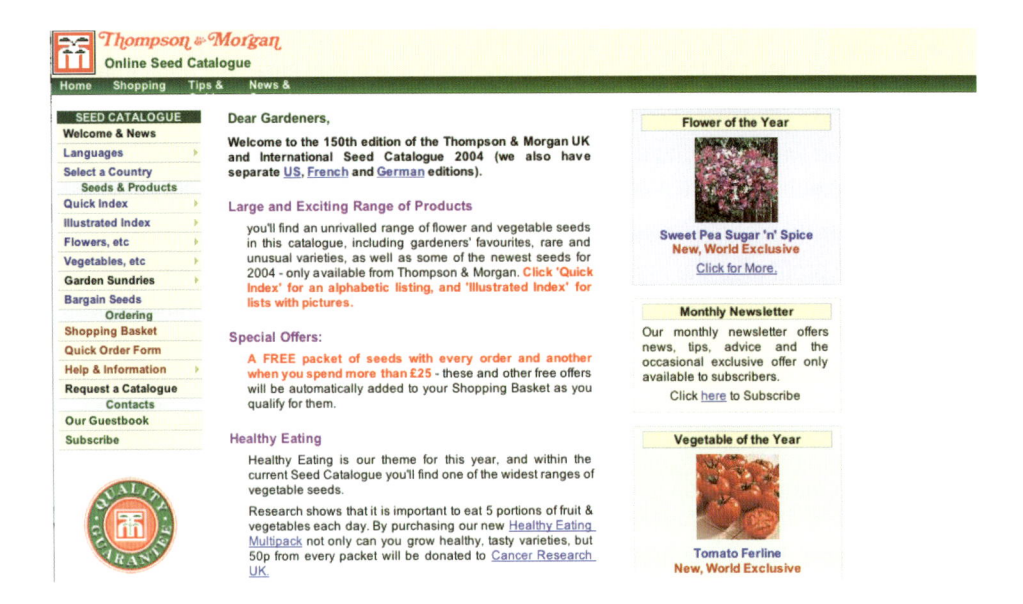

The home page for the Thompson & Morgan website

http://seeds.thompson-morgan.com/uk/en

Below is the web page for pansies. Notice that this web page includes growing instructions as well as the costs for different amounts of seed.

Instructions for growing pansies

http://seeds.thompson-morgan.com/uk/en/product/3252/2

~ Pansy : Universal Mixed ~

Code	Description	Price	Status
3252	1 packet (35 seeds)	£2.99	ADD

Half-hardy Annual / Hardy Perennial

Flowers: Dependent on sowing time

Height: 9 inches

Position: Sun or Partial Shade

Germination: Experience Useful

Aftercare: Easy

Description: Wonderful for summer bedding or if sown in summer will flower through the winter in mild spells. Compact and in a very wide range of blotched and clear colours and good flower size. Flowers winter or summer, Height 6-9in.

Sowing Instructions: For winter flowers sow in mid summer 1.5mm (1/16in) deep in good seed compost excluding light as darkness is beneficial. Germination usually takes 14-21 days at 19-24C (65-75F). Keep the soil just moist and avoid high temperatures which will prevent germination. For summer flowers sow late winter/spring or late summer.

Growing Instructions: When seedlings are large enough to handle, transplant and grow cool and plant out in the autumn 23-30cm (9-12in) apart in most soils, sun or part shade.

Aftercare Instructions: The summer sowings should be moved to a coldframe and planted out in early spring.

Lesson 2 Understanding the problem and thinking about solutions

◀ FIND IT OUT ▶

Use the Thompson & Morgan website to find out about the growing conditions for the following bedding plants:

- Alyssum
- Lobelia
- Marigold.

Write brief notes on the growing conditions needed for each plant.

Make it happen

ACTIVITY 4: Identifying the parts of the project that ICT can help with

In this activity you have to think about those areas of the project that could use ICT to make the task easier.

Because it is much cheaper to buy in bulk, you will grow just a few popular types of bedding plants. These are the plants that you will grow:

- Pansies
- Alyssum
- Lobelia
- Marigold.

The plants in the above list are the most popular bedding plants and they are easy to grow.

Write a list of ways to use ICT to help with the project. Do not just think about growing the plants, think about selling them and keeping records of the orders.

ACTIVITY 5: Developing the project

Look at the information about pansies in the Thompson & Morgan on-line seed catalogue. This information is shown in the figure above.

1. What information in the above figure might help you when constructing a financial model?

205

Unit 5 Integrating applications to find solutions

2 You are going to create a financial model to determine the break-even point for selling the trays of plants. This is the number of trays you need to sell in order to cover all of the costs.

List the costs involved in producing the plants other than the cost of the electricity for the lights and heaters. All of the labour will be provided free by the students in your group.

3 Later on in the unit, a control flowchart will be produced to control the growing conditions in the greenhouse. State the ideal temperature for the following:

(a) Germinating the pansy seeds.

(b) Growing the young plants.

ACTIVITY 6: What activities are there in the project?

Your teacher will put you into small project groups. This will make it easier to work on the project as the group members will be able to discuss things amongst themselves.

The project is to grow pansies from seed, sell the plants and make a profit which will go towards paying for ICT equipment.

ICT will be used to:

- Construct a financial model to work out, before you start, whether you can make a profit from the project.
- Help advertise and market the plants.
- Control the growing conditions inside the greenhouse.
- Produce records to keep track of the customers.

Discuss with your project team and then write down the ways that ICT could be used to help with each part of the project listed above.

KEY WORDS

parameter – a limiting factor that dictates how wide or narrow a project needs to be

The parameters of the system

It is not always possible to develop the ideal or perfect system. Such systems take time and money to develop. You may need to limit the size of the project in some way. Factors that limit the scope of a project are called parameters.

Lesson 3: DEVELOPING A FINANCIAL MODEL FOR THE BEDDING PLANTS PROJECT

Before starting a project such as this it is important to model the money coming in and going out and forecast the expected profit/loss. This is called a financial model and you will be developing this model in the activities below.

In this instance, the most important thing to know is the cost of producing one tray of plants. To work this out you need to find out the price of the things required to get the project started.

!Note

Models can be created using spreadsheet software. To create a model from scratch you have to consider the variables and the rules.

KEY WORDS

financial model – a spreadsheet or other model used to show the likely profit or loss from a business or venture

forecast – a prediction of what might happen in the future

rule – a condition that must be obeyed in a computer model and which is expressed as a formula

variable – a quantity whose value is not fixed

What money will be needed to get going?

The head teacher has set a budget for the project. This budget is for all of the costs involved in setting up the project, such as:

- the cost of gardening tools
- advertising and marketing costs
- the cost of stamps for mail shots
- the cost of compost
- the cost of seeds
- the cost of seed trays.

Your head teacher has given you an initial budget of £500 to cover all of the above. All other expenses, not in the list above, will be met by the school. The head teacher will pay for all of the equipment to control the growing conditions in the greenhouse and also for the computer equipment and software.

Unit 5 Integrating applications to find solutions

The costs

You have managed to negotiate the best prices on the items listed above and the costs are as follows.

Gardening tools	= £165
Cost of stamps for mail shot (200 stamps at £0.20)	= £40
Advertising and marketing costs	= £75
Costs per tray of plants (i.e. based on 12 seeds per tray):	
Seed (12 seeds at £0.02 each)	= £0.24
Seed tray	= £0.35
Labels (to show what plants are in each tray)	= £0.02
Compost	= £0.19

Working out the break-even point

By working out the break-even point you will find out how many trays you would need to produce and sell in order to break even. In Unit 4 you learnt how to find the break-even point using various methods. If you are unsure about break even you may want to go back and read the relevant section in Unit 4.

REMEMBER!

Variable costs are those that depend on the number of trays produced. Fixed costs are those that do not depend on the number of trays produced.

Fixed or variable costs?

In order to work out the break-even point you need to separate the costs into fixed or variable costs.

Make it happen

ACTIVITY 7: Is it a fixed or a variable cost?

Copy the following table and then complete the right-hand column with either 'fixed' or 'variable'.

Your teacher will go through the answers with you as it is important when you set up the model that you get this right.

Cost	Fixed or Variable?
Seed	
Seed trays	
Advertising and marketing	
Stamps for mail shot	
Gardening tools	
Labels	
Compost	

Lesson 3 Developing a financial model for the bedding plants project

Using spreadsheet software to create models

You have had plenty of practice creating models as you learnt about them in Year 7 as well as in Unit 4 this year. If you are still unsure you should look back at these previous units. Before starting to create the models make sure that you understand the difference between absolute and relative referencing and that you know how to create formulae.

KEY WORDS

absolute cell referencing – in this type of reference, a particular cell is used in a formula, and when this formula is copied to a new address the cell address does not change

formulae – calculations used in a spreadsheet

relative cell referencing – when a cell is used in a formula and the formula is copied to a new address, the cell address changes to take account of the formula's new position

Make it happen

ACTIVITY 8: Setting up a model to determine the break-even point

The break-even point is the number of trays of plants produced at which point the costs of producing and marketing the plants minus the money from the sale of plants equals £0.

1 Load Excel and type in the headings and labels exactly as they appear here:

	A	B	C	D	E	F
1	Model for the Bedding Plants Project to determine the break-even point					
2						
3						
4	Selling price of tray of bedding plants	£1.40				
5						
6	**Fixed costs**					
7	Gardening tools	£165				
8	Advertising and marketing costs	£75				
9	Costs of stamps for mail shot	£40				
10	Total fixed costs					
11						
12						
13	**Variable costs (per tray)**					
14	Seeds	£0.24				
15	Seed tray	£0.35				
16	Compost	£0.19				
17	Label	£0.02				
18	Total variable costs (per tray)					
19						
20	Number of trays of plants sold	Variable costs (£)	Fixed costs (£)	Total costs (£)	Sales Revenue (£)	Profit/Loss (£)
21						
22						
23						
24						
25						
26						
27						

Unit 5 Integrating applications to find solutions

2 Put a formula in cell B10 to work out the total fixed costs and then put a formula in cell B18 to work out the total variable costs.

3 You now need to fill in the data for row 21 to work out the break-even point. You need a number of trays sold as a starting point.

Enter the number 300 into cell A21.

4 Now put a formula into cell B21 to work out the variable costs when 300 trays are produced. This formula should contain a reference to cell B4.

5 As the fixed costs do not change with the number of trays produced, put in a formula to take the contents of cell B10 and put them into cell C21. Look back at Unit 4 for a hint on how to do this.

6 Put a formula in cell D21 to add the costs in cells B21 and C21 together.

7 Put a formula in cell E21 to work out the amount of money from the sale of the number of trays of plants. This is called the sales revenue. This formula will need to contain both the selling price of a tray of bedding plants and the number of trays of plants sold.

8 Now put in a formula to work out the Profit/Loss (£). The Profit/Loss (£) can be calculated by subtracting the total costs from the sales revenue.

9 You should now check that your worksheet looks the same as the one below. If it does not you will need to find out which of the formulae are wrong and correct them.

	A	B	C	D	E	F
1	Model for the Bedding Plants Project to determine the break-even point					
2						
3						
4	Selling price of tray of bedding plants	£1.40				
5						
6	**Fixed costs**					
7	Gardening tools	£165				
8	Advertising and marketing costs	£75				
9	Costs of stamps for mail shot	£40				
10	Total fixed costs	£280				
11						
12						
13	**Variable costs (per tray)**					
14	Seeds	£0.24				
15	Seed tray	£0.35				
16	Compost	£0.19				
17	Label	£0.02				
18	Total variable costs (per tray)	£0.80				
19						
20	Number of trays of plants sold	Variable costs (£)	Fixed costs (£)	Total costs (£)	Sales Revenue (£)	Profit/Loss (£)
21	300	£240.00	£280	£520.00	£420.00	-£100.00
22						
23						
24						

10 Save your model using the file name 'Final bedding plants model'.

Lesson 3 Developing a financial model for the bedding plants project

ACTIVITY 9: Finding the break-even point

Having set up the model in the last activity, you can now determine the break-even point, which is the number of trays of plants that will give a Profit/Loss of zero.

You will remember finding the break-even point for the Aroma Coffee Bar in Unit 4. You used three different methods.

In this activity you have to find the number of trays sold in order to break even.

It is up to you which method you use to determine the break-even point. However, you may find that the goal-seek method is the easiest.

Save your worksheet using the file name 'Bedding plants model – break-even'.

KEY WORDS

goal seek – using spreadsheet software to find the input value needed to produce a certain output value

REMEMBER!

It is often best to use **Save As** rather than just **Save** because you can see where the file is being saved.

ACTIVITY 10: Exercising the model

1. Load the worksheet Final bedding plants model, if it is not already loaded.

2. One of the teachers is a keen gardener and has been shown this worksheet.

He says that you are planning to sell the trays of plants too cheaply.

He suggests that the selling price should be £2.00 per tray.

Make this change to the spreadsheet.

What profit/loss is made when 300 trays are sold?

3. The same teacher suggests that many people have old gardening tools in their sheds that they no longer use and they may be willing to donate them to the school. This would mean that you would not need to buy any gardening tools.

Delete the label and the amount set aside for gardening tools.

What profit/loss is now made when 300 trays are sold?

Why do you think this has made such a difference to the profit?

4. Some students offer to do some research by travelling around garden centres and pricing their bedding plants. They want the plants to be slightly more expensive.

After this, it is suggested that the selling price of the plants be increased to £2.30 per tray.

What profit/loss is now made when 300 trays are sold?

Unit 5 Integrating applications to find solutions

EXTENSION ACTIVITY

Using the model you have just created, determine the new break-even point.

ACTIVITY 11: Has the budget set by the head teacher been exceeded?

Here are two worksheets for the financial model. Both worksheets give the break-even point.

The head teacher has given the project an initial budget of £500.

Initial model

	A	B	C	D	E	F
1	Model for the Bedding Plants Project to determine the break-even point					
2						
3						
4	Selling price of tray of bedding plants	£1.40				
5						
6	**Fixed costs**					
7	Gardening tools	£165				
8	Advertising and marketing costs	£75				
9	Costs of stamps for mail shot	£40				
10	Total fixed costs	£280				
11						
12						
13	**Variable costs (per tray)**					
14	Seeds	£0.24				
15	Seed tray	£0.35				
16	Compost	£0.19				
17	Label	£0.02				
18	Total variable costs (per tray)	£0.80				
19						
20	Number of trays of plants sold	Variable costs (£)	Fixed costs (£)	Total costs (£)	Sales Revenue (£)	Profit/Loss (£)
21	466.6666667	£373.33	£280	£653.33	£653.33	£0.00

1 Look at the above screenshot of the initial model. All of the costs have to be paid before any money comes in from the sale of plants.

Is the project suggested by the above model feasible bearing in mind that the budget is £500? Explain your answer.

Final model

	A	B	C	D	E	F
1	Model for the Bedding Plants Project to determine the break-even point					
2						
3						
4	Selling price of tray of bedding plants	£2.30				
5						
6	**Fixed costs**					
7						
8	Advertising and marketing costs	£75				
9	Costs of stamps for mail shot	£40				
10	Total fixed costs	£115				
11						
12						
13	**Variable costs (per tray)**					
14	Seeds	£0.24				
15	Seed tray	£0.35				
16	Compost	£0.19				
17	Label	£0.02				
18	Total variable costs (per tray)	£0.80				
19						
20	Number of trays of plants sold	Variable costs (£)	Fixed costs (£)	Total costs (£)	Sales Revenue (£)	Profit/Loss (£)
21	76.66666667	£61.33	£115	£176.33	£176.33	£0.00

2 The screenshot for the final model is shown on the previous page. Is the project (as suggested by this spreadsheet) feasible bearing in mind that the budget is £500?

Lesson 4: KEEPING RECORDS

In this lesson you will be looking at keeping records on the customers and their orders.

The project in the past

The head teacher has told you that a similar bedding plants project was undertaken in the past and he still has the records of customers who bought the plants.

Although the project in the past was successful in terms of selling the plants and making a profit, the equipment to control the conditions in the greenhouse was very expensive compared with today. This meant that pupils or staff had to do the watering and take care of opening and closing windows and turning heaters on or off. This was fine when the pupils or staff were at school, but it needed to be done at weekends and in the school holidays. Not many pupils or staff wanted to tie themselves down over the holidays. Because of the hassle, the project was abandoned after three years. All of the materials such as seed trays etc. were sold and the large greenhouse was then used for storage.

QUESTIONS

1 In what ways can ICT help with the marketing of this bedding plants project?

2 Give the main reason for the failure of the bedding plants project in the past.

3 The head teacher gives you a disk containing a spreadsheet file that has a database showing past customer names and addresses along with details of their orders.

Why do you think spreadsheet software was used to create the database rather than specialist database software?

4 Use a dictionary to look up the definition of marketing. You can use either a traditional dictionary or one on the Internet.

Write down an easy-to-understand definition of the word.

Unit 5 Integrating applications to find solutions

Make it happen

ACTIVITY 12: The advantages of the new project compared with the old

In this activity you will identify the advantages that the new project has over the old one.

1 Write a short piece of word-processed text explaining how the new project will overcome the problems encountered with the previous project.

2 The teacher in charge of your project has said that the list of customers and the plants they ordered might be very useful.

This list was prepared using spreadsheet software and some of the details are shown here.

	A	B	C	D	E	F	G	H	I	J
1	Forename	Surname	Street	Area	Postcode	Telephone No	Pansy	Lobelia	Marigold	Alyssum
2	Dianne	Kennedy	49 Abbeyfield Drive	Old Swan	L13 7FR	(0151)547-1812	1	0	0	0
3	Ann	Hugh	93 Aspes Road	West Derby	L12 6FG	(0151)724-9880	3	3	2	0
4	Paula	Edwards	109 Pagemoss Lane	Old Swan	L13 4ED	(0151)228-3142	5	3	0	2
5	Fiona	Philips	3 Lake Avenue	Old Swan	L13 5FC	(0151)220-0861	10	0	0	0
6	Kirk	Kennedy	49 Abbeyfield Drive	Garston	L24 7HJ	(0151)547-1812	2	0	0	1
7	Joanne	Macmahon	18 Grassendale Court	Woolton	L35 6FD	(0151)426-9849	4	7	0	5
8	Barbara	Mckay	10 Crondoll Grove	Old Swan	L13 4GH	(0151)281-5074	2	3	3	3
9	Eamon	Holderness	111 Elmshouse Road	Garston	L24 7FT	(0151)280-6458	0	6	6	6
10	Irenee	Gant	34 Austin Close	Garston	L24 8UH	(0151)475-3351	1	1	0	0
11	Rita	Lynch	99 Astley Road	Old Swan	L13 5DF	(0151)289-9300	0	0	0	1
12	Paula	Martin	34 Richmond Avenue	West Derby	L12 3DE	(0151)489-3805	5	4	4	4
13	Marie	Marshall	50 Fairfield Cresent	West Derby	L12 4SD	(0151)709-9207	6	0	0	6
14	Nicola	Metcalf	35 Aigburth Hall Lane	West Derby	L12 8HG	(0151)475-5225	4	2	2	3
15	Margaret	Thomas	139 Hollow Croft	Old Swan	L13 9KL	(0151)449-3123	0	0	0	3
16	David	Jones	35 Speke Hall Road	Garston	L24 5VF	(0151)480-4589	0	5	0	5
17	Angela	Gerrard	66 Clough Road	Woolton	L35 6GH	(0151)708-3445	12	7	7	7
18	Gill	Martin	8 Crofton Road	Old Swan	L13 5DF	(0151)336-5050	6	6	6	6
19	Amy	Cheung	18 Rycroft Road	West Derby	L12 5DR	(0151)427-2384	1	1	0	1
20	Maureen	Criddle	42 Lawson Drive	West Derby	L12 3SA	(0151)722-6899	2	3	3	1
21	Raymond	Cropper	12 Coronation Street	Old Swan	L13 8JH	(0151)478-0371	0	0	0	2
22	Hugh	Davies	124 Inkerman Street	Old Swan	L13 5RT	(0151)478-0098	5	6	2	3
23	Amy	Jones	13 Cambridge Avenue	West Derby	L12 5RE	(0151)427-1011	8	0	0	0
24	Charles	Hughes	98 Forgate Street	West Derby	L12 6TY	(0151)427-4299	6	10	10	5
25	Lesley	Lee	222 Forge Street	Garston	L24 5RS	(0151)280-0011	12	6	6	10
26	Tom	Jackson	12 Leopold Drive	Garston	L24 6ER	(0151)280-9212	3	4	4	0
27	Heidi	Hutton	123 Edgehill Road	West Derby	L12 6TH	(0151)280-0088	1	1	1	1
28	Amy	Rimmer	12 Woolton Road	Garston	L24 7DR	(0151)280-7786	2	3	3	0
29	Fiona	Harper	43 Fort Avenue	West Derby	L12 7YH	(0151)427-8777	5	5	0	5
30	Freda	Quiggins	54 Coronation Street	Old Swan	L13 9YT	(0151)478-1142	2	2	2	2
31	Charles	Clare	1 Woodend Drive	Woolton	L35 8RW	(0151)426-9849	0	6	0	0
32	Andrew	Miles	49 Leopold Drive	Garston	L24 6SD	(0151)280-8009	5	5	0	0

The list (database) of customers and their orders

(a) Why might this list of past customers be useful with your new project?

(b) One pupil suggests that people may object to being sent mail through the post and for this reason you should not use the list. Do you agree? Give reasons for your answer.

Lesson 4 Keeping records

Keeping track of customers

It is usually easier to sell to your past customers than to get new ones, so having the information on customers and their orders is very useful even though it has been three years since they ordered the plants.

Not all of the customers in the list will order plants. Some past customers may have moved house or they may prefer to buy plants elsewhere.

It is helpful if customers can place their orders as early in the year as possible. This is so that plants can be grown to order. The orders are paid for when the customers collect their plants from the school.

The idea is that the customers place their order by filling in an order form and returning it to the school.

The data on the form can be organised by using spreadsheet software to create a new database for new customers. The details of those people from the customer file who have ordered in the past can be copied into the new database. This saves having to type their name and address details in again although you will still probably need to alter the details of their orders.

KEY WORDS

organise – to give an orderly structure to something

Why keep records?

You need to keep records so that you:

- know how may trays of each type of plant to grow
- can contact customers to tell them their plants are ready to pick up
- can send details of plants and order forms to past customers
- can work out how much to charge the customer when they pick up their order
- can deal with customer queries (e.g. customers who have forgotten what they have ordered).

Unit 5 Integrating applications to find solutions

KEY WORDS

database – a series of files stored in a computer that can be accessed in a variety of different ways

field – an item of data or space for data in a database

record – a set of related information about a thing or individual. Records are subdivided into fields

REMEMBER!

A list or simple database created with spreadsheet software is often referred to as a flat-file database. The other type of database, called a relational database, needs to be produced using specialist database software.

How are the records stored?

Simple databases are often set up using spreadsheet software for the following reasons:

- It saves having to learn about specialist database software.
- Spreadsheet software is easier to use than database software.
- More people have spreadsheet software on their computers than specialist database software.

Make it happen

ACTIVITY 13: Using the customer file

You are now going to look at the customer file which was prepared using the spreadsheet Excel. You will see how useful it might be to you.

1. Load the spreadsheet software Excel and the file called Customer and orders database.

2. Check that you have the right file by comparing what you see on the screen with the screenshot on the following page.

3. In cell K1 type the label *Number of trays ordered*. Can you find out how to make this cell appear like all the other labels? If you are unable to do this, ask for help.

4. Put a formula in cell K2 to work out the total number of trays that this particular customer has ordered.

Copy this formula down the column as far as cell K32.

5. It would be really useful for the project team to know how many trays of each type of plant were sold.

Add suitable labels and formulae to work this out.

6. Save this worksheet using the file name 'Customer and orders database v1'.

REMEMBER!

Landscape orientation is ideal for situations where the width of the data is much greater than the length.

216

Lesson 4 Keeping records

	A	B	C	D	E	F	G	H	I	J
1	Forename	Surname	Street	Area	Postcode	Telephone No	Pansy	Lobelia	Marigold	Alyssum
2	Dianne	Kennedy	49 Abbeyfield Drive	Old Swan	L13 7FR	(0151)547-1812	1	0	0	0
3	Ann	Hugh	93 Aspes Road	West Derby	L12 6FG	(0151)724-9880	3	3	2	0
4	Paula	Edwards	109 Pagemoss Lane	Old Swan	L13 4ED	(0151)228-3142	5	3	0	2
5	Fiona	Philips	3 Lake Avenue	Old Swan	L13 5FC	(0151)220-0861	10	0	0	0
6	Kirk	Kennedy	49 Abbeyfield Drive	Garston	L24 7HJ	(0151)547-1812	2	0	0	1
7	Joanne	Macmahon	18 Grassendale Court	Woolton	L35 6FD	(0151)426-9849	4	7	0	5
8	Barbara	Mckay	10 Crondoll Grove	Old Swan	L13 4GH	(0151)281-5074	2	3	3	3
9	Eamon	Holderness	111 Elmshouse Road	Garston	L24 7FT	(0151)280-6458	0	6	6	6
10	Irenee	Gant	34 Austin Close	Garston	L24 8UH	(0151)475-3351	1	1	0	0
11	Rita	Lynch	99 Astley Road	Old Swan	L13 5DF	(0151)289-9300	0	0	0	1
12	Paula	Martin	34 Richmond Avenue	West Derby	L12 3DE	(0151)489-3805	5	4	4	4
13	Marie	Marshall	50 Fairfield Cresent	West Derby	L12 4SD	(0151)709-9207	6	0	0	6
14	Nicola	Metcalf	35 Aigburth Hall Lane	West Derby	L12 8HG	(0151)475-5225	4	2	2	3
15	Margaret	Thomas	139 Hollow Croft	Old Swan	L13 9KL	(0151)449-3123	0	0	0	3
16	David	Jones	35 Speke Hall Road	Garston	L24 5VF	(0151)480-4589	0	5	0	5
17	Angela	Gerrard	66 Clough Road	Woolton	L35 6GH	(0151)708-3445	12	7	7	7
18	Gill	Martin	8 Crofton Road	Old Swan	L13 5DF	(0151)336-5050	6	6	6	6
19	Amy	Cheung	18 Rycroft Road	West Derby	L12 5DR	(0151)427-2384	1	1	0	1
20	Maureen	Criddle	42 Lawson Drive	West Derby	L12 3SA	(0151)722-6899	2	3	3	1
21	Raymond	Cropper	12 Coronation Street	Old Swan	L13 8JH	(0151)478-0371	0	0	0	2
22	Hugh	Davies	124 Inkerman Street	Old Swan	L13 5RT	(0151)708-0098	5	6	2	3
23	Amy	Jones	13 Cambridge Avenue	West Derby	L12 5RE	(0151)427-1011	8	0	0	0
24	Charles	Hughes	98 Forgate Street	West Derby	L12 6TY	(0151)427-4299	6	10	10	5
25	Lesley	Lee	222 Forge Street	Garston	L24 5RS	(0151)280-0011	12	6	6	10
26	Tom	Jackson	12 Leopold Drive	Garston	L24 6ER	(0151)280-9212	3	4	4	0
27	Heidi	Hutton	123 Edgehill Road	West Derby	L12 6TH	(0151)280-0088	1	1	1	1
28	Amy	Rimmer	12 Woolton Road	Garston	L24 7DR	(0151)280-7786	2	3	3	0
29	Fiona	Harper	43 Fort Avenue	West Derby	L12 7YH	(0151)427-8777	5	5	0	5
30	Freda	Quiggins	54 Coronation Street	Old Swan	L13 9YT	(0151)478-1142	2	2	2	2
31	Charles	Clare	1 Woodend Drive	Woolton	L35 8RW	(0151)426-9849	0	6	0	0
32	Andrew	Miles	49 Leopold Drive	Garston	L24 6SD	(0151)280-8009	5	5	0	0

The database of customers and their orders

7 Print a copy of your worksheet on a single page using landscape orientation.

Make it happen

ACTIVITY 14: Adding financial information to the worksheet

1 Open the previous spreadsheet, Customer and orders database v1, if it is not already open.

2 One of your project team has suggested that it would be useful if this worksheet showed the total number of trays sold. Add this in a suitable place with an appropriate label.

3 They also suggest that it would be useful to display the amount of money that each customer is due to pay for the plants.

Add this information in a suitable place on the worksheet.

4 Save your work using an appropriate file name.

Unit 5 Integrating applications to find solutions

ACTIVITY 15: Creating a customer order form

In this activity you are required to produce a customer order form using word-processing software.

1. Think carefully about what information needs to be included on this form.

You should use the fields in the customer database in Activity 14 as a guide, but there may be fields that were not in the original database that you feel it would be useful to include.

2. Write a list of all the items you need to include on this form.

You will find it easier to plan your design on paper and then discuss it with your project team before putting it on the computer.

3. Produce a final design using word-processing software. Save your design and then print out a copy.

!Note

The database for the new customers need not have the same structure as the one used for the previous project. You should always consider improving old systems rather than using them as they are.

EXTENSION ACTIVITY

1. Create a new database structure that will include any new fields that you have added. Use the order form created in the previous activity to guide you.

2. Put in three rows of typical data.

3. Add any calculations to the spreadsheet, for example to work out the total plants that it is necessary to grow and the amount of money to be paid by the customers etc.

4. Evaluate your new database structure by explaining how it is an improvement on the design used for the previous project.

What data are organisations allowed to keep?

Most people get lots of advertising material through the post every day. These letters appear personal because they are addressed to the intended recipient and use their name in the letter. Some people get annoyed by this mail and others find it useful. The people who are annoyed by it dislike the fact that organisations are able to hold this data and even sell it to other companies so that they can send more mail. Unwanted mail is often referred to as junk mail.

Lesson 4 Keeping records

Every time you give your details to someone they are likely to end up on their computer system. You can always tell them that you do not want your details to be passed to others, but you often forget to tick the relevant box on the form.

The way personal data can be stored and used is governed by a law called the Data Protection Act 1988. The Information Commissioner is the person who is in charge of the Act and helps protect us from the misuse of data.

KEY WORDS

Data Protection Act – a law that restricts the way personal information is stored and processed on a computer

misuse – using data in a way that is morally or ethically wrong or illegal

personal information – information about a person such as political beliefs, health records, creditworthiness, etc.

FIND IT OUT

You may already have learnt about the Data Protection Act in your Personal, Social and Health Education (PSHE) or Citizenship lessons.

Use the following website to discover more about the Act: **www.dataprotection.gov.uk** and then find the answers to the following.

1. Use the glossary feature in the website to find out what the following words mean. You must put the definitions into your own words and then copy them into your book.

    (a) Personal data.

    (b) Data subject.

    (c) Data controller.

2. When you are filling in a form the following symbol is present.

    Explain what this symbol means.

3. What are the main purposes of the Data Protection Act?

QUESTIONS

1. Write down three items of information that each of the following organisations would hold about you.

    (a) Dentist   (d) Doctor
    (b) School   (e) Fitness club
    (c) Library

2. Some data about you could be classed as personal.

    Write down five items of data that would be personal.

3. The older you get, the more information is stored about you.

    Write down the names of three organisations that do not hold personal data about you now but are likely to do so in the future.

4. Mistakes can be made and the personal data held on an ICT system could be wrong. How does the Data Protection Act protect you from wrong information?

219

Unit 5 Integrating applications to find solutions

Lesson 5: SENDING LETTERS TO CUSTOMERS

In this lesson you will learn how to perform a mail merge using the spreadsheet file of past customers and their orders and a document created using word-processing software.

What is mail merge?

Mail merge can be used to send the same basic letter, with just slight differences, to a large number of people. A mailing list is often used to supply the names, addresses and other details of the people to whom the letter is to be sent. Sometimes this list is created in Word, but it could also be obtained from another package such as Excel (the spreadsheet package) or Access (the specialist database package).

Before performing a mail merge ask yourself if the number of letters you intend sending out warrants the effort. If you had 10 letters to send then it may not be worth the trouble. You could simply create the letter with one set of details and then change these for the next letter and so on. If you need more than 10 letters or you need to send a similar letter to the same people in the future, then you should consider using mail merge.

If successful, the plants project will run indefinitely, so it will be useful to keep in touch with customers as it is always easier and cheaper to sell to satisfied existing customers rather than find new ones.

As the project has been carried out before, there is already a list of some past customers and their orders. You need to contact these customers first to let them know that you are producing the bedding plants again and to ask them if they would like to place an order.

In the following activity you will create a letter in Word and then add the variable information using the customer details in the spreadsheet file.

!Note

Two files are needed for a mail merge: the letter itself as a Word file and a data source such as a Word, Excel or Access file.

Lesson 5 Sending letters to customers

Make it happen

ACTIVITY 16: Setting up a mail merge

The first step is to create the letter.

1. Load Word and then create a new document. Click on **Tools** and the following menu drops down. Move down to **Letters and Mailings**.

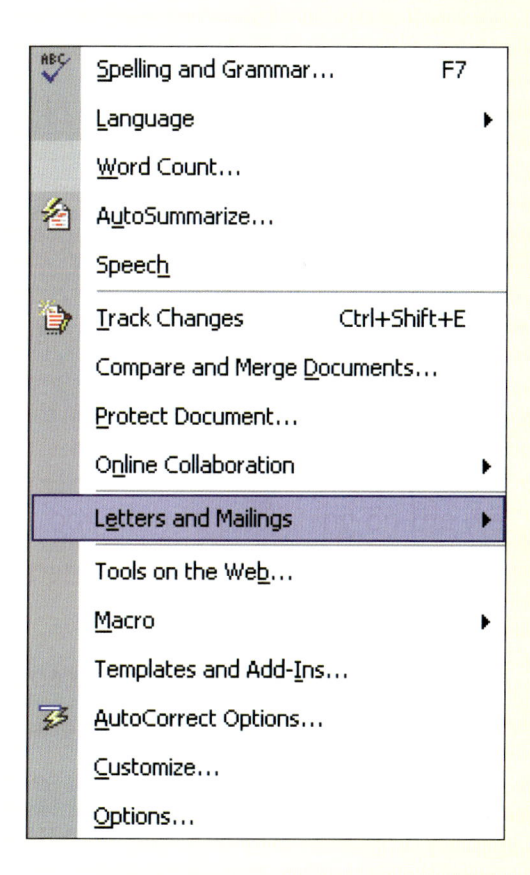

2. The following menu appears. You need to select **Mail Merge Wizard...** .

Click on **Mail Merge Wizard**.

221

Unit 5 Integrating applications to find solutions

3 The screen divides into two and on the right-hand side there are instructions for you to follow.

4 Make sure that **Letters** is selected. You can then start typing.

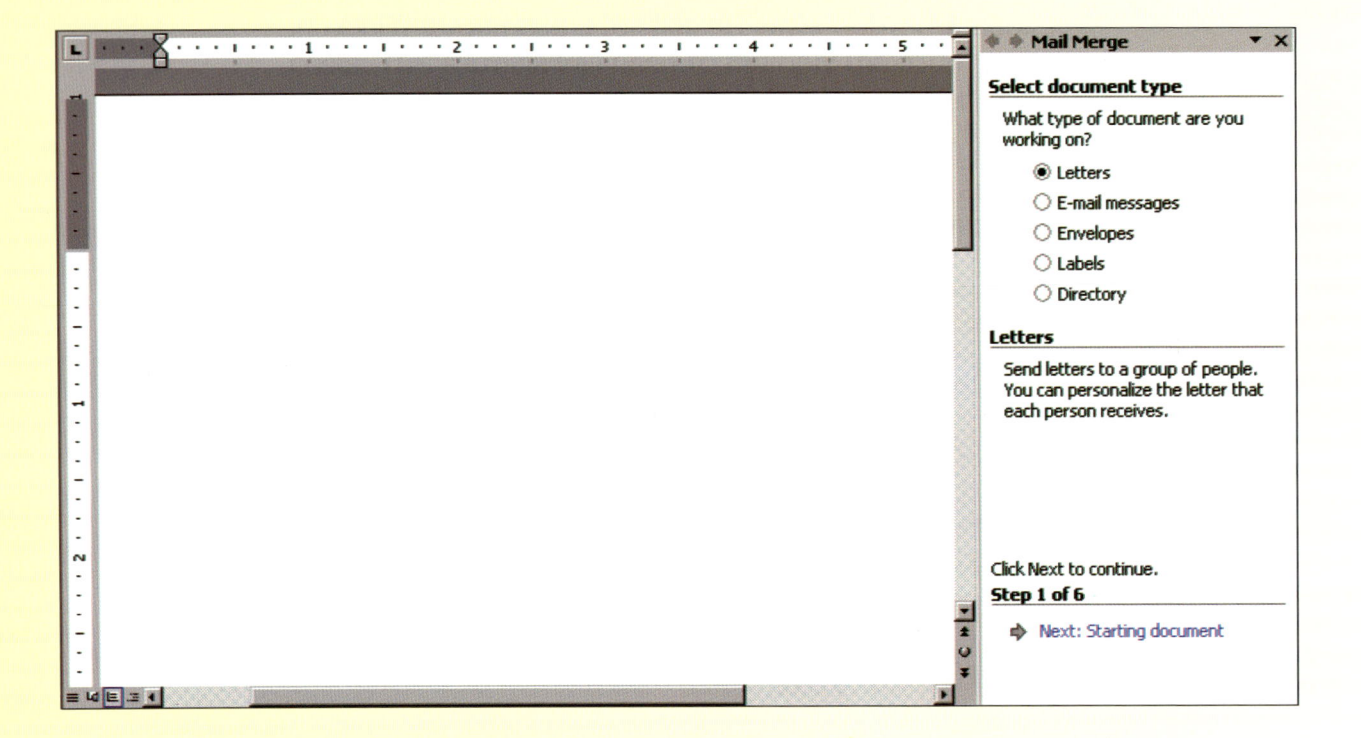

5 Type in the following letter.

> Dear
>
> Three years ago you ordered some bedding plants from our school and I hope you were happy with them. Unfortunately, we had to abandon the project because of the difficulties in watering and looking after the plants during the weekends and other holidays. We now have automatic controls in our greenhouses, so this problem has been eliminated.
>
> We are now re-starting this project and need your help again. We are going to produce a range of the more popular bedding plants by the tray.
>
> Before we start our project we need to be sure that we have some orders.
>
> Enclosed is an order form showing the varieties of plants available. All of the trays contain 12 plants and cost £2.00 per tray.
>
> We would really appreciate your order as all of the profit we make will be going to buy the latest ICT equipment which will benefit a lot of people in the community.
>
> We look forward to receiving your order.

Lesson 5 Sending letters to customers

6 Click on **Next: Starting document**.

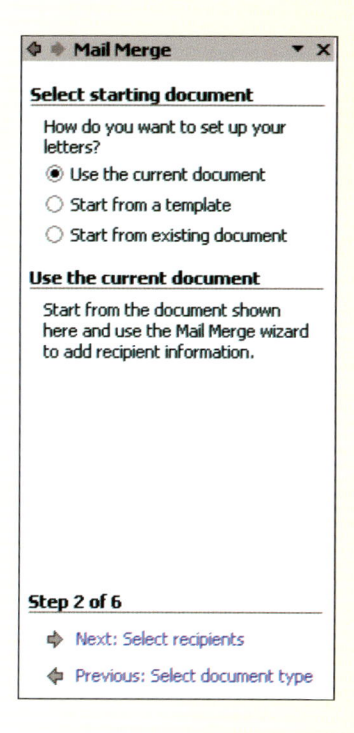

Make sure that the option **Use the current document** has been selected.

Click on **Next: Select recipients**.

7 In the following screen, select **Browse...**.

Unit 5 Integrating applications to find solutions

8   You now need to find the spreadsheet file called Customer and orders database. Your teacher will tell you where it is if you are unable to find it.

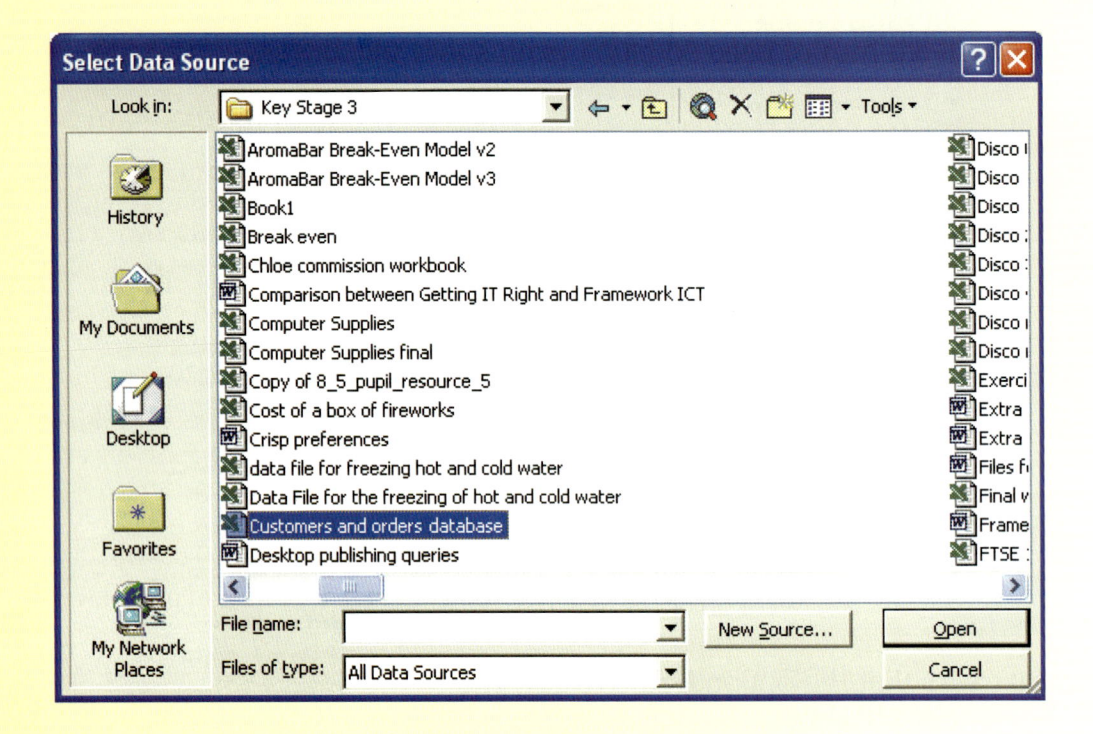

When you have located the file select it by double clicking on the name.

9   The following screen appears:

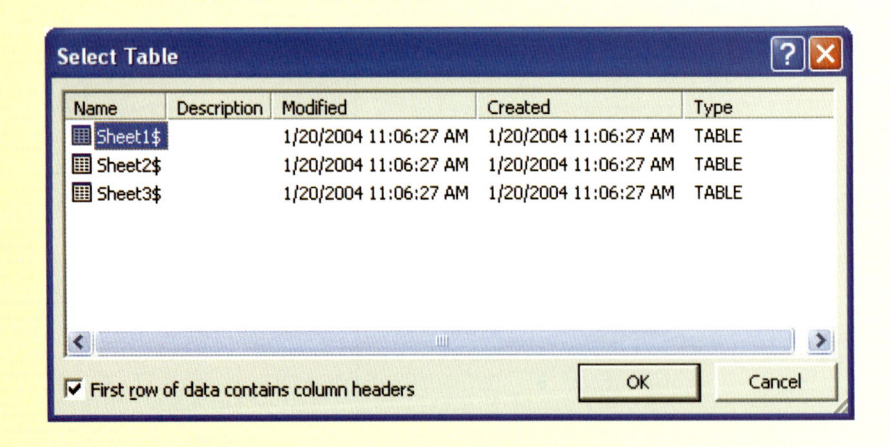

As you know, a workbook can contain more than one worksheet. Three different worksheets are shown in the above screen. Only worksheet 1 has been used to store the customer database so select it and then click on **OK**.

10 The following screen appears (opposite). It shows the data in the worksheet and gives you the opportunity to select certain past

Lesson 5 Sending letters to customers

customers. There are ticks in all of the boxes to the right of the surname and this shows that all of the past customers will be sent letters.

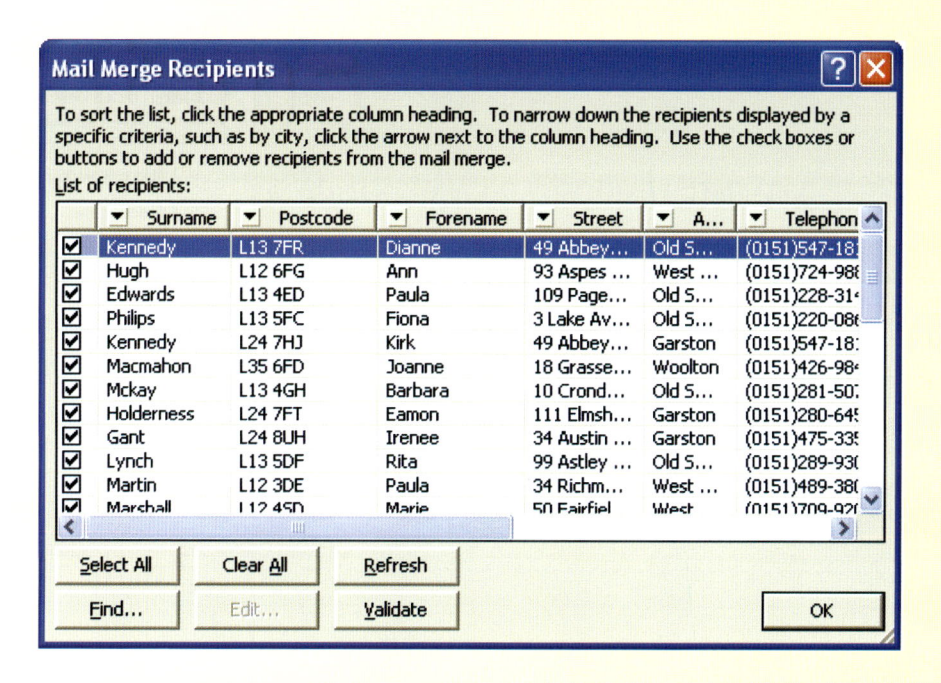

Now click on the **OK** button.

11 Notice that the right-hand side of the screen contains the following information (right):

Click on **Next: Write your letter**.

Unit 5 Integrating applications to find solutions

12 The following appears on the right of the screen.

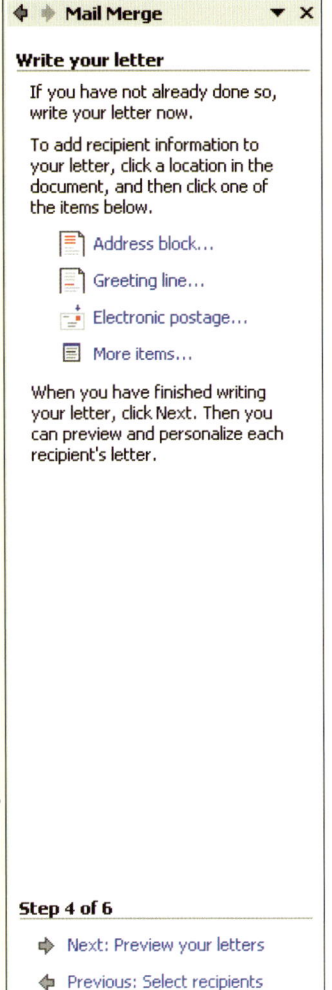

> **Mail Merge**
>
> **Write your letter**
>
> If you have not already done so, write your letter now.
>
> To add recipient information to your letter, click a location in the document, and then click one of the items below.
>
> 📄 Address block...
> 📄 Greeting line...
> 📄 Electronic postage...
> 📄 More items...
>
> When you have finished writing your letter, click Next. Then you can preview and personalize each recipient's letter.
>
> **Step 4 of 6**
>
> ➡ Next: Preview your letters
> ⬅ Previous: Select recipients

13 Go to the part of the screen where your letter is and insert about five blank lines at the top of the page. This is so that enough room is left for the recipients' name and address details to be inserted.

When you have done this, the part of the screen containing the letter will look like this:

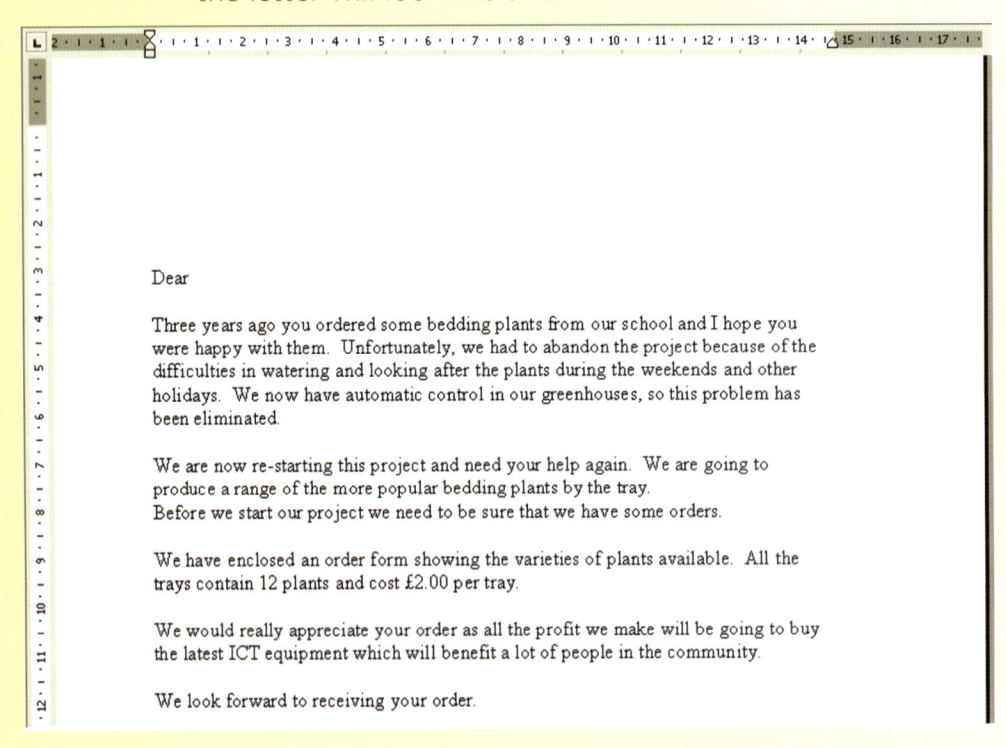

Dear

Three years ago you ordered some bedding plants from our school and I hope you were happy with them. Unfortunately, we had to abandon the project because of the difficulties in watering and looking after the plants during the weekends and other holidays. We now have automatic control in our greenhouses, so this problem has been eliminated.

We are now re-starting this project and need your help again. We are going to produce a range of the more popular bedding plants by the tray.
Before we start our project we need to be sure that we have some orders.

We have enclosed an order form showing the varieties of plants available. All the trays contain 12 plants and cost £2.00 per tray.

We would really appreciate your order as all the profit we make will be going to buy the latest ICT equipment which will benefit a lot of people in the community.

We look forward to receiving your order.

Lesson 5 Sending letters to customers

14 On the screen move your cursor onto the first line of the page. This is where the recipient's name is to go.

Now go to the right-hand part of the screen and click on

☰ More items...

The following window appears. Here you can select the fields that you want to go in your letter.

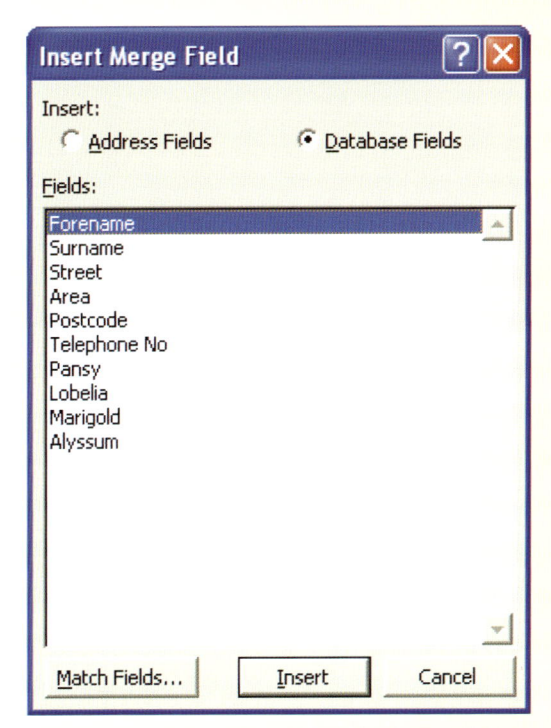

Insert Merge Field

Insert:
○ Address Fields   ● Database Fields

Fields:
- Forename
- Surname
- Street
- Area
- Postcode
- Telephone No
- Pansy
- Lobelia
- Marigold
- Alyssum

Match Fields...   Insert   Cancel

Make sure that the first field **Forename** is selected and then click on the **Insert** button.

15 The Forename field is now inserted and looks like this on the screen.

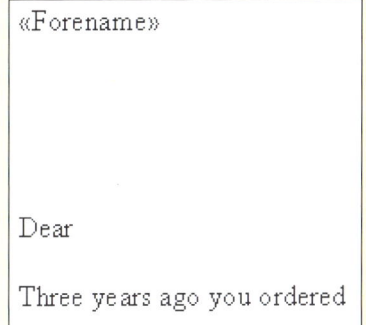

«Forename»

Dear

Three years ago you ordered

16 Click on **Close** so that the window disappears.

You now need to insert a space after the Forename field because you want to insert the Surname field but you do not want them joined together.

Then click on ☰ More items... and select **Surname** from the list of fields. Click on the **Insert** button.

The top of the word-processed document will now look like this:

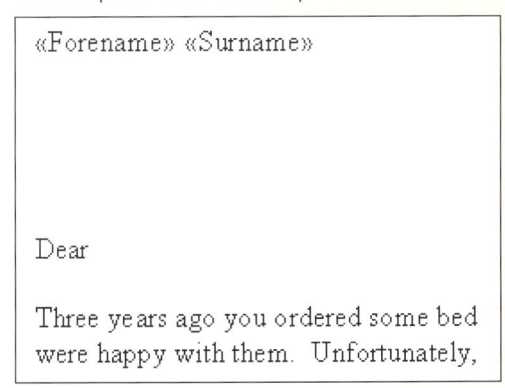

«Forename» «Surname»

Dear

Three years ago you ordered some bed
were happy with them. Unfortunately,

Unit 5 Integrating applications to find solutions

Press **Enter** to move to the line below so that you are ready to insert the first line of the address.

17 Insert the **Street** field on this line.

Move down a line and then insert the **Area** field.

On the next line insert the **Postcode** field.

The top of your document should now look like this:

```
«Forename» «Surname»
«Street»
«Area»
«Postcode»


Dear

Three years ago you ordered some bed
were happy with them. Unfortunately,
```

18 You now need to add the person's forename and surname after the word Dear.

Do this and the top of the document should look similar to this:

```
«Forename» «Surname»
«Street»
«Area»
«Postcode»


Dear «Forename» «Surname»

Three years ago you ordered some bed
were happy with them. Unfortunately,
```

19 Click on

➡ Next: Preview your letters   near the bottom right of the screen.

The letter will now appear with the name and address details merged into it. Check that your letter looks like this:

Lesson 5 Sending letters to customers

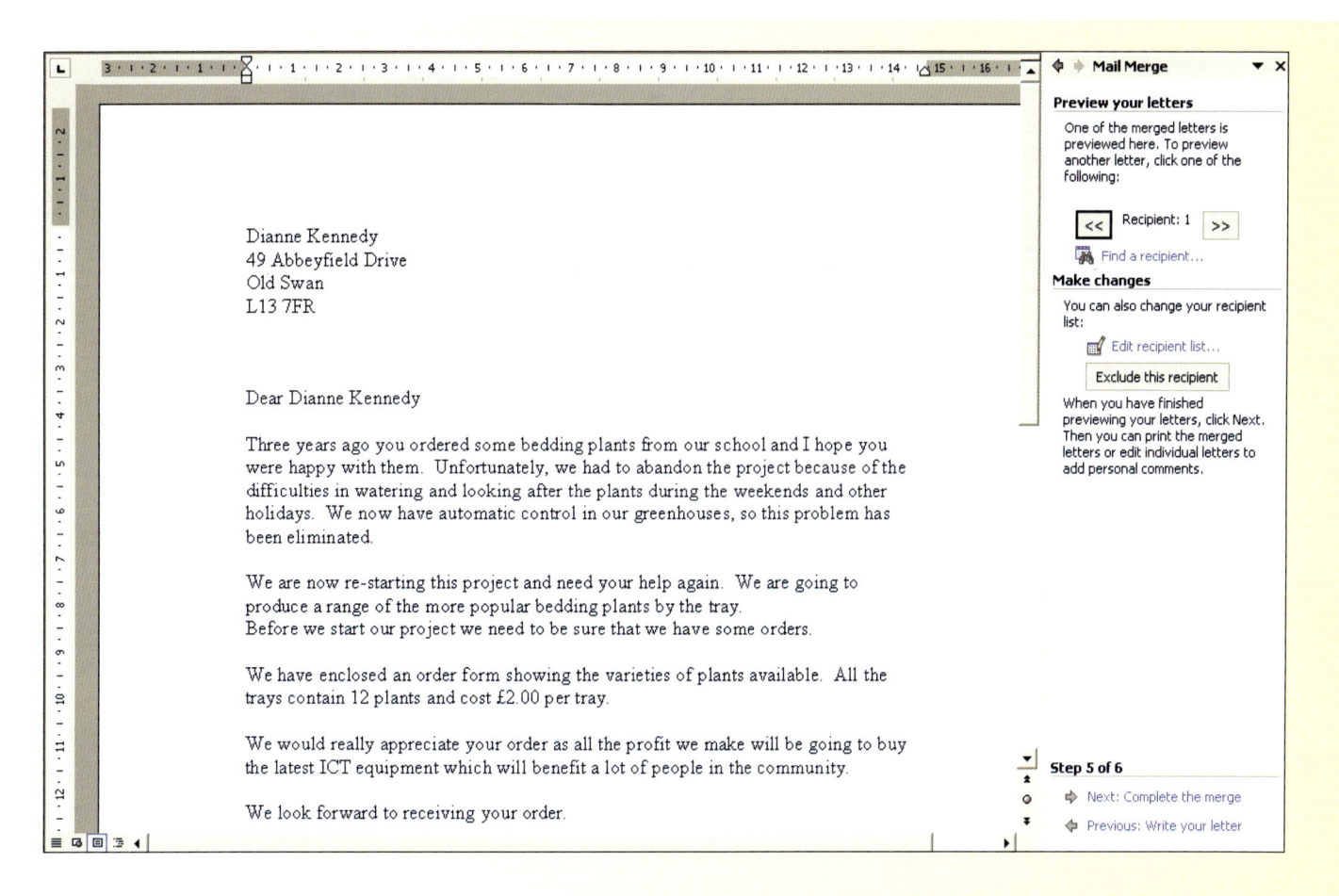

> Dianne Kennedy
> 49 Abbeyfield Drive
> Old Swan
> L13 7FR
>
> Dear Dianne Kennedy
>
> Three years ago you ordered some bedding plants from our school and I hope you were happy with them. Unfortunately, we had to abandon the project because of the difficulties in watering and looking after the plants during the weekends and other holidays. We now have automatic control in our greenhouses, so this problem has been eliminated.
>
> We are now re-starting this project and need your help again. We are going to produce a range of the more popular bedding plants by the tray.
> Before we start our project we need to be sure that we have some orders.
>
> We have enclosed an order form showing the varieties of plants available. All the trays contain 12 plants and cost £2.00 per tray.
>
> We would really appreciate your order as all the profit we make will be going to buy the latest ICT equipment which will benefit a lot of people in the community.
>
> We look forward to receiving your order.

20 You can now check each of the letters one by one by clicking on the arrows pointing right on the following part of the screen:

21 When you have checked through all of the letters, click on

⇨ Next: Complete the merge

22 The right-hand part of the screen changes to the following where you have a choice of editing individual letters or printing all of the letters.

Unit 5 Integrating applications to find solutions

Mail Merge

Complete the merge

Mail Merge is ready to produce your letters.

To personalize your letters, click "Edit Individual Letters." This will open a new document with your merged letters. To make changes to all the letters, switch back to the original document.

Merge

- Print...
- Edit individual letters...

Step 6 of 6

← Previous: Preview your letters

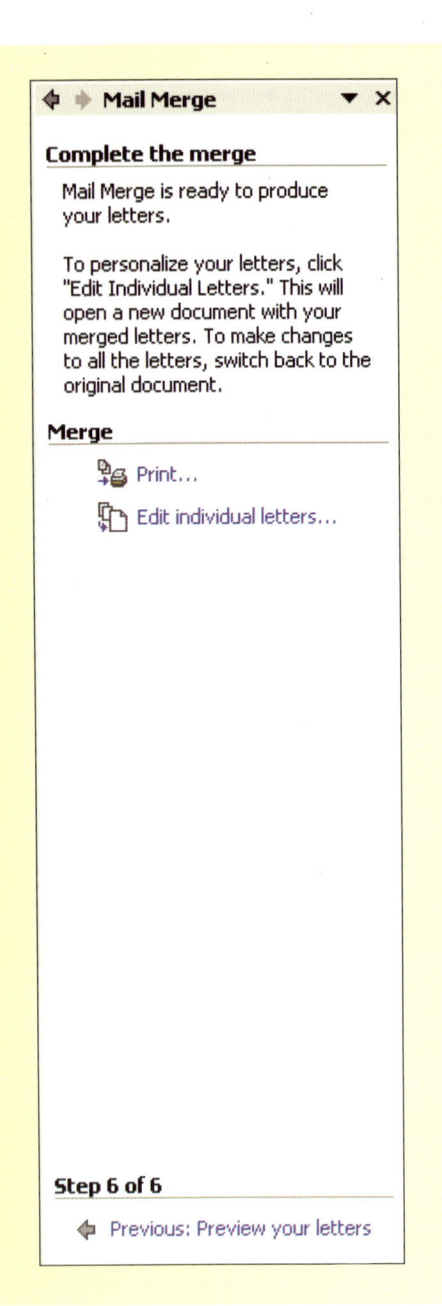

Notice on this screen that you can always go back through the steps in the opposite direction to make changes.

23 You could print out all of the letters, but as we have already looked at each letter to check it, printing them would be a waste of paper.

24 Well done! You have now completed your mail merge.

Using ICT to help print names and addresses

Once all of the letters have been produced, you need to decide how to put the names and addresses on the envelopes. Luckily there are two quick ways of doing this using word-processing software.

Printing envelopes and mailing labels

There is not much point in getting the computer to write hundreds of letters for a mail merge if you then have to sit down and write all of the envelopes by hand. You can use the data source file to get the

Lesson 6 Monitoring and controlling conditions in the greenhouse

computer to either type the addresses onto self-adhesive mailing labels or print directly onto the envelopes.

> **EXTENSION ACTIVITY**
>
> Find out how to put the names and addresses onto envelopes by either printing directly onto the envelopes or using labels.
>
> Use the Help facility in Word to guide you through the process.
>
> Ask your teacher for a couple of envelopes and some labels in order that you can test your solution.

QUESTIONS

1. Explain what is meant by the term 'mail merge'.
2. What are the advantages of performing a mail merge compared with altering each word-processed letter individually?
3. Describe one way that the mail merge could be used with the database of customers who place orders for the new project.
4. Some customers may object to these personalised letters. Explain why they might object.
5. Sending information to the customers by post is expensive.
   (a) What costs are involved in sending a letter?
   (b) Is there a cheaper and more cost-effective way of sending information about the plants to customers? Explain your answer.

Lesson 6: MONITORING AND CONTROLLING CONDITIONS IN THE GREENHOUSE

Because of the problems with the previous project (i.e. looking after the plants during holidays), it has been decided to automate some processes such as watering the plants, switching the heater on and off, etc. This will be done using computer control and will be a continuous repetitive process. Computer control is ideal for repeated processes where the same thing is done over and over again.

In this lesson you will learn how control systems can be used to automate processes in the greenhouse. Before a condition can be controlled it needs to be monitored, and sensors are used to collect data about the current conditions. Each sensor is designed to monitor a physical quantity such as temperature. A decision can

KEY WORDS

automate – to enable a process to be performed without human intervention

continuous – without end

control – switching devices on or off or making adjustments on the basis of data obtained from sensors

Unit 5 Integrating applications to find solutions

KEY WORDS

monitor – take readings of conditions using sensors

repeated processes – processes in a flowchart that are carried out again and again or for a set number of times

repetitive – unvarying or unchanging

sensors – devices which are used to sense or measure physical quantities

sequence of instructions – instructions, such as in a flowchart, where the instructions need to be obeyed in a certain order

then be made about what to do next and the output can be altered if necessary. A control program is written and this is a sequence of instructions that are followed.

Automating processes such as watering the plants and keeping the greenhouse at the ideal temperature is essential to the success of the project.

Ideal conditions are needed in order to grow strong healthy plants

The project to grow and sell the bedding plants failed in the past because the staff and students did not want to be tied to looking after the plants during holidays and at weekends. The equipment required to automate basic processes is cheap and readily available and the head teacher has offered to pay for it.

WORKSHEET WORKSHEET WORKSHEET WORKSHEET WORKSHEET

WORKSHEET 8.5.3 Human or computer

You may be given a worksheet on which to write your answers or you may be asked to write your answers in your book. When you have finished, your teacher will either go through the answers or give you an answer sheet so that you can check the answers yourself.

Some jobs are performed easily by computers or computer-controlled devices whilst others are best performed by humans.

Here is a list of jobs. You have to decide whether they are best performed by a computer or a human.

Lesson 6 Monitoring and controlling conditions in the greenhouse

Job	Best performed by computer or human?
Painting the outside of a house	
Checking recyclable glass bottles to make sure they are fit for re-use	
Filling a tooth at the dentist's surgery	
Washing and drying a batch of clothes	
Spray painting a car body in a car factory	
Checking a suspicious car that may contain a bomb	
Welding the spouts on kettles in a factory	
Handling customer complaints in a shop	
Controlling the temperature, moisture, ventilation, etc. in a greenhouse	
Controlling a set of traffic lights at a junction	
Teaching a class PE at school	
Continuously monitoring patients in an intensive-care unit	

WORKSHEET 8.5.4 **Reasons for using ICT for control**

You may be given a worksheet on which to write your answers or you may be asked to write your answers in your book. When you have finished, your teacher will either go through the answers or give you an answer sheet so that you can check the answers yourself.

Here are some reasons why computers are used for control. Complete the table below by writing the most appropriate letter in the right-hand column.

- A   Requires creativity
- B   Computers can work 24 hours per day
- C   It is expensive to pay people
- D   It is dangerous for people to do the job
- E   Simple rules need to be obeyed

Job	Main reason for using computer control rather than humans
Recording a TV programme on a video when you are out	
Landing an aircraft in thick fog	
Controlling the lifts in a very tall building	
Filling bottles with beer	

233

Unit 5 Integrating applications to find solutions

Job	Main reason for using computer control rather than humans
Paint spraying in a car production plant	
Controlling the traffic lights at a very busy junction	
Controlling the fuel rods in a nuclear power station	
Controlling the fog warning system on a motorway	
Controlling the temperature inside a freezer	

What are the ideal growing conditions?

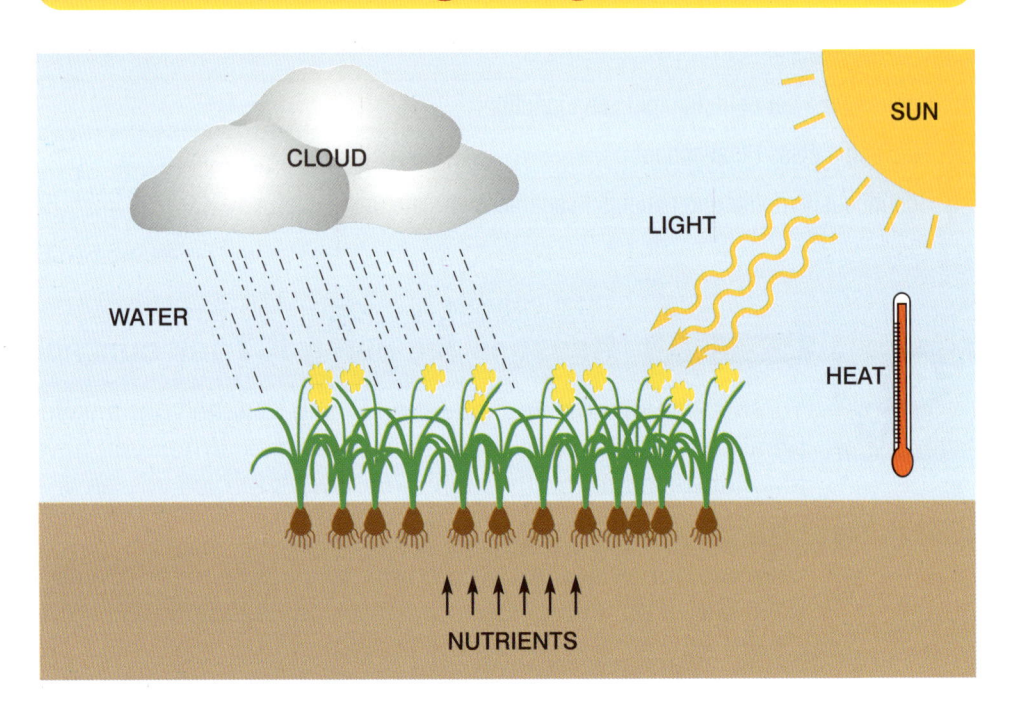

What do the plants need in order to grow?

Plants need the following in order to grow.

Light

Plants need light in order to photosynthesise. Artificial light can be used to supplement the natural light on dull days.

Heat

The ideal temperature for growing bedding plants is 15°C. This temperature is needed to germinate the seed and to grow the young plants.

There will be days when the greenhouse will need to be heated.

Lesson 6 Monitoring and controlling conditions in the greenhouse

There will also be some days when the temperature may rise much higher than 15°C, so the greenhouse will need to be cooled by opening windows.

Nutrients

The plants need food to grow and the nutrients in the compost supply these. There will be enough nutrients in the compost so it is not necessary to give the plants extra food.

Water

Plants need water in order to grow. They will need to be watered when the soil becomes dry. A water pump will be used to create a fine mist that will not damage the delicate plants.

QUESTIONS

Here is a list of the things that plants need in order to grow.
- Light
- Heat
- Nutrients
- Water.

1 The conditions can change in a greenhouse. Which one of the above do you not have to worry about monitoring and controlling? Give a reason for your answer.

2 Which two in the list are supplied by sunlight?

3 Here is a list of sensors: temperature sensor; moisture sensor; light sensor.

Choose one of these sensors to monitor each of the following.

(a) How wet or dry the soil is.

(b) How hot or cold the air in the greenhouse is.

(c) Whether the artificial lights inside the greenhouse, which help the plants grow, need turning on or off.

How often should the conditions be monitored?

Some conditions such as light can change very rapidly. For example, the sun can go in and the light and temperature can suddenly change. It is possible to change the rate at which the sensors take their measurements (known as the sample rate).

KEY WORDS

sample rate – the rate at which data is measured using a sensor

The two types of sensor: analogue and digital

There are two different types of sensor used in the greenhouse: an analogue sensor and a digital sensor. Each of the sensors measures the quantities in a different way.

Unit 5 Integrating applications to find solutions

KEY WORDS

analogue – data that can have an infinite number of values

digital – data that can have only two values. This means the value can be either correct or incorrect

Analogue sensors

This type of sensor measures values that change constantly and can have an infinite number of values. For example, temperature does not change in whole units, say from 10 °C to 11°C. It rises and falls through lots of values such as 10.5°C, 10.75°C, 10.9999°C, etc.

Digital sensors

These sensors can record conditions that are correct or incorrect, such as the amount of moisture in the soil or the water level in a washing machine. In order to do this, they check whether a set value has been exceeded.

Why use computer control?

To successfully grow plants from seeds it is necessary to give them the correct conditions and to keep these conditions constant.

To germinate the seeds a temperature of between 15°C and 18°C is required. Once the seeds have germinated (i.e. sprouted and started to grow) an ideal temperature of 15°C is needed.

The inputs and outputs for the greenhouse control system

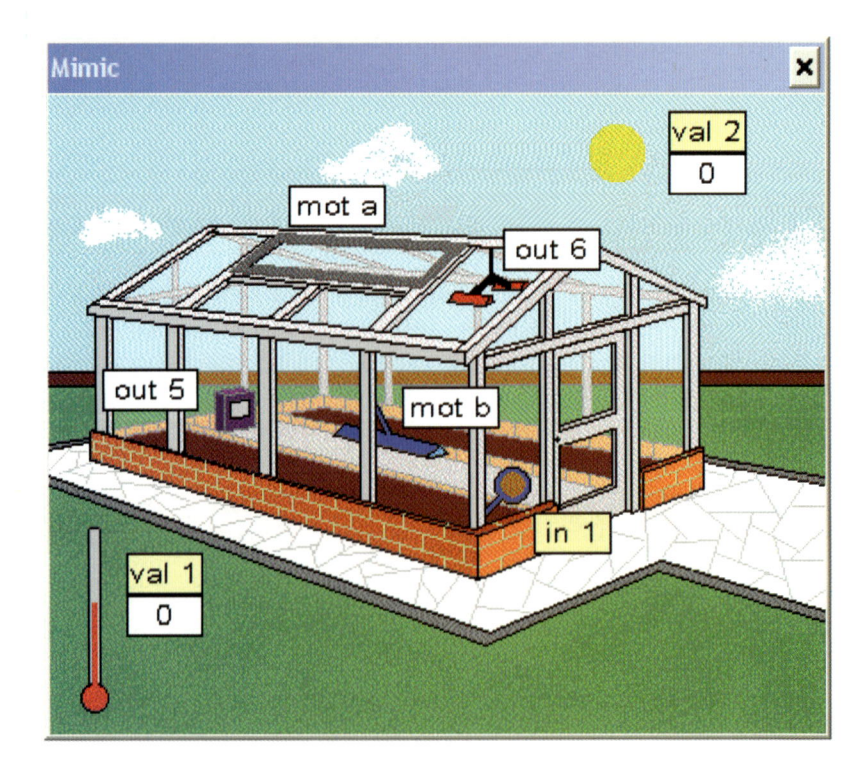

The sensors, inputs and outputs in the greenhouse control system

Source: Data Harvest

Lesson 6 Monitoring and controlling conditions in the greenhouse

Take a look at the diagram of a greenhouse on the previous page. Look at the labels.

Val 1 is an analogue temperature sensor.

Val 2 is an analogue light sensor.

In 1 is a digital moisture sensor.

Out 6 is a light.

Out 5 is a heater.

Mot a is a motor to open and close the window.

Mot b is a motor that turns a sprinkler on/off to water the plants.

Controlling the conditions remotely

It is possible to monitor and control the conditions in the greenhouse remotely. This means that the computer equipment used to control the greenhouse need not be in the same place as the greenhouse. The advantage of this is that you can control the conditions from a distance. There will be a delay between the data being recorded by the remote sensor and the value appearing on the computer because the signal takes a short time to arrive. The amount of time will depend on the transmission speed.

Remote sensors can be used to transmit data to the computer for processing. The computer will use this data according to the control program (Flowol) and will send data signals back to alter the output if necessary. The data is transmitted using radio signals which travel from the greenhouse to the computer and back.

It is important to check that the control program is controlling the conditions inside the greenhouse properly. The live data can be logged by using remote data logging.

A measure of the efficiency of the system is how well the control program maintains the conditions.

KEY WORDS

data logging – the collection of data automatically over a period of time. Remote weather stations use data logging

efficiency – how well the system performs

live data – data currently being used

remote data logging – data logging performed at a location that is away from the computer used to process the data

remote sensor – a sensor used to sense a physical quantity (temperature, pressure, rainfall, wind speed, etc.) where the sensor is situated away from the computer

transmission speed – the speed at which data is passed along a wire/cable or through the air

Make it happen

ACTIVITY 17: Using Flowol to control the light in the greenhouse

It is important to break down the control operation into small separate programs or use subroutines.

Unit 5 Integrating applications to find solutions

KEY WORDS

flowchart – a chart or diagram used to break down a task into smaller parts. It can also show the order of the tasks and any decisions which need to be made

subroutine – a section of a program that can be called upon when needed

The following flowchart has been designed to monitor the light level (called Val 2) inside the greenhouse. The light level is monitored continuously and when it falls below a certain value (a light level of 40 in this case), the electric light (called Output 6) is turned on. When the light levels rises to a value of 40 or over, Output 6 (the light) is switched off. This control program will ensure that the light level in the greenhouse never falls to a value less than 40.

The Flowol flowchart to monitor and control the electric light in the greenhouse

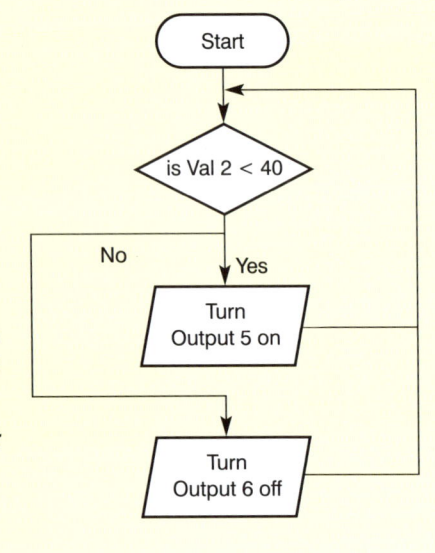

① Load the Flowol software.

② Create the above flowchart using the software.

③ Click on **Window**.

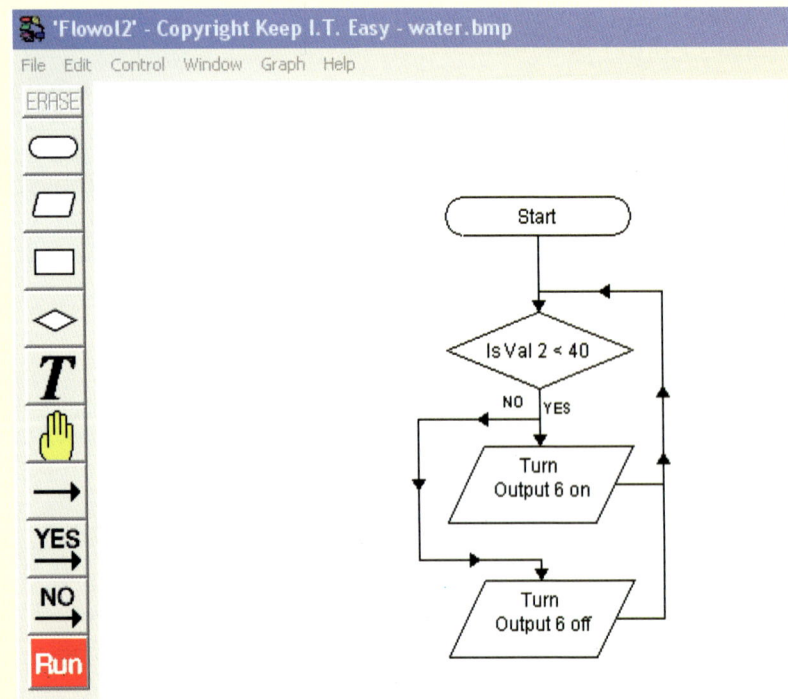

238

Lesson 6 Monitoring and controlling conditions in the greenhouse

The following pull-down menu appears. Click on **Mimic…**.

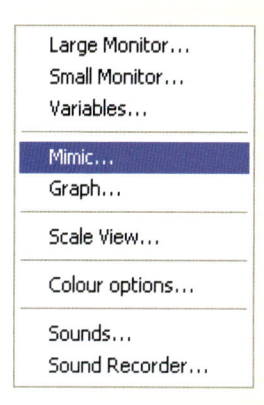

```
Large Monitor...
Small Monitor...
Variables...
Mimic...
Graph...
Scale View...
Colour options...
Sounds...
Sound Recorder...
```

4 A list of mimics will appear. Mimics are the animated pictures of the simulation.

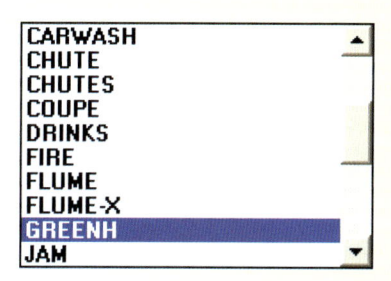

```
CARWASH
CHUTE
CHUTES
COUPE
DRINKS
FIRE
FLUME
FLUME-X
GREENH
JAM
```

Select the mimic **GREENH** and then click on **OK**.

5 The mimic now appears next to the flowchart as shown here:

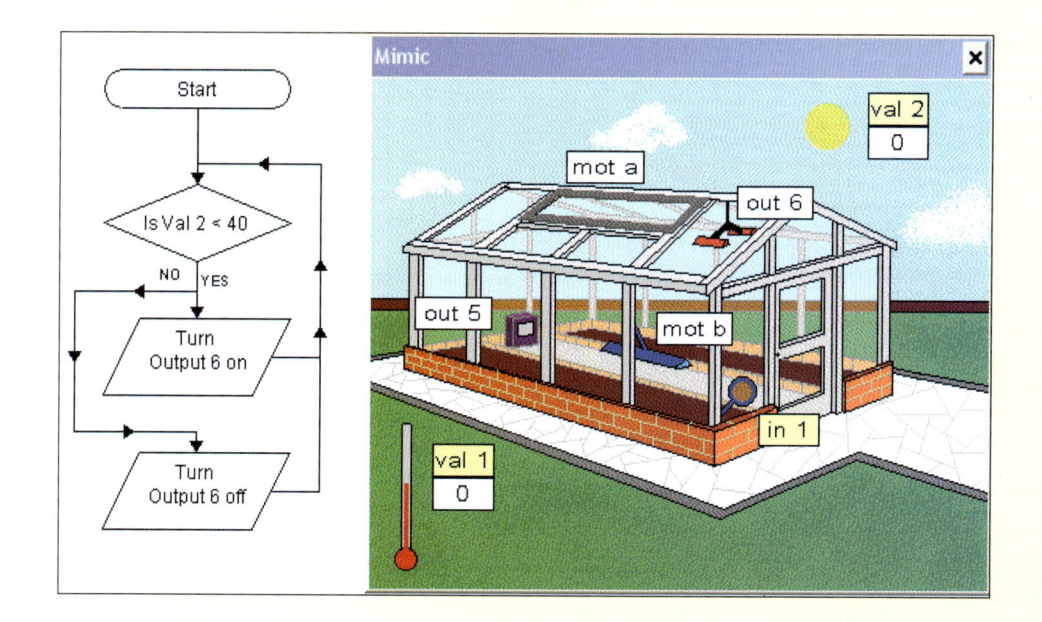

239

Unit 5 Integrating applications to find solutions

6 Now run the simulation by clicking on the **RUN** button.

7 You will see that the decision box and the first output box go yellow in turn, but this happens so quickly they just flicker. You can slow this side so that it is easier to see what is going on. To do this, click on **Control** in the menu at the top of the screen.

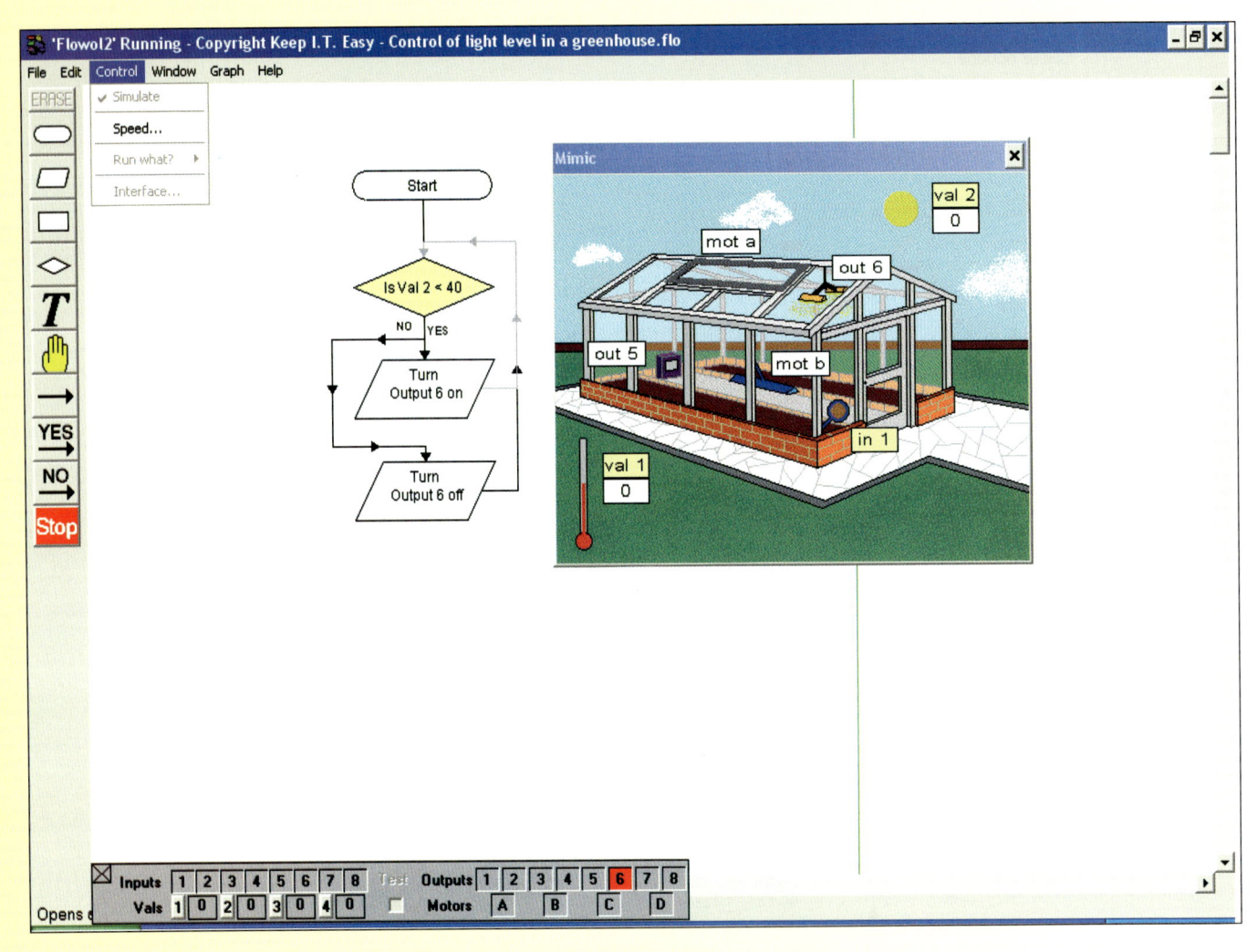

On the pull-down menu, click on **Speed...**.

The following window appears and you can click and drag the slider to the left to slow down the rate at which the light level is monitored.

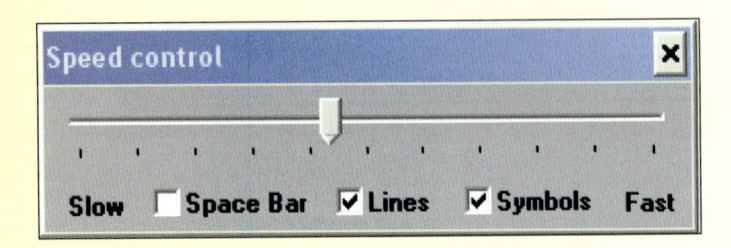

240

Lesson 6 Monitoring and controlling conditions in the greenhouse

It is now easier to see the instructions represented by the flowchart being carried out.

8 Test the flowchart by altering the value of the light level.

Do this on the number under the val 2 box.

To increase the value left click on the mouse, and to decrease the value right click on the mouse.

Test your flowchart by changing the values and make sure that the control program behaves as it should.

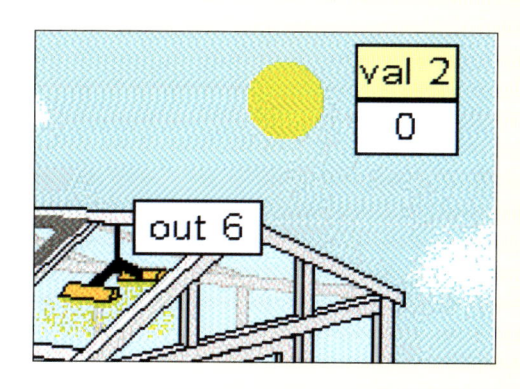

The light value is zero so the light will be on. It will stay on until the light value is 40 or above when the light will be switched off

When the light increases to a value of 40 or over, the light is switched off and it stays off until the light level is less than 40 at which point the light is switched on again

9 You have now completed the control program for the light.

Save your program using the file name 'Control of light level in a greenhouse'.

10 Produce a printout of the flowchart and annotate it explaining what the flowchart does.

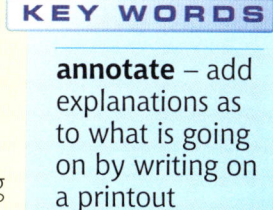

KEY WORDS

annotate – add explanations as to what is going on by writing on a printout

ACTIVITY 18: Improving the control system: turning the light off during the night

In the previous activity the control program turned the light on when the light level fell below a certain value. This meant that there was light (either natural or artificial) 24 hours per day.

Unit 5 Integrating applications to find solutions

However, plants grown in permanent light do not develop properly. They tend to be thin and straggly.

This means that the light needs to go off at night.

1 At first it was thought that a timer could be used to turn the light off at night. This idea was rejected. Give one reason why you think this was rejected.

2 It is possible to add another decision box to the flowchart so that the light was on during dull days but off at night.

Where should this decision box be placed and what text should it contain?

3 Think about following through the steps of the flowchart to check it before building it using the Flowol software. When you do this, you are said to be performing a dry run.

4 Using the Flowol software and the file created in the last activity called Control of light level in a greenhouse, add the decision box to the flowchart and add the flowlines.

5 Test your control program using the Mimic to make sure that the program behaves as expected.

6 Your teacher will put up a picture showing what this final flowchart should look like. Yours may look different yet still be correct. It depends on how dark it has to be for the light to turn off at night.

KEY WORDS

dry run – working through a flowchart manually to check its logic. Used as a test

Lesson 7: CONTROLLING MORE CONDITIONS IN THE GREENHOUSE

In the last lesson you used a control program to manage the light conditions in the greenhouse. In this lesson you will look at controlling some of the other conditions in the greenhouse such as soil moisture and temperature.

Lesson 7 Controlling more conditions in the greenhouse

Controlling the sprinkler system

The sprinkler system makes sure that the soil remains moist. When the moisture level in the soil drops to a certain level, the soil is too dry for the plants and they need to be watered. The watering is carried out by a sprinkler system.

The sprinkler system has one input and one output as follows:

- Input: in 1 is a digital moisture sensor.
- Output: mot b is an electric motor which works a sprinkler. The sprinkler sprays the plants with water.

The input

Here is the digital moisture sensor used in the greenhouse. When the inside circle of the sensor is blue it is detecting a suitable amount of moisture.

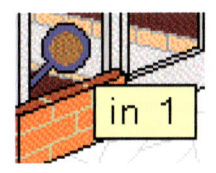

If you click on the sensor with the left mouse button you can change the conditions from wet to dry. When the inside circle of the sensor is brown it is detecting dry conditions so the plants need watering.

The output

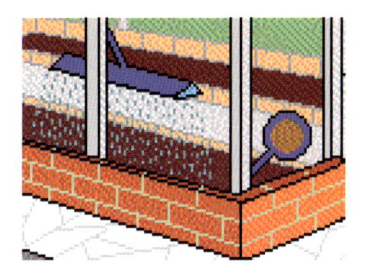

When 'in 1' is on, the sensor detects dry conditions and the motor (i.e. the sprinkler) is turned on.

243

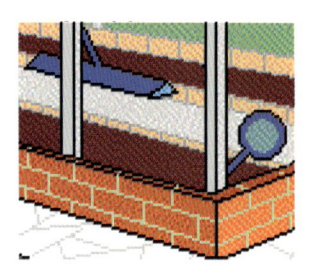

Unit 5 Integrating applications to find solutions

When 'in 1' is off, the sensor detects moist conditions and the motor (i.e. the sprinkler) is turned off.

Make it happen

ACTIVITY 19: Using Flowol to control the sprinkler system to water the plants

In this activity you will use the Flowol software to create a control program to control the operation of the sprinkler system.

1. Here are the boxes that are used in the flowchart to control the sprinkler.

   Turn Motor b off | Turn Motor b fd | Start | Is Input 1 on

2. Put these boxes into the correct order and connect them with flowlines (each box is to be used once only).

3. Thoroughly test your flowchart by using the Mimic.

Controlling the temperature inside the greenhouse

The bedding plants need to be kept at a constant temperature of 15°C.

A heater is provided and it needs to be turned on when the temperature drops below 15°C. This temperature is called the threshold temperature. The heater can be turned on and off according to the control program.

The greenhouse heater can be turned on and off by the control program

KEY WORDS

threshold – the minimum value of a quantity (such as temperature) which causes an event to take place (such as turning on a heater)

244

Lesson 7 Controlling more conditions in the greenhouse

There may be occasions in the summer, when the sun is shining, when the temperature with the heater off will rise well above the ideal of 15°C. When the temperature inside the greenhouse rises above the ideal temperature a motor, called mot a, is used to open the window. This motor can go forwards to open the window and backwards to close the window. It is also possible to stop the motor.

The temperature control system for the greenhouse can be divided into two control programs:

- A program to switch the heater on and off.
- A program to open and close the window.

An electric motor is provided which opens or closes the window as required by the control program

Out 5 (the heater) is on, as shown by the red filament

Out 5 (the heater) is off, as shown by the blue filament

Make it happen

ACTIVITY 20: Drawing a flowchart to control the heater

The flowchart to control the heater is very similar to the program for controlling the light.

Val 1 is an analogue temperature sensor used to measure the temperature inside the greenhouse.

Out 5 is a heater that can be switched on or off.

Here are the symbols that are used in the flowchart to control the heater.

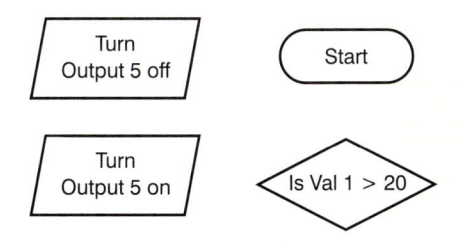

Using the symbols and the software Flowol, put them into the correct order and then connect them up using flowlines.

Test the working of this flowchart using the Mimic.

Unit 5 Integrating applications to find solutions

Keeping the greenhouse cool

If the temperature in the greenhouse rises above 15°C the plants could be damaged by the heat.

The greenhouse can be fitted with an automatic window-opening system that opens the window when the temperature rises above 15°C. If the temperature drops below this, then the window will need to be closed.

The output device used to open and close the window is an electric motor. The electric motor can be operated forwards or backwards to either open or close the window.

Make it happen

ACTIVITY 21: Draw a flowchart to control the window

Your task is to produce a separate flowchart that can be used to open and close the window.

This system will use:

- Val 1, the analogue temperature sensor used to measure the temperature inside the greenhouse.
- Mot a, the electric motor that can go forwards or backwards to open or close the window.

Use Flowol to produce a flowchart and make suitable adjustments to the flowchart so that it operates properly. This flowchart needs to operate alongside the other control systems in the greenhouse.

QUESTIONS

A tomato grower uses an environmental control system in the greenhouses to make the conditions ideal for the growing of tomatoes. The air inside the greenhouse needs to be kept at constant temperature and humidity. The environmental control system is monitored and controlled by a computer.

The temperature inside the greenhouse can be controlled by both a heater and a fan.

The humidity is controlled either by a pump that sprays a mist of water when the humidity is too low, or by a motor that opens windows in the greenhouse if the humidity is too high.

1. Name two sensors that are used as inputs into the system.
2. Give the name of an output device that would be needed for this system.

Lesson 8: MARKETING THE PLANTS

In this lesson you will be looking at how you can use ICT to develop materials for marketing the plants.

Marketing involves making sure that you have the right product at the right price and also involves letting people know about your product. Letting people know about your product is called advertising.

Marketing involves letting people know about the plants you are growing, comparing the price of your bedding plants with others, convincing people that yours are better and so on.

There are a number of suitable ways to market the bedding plants.

KEY WORDS

audience expectation – what the audience might expect in your document or presentation

flyer – a short, small document used to advertise something. Flyers are usually put through letterboxes, on car windscreens or given out on the street

intended audience – the people who will be looking at and reading the information on the web page or other document

Posters

Flyers/leaflets

MARKETING

Newspaper

Mailshots

Internet/Website    *Local radio*    *Telephone selling*   **Marketing methods**

247

Unit 5 Integrating applications to find solutions

When thinking about your marketing materials you must consider your intended audience. Consider the audience expectation. What information would they like to see in your marketing material? Think about the people who will be buying your plants – are they young, old or middle aged?

Targeting your marketing

If you have only a certain amount of money for marketing (i.e. a budget), it makes sense to initially target your marketing at those customers who have ordered bedding plants in the past. This is why it is best to send the previous customers a mail-merged letter along with a price list.

Developing a corporate image

Large companies and organisations need to have an image that is readily recognised. They usually develop a logo as part of this corporate image.

As well as the logo, companies often write down a list of the things that they are in business to do. This is called a mission statement. It focuses on the main purpose of the business.

> **KEY WORDS**
>
> **corporate image** – the image that a company or organisation would like to present to others

Make it happen

ACTIVITY 22: Creating the mission statement

In this activity you have to write a list of the main objectives or purposes of the project.

Here are a couple to start you off:

- To raise as much money as possible for the purchase of ICT equipment.
- To let the pupils experience running a business.

Your task is to finish this list off by adding four more sentences.

Lesson 8 Marketing the plants

ACTIVITY 23: Designing and creating a logo

In Year 7 you saw how companies and organisations produced logos so that they are instantly recognisable.

Designer labels are often logos

249

Unit 5 Integrating applications to find solutions

Companies and organisations, large and small, like to have a corporate image and they often develop a logo that is distinctive and easily recognisable.

REMEMBER!
The logo needs to convey something about the project.

1. Using a pencil and paper sketch a couple of logos that might be suitable for this project.

2. After showing your draft designs to others, choose one that you think will work.

3. Using suitable software (your choice), produce this logo on the computer. Use text and colour where appropriate and then save your design in a suitable file format.

4. Check that it is easy for you to load your logo into a word-processed document or a spreadsheet.

5. Print out a copy of your design.

ACTIVITY 24: Designing and creating the price list

It is proposed to send a price list with the mail-merged letters. If the recipient wants to place an order then they write the number of trays of each plant on the form and post the form back to the project manager at the school. Customers could be given a stamped addressed envelope to encourage them to place an order. They could also e-mail their order using the Internet or use the school's website.

1. Write a list of the information that the order form must contain in order for it to serve its purpose.

2. Write a list of the information it would be desirable to include on the form.

3. On paper plan a design for the form. Play around with the design until you are happy with it.

4. Check that you have not forgotten any important aspect of the form. One way of doing this would be to get someone to make an order.

5. Using suitable software (your choice!), implement your design.

6. Save your file using a suitable file name and then print a copy of the order form.

Lesson 8 Marketing the plants

FIND IT OUT

It will be useful for you to collect a range of images to include in the documents that you will be creating in the next activity.

Use the Internet to collect some photographs of the following types of bedding plants:

- Pansy
- Lobelia
- Marigold
- Alyssum.

Make it happen

ACTIVITY 25: Creating marketing documents

In this activity you have to work as a group and produce a range of marketing documentation to market your plants to the local community.

Each person in the team should be assigned the task best suited to their capabilities.

Here is a list of the documentation you will need:

- Flyers (these are small posters to be put through letterboxes or on windscreens of cars).
- Posters.
- An advertisement to go in the local paper.

Save the file for each of these using a suitable file name and print enough copies so that all of the members of your team have a complete set of the documents.

Your teacher will show your designs to other groups and they can comment on what they liked or disliked about your design. Of course, you will be asked to comment on their designs as well.

EXTENSION ACTIVITY

Add to your documents the logo created in Activity 23.

Unit 5 Integrating applications to find solutions

Lesson 9: LOOKING AT THE FEASIBILITY OF THE PROJECT

KEY WORDS

feasible – whether a system is worth creating within the constraints of time, money and other resources

Whenever a project is proposed, it should be assessed to see if it is feasible. Basically, if a project is said to be feasible, then it is worth going ahead with it. Not all projects are worth going ahead with, so this report will look to see if the advantages of the project outweigh the disadvantages such as the costs and the time.

Although a project may be feasible in one area, it may not be feasible in other areas. For example, it may be possible to manage the growing conditions using computer control, but you might consider that the number of trays that you would need to sell to break even is so large that the project is not feasible financially.

ACTIVITY 26: Writing up the feasibility report

The head teacher has asked you to investigate the project's feasibility. You have now considered all the various parts of the project and should be in a position to decide whether you think the project is feasible or not.

The head teacher has asked you for a report on the project's feasibility. She has provided you with the following document to make this easier.

Fill in this document and hand it in.

The whole project has been broken down into the following three systems: • The finance system. • The greenhouse control system. • The marketing system.	
What the finance system involves	What the problem was and how I solved it
What the greenhouse control system involves	What the problem was and how I solved it
What the marketing system involves	What the problem was and how I solved it
Project recommendations	

Report into the feasibility of the whole project

Lesson 10: THE FINAL REPORT

The feasibility report conclusions should have stated whether it was worth developing the project to grow bedding plants to raise money for school equipment.

The final report will be given to the head teacher and will state how you will use ICT to help you with the project. The report outlines how the solution to the project should be developed.

Make it happen

ACTIVITY 27: Assessing performance

If you were a premiership footballer you would have an idea as to whether you performed well. You would not need other people to tell you as you would know yourself.

Imagine you are a premiership footballer. Write down how you would assess your performance if you played as:

1. a striker (i.e. a player who plays up front and tries to score goals)

2. a defender (i.e. a player who prevents the opposition players from scoring goals)

3. a goalkeeper.

ACTIVITY 28: Assessing your own performance in working through the project

When you have completed each of the lessons in this unit you need to think about how effective your work has been.

In this activity you need to reflect on the whole project. Evaluate your performance under the following headings:

- What I learnt about working on this project.
- How the financial model allowed me to decide whether the

Unit 5 Integrating applications to find solutions

project was feasible financially.

- How happy or otherwise I was about my efforts to control the conditions in the greenhouse.
- How good I think my marketing materials were and how appropriate they were to the audience.
- How well my mail merge performed.
- How well I worked with others in those parts of the project where I worked as part of a group.
- The improvements I might make to each part of the project if I had to do a similar task again.

ACTIVITY 29: **Producing the final report on the project**

In this activity you are required to produce a final report on the whole project.

The final report should include:

- An outline of the problem (the overall problem as well as the sub-problems).
- Examples of how each system was designed, developed, tested and evaluated.
- Labels and annotations on the printouts to explain them.
- Screenshots of what appears on the screen.
- Suggestions for the future development of each part of the system.
- A concluding report for the head teacher on the feasibility of the project.

Your report needs to follow the steps in the system life cycle for the development of a system.

The steps are as follows:

- Identify
- Analyse
- Design
- Implement
- Test
- Evaluate.

Lesson 10 The final report

You will need to explain the above steps for each of the three parts of the project:

- Financial
- Control
- Marketing.

It is important when writing up your final report that you include plenty of printouts to show how you completed each part.

REMEMBER!

You should annotate these printouts so it is clear to someone reading them what is going on.

Glossary

absolute cell referencing – in this type of reference, a particular cell is used in a formula, and when this formula is copied to a new address the cell address does not change

accessible – easy to get at and understand

accurate – absolutely correct (i.e. without any mistakes)

analogue – data that can have an infinite number of values

AND – a Boolean connector/operator used between two or more key terms when all of the terms need to be present

annotate – add explanations as to what is going on by writing on a printout

appraise – to decide on the quality or value of something such as information

appropriate – suitable or proper

audience expectation – what the audience might expect in your document or presentation

authentic – genuine. Not false or fake

automate – to enable a process to be performed without human intervention

biased – not balanced; favouring one side more than the other

Boolean connector/Boolean operator – the words AND, OR and NOT, placed between key terms when searching for specific information on the Internet or in a large database

continuous – without end

control – switching devices on or off or making adjustments on the basis of data obtained from sensors

corporate image – the image that a company or organisation would like to present to others

data logging – the collection of data automatically over a period of time. Remote weather stations use data logging

Data Protection Act 1988 – a law that restricts the way personal information is stored and processed on a computer

database – a series of files stored in a computer that can be accessed in a variety of different ways

digital – data that can have only two values. This means the value can be either correct or incorrect

dry run – working through a flowchart manually to check its logic. Used as a test

efficiency – how well the system performs

fact – truth or reality as distinct from mere statement or belief

feasible – whether a system is worth creating within the constraints of time, money and other resources

field – an item of data or space for data in a database

financial model – a spreadsheet or other model used to show the likely profit or loss from a business or venture

fitness for purpose – how well the information obtained matches the purpose to which it is to be put

flowchart – a chart or diagram used to break down a task into smaller parts. It can also show the order of the tasks and any decisions which need to be made

flyer – a short, small document used to advertise something. Flyers are usually put through letterboxes, on car windscreens or given out on the street

Glossary

forecast – a prediction of what might happen in the future

formulae – calculations used in a spreadsheet

Gantt chart – a horizontal time line used to plan and schedule activities

goal seek – using spreadsheet software to find the input value needed to produce a certain output value

Graphics Interchange Format (GIF) – a file format for saving pictures that can be sent and displayed easily on the Internet

hits – the number of times a particular page is visited. It can also mean the number of matches from a search condition that you set

home page – the page you normally start at when accessing a website

hyperlink – a link from a place in one document to a different place in the same document or a completely different document. If you click on a hyperlink it takes you to a different place

Hypertext Markup Language (HTML) – a series of instructions used to format and display text and images on the World Wide Web. You use it to specify the structure and layout of a web document

import – to put the data created in one package into a different package

intended audience – the people who will be looking at and reading the information on the web page or other document

Joint Photographic Experts Group (JPEG) – a file format mainly used for saving photographs

key words – words that can be searched on to find more information on a topic

live data – data currently being used

misuse – using data in a way that is morally or ethically wrong or illegal

model – the process of representing a real-world object or phenomenon as a set of mathematical equations

monitor – take readings of conditions using sensors

navigate – find your way around a website by making use of site maps and links

NOT – a Boolean connector/operator where you specify a term that you do *not* want to appear in your search results

opinion – a belief or judgement that is likely to be true but is not based on proof

OR – a Boolean connector/operator used between two or more key terms when one or more of the terms needs to be present

organise – to give an orderly structure to something

parameter – a limiting factor that dictates how wide or narrow a project needs to be

personal information – information about a person such as political beliefs, health records, creditworthiness, etc.

plausible – the information is reasonable or likely to be true

precise – exact, clear and detailed

primary data – data you have collected yourself

public information system – a system that the public can use to access information in a form that they can understand and use, for example weather forecasts, tables of share prices, details of foreign exchange rates

query – a request for information from a database

random number – a number that is impossible to predict

random number generator – a spreadsheet function that produces random numbers automatically

record – a set of related information about a thing or individual. Records are subdivided into fields

relative cell referencing – when a cell is used in a formula and the formula is copied to a new

Glossary

address, the cell address changes to take account of the formula's new position

reliable – the information is dependable or trustworthy

remote data logging – data logging performed at a location that is away from the computer used to process the data

remote sensor – a sensor used to sense a physical quantity (temperature, pressure, rainfall, wind speed, etc.) where the sensor is situated away from the computer

repeated processes – processes in a flowchart that are carried out again and again or for a set number of times

repetitive – unvarying or unchanging

rule – a condition that must be obeyed in a computer model and which is expressed as a formula

sample rate – the rate at which data is measured using a sensor

secondary data – data collected by someone else

sensors – devices which are used to sense or measure physical quantities

sequence of instructions – instructions, such as in a flowchart, where the instructions need to be obeyed in a certain order

simulation – seeing how the model behaves under different circumstances by altering the variables

subroutine – a section of a program that can be called upon when needed

synonym – a word that has the same meaning or almost the same meaning as another

system – a set of interconnected parts that work together to perform an overall task

system life cycle – the series of steps carried out during the creation of a new system

tags – special markers used in HTML to tell the computer what to do with the text. A tag is needed at the start and end of each block of text to which the tag applies

threshold – the minimum value of a quantity (such as temperature) which causes an event to take place (such as turning on a heater)

transmission speed – the speed at which data is passed along a wire/cable or through the air

URL (Uniform Resource Locator) – the address that defines the route to a file on the Internet. This is the website or web page address that you type in (e.g. www.oxfordsecondary.co.uk)

variable – a quantity whose value is not fixed

viewpoint – an opinion or point of view

web browser – a program used to search and display web pages on the Internet

web page – a single document on the World Wide Web, usually containing links to other web pages

web query – a query that gets data from the Internet. The data is usually in the form of a table

website – a site on the Internet containing information. It consists of one or more web pages

wizard – a program provided as part of the software package that provides step-by-step guidance through a process and allows you to personalise the layout and content

workbook – a file that contains one or more worksheets

worksheet – a single page showing the spreadsheet grid

World Wide Web (www) – a huge collection of web pages and other material, such as files for downloading, that you can access. This material is held on millions of computers all around the world

Index

absolute cell referencing, spreadsheets 209
accessible, defined 134
accuracy of information 131–4
acknowledging sources of information 156
advertisements 130–1
analogue sensors 235–6
animation, weather data/information 4, 10
annotate
   defined 241
   reporting 255
appraise, defined 134
appropriate, defined 155
assessing performance 253–4
audience expectation, defined 247
audience, intended 154–7, 247
automate, defined 231
automating processes, share prices system 34–42

bedding plants project 203–55
   break-even 208, 209–13
   control/controlling 231–46
   costs 208
   feasibility 252–3
   financial model 207–13
   marketing 247–51
   monitoring 231–42
   parameters 206
   price lists 250
   purchasing 203–4
   record keeping 213–19
   reporting 254–5
   sprinkler system 243–5
   temperature 244–6
   website creation 86–121
   websites 204
biased information 133–4
bogus information 127–8
books, cf. websites 51
Boolean operators
   key words 147
   searching 147–9
break-even
   bedding plants project 208, 209–13
   coffee bar 172–80

   defined 172
   goal seek 182–3
   graphs 180–2
   models 172–80, 180–4
broadband 51–2, 59
browsers, web 62

charts
   dice throwing 188–9
   flowcharts 238–42, 245–6
   Gantt charts 200–1
   output worksheets 28–34
   share prices system 39–40
   weather data/information 5, 28–34
coffee bar
   break-even 172–80
   fixed costs 172–80
   variable costs 172–80
coffee making, sequencing events 198
commission, clothes shop, goal seek 166–9
computing stages, input-process-output 21–34, 165, 194–6
continuous, defined 231
control/controlling
   bedding plants project 231–46
   defined 231
   flowcharts 238–42, 245–6
corporate image 248–50
Corporate Presence Wizard 86–105
counters, websites 131
criteria, evaluation 43–4, 120
customers
   letter sending 220–31
   order form 218
   record keeping 214–17

data
   automating processes 41–2
   importing 13–17, 21–34
   cf. information 11
   primary 11
   refreshing 41–2
   secondary 11
   from websites 21–34

Index

data logging
   defined 237
   weather data/information 7–10
Data Protection Act 219
data sources, weather data/information 11–17
database, defined 216
dial-up 51–2
dice throwing, random numbers 186–92
digital sensors 235–6
displaying *see* presenting
Dr Who, searching 138–9
dry run, defined 242

efficiency, defined 237
evaluation
   criteria 43–4, 120
   information 134
   public information systems 42–6
   websites 57–9, 119–21
Excel *see* spreadsheets

F9 key, recalculating data 186
facts 122–7
feasibility, bedding plants project 252–3
feedback forms, publishing on the web 110–16
field, defined 216
financial model
   bedding plants project 207–13
   defined 207
Finding Nemo, fish information 157
finding out and learning 154–7
fish information, Finding Nemo 157
fitness for purpose, defined 155
fixed costs
   bedding plants project 208
   coffee bar 172–80
flowcharts
   control 238–42, 245–6
   defined 238
flyers, defined 247
forecast, defined 207
formulae, spreadsheets 209
FrontPage, publishing on the web 80–5

Gantt charts, sequencing events 200–1
GIF (Graphics Interchange Format), images 62
glossary 256–8
goal seek
   break-even 182–3
   commission, clothes shop 166–9
   defined 166, 211
   spreadsheets 164–71

Google™, searching 138–42, 148–9
graphs
   break-even 180–2
   output worksheets 28–34
   weather data/information 5, 28–34
hits, websites 59, 131
home pages, websites 60–1
HTML (Hypertext Markup Language)
   looking at 63–4
   using 64–72
   websites 62–72
hyperlinks 70, 130

images
   searching 153
   websites 62, 70
importing data
   automating processes 35–7
   share prices system 35–7
   weather data/information 13–17
   from websites 21–34
information
   acknowledging sources 156
   cf. data 11
input/output, spreadsheets 164–71
input-process-output
   computing stages 21–34, 165
   identifying 195–6
   systems 194–6
   workbooks/worksheets 21–34
input worksheets
   share prices system 35–7, 41–2
   weather data/information 22–5
intended audience 154–7
   defined 247
investigating public information systems, weather data/information 18–20

JPEG (Joint Photographic Experts Group), images 62

key words
   Boolean operators 147
   searching 144–9

learning and finding out 154–7
leeches 145–6
letter sending, mail merge 220–31
life cycle, systems 197–8
links (hyperlinks) 70, 130
live data, defined 237

260

Index

Liverpool, searching 141–2
logos 249–50

maggots 145–6
mail merge 220–31
maps, weather data/information 4
marketing, bedding plants project 247–51
mission statement 248
misuse, defined 219
models 158–92
   break-even 172–80, 180–4
   defined 158
   financial, bedding plants project 207–13
   goal seek 164–71, 182–3
   good 183
   input-process-output 21–34, 165
   numeric data 158–64
   pets costs 170–1
   randomness 184–92
   spreadsheets 159–92
   terms 160
modems 52
monitor, defined 232
monitoring, bedding plants project 231–42

navigating, websites 59, 116–18, 131
numeric data, models 158–64

opinions 122–7
order form, customers 218
organise, defined 215
output worksheets
   share prices system 38–42
   weather data/information 28–33

parameters 206
paste special
   share prices system 38–9
   weather data/information 26–7, 32–3
performance, assessing 253–4
personal information, defined 219
pets costs, models 170–1
a place in the sun, public information systems 45–6
plagiarism, searching 147
plants *see* bedding plants project
plausible information 127
precise, defined 134
presenting, weather data/information 3–7, 15–17
price lists, bedding plants project 250
primary data 11
process worksheets
   share prices system 38–42
   weather data/information 26–7
processes, automating 34–42
public information systems 1–46
   defined 1
   evaluation 42–6
   examples 1–2
   investigating 18–20
   a place in the sun 45–6
   setting up 20–5
publishing on the web 47–121
   bedding plants website 86–121
   checking 116–19
   completing websites 106–10
   creating websites 56–105
   feedback forms 110–16
   FrontPage 80–5
   HTML 62–72
   navigating 116–18
   publishing 116–19
   wizards 86–105
   Word 73–80
   see also websites

queries
   searching 135
   'what if...?' 158

randomness
   models 184–92
   random number generators 184
   random numbers 184
recalculating data, F9 key 186
record, defined 216
record keeping
   bedding plants project 213–19
   customers 214–17
   reasons 215
refreshing data, automating processes 41–2, 186
relative cell referencing, spreadsheets 209
reliability of information 128–31, 132–4
remote data logging, defined 237
remote sensors, defined 237
repeated processes, defined 232
repetitive, defined 232
reporting, bedding plants project 254–5
roast dinner, sequencing events 199–200
rule, defined 207

sample rate, defined 235
save as/save 211

Index

schools, websites 57, 71–2
searching 135–53
   Boolean operators 147–9
   Dr Who 138–9
   Google™ 138–42, 148–9
   images 153
   key words 144–9
   Liverpool 141–2
   plagiarism 147
   search engines 135, 150–3
   synonyms 136–7, 142
   thesauri 136–7
   using searches 135–43
   Yahoo!© 150–1
secondary data 11
sensors
   defined 232
   types 235–6
   weather data/information 7–10
sequence of instructions, defined 232
sequencing events
   Gantt charts 200–1
   systems 198–200
share prices system
   automating processes 34–42
   evaluation 44
simulation 159
   defined 158
sources of data, weather data/information 11–17
sources of information, acknowledging 156
spreadsheets
   absolute cell referencing 209
   benefits 159–63
   cell referencing types 209
   formulae 209
   goal seek 164–71
   importing data 13–17
   input/output 164–71
   models 159–92
   random numbers 185–92
   recalculating data, F9 key 186
   relative cell referencing 209
   weather data/information 13–17
   workbooks/worksheets 20–1
sprinkler system, bedding plants project 243–5
subroutine, defined 238
synonyms, searching 136–7, 142
systems 193–202
   components 197
   defined 193
   examples 193–4

input-process-output 194–6
   life cycle 197–8
   sequencing events 198–200

tags, websites 62
target value, defined 166
temperature, bedding plants project 244–6
templates, websites 74–80, 80–5
terms, models 160
thesauri, searching 136–7
threshold, defined 244
transmission speed, defined 237

updating data, automating processes 41–2
URLs (Uniform Resource Locators) 21, 128–30

validity of information 134
variable costs
   bedding plants project 208
   coffee bar 172–80
variable, defined 207
viewpoints, defined 133

weather data/information 1–34
   animation 4, 10
   charts 5
   data loggers 7–10
   evaluation 43–4
   graphs 5
   importing data 13–17
   investigating public information systems 18–20
   maps 4
   presenting 3–7, 15–17
   purposes 16–17
   remote weather stations 12–13
   sensors 7–10
   sources of data 11–17
   Weather Reporter 8, 12–13
   weather stations 7–10
   websites 3, 4, 6, 8, 11, 12, 14, 18, 19, 23
web browsers 62
web queries
   automating processes 34–42
   defined 21
   menu location 23
websites
   activities 53–5
   bedding plants project 204
   cf. books 51
   completing 106–10
   counters 131
   creating 56–105

Index

Data Protection Act 219
deconstructing 50–1
evaluation 57–9, 119–21
expectations 54–5
feedback forms 110–16
format 49–51
FrontPage 80–5
getting data from 21–34
hits 59, 131
home pages 60–1
HTML 62–72
hyperlinks 70, 130
images 62, 70
investigating 53–5, 59–60
navigating 59, 116–18, 131
schools 57, 71–2
share prices system 35
tags 62
templates 74–80, 80–5
types 48–9
weather data/information 3, 4, 6, 8, 11, 12, 14, 18, 19, 23
web pages 47
white space 61
Word 73–80
see also publishing on the web
'what if…?' queries 158
white space, websites 61
Word, publishing on the web 73–80
workbooks/worksheets
   input-process-output 21–34
   spreadsheets 20–1

Yahoo!©, searching 150–1